THE APOSTLE PAUL, A BONDSERVANT OF CHRIST JESUS

A Biographical Commentary On His Life And Letters
Volume I

JOHN C. SCHNEIDERVIN

"For I am the least of the apostles, who is not fit to be called an apostle, because I persecuted the church of God; but by the grace of God I am what I am, and his grace to me was not to no avail; on the contrary, I labored even more than all of them, yet not I but the grace of God with me. " (1 Corinthians 15:9, 10)

"To the only wise God be the glory forever through Jesus Christ! Amen." (Romans 16:27)

The Apostle Paul
A Bondservant of Christ Jesus
Written In Late A.D. 55 & Early A.D. 57

COPYRIGHT

© 2019 by John C. Schneidervin
All rights reserved.

No part of this book may be reproduced in any form or by any electronic or mechanical means, including information storage and retrieval systems, without written permission from the author, except for the use of brief quotations.

All New Testament verses in this book are from the author's *The New Testament —Vivid English Translation*. Copyright © 2015; May 2019. All Rights Reserved. All Old Testament verses are the author's own translations.

❦ Created with Vellum

In memory of my beloved wife and lifelong best friend, Sandy, who so wanted me to finish writing this book and to publish it.

John C. Schneidervin
August 15, 2019

FOREWORD

Pastor John Schneidervin is a "missionary at heart." Even in retirement he is sharing the gospel around the world from his home in Waupun with his www.christianinconnect.com. He also began a ministry to Sunday School children in Pakistan which continues to this day under the auspices of the Wisconsin Evangelical Lutheran Synod.

Thousands of Pakistani and Nepali Christians love his adult confirmation course, "Your Word Is Truth" While both mission fields have several wonderful options for adult confirmation courses, each prefers his thorough course on Christian doctrine. What is interesting is that both mission fields reached this conclusion without consulting one another and without any promotion of Pastor Schneidervin's course over others. This master-work is now available in Urdu, the main language of Pakistan, and in Nepali.

With his missionary spirit he has written a book on the Apostle Paul, who is likely the greatest missionary in the history of the world. Pastor Schneidervin's words have been a special blessing to me in my work as a missionary. What I especially appreciate about his work is how solid, practical, encouraging and edifying his exposition is. He digs into the text. He expounds what God the Holy Spirit teaches us with rich insight. He also gives extensive historical background on many of the cities Paul visited. This adds to our understanding of the events described in the Book of Acts.

While he is a scholar, he is first and foremost a good pastor who sits at your side and simply tells you what the Word of God says. We are reproved and challenged by the law. We are comforted and inspired by the gospel. He spreads a table of God's word for us to feast on.

His biography shows how the Apostle Paul used every situation as a platform to exalt Christ – whether it was a stoning in Lystra (Acts 14), a beating and severe flogging in Philippi (Acts 16), a riot at the temple in Jerusalem (Acts 21,22) or a 2-year imprisonment in Caesarea and another 2-year imprisonment in Rome (23-28) or even a shipwreck in between (Acts 27,28).

In his own life Pastor Schneidervin has modeled this spirit. He retired early from the ministry he loved to care for his wife who suffered from multiple sclerosis for many years until the Lord called her home. In spite of personal challenges in the long-term care of his beloved wife, Sandy, he has used every situation – good and bad – to proclaim Jesus. From their humble home in Waupun he has been a prolific writer, even producing his own translation of the New Testament – The Vivid English Translation – and he is still reaching out to the world with the gospel. Perhaps he has reached more people because of this turn of events in his life than if he had continued in the parish ministry. For him the words of Paul have become his life's motto – "For me to live is Christ and to die is gain." May we catch his spirit.

Pastor Michael Duncan
Missionary to Nepal and Pakistan

ABOUT THE AUTHOR

Rev. JC, as he refers to himself in his literary works, graduated from Bethany Lutheran College, Mankato, MN. He then studied at Wisconsin Lutheran Seminary, Mequon, WI, from which he graduated with honors and a master's degree . Upon his ordination he first served as a parish pastor of Rock Of Ages Ev. Lutheran Church and as a home missionary in Kansas City North, MO. He then accepted a call to serve as the pastor of Crown Of Life Ev. Lutheran Church, Hubertus, WI, which was a mission congregation at the time. During this time he wrote many Bible studies and Christian materials for his congregations, which included an adult Bible instruction course entitled <u>Your Word Is Truth</u>. He was asked to be a contributing writer to a volume of sermon studies and also to the Meditations periodical. As a part of his ministry he spent a great deal of time in counseling, especially premarital and marital counseling. He wrote and then conducted for several years free marriage enrichment seminars as a service to couples. He also wrote materials for conducting premarital and marital counseling sessions with couples. He was asked to present to his fellow pastors at their seminars papers on how to conduct biblically sound premarital and marital counseling. He then wrote <u>Deepening Love For Marital Happiness</u>, which was published by Northwestern Publishing House in 1992. During the author's years in the active ministry he also created the Christian Inconnect website, which was about the first Christian website to go up on the internet, and for which he wrote all of its materials.

He retired to take care of his wife who was severely handicapped by multiple sclerosis. During his retirement he started and then administered for ten years a Sunday School Mission Ministry in Pakistan. In connection with that foreign missionary work and to aid the Pakistani Christians he simplified the language of his adult instruction course mentioned above. It was then translated into the Urdu language of Pakistan and afterwards into Nepali of neighboring Nepal by the Christian leaders of those countries. It is now the favorite course of Christian instruction of thousands of adult Christians in both countries. He also translated The New Testament – Vivid English Translation.

Having had forty-one years of theological and ministerial experience, he now turns to publishing some of his biblical Christian works as well as writing more for publication. He does so, not as a representative of any church body, but as an independent writer and publisher.

If you would like to be notified when he comes out with his next release, you can email him: mailto:jcschneidervin@gmail.com

ACKNOWLEDGMENTS

Pastor and Missionary Michael Duncan squeezed into his full schedule of overseeing the mission work in Pakistan and Nepal, as well as traveling extensively to the Middle East and the Far East, the reading of much of my manuscript. In the process of his reading he made a great many encouraging comments that bolstered my commitment to continue studying, researching, and writing. Throughout the two and a half years that it took me to write my biography of Paul, he remained a source of encouragement and a good friend. And when I had finished my manuscript, he was happy to write the Foreword for the book. For all the time he expended, for all the helpful, encouraging comments he made, and for all his many favorable statements in the Foreword — I thank him most heartedly.

My book cover designer Kristine Borneman, a long time friend, has again taken time out of her busy professional life as a commercial artist and out of her personal family life to help me by designing the covers for this three volume set of biographical commentaries about the apostle Paul. Without her artistic handiwork these volumes would not have been completed, because, needless to say, one cannot publish books without the covers to go with them. As I did previously in my book <u>Jesus' Last Week And Words</u>, so I again do now, I extend my thanks to her for her time and excellent work.

High on my list of things to give thanks to God for in connection with this biography are the proofreaders who spent hours reading chapters and scrutinizing line after line to ferret out my typos and bring them to my attention. At times they also made helpful insights that enabled me to improve the wording of a phrase or a paragraph for greater clarity and conciseness. Among my dedicated proofreaders were my daughter Virginia Voigt and my Christian friends: Annette Miller, Darlene Almandi, Carla Stanossek, Karen Bartman, Donald Koch and Charles Schranz. For their many hours of careful scrutinizing, and for their helpful suggestions, not to mention for all that they personally mean to me, I thank them. The final quality of the manuscript of this biographical commentary would not have been possible without their keen eyes picking out the typos that my degenerating eyesight has great difficulty seeing. I cannot thank them enough for their assistance.

Finally, but above all, I acknowledge my Lord's having supplied me with everything, and with every good blessing, that made the writing of this biographical commentary on Paul possible. He surely heard my many prayers for his aid, guidance and gifts. Among his many answers to my prayers were his preserving my eyesight to the extent that with technological aids I could still see well enough to read and write on my computer. May it please him to put this biographical commentary to good use in his kingdom of grace for the spiritual benefit of many others. To him then, the one and only true God of heaven and earth — Father, Son, and Holy Spirit — be the praise and the glory forever and ever! In Christ Jesus, Amen!

INTRODUCTION

Paul —
  The Beneficiary Of The Lord's Preparations
  And The Target Of The Devil's Opposition

A biographical commentary on the life of Paul, if it is to give honor to whom honor is due, must begin with the Lord God and his divine plan and preparations for Paul's life of service as his apostle. God's plan began in eternity before the creation of the heavens and the earth. It was a plan for the salvation of the world's sinners through the redeeming work of his Son, the Christ (Messiah). Already then in eternity before the beginning of time the Lord God chose those whom he would bring to believe in that gift of salvation through the preaching of the gospel of his Son Jesus Christ. God made his divine election to faith for salvation known very clearly through his apostle and bondservant Paul. In Ephesians 1:4, 5 God the Holy Spirit inspired Paul to write:

4 (God the Father) chose us in (our Lord Jesus Christ) before the foundation of the world, that we should be holy and blameless before him. In love

5 he predestined us for adoption as sons to himself through Jesus Christ, according to the good pleasure of his will, ...

And in 2 Thessalonians 2:13, 14 God again inspired Paul to write:

13 As for us, we ought to always give thanks to God for you, brothers loved by the Lord, because God chose you from the beginning for salvation by the sanctifying work of the Spirit and faith in the truth,

14 for which he called you through our gospel, for obtaining the glory of our Lord Jesus Christ.

Throughout the ages of the Old and New Testament eras of history the Lord has raised up many men to be his spokesmen to proclaim his gospel plan of salvation through faith alone in Jesus Christ. While all the men whom God had proclaim his gospel of Christ were chosen servants of God – whether patriarchs or prophets or apostles or pastors or teachers or evangelists, this biographical commentary directs its attention to just one such chosen servant whom God had set apart for the gospel from his mother's womb (ref. Galatians 1:15) – the apostle Paul.

It is evident from history that the Lord had made all the preparations necessary to enable Paul to labor tirelessly as he did in the cause of the gospel. As was stated above, God made his plan of salvation in eternity and started the preparations to carry it out. Then as Paul stated in Galatians 4:4, 5,

"When the fullness of the time came, God sent forth his Son, born of a woman, born under law, to redeem those under law ..."

That fullness of the time came when God had all his preparations made for the gospel of redemption to be fulfilled by Jesus Christ and to have that gospel then proclaimed to the world. And it was then, in that fullness of time, that Christ called and commissioned Paul to be his apostle to the Gentiles.

To complete his preparations for the coming of his Son Jesus Christ and for the preaching of his gospel in all the world, God had done many things. He had established the Jewish nation in Palestine, which lay on the land bridge between the two continents of Africa and Asia where he had his Son Jesus Christ born into the world, and from where his gospel was spread throughout Judea, Samaria, and to the end of the earth (Acts 1:8). God had shifted the center of secular power from the East (Assyria, Babylon, and Persia) to the West (Greece and then Rome). God had seen to it that the Greek influence of philosophy had diminished into skepticism while the mythology of the Greek gods had slipped into bankruptcy and moral decay. God had raised up Alexander the Great's army and through it the Koine (which means "common") Greek language. As Alexander's army marched, that Koine Greek was carried throughout the Mediterranean world and into the East. That Greek became the language through which the apostles were then able to converse wherever they went to spread the gospel of Christ. That Greek also became the language of the original New Testament Scriptures. What is more, God had then raised up the Roman Empire, using its legions to keep the Roman peace and to preserve safe passage by roads and by the sea for travelers, which enabled the apostles to then travel throughout the Mediterranean World and the East and into Europe to spread the gospel. God had also scattered the Jews throughout the Mediterranean World, who then established the synagogues where the apostle Paul could begin his mission work of spreading the good news about Jesus.

And so, having his plan of salvation brought to completion by the appearance of Christ Jesus into the world and by his redeeming sacrifice for the sins of all people, all was ready for God to raise up and to send out the apostle Paul together with the other apostles to spread God's good news – all sins had been paid for by Christ and the gates of heaven had been flung open!

To what extent Paul was able as the Lord's bondservant to spread the gospel will be observed through the course of this biographical commentary. That extent to which Paul did spread the gospel was to the credit of God. It was to the credit of God, for the reader should be aware that throughout the years of Paul's life and ministry a war was being waged, a war for the minds of mankind and thus ultimately for their souls. It was a war that Satan had started, as the Lord God had known beforehand in eternity that Satan would do. It was a war that

Satan had already been waging throughout the history of mankind since the Garden of Eden, where and when Satan in possession of a serpent said to the woman, "Is it even so that God said? . . . You shall not surely die. For God knows that in the day you eat from it your eyes will be opened and you will be like God knowing good and evil." Satan started the war by casting doubt over what God said, then denying the truthfulness of God's word, and finally blatantly contradicting it. It was a war of Satan's lies versus the truth of God's word. At the time of Paul Satan was continuing his battle to maintain his control over the minds of mankind that he had enslaved in the spiritual darkness of unbelief and sin beginning with Adam and Eve. Through the power of his gospel God was meanwhile setting men and women free from that dominion of darkness and bringing them into the light of the kingdom of his Son Jesus Christ for eternal life and salvation. It was to accomplish this purpose that the risen Lord Jesus told Paul on the road to Damascus:

16 For this reason I appeared to you, to appoint you a minister and a witness both of the things which you have seen and of the things which I will show you,

17 rescuing you from the *Jewish* people and from the Gentiles, to whom I am sending you,

18 to open their eyes, to turn *them* back from darkness to light and from the power of Satan to God, in order that they may receive forgiveness of sins and a share among those who have been sanctified by faith in me. (Acts 26:16-18)

So, behind the scenes that this biographical commentary presents on the life of Paul the reader should be aware that Satan was instigating and doing everything in his power to extinguish the gospel and to destroy the Church from without by persecution and from within by false teachings. He hardened the hearts of the majority of the Jews to the gospel of Jesus Christ and incited them to a blind fury of hatred and violence both against Paul and all who believed that gospel. He blinded the minds of the pagans so they could not perceive the truth of the gospel (2 Corinthians 4:3, 4), and then aroused them to oppose the good news of God's word about Jesus of

Nazareth to preserve their ways of ungodly spiritual darkness and idolatry. He combated the truth of God's word and gospel with the falsehoods of false teachers, who in Satan's service attempted to empty the gospel of its simple truth that eternal life and salvation were received not by any human efforts or works but solely by the undeserved grace of God through faith alone in his Messiah and Christ, Jesus of Nazareth.

In this war for minds and souls Paul fought, not on just one side, but on both sides! He fought first on Satan's side in opposition to the gospel of Jesus of Nazareth. Paul did so as a soldier lashing out blindly in ignorance and unbelief and wholly committed to eradicating the name of Jesus by persecuting those Jewish men and women who had come to believe in Jesus. Paul did so only for a short time, however; he did so only until the resurrected and glorified Jesus of Nazareth himself appeared to him, confronted his murderous persecution, and revealed the truth of God's gospel to him. Jesus afterwards stated,

"This man is my chosen instrument to carry my name before both Gentiles and kings, and the sons of Israel" (Acts 9:15).

To carry the name of Jesus meant nothing other than proclaiming Jesus' gospel, which is the word of God. Paul was to be Jesus' point-man to make that gospel known as far as to the end of the earth, meaning Rome especially. From that time on Paul fought as a committed soldier going into the battle to illuminate both Jews and Gentiles with the truth of their eternal life and salvation through faith in Jesus Christ.

The following biography of Paul's life is filled with his crusade in Christ's service to carry the gospel forward to Jews and Gentiles, to endure the persecutions instigated by Satan, and to fight off Satan's many falsehoods that he spawned through the Judaizers and false Christians like Hymenaeus and Philetus (2 Timothy 2:17). As an enlightened soldier of the cross Paul was well aware of the devil's power, cunning, and activities to deceive and to mislead the believers in Jesus, as Paul knew Satan was attempting to do to the Christians in Corinth. Paul wrote to the Corinthians,

"I am afraid lest in some way, as the serpent utterly deceived Eve in craftiness, your thoughts might be led astray from the singleness of purpose and purity in regard to Christ" (2 Corinthians 11:3).

Such deception and leading astray was Satan's aim in every place where Paul carried the gospel of Jesus Christ.

This biographical commentary does not point out the above information in the course of its explanations and comments. It is hoped this introduction will prepare the reader to know what to look for and to enable him or her to understand what was going on behind the scenes in Paul's life and ministry – a war for the minds of mankind, and Paul was in the thick of it!

CONTENTS

PART I
ABOUT THIS COMMENTARY'S CHRONOLOGY OF THE LIFE OF PAUL

1. The Problem In Compiling A Chronology Of The Life Of Paul — 3
2. The Basis Of This Chronology Of The Life Of Paul — 15
3. The Chronology For This Biographical Commentary — 23

PART II
PAUL – THE MAN

4. Paul's Birth And Early Life — 37
5. Paul's Conversion And Call To Be An Apostle — 69
6. Paul's Characteristics After His Conversion — 103

PART III
THE INITIAL YEARS OF PAUL'S SERVICE

7. Paul In Damascus And Arabia; Paul's First Visit To Jerusalem — 175
8. Paul In Tarsus, Syria, And Cilicia; Paul's Vision Of Heaven — 189
9. The City Of Antioch, Syria; King Herod & His Death; The Famine In Jerusalem — 211

PART IV
PAUL'S FIRST MISSIONARY JOURNEY

10. Paul's Divine Call Through The Church; His Mission Work On Cyprus — 239
11. Paul's Mission Work In Southern Galatia — 275

PART V
THE APOSTOLIC COUNCIL

12. Paul's Participation In The Apostolic Council Meeting; Paul's Rebuke Of Peter In Antioch, Syria — 357

I
ABOUT THIS COMMENTARY'S CHRONOLOGY OF THE LIFE OF PAUL

I
THE PROBLEM IN COMPILING A CHRONOLOGY OF THE LIFE OF PAUL

There were many bondservants of the Lord in the past, as there are many bondservants of the Lord to this day. But this biographical commentary is about just one of them – "The Apostle Paul, A Bondservant Of Christ Jesus."

Paul identified himself in his opening greeting in the majority of his letters as "an apostle". "An apostle" identified Paul according to his office. He was one who was sent out by God and the Lord Jesus Christ. He was a messenger who was commissioned to proclaim the gospel of God. But in three of the opening greetings in his letters he called himself a "bondservant" of Christ Jesus and of God (ref. Romans 1:1, Philippians 1:1, Titus 1:1). The Greek word that Paul used for himself in those three opening greetings was "doulos". He also identified himself as a "doulos" in Galatians 1:10. Its primary meaning was a slave, a man in bonds and servitude who was the property of someone else.[1] [2] Paul used this term in its secondary sense of one who as a fruit of his faith, in loving thanksgiving, gave himself over fully to the service and will of Christ Jesus, his beloved Lord and Savior, who used Paul's service to accomplish his purpose of spreading the gospel to Jews and Gentiles alike. The Greek word doulos is a sermon about the faith and life and love and commitment and servitude of the man Paul, whom God called in Christ Jesus to be his apostle and spokesman of the gospel of salvation by grace through faith alone in Jesus Christ.

Over the 2,000 years since Paul lived and loved and labored in the service of his Lord Jesus Christ, an innumerable amount of books and documents and sermons have been written about the apostle Paul. In them Paul has been praised for who and what he was and for the tremendous work he did as the greatest of missionaries to establish the Christian Church in its infancy. And indeed such books and writings should speak so highly of him. But if Paul could see now all those literary works praising him, he would likely adapt the Old Testament verse of Psalm 115:1 and apply it to himself, saying, "Not unto me, O Lord, not unto me, but to your name be the glory!" Yes, Paul, a bondservant of Christ Jesus, would not take any credit for what his God and Lord had accomplished through him. He would give all credit to God, which he did in his Pauline letters. Referring to the gospel and its power to enlighten people and convert them, Paul wrote, "We have this treasure in clay vessels, in order that the extraordinary greatness of the power may be of God and not from us" (2 Corinthians 4:7). Crediting the power of the gospel to God and not to any powers of his own, Paul stated in Romans 1:16, "For I am not ashamed of the gospel, for it is the power of God for salvation for everyone who believes, first of all not only to the Jew but also to the Greek." Paul also told the Romans, "I will not presume to say anything except what Christ accomplished through me by word and deed for the obedience of the Gentiles" (Romans 15:18). And in one of his spontaneous, Spirit-generated outbursts of praise for God Paul wrote, "For from him and through him and to him are all things. To him be the gory forever! Amen" (Romans 11:36).

Paul has probably become one of the most written about men of ancient history. Historian Kenneth Scott Latourette[3] wrote that Paul's "letters are usually self-revealing and we know him better than we do any other early Christian and, indeed, almost as well as we do any figure of antiquity." What we know about Paul and the order of events in his life may be gleaned from Luke's Book of Acts and from details that Paul supplied in his letters, such as in Galatians 1:13-2:1; 1 Corinthians 16:8; 2 Corinthians 11:32, 33 & 12:2; Romans 15:23-25, and Philemon 9 & 22. Having had these sources handed down to us, we have been blessed by the Lord with true historical facts and information as well as the life, work, and teachings of the apostle Paul that are absolutely trustworthy and reliable, for they are, after all, the inspired Word of God, who does not lie or make any mistakes (ref. 2 Timothy 3:16; John 17:17; Numbers 23:19).

Having God's word for the accuracy and trustworthiness of the Book of Acts and the Pauline epistles is sufficient for the Bible-believing Christian. He needs no further evidence to substantiate this fact. Be that as it is, he may find from time to time even an author of a non-biblical work who vouches for the accuracy and trustworthiness of the biblical text. In addition to some Bible-believing archaeologists he finds such an author in James Smith. James Smith in his classic work entitled The Voyage and Shipwreck of St. Paul,[4] published in 1856, commended Luke as having been a most accurate writer. With regard to Luke's narrative about the voyage and shipwreck of Paul that is recorded in Acts 27 Smith stated:

> St. Luke . . . possesses two qualifications as a writer, which in a great degree compensate for his omissions, and which enable us to supply many of them with the greatest certainty. The first of these is his perfect acquaintance with his subject, and second his accuracy. No man who was not in an eminent degree gifted with this quality could have given a narrative capable of being tested as his has been in the following examination. He must not only have been an accurate observer, but his memory must have been accurate, and his habits of thought and reasoning not less so. Hence his facts afford the firmest grounds for resting inferences upon, and these, in their turn, furnish data for mathematical reasoning. The reader may give an incredulous smile at working the dead reckoning of a ship from such disjointed and apparently vague notices: yet I have done so, and the result is nearer than I could have expected beforehand, had it been the journal of a modern ship, and had her log book been lying before me.

But even though we have the accurate, trustworthy sources mentioned above, setting forth the actual dates of the events in Paul's life is difficult, to say the least, and depends upon the calculations of dates that are based on thorough, intensive study, but are in the end still educated human conclusions. They are not to be confused with, or put on the same level of authority as, the inspired Scriptures of the Old and New Testaments. Conybeare & Howson, p. 91 states, "Theologians are well aware of the difficulties with which such (chronological) inquiries are attended, in the beginnings of St. Paul's biography. The early chapters in the Acts are like the narratives in the Gospels. It is often hardly possible to learn how far the events related were contemporary or consecutive."[5] In spite of this difficulty a reasonably accurate chronology is possible. The New Schaff-Herzog Encyclopedia of Religious Knowledge, Vol. VIII, in its discussion of "Paul, The Apostle" states, "Actual dates depend upon data which do not afford a single indisputable conclusion, yet, taken together, set definite limits to the field of science. The data and the events which they thus approximately determine are as follows: . . ."[6] Similarly, W. M. Ramsay in his St. Paul The Traveler And Roman Citizen spoke of Luke's "careful attention to order of events, and inattention to the stating of the lapse of time"; but then he added, "knowledge acquired from other sources, and attention to the author's order and method, enable us to fix the chronology with great accuracy; . . ."[7]

Except for Paul's own statements about his life and work in his letters, our knowledge of the life of Paul is totally dependent upon Luke's accounts in his Book of Acts. And his historical presentation of Paul's life, as trustworthy as it is, does not provide us with the definitive evidence we would like to have to establish the exact dates of many of the events in Paul's life.

W. M. Ramsay described the nature of the problem the biographer faces:

> Luke was deficient in the sense of time; and hence his chronology is bad. It would be quite impossible from *Acts* alone to get a true idea of the lapse of time. That is the fault of his age; . . . Luke had studied the

sequence of events carefully, and observes it in his arrangement minutely, but he often goes back in time to take up another thread; and these transitions are sometimes harsh. Yet, in respect of chronology, he was, perhaps, less careless than would appear.[8]

Ramsay acknowledged Luke to be a trustworthy historian. He said that he had "reasons for placing the author of *Acts* among the historians of the first rank."[9] And Ramsay then approached Luke's Book of Acts as a trustworthy work of history[10] as a historian who was using a "work of history". Ramsay stated, ". . . we . . .work on the hypothesis that *Acts* is a history."[11] He then evaluated Luke's work in the Book of Acts as a historian would, going so far as to say,

> . . . no one can accept the ending of *Acts* as the conclusion of a rationally conceived history[12] . . . We shall argue that the plan of *Acts* has been obscured by the want of the proper climax and conclusion, which would have made it clear, and also that the author did not live to put the final touches to his second book (referring to Acts). Perhaps we may thus account for the failure of chronological data. . . If the work was left incomplete, the reason, perhaps, lay in the author's martyrdom under Domitian.[13]

Ramsay was a historical scholar of no small reputation. For this reason this writer is reluctant to say anything contrary to his assessment. But this writer begs to respectively disagree that the plan of Luke's Book of Acts was obscured by the lack of a proper climax and conclusion. In this instance Ramsay did not correctly assess Luke's purpose in writing the Book of Acts and its theme. In contrast to Ramsay's assessment of Luke's Book of Acts, F. F. Bruce said, "He (Luke) has achieved the aim of his writing when he has brought Paul to Rome and left him there carrying on his apostolic task without let or hindrance under the eyes of the imperial authorities. But he has left us asking questions which he did not regard it as his business to answer, and to which no other writer provides a satisfactory answer."[14]

The Book of Acts is history, but it is not a history book. Professor Dr. Martin H. Franzmann, wrote this about the Book of Acts:

> The book does not pretend to be a history of the first church or even a history of early missions. It would be woefully incomplete as either of the two. It is the continuation of the story of the Christ, and can therefore be as selective in recording the facts of history as the Gospel itself. Of all the ways which the Gospel went, Luke selects just one, the high road to Rome.[15]

Dr. Franzmann went on to speak of large gaps in the record of Paul and said that "the whole work illustrates rather than chronicles the course of the word which proclaims and presents the Christ."[16]

Luke wrote the Book of Acts as a continuation of his Gospel of Luke. This intended continuation is evident from the first verse of Acts: "To be sure, the earlier written account I made, O Theophilus, was about all that Jesus began both to do and to teach." Note well Luke's words regarding his gospel as being "about all that Jesus **began** both to do and to teach." The Gospel of Luke relates what Jesus began to do and to teach during his three-year ministry and then Luke's Book of Acts relates what Jesus continued to do and to teach by means of the apostles whom he had chosen to "go into all the world and preach the gospel to all creation" (Mark 16:15).

Luke then wrote Acts with a definite purpose and theme in mind based on Jesus' commission in Acts 1:8: "You will be my witnesses both in Jerusalem, and in all Judea and Samaria, and even as far as the end of the earth." Luke's theme and purpose of the Book of Acts, then, "could be stated as tracing the progress of the Word of Jesus and the growth of the church from Jerusalem to Rome"[17]

Since that was Luke's theme and purpose for the Book of Acts, he picked and chose carefully what to include and what to exclude. He focused his narrative on the spread of the gospel from Jerusalem to Rome. He relates the successes of that spread of the gospel and the continued growth in the number of believers. He also relates the opposition that that gospel stirred up in those who tried to hinder and stop the spread of Jesus' gospel. Luke's style of historical narrative was to dwell on and elucidate those events in which the gospel of Jesus was spread and opposed and to brush over other events and periods of time that did not illustrate that spread and opposition. Thus the events he passed over did not fit into the scheme of the historical narrative of how Jesus continued to spread his gospel through his witnesses from Jerusalem to the end of the earth. This is very evident in his brief narrative style that omits amounts of time that elapsed between events and the omission of the names of men or places and other such details. The biographer of the life of Paul most desperately looks for such information, but very often Luke did not include it because it did not advance his theme and purpose. And so, contrary to Ramsay's theory that the Book of Acts is incomplete without a proper climax, the book is indeed complete from the perspective of Luke's purpose and theme of the book – the spread of the gospel of Jesus Christ from Jerusalem, the capital of Judea in the East, to Rome, the capital of the Roman Empire in the West.

One weakness of this writer's above explanation of Luke's style of historical narrative is Luke's failure to even mention Paul's early mission work in Syria and Cilicia from late A.D. 35 to the fall of 43. That was eight years! the longest period of time that Paul spent in any one region doing mission work, and yet Luke never even mentioned it! Perhaps the reason for this omission was that Paul never informed him of the details of those years, in which case Luke could not include them in his narrative.

Here are three examples of the problem that is faced chronicling the life of Paul on the basis of Luke's Book of Acts alone:

1) An important date for establishing the chronology of Paul's life is the date for Paul's conversion not long after the stoning of Stephen recorded in Acts 7:54-60. This date, however, cannot be established conclusively from the information Luke provides in the Book of Acts. The reason being that Luke does not indicate the length of time between the Pentecost event recorded in Acts 2:1-41 and the apostolic church's selection of the seven deacons recorded in Acts 6:1-6, nor the

amount of time that elapsed between the selection of those seven deacons and the stoning of Stephen. Thus, because of this lack of information, the date of Stephen's stoning and Paul's conversion shortly afterwards cannot be determined exactly on the basis of the Book of Acts alone.

2) When Paul returned from his second missionary journey, Luke reports, "And when he had put in at Caesarea, after he went up and greeted the church, he came down to Antioch" Acts 18:22. As will be explained in detail in the following body of this biographical commentary, this verse indicates that Paul went up to Jerusalem to greet the church. Luke reports this with just one word in the Greek text and never mentioned the city of Jerusalem, for he assumed everyone would know that "going up" was a common manner of speaking of going up to Jerusalem.

3) When Paul left Ephesus near the end of his third missionary journey and went into Macedonia, Luke reports in Acts 20:2, "And after he had passed through those parts and encouraged them with a long speech, he came into Greece." As this will also be explained in detail in the body of this commentary with that one sentence Luke reported a seven-month journey of Paul through Macedonia visiting the churches in Philippi, Thessalonica, and Berea to encourage them. And then at the end of seven months Paul entered Achaia and visited the church in Corinth.

One additional note for the benefit of the reader: If one undertakes the study of the life of Paul and begins to research the information available to him from recognized historians and sources, one soon learns that at nearly every juncture and time in the life of Paul as set forth in the Book of Acts and the Pauline epistles, there are differing opinions, conjectures, hypotheses, and arguments of the historians, biographers, and commentators. The location of Paul's shipwreck is one example. Luke said it occurred on Malta (Melita in the Greek text) in the part of the Mediterranean Sea called the Adria. Yet it has been asserted that his ship was wrecked on a different island named Melita (Melita Illyrica) at the northern tip of the Adriatic Sea, far north of Malta and the part of the sea in which Paul's ship sailed. How Paul came to know the gospel is another example of an erring opinion the reader will run into. Paul very plainly stated, and by the inspiration of God the Holy Spirit no less, that the gospel he preached he had received from no man:

> 11 For I make known to you, brothers, that the gospel that was preached by me is not according to man;
>
> 2 for indeed I neither received it from a man, nor was I taught it, but I received it by revelation of Jesus Christ. (Galatians 1:11, 12)

Yet New Testament historian F. F. Bruce qualifies Paul's plain and clear statement and asserts that Paul received by revelation only the essence of the gospel but not its factual details, which he needed to learn from the firsthand, eyewitness Peter.[18]

In addition to the differing opinions and conjectures that one runs into is erroneous information that is supposed to be credible, historical evidence but is actually contrary to what the inspired, inerrant Word of God in the Bible says. Here is an erroneous bit of information this writer came across in doing his research: According to the Turkish Archaeological News[19] the earliest archaeological finds from the area of the acropolis in ancient Perga are dated to the end of the fifth millennium B.C. But according to the chronological information given in the Book of Genesis, which is a part of the inspired, inerrant Word of God, the late fifth millennium B.C. would put those earliest archaeological finds before the date of the creation of the world, which occurred in the year 5,139 B.C. Beyond all doubt God's Word makes those fifth millennium finds an impossibility! The next claim of the Turkish Archaeological News' article said that the oldest traces of a continuous settlement at Perga were in the third millennium B.C. This, too, is just as false. For that time of the third millennium B.C. falls between the time of Seth at 4,000 B.C. and the time of Enoch at 3,282 B.C. and before the time of the universal flood of Noah in 2,613 B.C. So that dating of the third millennium is also an impossibility! For the complete chronological timetable for the age of this world beginning with creation through the time of Joseph, see <u>An Overview Of The Book Of Genesis</u> on the Christian Inconnect website.[20]

It is not the aim or the intention of this writer to examine and evaluate each and every one of the different opinions, hypotheses, arguments, or informational errors. Rather this biographical commentary will for the most part simply present the information that the inspired, inerrant Word of God in the Book of Acts and the Pauline epistles present, together with credible ancient Christian traditions and historical findings where applicable, as this writer has found them in the course of his biblical studies and research. In the process of writing this biographical commentary with its chronology this writer then, where called for, on the basis of those sources just mentioned, presented his best understandings, datings, and possible explanations of what took place and when in the life of Paul. As much as possible sources of information were noted. This commentary was written for Christian men and women who are looking for biblically sound information that unfolds the life of Paul to the best extent possible. This was not written to be a dissertation that examines and argues about all the historical hypotheses and conjectures that have been presented over the centuries.

---

1. Gingrich, F. Wilbur; Shorter Lexicon Of The Greek New Testament; The University of Chicago Press; Chicago, Illinois; p.55
2. Thayer, Joseph Henry, PhD.; Greek-English Lexicon of the New Testament; Zondervan Publishing House; Grand Rapids, Michigan; p. 157 & 158
3. Latourette, Kenneth Scott: A History of the Expansion of Christianity Volume 1; The First Five Centuries; Zondervan Publishing House; Grand Rapids, Michigan; p. 74
4. Smith, James; The Voyage and Shipwreck of St. Paul; Published: Longman, Brown, Green, Longmans, & Roberts, 2nd edition: London, England; p.34 & 35
5. Conybeare, W. J. & Howson, J. S.; The Life And Epistles of St. Paul; Wm. B. Eerdmans Publishing Company; Grand Rapids, Michigan; p. 91
6. The New Schaff-Herzog Encyclopedia of Religious Knowledge, Vol. VIII,; "Paul, The Apostle"; Jackson, Samuel Macauley, editor-in-chief; Baker Book House; Grand Rapids, Michigan; p. 398
7. Ramsay, W. M.; St. Paul The Traveler And Roman Citizen; Baker Book House; Grand Rapids, Michigan; Preface p. xvi
8. ibid. p. 18
9. ibid. p. 4

10. ibid, p. 1
11. ibid. p. 352
12. ibid. p. 352
13. ibid. p. 23
14. Bruce, F. F.; New Testament History; Doubleday; New York, London, Toronto, Sydney, Auckland; 1969; p. 361
15. Franzmann, Martin H.; The Word Of The Lord Grows; Concordia Publishing House, St. Louis, Missouri; p. 207
16. ibid.
17. Schneidervin, John C.; Christian Inconnect; Overview Of The Book of Acts, Vivid English Translation Of The New Testament, http://www.christianinconnect.com/book-of-acts.html)
18. Bruce, F. F.; New Testament History; Doubleday; New York, London, Toronto, Sydney, Auckland; 1969; p. 243, 244
19. Turkish Archaeological News; Perge; http://turkisharchawonews.net/site/perge
20. Schneidervin, John C.; Christian Inconnect; An Overview Of The Book Of Genesis; http://www.christianinconnect.com/overview-of-the-book-of-genesis.html

2

THE BASIS OF THIS CHRONOLOGY OF THE LIFE OF PAUL

Having described the problem of assembling an accurate chronology of Paul's life, an explanation of how this biographical chronology was established is in order. There are a number of key dates that form a basic skeleton for a chronology of the life of Paul upon which this writer was able to "flesh out" this historical, biographical narrative. Here is a listing of those dates as this writer has ascertained them:

1. The death of Herod the Great in 4 B.C.
2. Pontius Pilate's becoming governor of Judea in A.D. 26
3. The reign of Emperor Tiberias from A.D. 14-37
4. The beginning of John the Baptist's ministry in the 15th year of Tiberias in A.D. 28, Luke 3:1-3
5. The forty-sixth year of the building of the temple in Jerusalem, which was the first year of Jesus' three-year ministry and the time of Jesus' baptism by John in A.D.28; John 2:20, Luke 3:21, Mark 1:9, Matthew 3:13
6. The crucifixion, resurrection, and ascension of Jesus in the third year of his ministry in A.D. 31.(His three-year ministry spanned the four calendar years of A.D. 28, 29, 30 and 31.) See the four gospels and the Book of Acts

7. The death of Herod Agrippa in A.D. 44 in the third year of his reign over Judea under Emperor Claudius, Acts 12:1-23; Josephus, Antiquities, 19.8.2; Wars of the Jews, 2.11.6 (Josephus was a Jewish historian who is thought to have written his Antiquities and Wars of the Jews around A.D. 75)

8. The proconsulship of Gallio over Achaia in A.D. 51 & 52

9. Porcius Festus replaces Felix as governor of Judea at Pentecost, which was between mid-May to June 10th in A.D. 59, Josephus' Antiquities 20.7.1 & Acts 24:27.

An explanation would be beneficial for the year A.D. 28, which according to this chronology was the forty-sixth year of the building of the temple in Jerusalem, which was also the first year of Jesus' public ministry. Josephus in his Antiquities 15:11.1 stated King Herod the Great began the reconstruction of the temple in Jerusalem in the eighteenth year of his reign. His reign began in 37 B.C. after he finished conquering the city of Jerusalem. The eighteenth year of his reign, then, was 19 B.C. F.F. Bruce indicates these same dates.[1] Nineteen B.C. was the year when Herod addressed the Jews and proposed his reconstruction of the temple. Josephus marks that eighteenth year of Herod's reign when he proposed the reconstruction of the temple as the beginning of that reconstruction. Following Josephus, F. F. Bruce also marks the eighteenth year as the beginning of the reconstruction. The actual reconstruction of the temple, however, did not begin until sometime later according to Josephus' Antiquities 15.11.2. Before the actual reconstruction began Josephus indicated the resistance of the Jewish population had to be overcome, because the Jews were afraid Herod would tear down their existing temple and would fail to build a new one in its place, for the reconstruction would be such a gigantic undertaking. What is more, Josephus indicated that before the reconstruction began Herod assembled one thousand wagons for hauling the needed stone, chose ten thousand of the most skillful workmen, and bought a thousand sacerdotal garments for the priests and trained some of them in the arts of stonecutting and carpentry. And Josephus stated that then Herod began to build, but that building did not happen until "everything was well prepared for the work." All of those preparations just mentioned would have taken some time to complete. Allowing a year for all those preparations would be a good estimate, which would date the actual start of the reconstruction in 18 B.C., not 19 B.C. When Jesus cleansed the temple for the first time during the first year of his ministry, the Jews told him that the temple was in its forty-sixth year of reconstruction (John 2:20). Forty-six years from 18 B.C. would make the date of Jesus' cleansing the temple and the first year of his ministry A.D.28. This date coincides with the dating Luke provides in Luke 3:1-3 for the beginning of John the Baptist's ministry. John must have begun his public ministry in the early part of A.D. 28 and Jesus began his ministry some months later in the same year.

Another important part of the skeletal underbody of this chronology is based on a statement attributed to Chrysostom (c. A.D. 349-407). Chrysostom is credited as having said that Paul served the Lord for 35 years and was 68 years old when he was martyred.[2] Both Eusebius of Caesarea (c. A.D. 275-340) and St. Jerome (died September 30, A.D.420) indicated that Paul was martyred in the last year of Roman Emperor Nero. Nero died on June 9th A.D. 68. Putting this information together, Paul would have been born in A.D.1, his conversion would have taken place in A.D. 33, not too long after Stephan's martyrdom recorded in Acts 7:54-60, and Paul would have been martyred in A.D. 68.

The date of A.D. 33 for Paul's conversion agrees with the information that Paul himself provided in his Letter to the Galatians. In Galatians 1:18 Paul stated that three years after leaving Jerusalem and going to Damascus, at which time he was converted, he returned to Jerusalem. Then in Galatians 2:1 Paul stated that after fourteen years, he again went up to Jerusalem. That is a total of seventeen years from his conversion to his second visit to Jerusalem to attend the Apostolic Council. If he was indeed converted in A.D. 33 that seventeen years later dates the Apostolic Council Meeting at A.D. 50, which is the accepted date for that meeting. So it is that the information attributed to Chrysostom and the information provided by Paul are in agreement – Paul's conversion occurred in A.D. 33.

The above date of A.D. 51 & 52 for the proconsulship of Gallio has documented support.[3] [4] It is widely known that Emperor Claudius sent a letter to the city of Delphi, Greece, after Proconsul Gallio's term of office ended. The contents of the letter were engraved into a stone tablet and attached to a wall of a public building. The letter contains the name of "Gallio Proconsul of Achaia", as well as the name of Emperor Claudius, with dates for his reign. The date of the letter has been set as A.D. 52. It is known that since proconsuls were required to leave Rome for their posts no later than the middle of April, Gallio probably began his term of office in May A.D. 51, or at least no later than May. The chronology of this biographical commentary places Paul's arrival in Corinth around August of A.D. 51, which means Paul arrived in Corinth about three months after Gallio assumed his duties as the proconsul of Achaia. This dating allows time for Paul to have been brought before Gallio before the end of Gallio's term of office and to have remained in Corinth for a "considerable number of days longer"[5] before leaving Corinth himself.

In addition to the dates shown above, this chronology took into consideration what has been determined as the probable dates when Paul wrote his thirteen letters of the New Testament, beginning with his Letter to the Galatians written in the fall of A.D. 51 and ending with his Second Letter to Timothy written about mid A.D. 67.

The dates for the events of Acts 11:27-30 and 12:1-23 require some explanation. In Acts 11:27-30 Luke reports the prophet Agabus foretelling the great famine during the reign of Emperor Claudius and the ensuing collection taken by the church in Antioch to aid the Christians in Judea. In Acts 12:1-23 Luke informs us of Herod's persecution of Christians, his killing of the apostle James the brother of the apostle John, his arrest of Peter, and Herod's being put to death by an angel of the Lord. The dates of these events can be calculated on the basis of the famine foretold by Agabus in Acts 11:28. Josephus in his Antiquities 20.5.2 states the famine occurred during the terms of office of Fadus Cuspius and Tiberias Julius Alexander as procurator of Judea. Fadus was procurator from around October A.D. 44 into the year A.D. 46; Tiberias Alexander was procurator from A.D. 46 to 48.

This information enables us to see that that famine started with the spring harvest of March to June A.D. 45 for the barley and wheat crops and then the summer and fall harvests of the fruit crops of grapes, figs, and olives from July to November of the same year. This period was, as Agabus, had foretold, during the reign of Claudius, who was emperor from A.D. 41-58. This information made possible the indication or the calculation of certain events or periods of time: It narrowed the month of Herod Agrippa I's death to around August A.D. 44, which year is established by Josephus' Antiquities 19:8.2. The dating of the famine also made it possible to calculate the period of time that Paul and Barnabas worked for the famine relief in Jerusalem. The information also made it possible to indicate or to calculate the various months of certain events in the years A.D. 44 and 45 in the following chronology.

The dating of the reign of Aretas, the Nabataean king, whom Paul mentioned in 2 Corinthians 11:32 in connection with his escape from Damascus, was considered but not used to calculate the date of that escape. This writer did not think that the date of Aretas' reign from 9 B.C. to A.D.39 (a span of 48 years) and the date of Aretas' control over Damascus and the information about his "ethnarch/governor" over Damascus (which date and information are conjectural suppositions at best), were conclusive enough to date Paul's escape from Damascus, as helpful as that date would have been.

No definitive date can be attributed either to Paul's evangelizing Sergius Paulus on the island of Cyprus. The archeological evidence pertaining to Sergius Paulus is scanty and does not conclusively indicate the years during which he served as proconsul on Cyprus.

An explanation for the year A.D. 59 when Porcius Festus replaced Felix as procurator, or governor, of Judea is also needed. This chronology dates this change of procurators as Pentecost, which was between mid-May to June 10th, in A.D. 59. The year of A.D. 59 has support. F. F. Bruce indicated the year for this change was A.D. 59. He wrote, "The date of his (Felix') recall and replacement by Porcius Festus is disputed, but a change in the provincial coinage of Judea attested for Nero's fifth year points to A.D. 59."[6]

The year of A.D. 59 also fits into the frame of time indicated by Josephus and allowed by Acts 24:10. Josephus in his Antiquities 20.7.1 reports Claudius sent Felix "to take care of the affairs of Judea" at the time when "he had already completed the twelfth year of his reign . . ." Claudius became emperor of Rome in January of A.D. 41. In counting to the completed twelfth year of his reign one must count A.D. 41 as the first year. The twelfth completed year, then, would have been A.D. 52 when Claudius made Felix procurator of Judea. In Acts 24:10 Paul acknowledged that Felix at that time was the procurator of Judea "for many years." How many years are many years is, of course, debatable. What length of time might Paul have had in mind? To answer this question we can try to look at it from the perspective of Paul's timeframe. For how many years had the various procurators of Judea remained in office? Except for Pontius Pilate, who held the office for ten years, and Valerius Gratus before him, who held the office for eleven years, the procurators from A.D. 6 to Felix in A.D. 52 held the office for only two to three years. Felix took office in A.D. 52. Figuring A.D. 59 was the year that Felix was deposed and subtracting two years for the two years of Paul's imprisonment under Felix, the year of Paul's trial before Felix when Paul acknowledge the "many years" was A.D. 57. So Felix would have been procurator for five years at the time Paul acknowledged the "many years". Five years was two to three years longer than the majority of the previous procurators, and therefore the reason Paul referred to Felix' term of office as "many years". So the year of A.D. 59 does fit the timeframe indicated by Josephus and allowed by Acts 24:10.

---

1. Bruce, F. F.; New Testament History; Doubleday; New York, London, Toronto, Sydney, Auckland; 1969; p. 14 & 21
2. Ramsay, W. M.; St. Paul The Traveler And Roman Citizen; Baker Book House; Grand Rapids, Michigan; Preface p. xvi; see also Conybeare & Howson who mention this information attributed to Chrysostom; Conybeare, W. J. & Howson, J. S.; The Life And Epistles of St. Paul; Wm. B. Erdmann Publishing Company; Grand Rapids, Michigan; p. 37)
3. Archaeology and the Bible – NAMB; Archaeology and the Bible, 03.30.16, Blog; p. 3; https://www.namb.net/apologetics-bl;blog/archaeology-and-the-bible

4. Bruce, F. F.; The Acts Of The Apostles; William B. Eerdmans Publishing Company; Grand Rapids, Michigan; Third Revised And Enlarged Edition; 1990; p. 395
5. Acts 18:18
6. Bruce, F. F.; New Testament History; Doubleday; New York, London, Toronto, Sydney, Auckland; 1969; p. 345 & 346

THE CHRONOLOGY FOR THIS BIOGRAPHICAL COMMENTARY

Notes *For This Chronology:*
Pentecost occurred about mid-May to June 10th; this time period will be rounded off to "about June 1st".

The Feast of Unleavened Bread occurred about early March to the end of April; this time period will be rounded off to "about April 15th".

The following paragraphs give the dates of their respective events and/or the dates when Paul's letters were written. Note: The letter "c." in connection with a date means "about".

37 – 4 B.C.
   Reign of King Herod the Great

27 B.C –A.D.14
   Reign Of Roman Emperor Caesar Augustus

4 B.C.
   Birth of Christ; Luke 2:1-20

. . .

4 B.C.
Eight days after Jesus ' birth, he is circumcised and given the name of Jesus; Luke 3:21

4 B.C.
After 40 days had passed from the day of Jesus' birth, in keeping with the law of Moses, Mary and Joseph take Jesus to Jerusalem to present him to the Lord as a firstborn son, and to make a burnt offering and a sin offering for Mary; Luke 2:22-38

4 B.C.
The visit of the wise men, the flight into Egypt, and Herod the Great's slaughter of the male infants in Bethlehem; Matthew 2:1-18

4 B.C.
Death of Herod the Great; Mthew 2:19

4 B.C.
Upon the death of Herod the Great, Joseph brings Mary and Jesus back to Judea and they go to Nazareth in Galilee
Reign of Archelaus' begins; Matthew 2:19-23, Luke 2:39, 40

A.D. 1
Birth of Paul of Tarsus in Cilicia

September A.D. 14 – March 37
Reign of Roman Emperor Tiberias

. . .

A.D. 26
Pontius Pilate becomes governor of Judea

A.D. 28
John the Baptist's ministry begins in the 15th year of Tiberius Caesar and when Pilate is governor of Judea; Luke 3:1-20

In the 46th year of the temple's reconstruction in A.D. 28 (John 2:20; Josephus' Ant. 15:11:1 & 2) Jesus is baptized and begins the first year of his ministry when he is about 30 years of age. He then cleanses the temple; Luke 3:1, 21-23

End of March to about May 1st A.D. 31
Jesus' crucifixion, resurrection, and his ascension 40 days after his resurrection; Acts 1:3 and the gospel accounts

May A.D. 31
The day of Pentecost occurs 10 days after Jesus' ascension.

Pentecost marks the birth of the Christian church. The Holy Spirit comes miraculously upon Jesus' disciples, and Peter then preaches to the crowds, at which time 3,000 are converted and baptized and added to the church; Acts 2:1-41

c. A.D. 32
The martyrdom of Stephen. Paul approves of his murder by stoning; Acts 7:58-8:1. Paul then begins persecuting the church, which lasted for about a year.

A.D. 33

Paul's conversion; Acts 9:1-19

c. A.D. 33 to 35

During this three-year period of time Paul leaves Damascus and travels to Arabia, where he spends some period of time. Then he returns to Damascus where he preaches until he is compelled to flee. He flees from Damascus to Jerusalem; Acts 9:23-25; 2 Corinthians 11:32, 33

These preceding events in Paul's life as told in Galatians 1:17, 18 are wedged in between the end of Acts 9:22 and the beginning of Acts 9:23.

c. late A.D. 35

Paul's first visit to Jerusalem after his conversion at which time he visits with Peter for fifteen days; Galatians 1:18-20. He also sees James the Lord's half-brother, and debates with Hellenistic Jews until they plot to kill him. In the temple Jesus speaks to Paul in a vision. He is forced to flee to Tarsus; Acts 9:26-30

A.D. 36

Pontius Pilate is deposed as governor of Judea

c. late A.D. 35 to the fall of 43

Paul conducts his ministry in Tarsus of Cilicia and in the regions of Syria and Cilicia; Acts 9:30; Galatians 1:21

March A.D. 37 to January A.D. 41
Reign of Emperor Caligula

. . .

January A.D. 41-October A.D.54
   Reign Of Emperor Claudius

A.D. 41-44
   Reign Of King Herod Agrippa over all of Judea and Samaria; Josephus' Antiquities 19.5.1 & 19.8.2

A.D. 42
   Paul is given a revelation of heaven; 2 Corinthians 12:1-4

Fall of A.D. 43
   Paul's mission work in Syria and Cilicia ends when he is brought to Antioch to begin working with Barnabas for one year

c. December A.D. 43
   The prophet Agabus comes to Antioch and foretells a famine is coming; the church in Antioch then begins a collection for famine relief; Acts 11:27-30

c. January & February A.D. 44
   King Herod Agrippa I begins his persecution of Christians and kills the apostle James, the brother of the apostle John; Acts 12:1 & 2

c. March A.D. 44
   Herod arrests and imprisons Peter, but an angel frees him; Acts 12:3-17

c. April to August A.D. 44

Herod leaves Judea and goes to Caesarea where he is killed by an angel of the Lord at age 54; Acts 12:18-23; Josephus' Ant. 19.8.2

c. October 1st A.D. 44

To fill the vacancy of a ruler over Judea after the death of King Herod Agrippa I, Emperor Claudius appoints Fadus Cuspius as procurator of Judea. He rules over Judea into the year of A.D. 46.

The famine in Judea begins during Fadus' term in office; Josephus' Ant. 20.5.2.

c. March A.D. 45

Paul and Barnabas are sent by the church in Antioch to Jerusalem on a famine relief mission at the start of the harvest season that then fails, Acts 11:29 & 30. They remain to assist with the relief mission.

This is Paul's 2nd visit to Jerusalem after his conversion.

A.D. 46

Tiberias Julius Alexander is appointed by Emperor Claudius as procurator of Judea to replace Fadus Cuspius. He rules into the year A.D. 48.

The famine in Judea continues into his term of office; Josephus ' Ant. 20.5.2

c. early A.D. 46

Paul and Barnabas return to Antioch with John Mark, Acts 12:25

c. A.D. 46 to 49

Paul's first missionary journey with Barnabas to Cyprus, Pamphylia, and Galatia in Asia Minor; Acts 13:4-14:28

. . .

Early A.D. 50

Seventeen years after Paul's conversion he makes his third visit to Jerusalem for the Apostolic Council Meeting; Galatians 1:18 & 2:1; Acts 15:1-33

Paul returns to and remains in Antioch with Barnabas teaching and preaching for some period of days; Acts 15:30 & 35, 36

While remaining in Antioch Paul rebukes Peter for compromising the pure gospel by not associating with the Gentile Christian converts there; Galatians 2:11-21

c. The spring A.D. 50 to late March 53

Paul and Barnabas separate

Paul's second missionary journey through Galatia into Greece to Philippi, Thessalonica, Berea, Athens, and Corinth, Acts 15:36-18:22. Paul works in Corinth 1 1/2 years per Acts 18:11.

Paul arrives in Philippi around August, A.D. 50

Paul arrives in Corinth around August, A.D. 51

Gallio is proconsul of Achaia in A.D. 51-52

Paul sails back to Caesarea, goes up to Jerusalem to visit the church there, then goes down to Antioch; Acts 18:22. This is Paul's fourth visit to Jerusalem after his conversion.

Paul writes Galatians in the fall of A.D. 51

Paul writes 1 Thessalonians in the fall of A.D. 51

Paul writes 2 Thessalonians in early A.D. 52

A.D. 52

Felix becomes governor (procurator) of Judea in the 12th year of Claudius' reign; Josephus Ant. 20.7.1

May A.D. 53 to October A.D. 54

The first portion of Paul's third missionary journey through

Galatia and Asia Minor to Ephesus (Acts 18:23-20:6) where he worked for three years per Acts 20:31

October A.D. 54 – June A.D. 68
    Reign of Roman Emperor Nero

November A.D. 54 to Pentecost, about June 1st, A.D. 56 (ref. 1 Corinthians 16:8)
    The remaining portion of Paul's third missionary journey and work in Ephesus, including his brief visit to Corinth and the churches in Macedonia around April 1, A.D. 55
    Paul writes 1 Corinthians in late A.D. 55

Pentecost, about June 1st, A.D. 55 to mid-December A.D. 56
    Paul leaves Ephesus and visits Troas, 2 Cor. 2:12, 13; he then goes to Macedonia where he visits the churches in Philippi, Thessalonica, and Berea; Acts 19:21, 20:1, 2
    Paul writes 2 Corinthians in late A.D. 56
    It is possible that Paul also traveled at this time northward into Illyricum for a short time after writing Second Corinthians
    Paul travels on foot to Corinth to visit it for the 3rd time; 2 Corinthians 12:14-21 & 13:1, 2

c. December 15th A.D. 56 to March 15th A.D. 57
    Paul spends 3 months in Corinth; Acts 20:3
    Paul writes Romans in early A.D. 57

c. March 15th to Pentecost, about June 1st, A.D. 57
    Paul leaves Corinth, walks to Philippi, then sails to Troas, Miletus in Asia, and Tyre, and then travels to Jerusalem; Acts 20:3-21:17

. . .

Pentecost, about June 1st, A.D. 57
   Paul's fifth visit to Jerusalem
   He visits with James and the elders of the church
   He is then mobbed by the Jews at the temple and taken into Roman custody

Pentecost, about June 1st, A.D. 57 to A.D. 59
   Paul is imprisoned in Caesarea for two years up to the time Porcius Festus became governor (Acts 24:27).
   During this time Paul stands trial before the Roman Tribune Claudius Lysias in Jerusalem, Governor Felix in Caesarea, Governor Porcius Festus in Caesarea at which time Paul appeals his case to Caesar in Rome, and finally stands before King Herod Agrippa II in Caesarea; Acts 21:17-26:32.
   All-total Paul was in Roman custody for more than two years, for Acts 25:13 says some days passed before he stood before Festus and then Acts 25:14 says Agrippa was spending many days in Caesarea before Festus had him hear Paul's case.

Pentecost, about June 1st, A.D. 59
   Porcius Festus replaces Felix as governor

c. mid-August to mid-December A.D. 59
   Paul is transferred to Rome by ship under Roman guard but is shipwrecked on Malta; Acts 27:1-44

c. mid-December A.D. 59 to mid-March A.D. 60
   Paul winters on Malta for three months; Acts 28:1-10

. . .

Mid-March to beginning of April A.D. 60
Paul sails from Malta, arrives in Puteoli, Italy, where he finds fellow Christians who invite him to remain for seven days; he then travels on to Rome under guard; Acts 28:11-16

April A.D. 60 to April A.D. 62
Paul's first Roman imprisonment in his own quarters; Acts 28:16-31
Paul writes Ephesians, Philippians, Colossians, Philemon in the latter part of A.D. 60 to 61

April A.D. 62 to about March 63
Paul is acquitted & released from imprisonment
Paul begins his first post-imprisonment journey to the churches: possibly first to Corinth and to Crete (Titus 1:5), then to the churches in Asia Minor and Ephesus in the province of Asia; 1 Timothy 1:3 & 3:14

c. March A.D. 63 through the winter of A.D.63-64
Paul travels to Macedonia and revisits Philippi, Philippians 2:24; 1 Timothy 1:3
Paul spends the winter in Nicopolis of Epirus, Titus 3:12
Paul writes 1 Timothy & Titus in the fall of A.D. 63

c. spring A.D. 64 through winter of A.D.65-66
Paul makes a second post-imprisonment journey to Spain and conducts mission work there

July 19th - 24th A.D. 64
Emperor Nero burns the city if Rome

Shortly afterwards he begins his persecution of Christians

c. spring A.D. 66 to mid-67
Paul makes a third post-imprisonment journey to the East, including Corinth (2 Timothy 4:20), Miletus which was south of Ephesus, (2 Timothy 4:20), Ephesus, and then Troas north of Ephesus (2 Timothy 4:13)

c. late A.D. 66 to sometime in A.D. 67
Peter's martyrdom in Rome

c. A.D. 67
Paul's second Roman imprisonment under Nero begins

c. mid A.D. 67
Paul writes his Second Letter to Timothy and states that he wants Timothy to come quickly before winter; (2 Timothy 4:9 & 21)

First half of A.D. 68
Paul is martyred in Rome in the last year of Nero
Nero died June 9, A.D. 68

II
PAUL – THE MAN

❦ 4 ❦

PAUL'S BIRTH AND EARLY LIFE

PAUL'S AGE: 1-32 DATE: A.D. 1-32

In This Chapter: Its Source Of Information; Paul's Birth And Pharisaical Membership; His Home; His Early Childhood Training And Formal Education; His Names, His Tarsian And Roman Citizenships, Family Background And Trade; His Young Adult Life As A Pharisee

---

The Source Of Information For This Chapter

What we know from the Book of Acts and from Paul's letters about his birth, his early years, and his family background is very valuable but very sketchy. In all honesty we must say that the New Testament tells us almost nothing about Paul and his life from his birth to the time he suddenly appears on the pages of the Book of Acts guarding the cloaks of those who stoned Stephen to death. Such lack of information should not surprise us, however; for the New Testament was written to proclaim the good news about Jesus Christ and his gospel. It was never intended to provide peripheral details about the life of the apostle Paul.

The sketchy information in the New Testament on the early years of Paul's life is valuable, however, for it provides a skeleton on which we can flesh out the details of his birth, family background, formative years, and early life. Those details are based upon the historical information available to us on the time and places where Paul was born and raised, as well as what we know about the social life of the people at that time.

Having said this, the reader should know that the bulk of the information on Paul's formative years and early childhood training in this chapter is based on an assumption of this writer. His assumption is that Paul was raised in what would have been a typical, early first century Jewish family of Pharisees, and that his family, even though in Tarsus of Cilicia, would have followed the typical lifestyle pattern of ancient Jewish families of Pharisaic convictions in Judea. The assumption is that what can be known about such Pharisaic families in Judea would have for the most part been true of Paul's family and upbringing in Tarsus as well. This assumption can be safely made, for Paul's family was an Aramaic Jewish family, not a Hellenistic Jewish family influenced by Greek culture.

Thanks to Alfred Edersheim's years of research on ancient Jewish social life, much is known about the lifestyle of first century Jewish Pharisaic families in Palestine. That information enables this writer to paint a portrait of what Paul's family and upbringing were probably like.

For the sake of the reader a little information about Alfred Edersheim is in order. He lived from 1825 to 1889. He was born into a Jewish family and in his adult life converted to Christianity. Before his conversion he studied the Jewish Talmud and Torah at a Hebrew school. He was therefore well versed in the Jewish teachings and writings. After his conversion he became a true biblical scholar with a Doctor of Divinity Degree as well as a Ph.D. He paid meticulous attention to details. He devoted years of his life to biblical studies in preparation for the writing of his classic work entitled <u>The Life And Times of Jesus The Messiah</u>. He wrote two books that were forestudies to that classic work, as he called them in the preface of that classic work. The first was <u>The Temple, Its Ministry and Services</u>. The second was <u>Sketches of Jewish Social life</u>. It is this second book that is the basis of much of this chapter's information on the upbringing and education of the apostle Paul as well as about the first century Pharisees. Edersheim was able to assemble that information because he researched his ancient Jewish ancestors' social life at the time of Christ, of whom the apostle Paul was a contemporary. So what was true of the Jewish families at the time of Christ would also have been true of the Jewish families at the time of Paul, including Paul's own family. Having explained these details about Edersheim and his work, you, the reader, can understand what a truly reliable source was used for the information in much of this chapter.

Paul's Home In Tarsus Of Cilicia

There is no information available on what a Jewish home in Tarsus in the early part of the first century was like. If the Jews in Tarsus had houses similar to those in Judea, we could expect that their houses were built with a spacious room where the family cooked, ate their meals, and spent most of their time when indoors. There would have been some sleeping quarters and possibly a reception room in which they visited with relatives and friends. The houses may have been constructed with flat roofs, slightly pitched for drainage, where members of the family could sit in the evening in the cool of the day. In Judea the Jewish families often had their guest room up on the roof, perhaps the Jews in Cilicia did as well.

The family's furniture most likely consisted of a large dining table around which they sat on chairs, or, as in Palestine, they reclined at meal times on dining couches that were arranged around the table. They may have had comfortable cushions, especially for the dining couches if they had them. They would likely have had a smaller table or two in the various rooms on which they set their candles, candlesticks, and oil lambs. These furnishings would have varied in luxury or austerity depending upon the wealth and social status of the individual families. Perhaps the family had a few pictures, but heeding

God's law in Exodus 20:4, Paul's family would not have had pictures or carvings or statues of any kind of animals or birds upon the earth, nor of the sun, moon, or stars in the heavens above.

The lifestyle of Paul's family would have been very different from that of a pagan family in Tarsus, for the members of Paul's family were Pharisees, which means "The Separated". They would have been very exclusive, then, which will be discussed in some detail shortly. Being strict Pharisaic Jews, Paul's family would have been dedicated wholly to God. Their lifestyle would have reflected that dedication. They would have had times for their morning and evening prayers, for the ceremonial washing of their hands[1] and for prayers before meals, and the giving of thanks after meals. Their home would have been characterized by a holy manner of living together as parents and children in accordance with God's commandments. They would have abided by God's ceremonial laws of Leviticus 11 pertaining to the eating of only edible creatures that were labeled "clean" and abstaining from all inedible creatures that were labeled "unclean". They would have obeyed the other ceremonial ordinances of God's law as well. Every week they would have observed the Sabbath starting at six o'clock in the evening on Friday and lasting throughout the day of Saturday. The Sabbath would have been welcomed as a holy day of rest for communion with God. No work would have been done, not even cooking. All preparations for the Sabbath would have been made beforehand. According to Edersheim on the eve of the Sabbath the head of the house would have returned home from the synagogue service to find the house festively adorned, the Sabbath lamp lit, and the table set for the best of meals the family could afford.[2] [3] The father would have blessed each child with the blessing of Israel before the family dined. On Saturday evening the Sabbath would have drawn to a close and the next workweek would have then begun.

Paul's Birth And Pharisaical Membership; His Early Childhood Training And Formal Education

Edersheim noted[4] a number of terms from the Hebrew Old Testament that affectionately pictured what Jewish parents witnessed of the various stages of their child's life. Applying those terms to Paul, when he was born, he would have been considered a "jeled", which means a "babe". After his newborn status Paul would have become a "jonek", a "suckling" who nursed at his mother's breast. When he grew enough to begin eating and digesting solid food, he would have become an "olel" who was still a "suckling" but who was also asking for bread to eat. At the end of his second year he would have entered the next stage of his life, at which time his mother would have weaned him. A feast would then have been celebrated to mark the event. Paul would then have been called a "gamul", which meant one who was weaned. At about that same time he also would have been a "taph", meaning a child that clings to his mother. We can appropriately imagine Paul standing beside his mother with his little arms wrapped around her legs and holding on to her. Afterwards Paul would have entered that time in his life when he would have affectionately been known as an "elem". He was then a child who was becoming strong and firm. Upon the completion of those growing years Paul would have been a "naar", meaning a youth who "shakes off" and shakes himself free. This time of Paul's life was probably something like we see in children today, who, starting around the age of twelve and thirteen, begin to assert their independence that then extends through their teenage years. And finally Paul would have reached the age of being a "bachur", which meant a "ripened one". By that time he had grown to his young adulthood and reached the age when a young man could be a warrior of Israel.

Now the date of Paul's birth is unknown. Based on the traditions of the church as explained in Chapter 2, it appears that Paul was born in A.D. 1. He was a Jew born in Tarsus of Cilicia, a natural son of the Jewish nation, was descended from the tribe of Benjamin, was educated as a Pharisee in a Pharisaic household and by Gamaliel, and brought up also in Jerusalem. Paul himself informs us of these personal facts in the following verses.

> I myself am a Jewish man, born in Tarsus of Cilicia, then brought up in this city (of Jerusalem), educated at the feet of Gamaliel strictly according to the law of our forefathers, being a man zealous for God . . . (Acts 22:3)
> . . . circumcised on the eighth day, out of the people of Israel, of the tribe of Benjamin, a Hebrew of Hebrews; with respect to the law – a Pharisee; . . . (Philippians 3:5)
> I myself am a Pharisee, a son of Pharisees! (Acts 23:6)

Paul was a son of Pharisees. The Pharisees were a small[5] religious and political "order", a brotherhood. A man became a member when in the presence of three members he pledged himself to the strict observance of Levitical purity.[6] [7] It was a purity that was to be maintained even to the extent of avoiding association with the rest of the common Jewish people, who were considered an accursed people ignorant in the knowledge of the Mosaic Law.[8] This assessment of the common Jewish population as an ignorant, accursed people is made very evident by the Pharisees' who said in John 7:49: "But this crowd, which does not know the law – they are accursed people!" For good reason the Pharisees bore the name "Pharisees", "The Separated."[9] They separated themselves not only from the Gentile pagans but even from the rest of the Jewish population! In spite of their separation from the Jewish people and their extremely small membership, the Pharisees exerted a most powerful, dominating influence over the teachings and the practices of the synagogues.[10] The Pharisees were scrupulous observers of the law as interpreted by the experts in the law, who were also called scribes.[11] The experts in the law hedged in the law with their oral traditions and the Pharisees carried out those traditions to the extreme.

Edersheim used the term 'fraternity" to describe the Pharisees. "Fraternity" is a good description because it conveys the meaning that the Pharisees were a body of men who were united for the sake of their common beliefs and aims, which they were devoted to preserving and advancing.[12] The Pharisees were a fraternity that consisted in various degrees of membership that began with the novitiate and progressed to the next three levels that were ranked under the name "Purifications",[13] whom Edersheim also called "pietists".[14] As a fraternity the men were bound by special vows and obligations. They were bound especially by the vows to abide by the Levitical laws of tithing and purifications,[15] and the higher degrees made increasingly stricter vows.[16] And membership in the fraternity was hereditary.[17]

Accordingly, Paul became a Pharisee when he was born. According to the rules of the fraternity the wife and all the children of a member of the Pharisees became members of the Pharisees as well. In the case of a girl born to a Pharisee, she also became a member of the Pharisees, and according to the rules of the Pharisees she would have to marry a Pharisee.[18] Men and women who were not Pharisees and became members of a Pharisaic family through marriage had to seek admission into the fraternity as well.[19]

Paul said he was born into a family of Pharisees in Tarsus of Cilicia. More will be said about this city and Roman province shortly. According to Philippians 3:5 above he was circumcised on the eighth day. He was circumcised in compliance with the rite that the Lord initiated with Abraham,[20] and which rite God also commanded in the Law of Moses.[21] It was likely that the scene at Paul's circumcision was similar to the scene that took place at the circumcision of John the Baptist.[22] So likewise, the relatives and friends of Paul's family were present for the celebration of the special day of Paul's circumcision. According to Edersheim those who were present were likely to have congratulated the parents with words something like: "As this child has been joined to the covenant, so may it also be to him in reference to the 'torah', the 'chuppah' (a reference to the marriage ceremony), and to good works."[23] And if Paul had been the firstborn son of his father and mother, he would have also been presented to the Lord and redeemed according to the Law of Moses in Exodus 13.

When Paul was circumcised on the eighth day he was given the name "Saul", his Hebrew name. He was perhaps named Saul after his Hebrew father. Or, perhaps, as was the custom common in the tribe of Benjamin of which Paul was a descendant, he may have been named Saul after the first king of Israel who was from the tribe of Benjamin.

Paul was born into the sect of he Pharisees. It was only one of the Jewish sects at the time. There were two others – the Essenes and the Sadducees. The Pharisees were the strictest of the three, as Paul himself said at his hearing before King Herod Agrippa II in Acts 26:5: "... I lived as a Pharisee according to the strictest sect of our religion." The Pharisees abided strictly by the Law of Moses as it was interpreted by the experts in the law. Since Paul said that he was a son of Pharisees, it is obvious that his father was a Pharisee before him. And it is not unlikely that Paul's family line were Pharisees going back to the rise of the Pharisees. Their name "Pharisee" appeared in history for the first time during the Jewish leadership of John Hyrcanus (135-105 B.C.).

Edersheim commented that it would have been difficult to say when the instruction of a Hebrew child began.[24] The difficulty lies in this: Does one consider only when actual formal teaching was begun? Or, does one really need to take into consideration the child's whole upbringing from the time he was born? This writer is of the opinion one must take into consideration Paul's Jewish upbringing from the time he was born. He had been born into a Jewish Pharisaic family that would have begun raising him as such from the day of his birth. This opinion that instruction in God's Word began for Paul from his birth has some support from the first century Jewish historian Josephus. Josephus wrote that from birth the Jews respected the Old Testament Scriptures as the divine teachings of God, and that the principle concern of the Jews was the religious education of their children. He wrote:

> ... how firmly we have given credit to those books (meaning the books of the Old Testament) of our own nation is evident by what we do, for during so many ages as have already passed, no one has been so

bold as either to add anything to them or take anything from them, or make any change in them; but it becomes natural to all Jews, immediately and from their very birth, to esteem those books to contain divine doctrines, and to persist in them, and, if occasion be, willingly to die for them.[25]

Our principle care of all is this, to educate our children well; and we think it to be the most necessary business of our whole life, to observe the laws that have been given us, and to keep those rules of piety that have been delivered down to us.[26]

While the training of Paul would have been incumbent upon his father, in the earliest stages of Paul's life especially his training would have been carried out by his mother.[27] As soon as Paul's eyes were open to see and his ears to hear he would have looked up into the loving smile of his Jewish mother who was holding him oh-so-tenderly and speaking ever-so-softly and affectionately to him. From that very first moment and thereafter he would have begun to hear and to learn the sounds of the Hebrew words with their few syllables, some smoother sounding with labial consonants and others harsher sounding with their rough gutturals. And from time to time he would have heard his mother, as loving mothers tend to do with their beloved infants, sing softly to him – surely not the ungodly songs of pagan idolaters but the well-known songs of the Hebrews, the Psalms[28] that sung about the Lord, the God of Israel, and his words of truth, comfort, and hope. And from his mother's lips would have flowed the first stories he heard of the history of the patriarchs and the deliverance of Israel from slavery in Egypt. And every night it would have been his mother teaching him to pray his bedtime prayer before going to sleep.

At a very young age, likely before Paul could speak complete sentences and clearly understand what he was being taught, and from about the time he would have been an "olel" (a nursing child starting to eat solid foods), and most certainly by the time he would have been a "gamul" (a weaned child at the end of his second year of age), the image that would have impressed itself upon his little, untrained mind would have been the "Mesusah".[29]

Edersheim described the "Mesusah" as a phylactery. He says that if it had been according to the traditional "Mesusah" as known in the 1800's of his day, it would have been a parchment folded square on which twenty-two lines were written that were Hebrew quotations of Deuteronomy 6:4-9 and 11:13-21. It would have then been enclosed in a shiny metal case (no doubt to protect it from the weather) and fastened to the doorpost of the house "as a symbolical consecration of the home."[30] It could only be fastened to a house that was inhabited exclusively by Jews. Edersheim stated, ". . . there can be little doubt that, even at the time of Christ, this "Mesusah" would be found wherever a family was at all Pharisaically inclined."[31] The "Mesusah" served as a constant reminder to the Jews to be faithful and true to the Lord their God and to obey his commandments and teach them to their children. Isaiah wrote about the "Mesusah" already around 750 B.C. in Isaiah 57:8. And Josephus also wrote of the "Mesusah" in the first century A.D. in his Antiquities 4.8.13.

So at his very small age as a child being carried in his mother's arms, Paul would have observed that every time his father and his mother and their Jewish friends or relatives went in and out of their house, they reverently touched the "Mesusah", and afterwards they kissed their finger that had touched it while they spoke the benediction. From early Jewish times the presence of the "Mesusah" on the doorpost of the house "was connected with the Divine protection, this verse being especially applied to it: 'The Lord will guard your going out and your coming in from this time now and forevermore.' "[32] (Psalm 121:8).

Continuing now with the point of when Paul's training began: In addition to the impression that the "Mesusah" would have made on him during his youngest years, the religious services and observances in his Jewish home would have impressed themselves upon his little mind as soon as he could comprehend what was taking place around him. He would have observed all the family prayers and the weekly observances of the Sabbath and the observances of the annual Jewish festivals. All would have been training him as to what it meant to be a Hebrew descendent and a Jew. He would have begun to observe his family celebrating the Feast of Dedication, at which time his house was illuminated on the first evening with one candle for each member of his family. Then each succeeding night the number of the candles was increased so that by the eighth night there were eight candles lit for each family member. Paul's eyes would have opened wide with excitement over all the light that filled the room. Paul would have heard and seen the joyful, boisterous merry-making of "Purim", the Festival of Ester. Then, too, he would have been a part of the Feast of Tabernacles, at which time a booth was built and the youngest of the household had to live outside in the booth. Paul, too, would have had his turn of living out in the booth during the festival. And what is more, he would have been a part of his family's commemorating the very special Jewish festival – the Passover together with the Feast of Unleavened Bread. He would have seen his mother remove every speck of leaven from their house. He would have seen that everyone came dressed in festive attire for the Passover meal, which also would have told him that a very special festival was being commemorated. He would have witnessed that the Passover Supper was in fact a historical rite and service. In compliance with God's ordinance in Exodus 12:26, 27, Paul would have heard the retelling of the account of the first Passover in Egypt. At a specific time in the service the youngest at the Passover table would have arisen to ask what was the meaning of that Passover Supper service being conducted. At that time the father would have recounted the history of Israel beginning with the Lord's calling of Abraham down to the first Passover in Egypt when the angel of death passed over the firstborn sons of Israel but killed the firstborn sons of the Egyptians, and how God then led the Israelites as a nation out of Egypt in the exodus. And the time would have come when young Paul would have grown up enough to be the child who asked what was the meaning of the Passover. And he together with his family would have eaten of the paschal lamb that had been roasted whole and would have partaken of the unleavened bread and the bitter herbs. Year after year as an important part of his upbringing little Paul would have witnessed all of the weekly and annual Jewish observances and festivals. In the process he would have learned the history and the teachings of the Jews.

Edersheim said that without exaggeration Philo[33] was able to say that the Jews "were from their swaddling clothes, even before being taught either the sacred laws or the unwritten customs, trained by their parents, teachers, and instructors to recognize God as Father and as the Maker of the world" and that, "having been taught the knowledge (of the laws) from earliest youth, they bore in their souls the image of the commandments." [34] Josephus also stated that the Jews "beginning immediately from the earliest infancy" received verbal instruction in the laws of God.[35] Not long before his martyrdom Paul himself wrote of the instance of early childhood training that took place from infancy in the case of Timothy:

> I remember the genuine faith in you, which first lived in your grandmother Lois and your mother Eunice, and I am convinced that *lives* in you also... namely that from infancy you have known the holy Scriptures, which are able to make you wise for salvation through faith that *is* in Christ Jesus. (2 Timothy 1:5 & 3:15)

Now it is possible that Paul's father may also have possessed all or portions of the Old Testament Scriptures, for it was not uncommon already around 167 B.C. that Jewish families had them in their possession. This fact is known because 1 Maccabees 1:56, 57 of the Apocrypha state that during the persecution of Jerusalem and Judea by the Greek pagan king of Syria, Antiochus Epiphanes, he issued an order that a search was to be made for copies of the Old Testament Scriptures in order to destroy them, and that any Jew in possession of those Scriptures was to be put to death. Josephus in his Antiquities 12.5.4 reports the same information and that any who were found in possession of the Scriptures were "miserably punished." After the battle for independence from the Syrian king had been won by the Maccabees, Edersheim says that copies of the Old Testament would have multiplied greatly.[36] He further stated:

It is by no means an exaggeration to say that, if perhaps only the wealthy possessed a complete copy of the Old Testament, written out on parchment or on Egyptian paper, there would scarcely be a pious home, however humble, which did not cherish as its richest treasure some portion of the Word of God – whether the five books of the Law, or the Psalter, or a roll of one or more of the Prophets. Besides, we know from the Talmud that at a later period, and probably at the time of Christ also, there were little parchment rolls specially for the use of children, containing such portions of Scripture as the "Shema" (Deut. Vi. 4-9; xi. 13-21; Num. Xv. 37-41), the "hallel" (Ps. cxiii-cxviii.), the history of the Creation to that of the Flood, and the first eight chapters of the book of Leviticus.[37]

And so, there may have been the possibility for Paul as a little boy to have had access to one or more of those little scrolls from which he learned as well.

The Jews in the first century were extremely exclusive. One advantage of such exclusiveness in the case of the Aramaic Jews like Paul's family was this: it kept them apart from the outside influence of the pagan Greek culture that was all around them in Tarsus of Cilicia. Their exclusiveness pertained not only to their religion but also to their social and family life as well. Edersheim says that it even carried over to their knowledge. In the days of Christ, which was also the time of Paul, the Jew had no other knowledge to speak of other than the law of God, and he sought no other knowledge either. Even the pursuit of a trade or a business was considered to be subservient to the study and the gain of knowledge of God and his law. Every area of academics merged in some way into the study of God and theology, whether the field of medicine or mathematics or astronomy. And Edersheim notes that in the matters of history, geography and natural studies there was much outright ignorance. The whole aim and purpose of Jewish education was to prepare for the gaining of knowledge about God and his law and to teach it.[38] Such was the nature of the education in which Paul was trained.[39]

The religion of the Jews, then, and thus the religion of Paul's family, came down to two things Edersheim says – the knowledge of God and service, which service entailed the proper observance of God's laws, including the command to love one's neighbor.[40] Kaufman Kohler had this to say: "The aim and object of the Law, according to Pharisaic principles, are the training of man to a full realization of his responsibility to God and to the consecration of life by performance of its manifold duties."[41] For the Jew to have been right with God, then, he had to have known about God through study and then obeyed God's laws.

Such a religion amounted to a religion of work righteousness. And work righteousness describes very well the religion of the Pharisees at the time of Christ, and of Paul then too. Paul's family was a Pharisaic family, and so it was into that religion of work righteousness that Paul was being brought up and trained. The work righteousness of the Pharisees is evident in the Four Gospels. Jesus' Parable of the Pharisee and the Tax Collector clearly exposed the work righteous attitude of the Pharisees. In Jesus' parable the Pharisee prayed, which was really no prayer at all but merely a prideful boasting of how good he thought he was: "O God, I thank you that I am not like the rest of men: robbers, dishonest, adulterers, or even like this tax-collector. I customarily fast twice a week. I routinely give one tenth of all that I get."

Now that Paul's very early childhood training at home has been looked into, and it has been explained that the formal Jewish education was almost exclusively for the single purpose of enabling the students to gain a knowledge about God and his law, we can delve into the formal education Paul was likely to have gotten first in his home and then in a school.

According to the Mosaic Law the responsibility for the training of a child rested upon the father. If the father was incapable of teaching his child, the family employed a stranger, a tutor.[42] The formal home-schooling usually began at age three. But it is quite possible that even before the age of three Paul was being taught to memorize verses of the Old Testament in Hebrew, benedictions, and wise sayings such as proverbs. Beginning at age three Paul would have started learning to read Hebrew. The letters of the alphabet would have been written on a board for him to see until he could recognize them and learn how to write them. No doubt his father soon started to group the letters into words, then teach Paul how to pronounce new, unfamiliar words and to learn their meanings. As soon as possible Paul's father would have had Paul following with his eyes a pointer that moved along the lines from right to left in the Old Testament Hebrew text, sounding out the syllables of the words as he proceeded down the line and pronouncing the words. And, so that Paul would become a fluent reader, he would have been required to read the Hebrew lines aloud.

Customarily at age five the reading of the Hebrew Old Testament Scriptures was begun. At that young age of five Paul would have begun reading, not the first book of Moses, Genesis, with its history, but the Book of Leviticus. The history of the patriarchs and of Israel would have already been taught to Paul orally on the festive occasions mentioned above. So the formal reading of the Hebrew Scriptures began with the Book of Leviticus, because it taught the little children like Paul the laws of God that they needed to learn as early of an age as possible. And during this period of his education he would have continued to be taught the commandments and ordinances of God, as well as reciting the prayers that were said.

In Palestine a parent was legally bound to see to the education of his son at age six or seven.[43] So it is likely that at age six or seven Paul would have been sent to the local synagogue school for his elementary schooling. And in the years following, in his study of the Old Testament Scriptures, after Paul had completed his study of the Book of Leviticus, he would have proceeded to studying the other four books of Moses that together with Leviticus make up the Pentateuch, or the Law of Moses. Then his studies would have progressed to the Prophets. Surely the designation of the Prophets would have been according to the recognized Jewish cannon that included Joshua, Judges, 1 & 2 Samuel, and 1 & 2 Kings as well as the books of the Prophets listed in the Old Testament of our English Bibles. Then, after studying the Prophets Paul's Old Testament studies would have progressed to the Sacred Writings, as the Jews classified and called them, which included all the rest of the Old Testament Scriptures.[44]

Now at some point during his boyhood or adolescence Paul left the city of Tarsus and went to study in Jerusalem under the great Rabbi and renowned doctor in the Old Testament law, the Pharisee Gamaliel. Two Bible verses shed a little light on this period of Paul's life and studies. In A.D. 59 during his hearing before King Herod Agrippa II, Paul told him, "Now all Jews, to be sure, have known my manner of life from my youth, which from the beginning was among my nation and at Jerusalem." (Acts 26:4) Here Paul made it clear that his youth began in his nation of Cilicia where he resided with his family in Tarsus. Then in his youth he moved to Jerusalem. Next, in A.D. 57 when he addressed the angry mob of Jews in Jerusalem after being taken into Roman custody to save him from being killed, he told that Jewish assembly, "I myself am a Jewish man, born in Tarsus of Cilicia, then brought up in this city, educated at the feet of Gamaliel strictly according to the law of our forefathers, . . ." (Acts 22:3) The fact that Paul said he was brought up in Jerusalem indicates he moved to Jerusalem in the earlier years rather than the later years of his youth. Perhaps the years of his early adolescence would be a good guess. That age may fit into the years of his study under the great Gamaliel as well. Let it be said, however, that there is no historical document that this writer knows of that provides any information about a school or academy at which Gamaliel taught or what age group(s) he taught that would shed some light on what Paul's age might have been when he moved to Jerusalem and studied under Gamaliel. As a matter of fact Wikipedia has published this statement:

> There is no other record of Gamaliel ever having taught in public, but the Talmud does describe Gamaliel as teaching a student who displayed 'impudence in learning', which a few scholars identify as a possible reference to Paul.[45]

Age thirteen would have been a special time in the life of Paul. According to Edersheim a boy became "of age", or a "Bar Mizvah", meaning a son of the commandments, at that age. That was the legal age when religious obligations and privileges would have been bestowed on Paul and he would have become a member of the congregation.

Now another important part of Paul's education was his study of languages. Paul became trilingual. As explained in detail above, Paul learned Hebrew first of all. We know for certain that he could read, write, and speak Hebrew, or Aramaic. His ability to read and converse in the Hebrew/Aramaic language is evident on the basis of several Scriptural facts. In Acts 26:14 Paul stated that when Jesus appeared to him outside of Damascus, Jesus spoke to him in the Hebrew dialect. What is more, Paul studied in Jerusalem under Gamaliel, who was a renowned Pharisee and teacher of the Law of Moses. Gamaliel surely taught Paul the law from the Hebrew Old Testament Scriptures (ref. Acts 5:34 & 22:3). And, when Paul addressed the Jewish crowds in Jerusalem after he was taken into Roman custody, he spoke to them in Hebrew (ref. Acts 21:40). Paul also learned to read, write, and speak in Greek. This is evident from the fact that he wrote his thirteen letters in the New Testament in the Koine Greek language, and his Old Testament quotations in those letters were from the Greek Septuagint. Paul also spoke to the Roman Tribune Claudius Lysias in Greek (ref. Acts 21:37). Finally, Paul must have learned to read, write, and speak Latin as well, for all his Roman legal proceedings were written in Latin and he had to speak Latin in his trials before the Roman governors Felix (ref. Acts 24:1-23) and Festus (ref. Acts 25:6-12) and his trial before the court of Caesar in Rome.

An added note about Paul's above education is in order. It should be kept in mind that God had set Paul aside for his apostolic ministry from his mother's womb. The Holy Spirit testified to this through Paul in Galatians 1:15. This having been true, God was in charge of Paul's life from his birth to his calling as an apostle. All of Paul's education and training, then, in his childhood in Tarsus through his schooling under Gamaliel in Jerusalem, was given to him by the providence of God to prepare him for his apostolic ministry.

Paul's Names, Tarsian And Roman Citizenships, And Trade:

Paul had two names – Saul and Paul. His Hebrew name Saul was explained previously. But his Latin, Roman name was Paulus (Paulos in Greek), by which name he would have been known among his Gentile neighbors in Tarsus throughout his boyhood. Paul (Paulos) was the name he used for himself in his New Testament letters and among the Christians of the congregations he founded. His name Paul is found for the first time in the New Testament Scriptures in Acts 13:9. To prevent any possibility of confusion for the reader, this biographical commentary will only use his name Paul.

Acts 22:3 states that Paul was born in Tarsus of Cilicia. Years later when Paul was arrested in Jerusalem and taken into Roman custody, he told the tribune Claudius Lysias, "I am indeed a Jewish man of Tarsus of Cilicia, a citizen of no insignificant city." (Acts 21:39) Tarsus was the capital of the Roman province of Cilicia in the eastern part of what is now Turkey on the River Cydnus, which was about twelve miles inland from the Mediterranean Sea. Tarsus was an important center of philosophy and literature that rivaled the cities of Athens and Alexandria.[46] Tarsus was a Greek city in character where Greek was spoken and Greek literature was cultivated. For this reason Paul was able to learn to speak Greek in Tarsus from his youth.

When Paul stated he was born in Tarsus of Cilicia, he also said that he was a citizen of that city (ref. Acts 22:3 & 21:3). He also stated he was born a citizen of Rome (ref. Acts 22:27, 28). He was, then, both a citizen of the city of Tarsus and a citizen of Rome. Cilicia had been made a Roman province by Pompey in 64 B.C. The citizens of Cilicia, then, were subjects of Roman rule. The city of Tarsus, however, was not a Roman colony; thus their Tarsian citizenship was not tied to Roman citizenship. A person's citizenship in Tarsus did not make him a citizen of Rome.

Paul was a Roman citizen by birth. His father, then, had to have been a Roman citizen, and perhaps his grandfather before him. How Paul's father, or maybe his grandfather, came to have Roman citizenship is unknown. It is a subject of speculation. There were several possibilities. One possibility was that Paul's father or grandfather purchased his Roman citizenship, as Tribune Claudius Lysias said he had done for a substantial amount of money (ref. Acts 22:28). A second possibility was that Paul's father or grandfather was awarded his Roman citizenship for special service to the state. Military service was one service that has been mentioned, which was not likely in the case of Paul's father or grandfather. Another awarded service has been mentioned as well. It has been said that during the Roman Civil Wars of the 40s to 30s B.C. many Jews were enslaved. Afterwards they were freed. For services rendered to a powerful Roman during the time of enslavement a Jew could be granted Roman citizenship upon the fulfillment of the proper procedures.

However Paul's father or grandfather came into possession of his Roman citizenship, that Roman citizenship into which Paul was born would prove to be of immense value to him throughout the years of his apostolic ministry. From the New Testament Scriptures it is clear that Paul's citizenship entitled him to various rights he otherwise would not have had under Roman law. First, his citizenship entitled him to have a legal trial before a proper court and gave him the right to defend himself. This right made it possible for him to appeal to Caesar rather than stand trial before Festus and the Jews in Jerusalem where he would hot have gotten a fair trial or been able to defend himself. Second, according to Roman law a Roman citizen could not be chained up, tortured, scourged, or crucified. And death sentences could be commuted to voluntary exile except in the case of being found guilty of treason. This Roman law prevented Tribune Claudius Lysias from scourging Paul and was the reason that Paul was beheaded when he was martyred and not crucified like Peter.

How Paul's family came to live in Tarsus of Cilicia, and for how long the family had lived there prior to Paul's birth, and whether the family was a Jewish family of the dispersion that had been transplanted there, are also unknown.

Neither is it known on the basis of ancient historical evidence what the financial and social status of Paul's family was in Tarsus.

Whether his family's Roman and Tarsian citizenship meant the family was wealthy and held social stature cannot be asserted with certainty. Wm. M. Ramsay[47] and the New Schaff-Herzog Encyclopedia of Religious Knowledge[48] both considered Paul's family one of social distinction and of at least moderate wealth. It is true that if the Roman citizenship was purchased by a man, a great price had to be paid, as Tribune Claudius Lysias made clear in Acts 22:28. However, obtaining that citizenship was not dependent upon the person having a degree of wealth. A person could have been less than wealthy and still obtain a Roman citizenship. Furthermore, the assertion that Paul's family was affluent because it had a purchased Roman citizenship cannot be maintained because it is not known that Paul's father or grandfather had purchased the Roman citizenship. It may have been awarded for service to the state. F. F. Bruce stated that a requirement of property ownership was made a prerequisite to being able to exercise the rights of Tarsian citizenship,[49] but there is no ancient historical evidence to substantiate that assertion.

On the other hand, an argument cannot be made that Paul and his family must have been poor, or at least belonged to a lower financial and social class, because Paul had an occupational trade as a tentmaker. Paul did employ that trade to support himself during his missionary travels and ministry, as he did in Corinth and Thessalonica, and as he also did to give aid to the needy in Ephesus.[50] Such an assertion of poverty on the basis of Paul's having had a trade cannot be made because it was a Jewish practice for the boys of a family to learn a trade. Edersheim quoted this rabbinical principle on occupations: "It was indeed quite true that every Jew was bound to learn some trade or business. But this was not to divert him from study; quite the contrary."[51] Following that custom, Paul's father had Paul learn the trade of tent making. Whether Paul's father himself was a tentmaker is not known, but there was a Jewish principle that stated if possible a son was "not to forsake the trade of the father."[52] Whether Paul's father was a tentmaker or not, it is the opinion of this writer that Paul and his father before him were respectable, honest, hard-working men who labored to support themselves, as Paul's father must have undoubtedly done to support himself and his wife and Paul and Paul's sister (his sister is mentioned in Acts 23:16), and as Paul himself did rather than accept financial support from the congregations to which he ministered. Be those matters as whatever they were, one can only guess about the financial circumstances of Paul's family.

As for Paul's family after he became a Christian nothing is known about them. There are only unanswered questions. How did Paul's Pharisaic family react to his forsaking the Jewish religion and Pharisaism for Christianity that he had so viciously persecuted previously? Did they disown him? Did they in time accept Paul's new life and cope with the adjustments that the gospel of Christ brought into their own family and lives? Did they listen to the gospel of Christ that their son Paul began to preach and to teach? Did they then embrace the newfound Christianity of Paul and become Christians themselves? As much as we would like to know the answers to these questions, we simply do not have them.

If his family had turned against him for his having become a Christian, it would have been very hard for Paul to live in Tarsus with his family for the eight years that he evangelized that city and the regions of Syria and Cilicia. He would have had to endure his family's rejection. He may have had to live in Tarsus apart from his parents. Even to this day families disown their sons or daughters who become Christians. On the other hand, the fact that Paul did live and work out of the city of Tarsus for eight years may be an argument from silence that his family did not disown him but received him as their "Christian" son.

There is one scriptural fact that suggests Paul's family might not have disowned him. In A.D. 57, twenty-four years after his conversion, Paul's sister's son, Paul's nephew, hurried to inform him that a band of more than forty Jews had made a plot to kill him (ref. Acts 23:16). That information Paul's nephew brought to him saved his life. If Paul's family, including his sister, had disowned Paul twenty-four years earlier after his conversion, it is unlikely that his sister's son would have rushed to inform Paul of a plot against his life. The possibility must be granted, therefore, that Paul's family did not disown him and might have embraced the gospel of Jesus that Paul preached.

Paul As A Young Adult Pharisee

Having completed his education under Gamaliel, Paul entered upon his young adulthood. He was by this time an extreme zealot for the traditions of his fathers. Nothing is known about this period of Paul's life however. There is no definitive information on Paul's young adult life of which this writer is aware. For this reason this portion of his life raises some interesting questions. Where was Paul from the time he completed his education in Jerusalem to his appearing at the stoning of Stephen? Did he return to Tarsus where he worked as a tentmaker and taught in the synagogue services and school? If this were the case, what would have brought him back to Jerusalem afterwards? And what was he doing there in Jerusalem that he became recognized as a rising star in Judaism?

As for where Paul was after completing his education under Gamaliel, this writer can only conjecture, which is all anyone can do. This writer is of the opinion that other than occasional visits to Tarsus to see his parents, relatives, and friends, he remained in Jerusalem. This writer has several reasons for holding this opinion.

First, during his young adulthood Paul was climbing "the ladder of success" in Judaism. He was on fire to uphold the laws of God and the traditions that interpreted those laws. He was so aflame to uphold and to live by those traditions that he continued to be recognized more and more in the Judaic circles. He was moving ahead of other Jewish young men his age (ref. Galatians 1:14). Before the time that the high priest and the ruling members of the Sanhedrin (the supreme council and court) of the Jews in Jerusalem stoned Stephen to death, Paul was already well known by them and among them. This is clear from the fact that when they rose up and stoned Stephen, the witnesses to Stephen's supposed blasphemy "took off their cloaks and laid them beside the feet of a young man named Saul." (Acts 7:58) It is highly unlikely that Paul would have attained such recognition among those highest-ranking Jews in Judaism if he had been living in Tarsus of Cilicia. He would have needed to be living and working in Jerusalem.

Second, when those Jewish leaders began to carry out their persecution of the Christians in the area of Jerusalem, Paul became the chief persecutor. He would not have been given such authority if he had been a relatively unknown newcomer in Jerusalem and to those high ranking Jewish leaders. It is more reasonable to assume he had been in Jerusalem and had become a trusted underling. Nothing is said in the New Testament about what Paul's official position was, but it was a high position in which he could go directly to the high priest for orders of authorization for the persecution, as he did in obtaining letters from the high priest to persecute the Christians in Damascus. Being in such an official position, Paul was able to write in his Letter to the Galatians,

> 13 "For you have heard of my former way of life in Judaism, that I used to persecute the church of God to an extraordinary degree and was trying to destroy it,
>
> 14 and I kept advancing in Judaism over and above many contemporaries among the people, being more of an extreme zealot for the traditions of my fathers." (Galatians 1:13, 14)

Third, in the Galatians 1:13 verse just quoted, Paul wrote of his 'former way of life in Judaism." Those words indicate that Paul had a way of life in Judaism. That way of life must have led to his then becoming the chief persecutor of the church. For the reasons just stated above it must have been a way of life in Judaism in which he had already been advancing before the persecution started. Such a way of life in Judaism could not have happened in Tarsus of Cilicia. It would have had to have occurred in Jerusalem.

Fourth, as a committed Pharisee to the law and the worship of God, Paul would have wanted to be able to worship in the temple of Jerusalem and participate in all of its religious, festive services. Paul exhibited such a desire even after his conversion when in A.D. 57 he hurried back to Jerusalem to be there in time for the Pentecost celebration (ref. Acts 20:16).

Whether or not Paul did in fact remain in Jerusalem after completing his education under Gamaliel, we do know that throughout his adulthood Tarsus continued to be Paul's hometown where he maintained his citizenship. This is evident from a number of historical details that Luke provides in the Book of Acts. At the time of Paul's conversion in A.D. 33 when Jesus appeared to him, Jesus referred to him as "a man from Tarsus." (ref. Acts 9:11) About two or more years later in late A.D. 35 when Paul fled from Jerusalem, he returned to his hometown of Tarsus (ref. Acts 9:30). According to Paul's words in Galatians 1:21, it is clear that he remained in the area of Tarsus in the Roman provinces of Cilicia and Syria preaching and teaching, which he did from late A.D. 35 to the fall of 43. In the fall of A.D. 43 Barnabas left the growing mission congregation of Antioch, Syria, to go to Tarsus to get Paul and bring him to Antioch to help with the work there (ref. Acts 11:25). And in A.D. 57 when Paul was taken into Roman custody in Jerusalem, he told Tribune Claudius Lysias that he was a man from Tarsus of Cilicia (Acts 21:39).

Paul remained unmarried throughout his adult life. In A.D. 55 he wrote of his single, celibate lifestyle to the Corinthians and said,

> I wish that all men were even as *I* myself *am*; but each one has his own gift from God, one in this manner, and another in that manner. Now I say to the unmarried and to the widows, it is excellent for them if they remain as I am. (1 Corinthians 7:7 & 8)

In Philippians 3:5, 6 Paul provided some important facts about himself in his adulthood. He wrote that he was "a Hebrew of Hebrews; with respect to the law – a Pharisee; with respect to zeal – one who persecuted the church; with respect to the righteousness that is by the Law – one who was blameless."

According to Paul, he was a Hebrew of Hebrews. He was first of all according to his ancestral bloodline of pure Hebrew stock. Second of all, he was an Aramaean Jew who spoke the Hebrew/Aramaic language. Among the Jews in Paul's day there were two kinds of Jews, the Aramaen Jews and the Hellenistic Jews. The Aramaean Jews, on the one hand, were those of Palestine and Syria, together with those of Mesopotamia who lived along the Tigris and Euphrates Rivers, and spoke similar dialects of the language of Aram. Furthermore, they held closely to the traditional teachings of Moses and the Old Testament Scriptures. The Hellenist Jews, on the other hand, were those who spoke the Greek language, lived in Greek cities, and had been influenced by the Greek civilization and culture. They did not hold as closely to the traditional Jewish teachings and practices as did the Aramaean Jews. Interestingly enough, Paul to a great extent fit into both of those groups, which so well prepared him for his apostolic outreach to both groups. He was raised in a Pharisaic household that spoke Hebrew at home, and he was educated in Jerusalem by Gamaliel in the Hebrew language; yet he was born and raised in Tarsus, which was a city of Greek character, language, culture, and literature, and Paul spoke and wrote Greek fluently. What is more, in his letters Paul's quotations of Old Testament passages were from the Greek Septuagint translation of the Old Testament, which he appears to often have quoted from memory. Yet, in spite of all those Greek influences in his life, Paul's statement that he was a Hebrew of Hebrews indicates that he considered himself above all to be a member of the Aramaean Jews and not the Hellenist Jews.

With respect to the Mosaic Law and the righteousness that the Pharisees thought came through obedience to it, Paul said he lived according to the strictest sect of the Jewish religion and that he was blameless in it. Paul said,

> Now all Jews, to be sure, have known my manner of life from my youth, which from the beginning was among my nation (referring to Tarsus in Cilicia) and at Jerusalem, since they have known me for a long time, if they wish to testify, that I lived as a Pharisee according to the strictest sect of our religion. (Acts 26:4 & 5)
>
> ... with respect to the law – a Pharisee; ... with respect to the

righteousness that is by the Law – one who was blameless. (Philippians 3:5 & 6)

During his adult life, then, up until his conversion to faith in Jesus Christ, he obeyed the laws of Moses and observed the traditions of the elders and his fathers faultlessly. Those traditions of Paul's fathers were the 613 commandments that the Jewish rabbis had erected like a hedge around the Mosaic Law to insure that the purity of the Law and of Israel would be preserved. Those rabbinical commandments the Pharisees sought to uphold to the extreme in an effort to regulate every aspect of Jewish life. [53] Some of those traditions of the elders are mentioned in the gospels, such as the ceremonial washings of the hands before eating[54] and upon returning from the marketplace, and the prescribed washings of cups, pitchers, pots, and dining couches,[55] the tithing of garden herbs,[56] and the excusing of a son from giving financial support to his parents if he had previously pledged to make a sacrificial gift to God that was called "Corban."[57] Paul would have observed the Mosaic laws pertaining to the eating of only clean foods and abstaining from the unclean foods.[58] He would have observed the Sabbath days without working, and the Old Testament festivals of the Passover, the Feast of Unleavened Bread, Pentecost, the Feast of Tabernacles, the Day of Atonement, and the new moon festivals.[59] Following all the laws and traditions would have been the central part of his adult life in his eager quest for the righteousness that came by obedience to them.

The description that now follows describes the Pharisees as a fraternal body in general.[60] Allowances must be made for the individual variations from one Pharisee to another. There would have been varying degrees among the Pharisees, from the lowest novitiate to the most advanced degree of the "pietist.[61] Having been born and raised and trained as a Pharisee, we can safely assume that Paul would have been in a very advanced pietistic order of the membership.

On the inside Paul had been steeped in the ways of the Pharisees from his birth. And so in his young adulthood he would have looked and acted every bit like a Pharisee on the outside. When he stepped out onto the street and into the crowds, then, he appeared as a "peculiar and striking" individual who was different from all the people around him who were not Pharisees. He would have immediately attracted their attention.[62] His attire would have included a pointed cap on his head that was like a turban. Its material was wound in such a fashion that its ends hung down gracefully in the back. His beard would have been carefully trimmed and possibly anointed and perfumed. His beard clearly set him apart as a freeman, for slaves were not permitted to wear beards. An inner garment that covered his body hung down to his heels. It was covered by an outer robe with tasseled borders. These borders will be discussed further in the following paragraph. On his feet Paul would have worn sandals that consisted of soles that were held on by straps or thongs.

Not only did his attire just described set Paul apart from the crowds among whom he mingled, but also the tassels on the four corners of his outer robe and the phylacteries that made Paul ostentatious. The tassels themselves on the four corners of the Jews' robes were worn in accordance with Numbers 15:37 and Deuteronomy 22:12. Those tassels were blue in color, which was the symbolical color of the covenant. They were to be looked at to serve as a reminder of all the commandments that the Lord had given to the Israelites. But the Pharisees enlarged the size of the tassels to make them conspicuous to attract attention to themselves as being especially pious men.

Like the rest of the fraternity of Pharisees Paul also attracted attention to himself by wearing enlarged phylacteries. The non-Pharisaic Jews wore the phylacteries at prayers and solemn occasions. Paul, like the Pharisees in general, however, wore them all day. A phylactery was a small box containing verses from the Old Testament. The verses were Exodus 13:1-10, Exodus 13:11-16, Deuteronomy 6:4-9, and Deuteronomy 11:13-21. The phylacteries were worn on the left arm towards the heart and on the forehead. They were bound onto the left arm and forehead with black leather straps. The phylacteries plainly identified the wearer as a Pharisee. The Pharisees regarded the phylacteries as highly as the Old Testament Scriptures themselves.

Jesus spoke of both the tassels and the phylacteries when he exposed the hypocrisy of the Pharisees. Jesus had this to say about the Pharisees and their ostentatious use of the tassels and phylacteries: "They do all their deeds in order to be noticed by people, for they enlarge their phylacteries and lengthen the tassels *of their garments.*" (Matthew 23:5)

Being the conspicuous Pharisee that Paul made himself to be, when he was on the streets or in the market places, he was recognized by friend or foe of the Pharisees as a religious, political power, who belonged to the most influential, zealous, highly connected fraternity that was committed to its objectives and was unafraid.[63] As a Pharisee Paul was viewed among the Jewish population as a staunch individual. He moved among the Jewish crowds who respectfully got out of his way and often looked at him with curiosity. And when he walked along the street, he would suddenly halt to say prescribed prayers at certain specified times. This he would do even if he were in the middle of the street. When he had said a prayer or two, he would walk on for a time, then stop again to say some more of the prescribed prayers. And he made his devotional prayers quite obvious in the market places and on the street corners. When Paul entered a village, and again when he left it, he would have stopped to say at least one or two prayers. If he encountered any kind of danger, or saw something new or different or very beautiful, he would have stopped to pray. And the longer he made his prayers the better, for as a Pharisee he believed his long prayers were sure to be heard.[64] He also would have believed that each prayer that he closed with a benediction using the Lord's divine name had a special merit. And so, the more such prayers and benedictions he said each day, the greater the measure of his piety.[65]

In the typical Pharisaic manner Paul's face would have had a self-satisfied or an exaggerated appearance of humility that readily identified him as a Pharisee. His appearance would have been further marked by his raised eyebrows that expressed a scorn for the people in the crowd around him. He would have made every effort to avoid any kind of contact with those persons or the things that he considered to be unclean, lest he become defiled and unclean himself.⁶⁶ What is more, Paul would have avoided all contact with any person who was not a member of the Pharisaic party. And furthermore, he would even have avoided any Pharisee who was of a lesser, inferior degree of Pharisaism than himself.

For good reason our beloved Lord and Savior Jesus Christ who came to save sinners said:

> For I tell you that unless your righteousness greatly surpasses that of the experts in the law and the Pharisees, you will absolutely not enter into the kingdom of heaven. (Matthew 5:20)
>
> And when you pray, you shall not be like the hypocrites, because they love to stand in the synagogues and on the street corners praying, in order that they may be seen by people. Truly I say to you, they receive their reward in full. (Matthew 6:5)

We have now seen the young Paul that the Lord had raised up from his birth to his young adulthood. In the next chapter we will see what Paul then did and how the Lord changed the course of his life to mold him into the apostle and bondservant that the Lord wanted him to be.

---

1. Mark 7:3
2. Edersheim, Alfred; Sketches of Jewish Social Life – In The Days Of Christ; Wm. B. Eerdmans Publishing Company; Grand Rapids, Michigan; reprinted 1974; p. 97
3. "(The Pharisees') object was to render the Sabbath 'a delight', a day of social and spiritual joy and elevation rather than a day of gloom. . .the Pharisees . . . transformed the Sabbath and festivals into seasons of domestic joy, . . ." Kohler, Kaufman; Pharisees; Jewish Encyclopedia, The unedited full text of the 1906 Jewish Encyclopedia; jewish encyclopedia.com
4. Edersheim, Alfred; Sketches of Jewish Social Life – In The Days Of Christ; Wm. B. Eerdmans Publishing Company; Grand Rapids, Michigan; reprinted 1974; p. 97 p. 103, 104
5. The Pharisees only numbered just over 6,000 out of the entire Jewish population at the time of Herod according to Josephus' Antiquity Of The Jews, 17.2.4. Writers on occasion have called them a "kernel".
6. Kohler, Kaufman; Pharisees; Jewish Encyclopedia, The unedited full text of the 1906 Jewish Encyclopedia; jewish encyclopedia.com

7. Edersheim, Alfred; Sketches of Jewish Social Life – In The Days Of Christ; Wm. B. Eerdmans Publishing Company; Grand Rapids, Michigan; reprinted 1974; p. 235
8. Kohler, Kaufman; Pharisees; Jewish Encyclopedia, The unedited full text of the 1906 Jewish Encyclopedia; jewish encyclopedia.com
9. The New Schaff-Herzog Encyclopedia of Religious Knowledge, Vol. IX; "Pharisees And Sadducees"; Jackson, Samuel Macauley, editor-in-chief; Baker Book House; Grand Rapids, Michigan; p. 8
10. Edersheim, Alfred; Sketches of Jewish Social Life – In The Days Of Christ; Wm. B. Eerdmans Publishing Company; Grand Rapids, Michigan; reprinted 1974; p. 226
11. Kohler, Kaufman; Pharisees; Jewish Encyclopedia, The unedited full text of the 1906 Jewish Encyclopedia; jewish encyclopedia.com
12. Edersheim, Alfred; Sketches of Jewish Social Life – In The Days Of Christ; Wm. B. Eerdmans Publishing Company; Grand Rapids, Michigan; reprinted 1974; p. 226
13. Ibid., p. 235
14. Ibid., p. 215
15. Ibid., p. 236
16. Ibid., p. 235
17. Ibid., p. 226
18. Ibid., p. 228
19. Ibid., p. 236
20. Genesis 17:9-14
21. Leviticus 12:3
22. Luke 1:57-63
23. Ibid., p. 128
24. Ibid., p. 106
25. Josephus, Flavius; "Antiquity of the Jews – Flavius Josephus Against Apion, Book I.8"; Josephus – Complete Works; Kregel Publications; Grand Rapids, Michigan; Twelfth Printing, 1974; p. 609
26. Ibid, Book I.12
27. Ibid., p. 129
28. Ibid., p. 109
29. Ibid., p. 106
30. Kohler, Kaufman; Pharisees; Jewish Encyclopedia, The unedited full text of the 1906 Jewish Encyclopedia; jewish encyclopedia.com
31. Ibid., p. 107
32. Ibid., p. 107
33. Philo was a Hellenistic Jewish philosopher of Alexandria who lived from abound 20 B.C to A.D. 50
34. Ibid., p. 110, 111
35. Josephus, Flavius; Antiquity Of The Jews – Flavius Josephus Against Apion, II.18; Josephus – Complete Works; Kregel Publications; Grand Rapids, Michigan; Twelfth Printing, 1974; p. 630
36. Edersheim, Alfred; Sketches of Jewish Social Life – In The Days Of Christ; Wm. B. Eerdmans Publishing Company; Grand Rapids, Michigan; reprinted 1974; p. 117
37. Ibid., p. 117
38. Ibid., p. 124
39. "In establishing schools and synagogues everywhere and enjoining each father to see that his son was instructed in the Law, the Pharisees made the Torah a power

for the education of the Jewish people . . ."; Kohler, Kaufman; Pharisees; Jewish Encyclopedia, The unedited full text of the 1906 Jewish Encyclopedia; jewish encyclopedia.com

40. Edersheim, Alfred; Sketches of Jewish Social Life – In The Days Of Christ; Wm. B. Eerdmans Publishing Company; Grand Rapids, Michigan; reprinted 1974; p. 125
41. Kohler, Kaufman; Pharisees; Jewish Encyclopedia, The unedited full text of the 1906 Jewish Encyclopedia; jewish encyclopedia.com
42. Edersheim, Alfred; Sketches of Jewish Social Life – In The Days Of Christ; Wm. B. Eerdmans Publishing Company; Grand Rapids, Michigan; reprinted 1974; p. p.129
43. Ibid., p. 106
44. Ibid. p. 136
45. Wikipedia, Gamaliel; https://en.wikipedia.org/wiki/Gamaliel
46. Strabo; The Geogrpahy Of Strabo; Book XIV, Chapter 5, paragraph 13 on the webpage; published in Vol. V of the Loeb Classical Library edition, 1928; http://penelope.uchicago.edu/Thayer/E/Roman/Texts/Strabo/14E*.html
47. Ramsay, W. M.; St. Paul The Traveler And Roman Citizen; Baker Book House; Grand Rapids, Michigan; p. 31 & 34
48. The New Schaff-Herzog Encyclopedia of Religious Knowledge, Vol. VIII; "Paul, The Apostle"; Jackson, Samuel Macauley, editor-in-chief; Baker Book House; Grand Rapids, Michigan; p. 406 column 1
49. See Bruces's The Acts of The Apostles, p.245 & 453, and his New Testament History, p. 234. Bruce also asserted the property qualification was **probably** established by Athenodoros, which indicates Bruce had no specific ancient evidence on which to base that assertion. He also said that the holding of both a Tarsian and Roman citizenship indicated an aristocratic stature, but he did not cite ancient historical evidence to substantiate the claim. It appears from the context that Bruce had consulted the ancient geographer and historian Strabo for his information. In The Geogrpahy Of Strabo, Book XIV, Chaper 5, paragraph 14, Strabo wrote of the corrupt government administration being broken up by Athenodoros and his expelling the corrupt ringleader Boethus and his partisans, but that is all. Strabo said nothing about Athenodoros rewriting the constitution for Tarsus and making the owning of property a prerequisite to holding and exercising citizenship in Tarsus. The property qualification, then, as well as the new constitution as espoused by Bible Hub (Bible Hub; Tarsus; sections 6 & 7; http://bibleatlas.org/tarsus.htm) was an assumption, not a fact. On the basis of such an assumption one cannot make a definite assertion about the wealth and social status of Paul and his family. To the best of this writer's knowledge there is no ancient evidence that indicates Paul's family were landowners, wealthy to some degree, and aristocrats.
50. Acts 18:1-3; 1 Corinthians 4:12; 2 Thessalonians 3:6-12, Acts 20:33-35
51. Edersheim, Alfred; Sketches of Jewish Social Life – In The Days Of Christ; Wm. B. Eerdmans Publishing Company; Grand Rapids, Michigan; reprinted 1974; p. 126
52. Ibid., p. 185
53. The New Schaff-Herzog Encyclopedia of Religious Knowledge, Vol. XI; "Pharisees And Sadducees"; Jackson, Samuel Macauley, editor-in-chief; Baker Book House; Grand Rapids, Michigan; p. 12
54. "The same sanctity that the priests in the Temple claimed for their meals, at which they gathered with the recitation of benedictions and after ablutions, the Pharisees established for their meals, which were partaken of in holy assemblies after purifi-

cations and amidst benedictions. . . . A true Pharisee observed the same degree of purity in his daily meals as did the priest in the Temple, wherefore it was necessary that he should avoid contact with the 'am ha-arez' (the common Jewish people of the land)." Kohler, Kaufman; Pharisees; Jewish Encyclopedia, The unedited full text of the 1906 Jewish Encyclopedia; jewish encyclopedia.com

55. Mark 7:1-4
56. Matthew 23:23; Luke 11:42
57. Mark 7:9-12
58. Lev. 11:1-31
59. Leviticus 23; Colossians 2:16
60. The description is based on Edersheim's descriptions and discussions of Pharisaic attire. See Edersheim, Alfred; Sketches of Jewish Social Life – In The Days Of Christ; Wm. B. Eerdmans Publishing Company; Grand Rapids, Michigan; reprinted 1974; p. 216 f.
61. Ibid., p. 215
62. Edersheim, Alfred; Sketches of Jewish Social Life – In The Days Of Christ; Wm. B. Eerdmans Publishing Company; Grand Rapids, Michigan; reprinted 1974; p. 213
63. Ibid., p. 213
64. Ibid., p. 214
65. Ibid., p.215
66. Ibid., p. 215

5

PAUL'S CONVERSION AND CALL TO BE AN APOSTLE

PAUL'S AGE: 33 DATE: A.D. 33

In This Chapter: Did Paul See And Hear Jesus? The Pharisees' Opposition To Jesus; Paul's Attitude As A Pharisee Toward Jesus; Paul's Persecution Of The Church; Paul's Conversion And Divine Call – The Turning Point In His Life.

Did Paul See And Hear Jesus?

There is not a single verse in the New Testament that states Paul ever saw or heard Jesus during Jesus' three-year earthly ministry. But no thoughtful commentator would go so far as to say that Paul could "never" have seen or heard Jesus or that it was impossible for Paul to have seen and heard him. The possibility must at least be allowed that Paul might have been in Judea or Jerusalem or at the temple at a time when Jesus was there. There are two verses, one in the Book of Acts and the other in First Timothy, that suggest Paul may have been an eyewitness who saw and/or heard Jesus.

The first of those verses is Acts 26:16. It relates some of the words Jesus spoke to Paul on the road outside of Damascus. Jesus told Paul, "For this reason I appeared to you, to appoint you a minister and a witness of the things which you have seen and of things which I will show to you." The word for a "witness" in the original Greek text is "martus". First, "martus" denotes a person who is qualified, in a legal sense, to testify to what he has seen or heard with his very own eyes and ears. Secondly, it denotes a person who can testify to facts in general or to truths or views on the basis of his personal knowledge and experience.[1] Luke used the word "martus" thirteen times in the Book of Acts;[2] once the word was used to denote a man who testified to the truths of Jesus – Stephen before he was stoned. The other twelve times "martus" was used of a man who could testify on the basis of his personal knowledge and experience to the facts. Peter said he was a "martus" of the sufferings of Christ (1 Peter 5:1). Based on what is written in the four gospels there is no doubt that Peter personally witnessed the sufferings of Christ Jesus and could speak of them from firsthand knowledge and experience. So we can correctly understand that in Acts 26:16 Jesus clearly used the term "martus" to mean Paul was to be a witness who would testify on the basis of his personal knowledge to the facts of what he had seen up to that time and what he would yet be shown in the future.

According to that definition of "witness" Jesus appointed Paul to be an eyewitness who could testify from personal, firsthand experience to what he had seen and/or heard. The things that Paul had seen commentators readily understand to be what Paul saw and heard when Jesus appeared to him on the road outside of Damascus. And those words of Jesus are understood to mean that Paul was to testify as an eyewitness to the fact that he had seen Jesus resurrected from the dead. Such an understanding is in line with the New Testament Scriptures, for according to Acts 1:22 the original Twelve apostles were also to be witnesses to Jesus' resurrection.

That understanding, however, does not rule out the possibility that the things that Paul had seen and heard could also have included Paul's having been an eyewitness to Jesus' passion, particularly his trial before Pilate and his crucifixion. If Paul had to be an eyewitness in the sense of having personally seen the risen Lord Jesus in order to testify to and establish the fact that Jesus had been resurrected from the dead, it stands to reason that if Paul testified to Jesus' having been tried by Pilate, crucified and killed, he should have been an eyewitness in that same sense of having personally seen Jesus' trial, crucifixion, and death so that he could establish those facts, like Peter who said he was a witness of the sufferings of Christ. If Paul had not been an eyewitness to those facts, throughout his apostolic ministry all he could honestly have said was that he had been told that Jesus had been tried, crucified, died, and was buried, in which case his testimony would have immediately been subject to question and uncertainty. But if he had indeed been an eyewitness, then there could have been no arguments to the contrary. And Paul did indeed testify to Jesus' having been crucified and put to death on the cross as well as having witnessed to Jesus' having been raised from the dead. As evidence of this, consider how many times in his various letters Paul witnessed to Jesus' crucifixion and death. Here is a partial listing of such verses: Galatians 2:1 & 13; Romans 4:24, 25; 5:6 & 8; 1 Corinthians 1:23 & 2:2; Ephesians 5:2; Philippians 2:8; Colossians 1:20 & 22; 1 Thessalonians 2:14, 15 & 3:14; and Titus 2:14. Now since Paul witnessed to Jesus' crucifixion and death so often in his few letters, how many more times must he have witnessed to Jesus' crucifixion and death in his preaching and teaching over a period of about thirty-five years? Paul could hardly have testified as a valid witness to Jesus' crucifixion and death if in fact he had never witnessed those events himself.

The second of those verses that suggest Paul might have been an eyewitness to Jesus' suffering and crucifixion is 1 Timothy 6:13. In this verse Paul wrote to Timothy, "I charge you in the presence of God who gives life to all things and Christ Jesus who testified the good confession in the presence of Pontius Pilate . . ." Now someone might have told Paul that Jesus made a good confession before Pontius Pilate. That must be recognized as a possibility. But what kind of an eyewitness would Paul had been then? When Jesus appeared to Paul and called him to be an apostle, Jesus told him he was to be a firsthand witness who could establish the things he had seen. Paul could not have been such a firsthand witness to what he had not seen, could he? So, could Paul have been an eyewitness to what Jesus confessed to

Pilate, if Paul had not been there to see and to hear it for himself? Of course not! So, the possibility that Paul did witness Jesus' trial before Pilate and heard what Jesus said must be granted. What is more, F. F. Bruce's assertion that Paul had to learn such factual details of the gospel from the firsthand eyewitness Peter so he could then preach that gospel is groundless and contrary to Scripture, not only for the reasons just given but because Paul said he was not taught the gospel nor received it from a man (ref. Galatians 1:12) and because Paul started preaching the gospel immediately after his conversion in Damascus three years before he ever saw or met Peter! (ref. Galatians 1:18; Acts 9:19 & 20)

In support of the above comments that it does indeed seem apparent that Paul was an eyewitness to Jesus' trial, suffering, crucifixion, and death is the little relative pronoun "on" (pronounced hown) in the Greek text that Jesus used in Acts 26:16 above. The relative pronoun literally means "of which things", and is translated "of the things which". Jesus did not call Paul to be a witness of just the one thing commentators point to – the revelation outside of Damascus of the resurrected Jesus, but to be a witness of more than one thing – of the things which Paul had seen with his very own eyes. As stated above those things would have included Jesus' trial, crucifixion, and death as well as his resurrection. Further support of Paul's having been a witness as asserted in the preceding paragraphs is found in the words of Ananias to Paul when Jesus had Ananias restore Paul's sight. Ananias said to Paul, "You will be a **witness** to him (Jesus) to all mankind **of the things that you have seen and heard** (Acts 22:15).

Granting that Paul did see Jesus during his passion does not lessen the significance of Paul's statements in 1 Corinthians 9:1 & 15:8 that the risen Lord Jesus had appeared to him and that he had seen the Lord. For in those verses Paul was speaking of having seen the resurrected, living, glorified Lord Jesus Christ who appeared to him. That has no bearing whatsoever on Paul's having seen Jesus during his earthly life and passion that is the subject of this discussion. And those verses cannot be used as an argument that Paul could not have seen Jesus until the resurrected Jesus appeared to him on the road to

Damascus, because Paul never said in those verses that he had never seen Jesus before he saw the resurrected Lord Jesus.

And there is an additional point that should be kept in mind as well: It seems very evident that Paul had been lied to about Jesus' resurrection by the chief priests and elders. They must have told him that Jesus' disciples had stolen Jesus' body and then claimed that Jesus had risen from the dead (ref. Matthew 28:11-15). For if Paul had heard and known the truth that Jesus had risen from the dead, his attitude toward Jesus and the Christians who believed in him would surely have been much different. His persecution of the Christian Church might never have happened if he had known the truth, for it was the knowledge of that truth that converted him. More will be said about this in connection with Paul's conversion later in this chapter.

Now if Paul was indeed a witness to Jesus' trial, crucifixion, and death, as it seems he must have been, at that time Paul would have had no correct spiritual understanding of the significance and meaning of what he was witnessing, for at that time Paul was spiritually dead in the depths of his Pharisaic traditions, unbelief and rejection of Jesus of Nazareth. Based upon how Paul later hated and persecuted the name of Jesus, Paul must have thought at the time that Jesus was getting the sentence he deserved as a false teacher and blasphemer of God. Paul would not gain the correct understanding of Jesus' crucifixion and death until two years later, and then in a most shocking manner, as we are about to see in this chapter.

The *Pharisees Opposition To Jesus*

The Pharisees and the experts in the law sat in the chair of Moses as the recognized authoritative teachers of God's Law among the Jews (ref. Matthew 23:2). The experts in the law declared in their traditions what should and should not be done; the Pharisees saw to it those traditions were carried out to the extreme. Together they oversaw the doctrine and practice of the religion of the Jews at the time of Jesus' ministry. But then serious contradictions to their doctrines and practices began to arise with which they thought they must contend.

In A.D. 28 John the Baptist appeared as the prophet of God and the forerunner of the Messiah (Christ). Unlike the work-righteousness taught and upheld by the Pharisees as the way to eternal life, John the Baptist preached a baptism of repentance for the forgiveness of sins. And when he saw the Pharisees coming to his baptism, he labeled them as a brood of vipers and challenged them, "Who warned you to flee from the coming wrath?" (Matthew 3:7) Needless to say, John's preaching a message contrary to the Pharisees' legal work righteousness and his labeling them as a brood of vipers who were under the condemnation of God did not sit well with them. They, in turn, then rejected John and his message (Matthew 21:31, 32).

Then some months later Jesus of Nazareth appeared on the scene. As much as the Pharisees disliked the message of John, in a short matter of time they began to object to and reject the message of Jesus even more. The Four Gospels reveal how during the years of Jesus' ministry the Pharisees, the teachers of the law and the chief priests all continued to wage an ongoing war against Jesus and his teachings. The Four Gospels reveal that as the three years of Jesus' ministry progressed, the attacks on Jesus by the Pharisees continued and intensified.

The Pharisees' criticisms of Jesus began from nearly the outset of Jesus' public ministry. The Gospel of John reports that already early in the first year of Jesus' ministry the Pharisees began persecuting Jesus for breaking their Sabbath law and for saying that God was his Father. For such a blasphemy they wanted to kill him already then in the early months of his ministry.[3] And throughout the years of his ministry they continued to reject his claim that he was the Son of God. On one occasion when he spoke one of his "I Am" sayings, no doubt Pharisees were among those Jews present who hated him for identifying himself as the Lord who spoke to Moses from the burning bush (ref. Exodus 3:14). They then wanted to stone him (ref. John 8:58, 59). John 4:1-3 also tell us that during that first year of Jesus' ministry the Pharisees heard that Jesus was baptizing more disciples than John the Baptist.

They had become aware of Jesus' growing popularity and success. When Jesus learned of this fact, he withdrew from Judea and went into Galilee. This information makes it clear that already during that first year of his ministry Jesus saw that the Pharisees posed a dangerous threat to him and his ministry.

From then on the Pharisees kept criticizing and opposing Jesus. They detested Jesus' violating their traditions on how the Sabbath should be observed. Matthew 12:9-14 informs us that during the second year of Jesus' ministry the Pharisees tempted him by asking if it were lawful to heal on a Sabbath day. When Jesus made it clear in their synagogue that compassion and love came even before the observance of the Sabbath and then healed a man with a crippled hand, the Pharisees became so enraged that they went out and began plotting to kill him. The Pharisees resented the fact that Jesus criticized the traditions of the elders that they adhered to.[4] When Jesus told a paralytic that his sins were forgiven, the Pharisees accused him of blasphemy against God.[5] The Pharisees also accused Jesus of casting out demons by the power of the devil and being in league with the devil (ref. Matthew 12:22-37). What is more, they repeatedly demanded miraculous signs from Jesus to substantiate his authority and who he really was, for they refused to accept that he had the authority of God to do what he was doing.[6] They tempted Jesus on the doctrine of marriage and divorce and tried to justify their divorces of their wives (ref. Matthew 19:3-9). They were lovers of money and they sneered at Jesus when he said men could not serve both God and money (ref. Luke 16:14). They hardened their hearts and refused to reply when Jesus demonstrated from David's Psalm 110 that the Christ (meaning Jesus himself) was not only a man but David's Lord, and therefore the Christ was both the Son of David and the Son of God (ref. Matthew 22:41-46). Over and above all these complaints that the Pharisees had about Jesus was this: Jesus was not their idea of what Christ, the Messiah, was supposed to be. Jesus in their opinion did not look or act like a powerful political king who would restore the nation of Israel to the great prosperity and power it once had been under King David. For this reason on Palm Sunday when Jesus entered Jerusalem amid the shouts that were proclaiming him to be the long-awaited Son of David, the Messiah (the Christ), the Pharisees demanded that Jesus rebuke those disciples for making those proclamations (ref. Luke 19:39).

Now the apostle John was an eyewitness to the Pharisees', not to mention the other Jews' as well, rejection and abusive treatment of Jesus. By the inspiration of the Holy Spirit he summed up what took place during those three years of Jesus' ministry. He said in the following verses of John 1:

> 4 In him was life, and the life was the light of men.
>
> 5 And the light shines in the darkness, and yet the darkness did not overpower it.
>
> 10 He was in the world, and the world was made through him, and yet the world did not recognize him.
>
> 11 He came to his own land of Israel, and his own people did not receive him *favorably*.
>
> 12 But as many as received him, to those who believe in his name, he gave the right to become children of God,
>
> 13 who were begotten, not of blood, nor of the will of the flesh, nor of the will of man, but of God.
>
> 17 For the law was given through Moses – the grace and the truth came through Jesus Christ.
>
> 18 No one has ever seen God; the only begotten God who is in the bosom of the Father – that One has made him known.

As the apostle John stated, in Jesus was life – spiritual and eternal life, and that life was the light that enlightened individuals to believe in him. Jesus was the light of the world through whom came the grace and the truth that offered eternal life and salvation to all. And all who did believe in him became children of God. As that light of life, grace, and truth, Jesus stood up to the spiritual darkness of the Pharisees who tried to extinguish him and his light of life, but as the apostle John said, they did not overpower him. Throughout his ministry he rebuked the Pharisees to correct them in order to lead them to repentance and to uphold the grace and truth of his gospel. In his rebuking the Pharisees he was fulfilling what had been written about him in Psalm 45:6, 7, which was a Messianic psalm. The verses foretold that as the Messiah, meaning the Christ, the scepter by which Jesus ruled in his kingdom was a scepter of righteousness, for he loved righteousness and hated wickedness. Jesus did just that during his three-year ministry.

Accordingly we read in the Four Gospels that Jesus rebuked the Pharisees, their false teachings, and their wickedness repeatedly. Here are but a few such examples: He rebuked their self-righteous pride and contempt for those who were not Pharisees like themselves but were tax collectors and people they called "sinners". And he also rebuked their work righteousness by which they sought to be right with God and obtain eternal life.[7] He taught the Pharisees that God's law commanding compassion and love was a higher law than that of the Sabbath law and their legalistic observances of the Sabbath.[8] He corrected their thoughts that he did not have the divine authority to forgive sins by healing the paralytic and showing them in the process that he was God himself in the flesh.[9] When they accused him of casting out demons by the power of the devil, he rebuked their blasphemy against the Holy Spirit.[10]

The Pharisees continued to harden their hearts against the Word of God and the gospel that Jesus taught. So, by the third year of Jesus' ministry the Pharisees and the experts in the law became terribly hostile to Jesus and plied him with a great many questions (ref. Luke 11:53). Time and again they tempted him in the attempt to trap him into saying something for which they could accuse him and condemn him. And time and again Jesus corrected them and rebuked them. For those rebukes and because Jesus refused to knuckle under to their false teachings and practices but exposed them, the Pharisees as well as the other ranking Jews hated him and plotted how they might kill him.

There were yet two more reasons for their hating Jesus and wanting to kill him. First, by the time of Holy Week in A.D. 31 the Pharisees and the chief priests were worried about their own futures and the future of their positions as the rulers of Israel under the supervision of the Romans. They were afraid that if Jesus were not stopped and eliminated, the Romans would march in, take control of the unstable situation in Palestine, and remove them from their places of political power. Second, the Pharisees were jealous of the success of Jesus' ministry among the multitudes. The fact of this jealousy is made clear first by the Pharisees' own statements and then by the knowledge of Pontius Pilate. We are told:

> 47 So the chief priests and the Pharisees brought the Sanhedrin together, and began saying, "What are we doing, because this man performs many miraculous signs?
>
> 48 "If we let him go on in this manner, everyone will believe in him, and the Romans will come and take away both our place and the nation!" (John 11:47, 48)
>
> 19 Consequently the Pharisees said to one another, "See, you are accomplishing nothing! Behold, the world has just gone after him!" (John 12:19)
>
> 17 So when they had gathered together, Pilate said to them, "Whom do you wish that I release to you – Barabbas or Jesus, who is called Christ?"
>
> 18 For he knew that out of jealousy they had handed him over. (Matthew 27:17, 18)

This opposition to Jesus reached a climax by the time of Holy Week when the Pharisees together with the other ranking leaders of the Jews were doing everything they could to seize and arrest Jesus in order to kill him. Jesus' rebukes of the Pharisees came to a head on Tuesday of Holy Week when he exposed Pharisaism for the hypocrisy and the false teaching that it was. He pronounced seven woes upon them as a warning to them of the judgment of God that was coming upon them. Matthew informs us[11] that Jesus said the Pharisees were: Hypocrites! Hypocrites! Hypocrites! Those who loved the place of honor at the banquets and the seats of honor in the synagogues and the respectful greetings in the marketplaces and to be called, 'Rabbi'!

Those who bound heavy and hard to bear burdens of the law on others but were unwilling to raise a finger to move them themselves! Those who shut the kingdom of heaven in people's faces! Foolish and blind leaders! Neglecters of the important matters of the law – justice and mercy and faithfulness! Men full of plunder and a lack of moral restraint! Whitewashed tombs that were lovely on the outside but inside were full of death and every kind *of* impurity! Snakes! A brood of vipers!

A more scathing denunciation of religious leaders and teachers cannot be imagined!

Paul's Attitude As A Pharisee Toward Jesus

The Pharisees were a close-knit religious fraternity. Jesus' teachings, rebukes of the Pharisees' doctrine and practice, and claims that he was the Son of God would have made the headlines throughout the Pharisaic brotherhood. Paul, the Pharisee, would have also heard and known about all those things as well. The Pharisees' reasons, explained above, for opposing and hating Jesus would have been Paul's reasons for opposing and hating Jesus. The Pharisee Paul would have considered Jesus a false teacher for rejecting and overturning the traditions of the Jewish elders. Paul would have looked upon Jesus as a blasphemer of the very worst kind for claiming he was the Son of God. Paul would have looked upon Jesus as a false Christ (Messiah) who was nothing like the powerful, political king who was to restore the greatness of Israel. Paul would have taken Jesus' scathing denunciations of the Pharisees as scathing denunciations of himself. And Paul would have taken Jesus' stern rebukes of the Pharisees' doctrine and practice as stern rebukes of his doctrine and practice and as an insult not only to himself but also to his family and Pharisaic upbringing. For all of these reasons Paul would have thought that Jesus was the enemy of his beliefs and Pharisaic way of life. Paul would have been committed to stopping and eradicating Jesus and his teachings to the best of his ability.

Paul's Persecution Of The Church

Now Paul had a fiery temperament that especially flared up when confronted by teachings that stood in opposition to God and God's teachings. That temper also flared up when he was confronted with the persons upholding those heretical teachings. Thus Paul's fiery temperament flared up like an ignited blowtorch in the face of the beliefs and teachings of the "heretical man Jesus" and his followers. Being so zealous, and aroused to a furious indignation, Paul hated the very name of that false rabbi and blasphemer Jesus of Nazareth, as Paul considered him.

This being the case, Paul became a man on a mission with a crusade to carry out. He had to put a stop to that new, heretical religion of Jesus of Nazareth. He had to wipe out the name of that man Jesus. About twenty-six years later in A.D. 59 Paul told King Agrippa II: "To be sure, as for me, I thought within myself that it was necessary to commit many hostile acts against the name of Jesus the Nazarene."[12] And so, when the day came that the Jewish rulers of the Sanhedrin were holding a hearing for a follower of Jesus named Stephen, Paul was right there to hear all that was said. And Paul was right there when the Jewish rulers became infuriated at Stephen for blaming them for the murder of Jesus of Nazareth, the "Righteous One" who was the Christ whom God's prophets had foretold was to come. And when the Jewish rulers started plugging their ears and screaming to drown out Stephen's words and were dragging him out of the city to begin stoning him, Paul was right there, ready and eager to join in the stoning of Stephen. Paul guarded the rulers' coats while they stoned Stephen to death, and Paul gave his hearty approval to Stephen's murder![13]

Acts 7:58 tells us, "And after (the Jewish rulers) drove (Stephen) outside of the city, they began stoning him. And the witnesses took off their cloaks and laid them beside the feet of a young man named Saul." According to this verse Paul was a young man when he stood by and watched approvingly the stoning of Stephen. The Greek term for "young man" in this verse was a term used for men between twenty and forty years of age. Based on the chronology included in this biographical commentary of Paul's life, Paul would have been 32-33 years of age.

Luke then informs us. "Now on that day a violent persecution erupted against the church in Jerusalem." (Acts 8:1) In that religious uprising of the Jews against the followers of Jesus, Paul rose up to be the chief persecutor of the church. Luke reports, "Then Saul (Paul) began to destroy the church. Going into house after house and dragging away both men and women, he kept locking them up in prison." (Acts 8:3) Paul was carrying out this persecution of the followers of Jesus, because the chief priests had commissioned Paul to persecute them. Paul was acting upon their authority as Paul later stated in Acts 26:10:

> ... and many of the saints I myself even locked up in prisons, because I had received this authority from the chief priests, and when they were being put to death, I cast a vote against them.

In addition to the statements of Paul given above, years later in his life and in his letters, Paul confessed what he had done in persecuting the new, infant Church of Jesus Christ's believers:

> And when I was punishing them throughout all the synagogues, I kept forcing them to blaspheme; and because I was extremely enraged at them, I kept persecuting them even as far as foreign cities. (Acts 26:9-11)
>
> I used to persecute the church of God to an extraordinary degree and was trying to destroy it. (Galatians 1:13)
>
> I persecuted this Way (the name for the Christian faith) even to the point of putting them to death, binding not only men but also women and delivering them into prison. (Acts 22:4)
>
> ... in one synagogue after another I indeed used to imprison and beat those who were believing in (Jesus). (Acts 22:19)

In persecuting the church in those ways Paul was fulfilling the words of Jesus, as other Jews would later do also, for Jesus had told his disciples, "They will expel you from the synagogue; why, an hour is coming when everyone who kills you shall think he is offering a religious service to God!" (John 16:2) And so, Paul, in his misguided zeal for God and his misplaced devotion to the doctrines and practices of the Pharisees, also thought he was offering a religious service to God by persecuting the men and women of the Church in a most brutal, violent, cruel, hateful fashion.

For exactly how long Paul's furious persecution of the infant Church went on cannot be stated with certainty. It seems to this writer, as he indicated in the chronology shown in Chapter 3, that the stoning of Stephen occurred about A.D. 32. Based on the information credited to Chrysostom Paul's conversion happened in A.D. 33. Using this information it appears that Paul's persecution of the church lasted for about a year.

Paul's Conversion – The Turning Point In His Life

Luke informs us that when the violent persecution of the church in Jerusalem erupted, many believers in Jesus "were scattered throughout the country of Judea and Samaria except for the apostles." (Acts 8:1) The Lord in his infinite wisdom, who causes all things to work for the good of his Church,[14] did indeed cause this persecution to work for the good of his church. The Jews in their hatred of Jesus were attempting to stamp out the name of Jesus and his church with a violent persecution, but what the Lord accomplished through them instead was to scatter and spread the church out in different directions to different places. After Paul had been persecuting the followers of Jesus in Jerusalem for some period of time, it seems that he must have thought that a number of Jesus' followers had fled to Damascus in the neighboring country of Syria. For Luke reports in Acts 9:1, 2:

1 Now Saul (Paul), still breathing threats and murder against the disciples of the Lord, went to the high priest

2 and asked for letters from him to the synagogues in Damascus, in order that if he found anyone who belonged to the Way, not only men but also women, after he bound them in chains, he might take them along to Jerusalem.

Paul did receive letters of authorization from the high priest to persecute Jesus' followers in Damascus. Having that authorization, he then set out for Damascus.

Damascus was a very ancient city. It has been said that the city was founded by Uz the grandson of Shem.[15] It was in existence already at the time of Abraham around 2,100 B.C., for Genesis 15:2 states that Abraham's chief servant Eliezer was from Damascus. The city was located in a beautiful, fertile land where it was well watered by channels of the Abanah and Pharpar Rivers of which Naaman spoke in 2 Kings 5:12 and called the rivers of Damascus. Gardens and orchards were then able to flourish there, which set the city apart from the nearby desert. The city at the time of Paul was about two miles long and just under a mile wide. Running almost through the center of Damascus was "a street called Straight",[16] which ran east and west the full length of the city. The street at that time was a magnificent thoroughfare that was lined with Corinthian columns.[17] Straight Street past by the amphitheater on the west side of the city and then past the governor's palace that was a short distance to the east. There was another short straight street on the north side of the city that extended from the city's marketplace to the Temple of Jupiter.[18] The city was defended by a wall that surrounded it, as is also evident from Luke's report of Paul's later escape from the city (ref. Acts 9:23-25). There were five city-gates; one at each end of the colonnaded Straight Street, and three facing the Abanah River. Damascus was home to a large population of Jews at the time of Paul, for which reason there were several synagogues in the city. Such a large population of Jews in Damascus was reported by Josephus,[19] who stated that at the time of Nero years later ten thousand Jews of Damascus had their throats cut and were massacred. That having been true, perhaps the population of Damascus was 20 to 25,000 including the Gentiles. The city in A.D. 33 at the time of Paul was under the control of Aretas, who was a Nabataean king that ruled over the city through his appointed governor (ref. 2 Corinthians 11:32).

Such was the scene and situation of Damascus when Paul approached the city on the road. Luke then informs us in Acts 9:3-9:

> 3 And it happened while he was going and was drawing near to Damascus – suddenly a light out of heaven flashed around him!
>
> 4 And when he fell to the ground, he heard a voice saying to him, 'Saul! Saul! Why are you persecuting me?'
>
> 5 And he said, "Who are you, Lord?" and he said, "As for me, I am Jesus, whom you, yes you, are persecuting!
>
> 6 But get up and go into the city, and it will be told you what you must do."
>
> 7 Now the men who were with him and had been standing speechless, because they were hearing the voice, to be sure, but they were seeing no one.
>
> 8. Then Saul was helped up from the ground, and although his eyes were open, he could see nothing. And leading him by the hand, they brought him into Damascus.
>
> 9 And he was blind for three days, and he neither ate nor drank anything.

Paul also described in his own words what that most glorious moment in his life was like. Piecing his words to King Agrippa in Acts 26:13-18 together with his words to the Jewish rioters at the temple in Jerusalem in Acts 22:7-11, Paul described the scene on the road to Damascus as follows:

> I was proceeding to Damascus with the authority and permission of the chief priests. At midday, while going down along the road I saw a light flash around me from heaven much brighter than the brightness of the sun, . . . and those who were with me saw the light. . . . And after

we all fell to the ground, I heard a voice say to me in the Hebrew dialect,

"Saul! Saul! Why are you persecuting me? It is hard for you to kick against the goads."

. . .Those with me did not understand the voice of the One who was speaking to me. Then I myself said, "Who are you, Lord?"

And the Lord said, "As for me, I am Jesus the Nazarene, whom you, yes you, are persecuting!"

Then I said, "What shall I do, Lord?"

And the Lord said to me, "Get up! Stand on your feet! For this reason I appeared to you, to appoint you as a minister and a witness both of the things which you have seen and of the things which I will show to you, rescuing you from the Jewish people and from the Gentiles, to whom I am sending you 'to open their eyes, to turn them back from darkness to light and from the power of Satan to God, in order that they may receive forgiveness of sins and a share among those who have been sanctified by faith in me. . . Go into Damascus, and there it will be told to you concerning all the things that have been determined for you to do."

And since I was unable to see because of the brightness of that light, while being led by the hand by those who were with me I came into Damascus.

Suddenly, without any forewarning, a light flashed around Paul. It was not an earthly light that shown out of the sky. It came from heaven, the dwelling place of God Almighty. It was, then, a divine light. It suddenly started shining at midday when the sun was at its height of maximum brilliance. But this light was much brighter than the sun, which paled by comparison. It was flashing and dancing around Paul like numerous spotlights suddenly illuminating an actor on a stage amid the surrounding dark shadows. In the midst of that brilliant light Paul saw a figure of a man standing. He at once realized that figure had to be none other than the Lord himself, radiating a glorious light so white and bright it hurt the eyes to look at it. This was not the first time the Lord Jesus revealed himself in such a dazzling glory. He appeared in such a divine glory to his disciples Peter, James, and John on the Mount of Transfiguration.[20]

The men who were with Paul saw the light also. They stood there speechless, dumbfounded, when they heard a voice speaking but saw no one and could not understand what the voice was saying. They all, together with Paul, fell to the ground onto the hard-packed surface of the road. They were stunned and terror stricken at the sight of what was happening before their very eyes. Lying there on the road, helpless and weak before the divine figure of the Lord of glory, Paul then heard the voice speak to him in the Hebrew dialect: "Saul! Saul! Why are you persecuting me? It is dangerous for you to kick against the goads."

Paul's conscience was pricked. He had persecuted many men, starting with Stephen whose murderous stoning he approved. In Jerusalem and its surrounding area he had persecuted so many men, as well as women, and put them in prison and voted to put them to death. Of all those men upon whom he had inflicted so much pain and suffering and even death – which one of them had been the figure of the man in the dazzling light, the Lord himself, unbeknown to him? Ignorant of whom it was that he thought he was seeing, he asked, "Who are you, Lord?"

Then Paul heard the Lord say, "As for me, I am Jesus the Nazarene, whom you, yes you, are persecuting!" Jesus' voice was short, to the point, firm, and yes reprimanding, and deservedly so. For Jesus, the all-knowing Lord God, knew ever so well all the despicable deeds of which Paul was guilty in the process of persecuting Jesus' followers who confessed their faith in him. As the risen and glorified Lord to whom his heavenly Father had given all judgment (ref. John 5:22), Jesus could have most justly judged and condemned him long ago, and could rightly do so at that moment. But while speaking so emphatically and sternly and accusatively to Paul, Jesus was showing his divine restraint and compassion and mercy on a misguided Paul who had acted in ignorance, thinking that he had actually been acting to defend the honor of God's name. Coming to the realization at some later time of just how restrained, compassionate, and merciful to him the Lord Jesus had been on that day on the road, about thirty years later Paul wrote: "Even though I was formerly a blasphemer and persecutor and violent man, I was shown mercy, because I acted in unbelief while being ignorant." (1 Timothy 1:13)

Jesus' challenging question, "Why are you persecuting me?" and Jesus stern accusation, "I am Jesus the Nazarene whom you, yes you, are persecuting," were Jesus' manner of reaching out to save a lowly, terribly misguided sinner. Jesus' words were a call to Paul to repent. It would indeed be dangerous for Paul to resist Jesus' call. Accordingly Jesus told Paul, "It is dangerous for you to kick against the goads." Goads were sharp pointed sticks that the ancient oxen drivers used to prod the stubborn, less than willing oxen to move along in the direction they were supposed to go. The oxen, however, resisted the prodding by kicking back against the goads. In doing so they only hurt themselves. Jesus' words of his question and accusation of Paul were the goads. It was dangerous for Paul to resist and fight against those sharp, pointed words. In doing so he would only endanger and harm himself – eternally. His own soul was at stake. For as the Lord Jesus had told the Eleven after his resurrection, "The one who believed and was baptized will be saved; but the one who did not believe will be condemned," so it was for Paul. It was absolutely necessary for Paul's own salvation that he become one who believed and was baptized, and not remain one who did not believe to be condemned in the end.

Hearing that the Lord of glory standing before him was none other than Jesus of Nazareth whom he was persecuting had to have been a most astonishing revelation to Paul's mind. Jesus of Nazareth was Christ the crucified and resurrected Lord of glory and the Son of God! Paul could no longer deny it. He could not argue the point. The reason was simple – the glorious evidence in the figure and person of the Lord was standing there before him! And this was the point at which Paul ceased to be the spiritually dead, unbelieving Pharisee and became a spiritually alive, believing disciple of the risen Lord Jesus Christ. So ashamedly, humbly, timidly, but most willingly, Paul asked, "What shall I do, Lord?"

Paul's question was the evidence of his conversion in two ways.

First, Paul called the Jesus of Nazareth whom he had been persecuting "Lord". Paul no longer was seeing Jesus as a false teacher and blasphemer. He was seeing Jesus as the Lord God himself in the flesh of the man whom he had so hated and despised. Second, when people are converted and brought to faith in their Savior Jesus Christ, they want to serve him. They want to know what they can do to be in his service. So it was here in Paul's case. He wanted to know what he could do to serve his Lord and Savior Jesus Christ.

And so, Jesus said to him, "Get up! Stand on your feet! For this reason I appeared to you, to appoint you as a minister and a witness both of the things which you have seen and of the things which I will show to you, rescuing you from the Jewish people and from the Gentiles, to whom I am sending you 'to open their eyes, to turn *them* back from darkness to light and from the power of Satan to God, in order that they may receive forgiveness of sins and a share among those who have been sanctified by faith in me." (Acts 26:16-18).

How could Paul serve Jesus? By serving him as his apostle. For Jesus' appointing Paul was Jesus' call of Paul to be his apostle. As an apostle his duty would be to be Jesus' minister and witness. As an apostle of Jesus, Paul was also to be a witness to testify to whom Jesus was and what Jesus had done and the forgiveness of sins that Jesus had obtained for everyone. Jesus told Paul that he was to be a witness of the things which he had seen and of the things which Jesus was still to show him. The things that Paul had seen were previously discussed at the beginning of this chapter, so they will not be discussed again here.

As for the things that Jesus said he would show him, no specific details of what those things were are known. Those things have been thought to be future, additional revelations. Such an interpretation is scripturally possible, for in the years ahead Jesus would speak a number of times to Paul. He would speak to Paul while Paul was in a trance in the temple in Jerusalem;[21] he would speak to him again in a vision while Paul was in Corinth;[22] he also would stand by Paul and speak to him when Paul was imprisoned in Caesarea.[23] As the Son of God Jesus certainly would also have worked in unison with the Holy

Spirit, who is called the Spirit of Jesus, in giving to Paul the vision of a man beckoning him to come to Macedonia (Acts 16:9, 10). And then there would be the revelation of heaven that would be given to Paul by the Lord, who is Jesus, the Son of God as well as the Father and the Holy Spirit (ref. 2 Corinthians 12:1-4). These visions and revelations might also be included in the things that Jesus told Paul he would show him. And it is also possible that Jesus may have given Paul other subsequent visions that neither Acts nor the Pauline letters have told us about, in which Jesus gave Paul some kind of instructions.

Paul was not aware of the fact when Jesus called him to be an apostle, but his apostolic ministry would be fraught with danger. Since that would be the case, Jesus assured Paul beforehand that he would be rescuing him from the Jewish people and from the Gentiles. The persecution and hatred that Paul had dished out to Jesus' followers in the past he himself would have heaped upon him in the future. But Jesus would pluck him out of those dangers and rescue him. As the years of Paul's apostolic ministry progressed amid persecution after persecution from both Jews and Gentiles this assurance of Jesus was quite likely to have been a great source of spiritual strength for Paul that sustained him.

Now it was to those Gentiles especially that Jesus was sending Paul as his apostle. In the koine Greek of the New Testament the noun "apostle" means "one who is sent out." Such was Paul, the apostle who was sent out to the Gentiles. Jesus informed Paul what his mission among the Gentiles would be. Simply stated, that mission that Paul was to do for the Gentiles was what Jesus had just done for him, the Pharisee who had been in the depths of the darkness of unbelief and under the control of the devil. And so, Jesus said he was sending Paul to open the eyes of the Gentiles, to turn them back from the darkness of unbelief and lives of sin to the light of faith in Jesus Christ and godly living. In doing that Paul would turn the Gentiles from the power of Satan to God. Paul was to lead the Gentiles to such repentance and faith through his preaching and teaching of the gospel, in order that they might receive the forgiveness of their sins and have a share in the eternal life and salvation in the kingdom of heaven that belonged to all who had been sanctified, that is set aside as holy for God, as his own people. Such sanctification happened then as it does today – through faith in Jesus Christ, the Son of God and Savior of the world.

Then, just as suddenly as Jesus had appeared to Paul on the road, so he in like manner vanished once again. Paul later said that since he was unable to see because of the brightness of that light, he was led by the hand into the city of Damascus by those who were with him. He was led to the house of a man named Judas, who was a Jewish man and likely to have been a Pharisee like Paul. There in Judas' house Paul sat in the darkness of his suddenly inflicted blindness for three days. We have no way of knowing for certain what thoughts and emotions passed through Paul's mind during those three days. But he surely had a lot to think about and to reflect upon in order to come to grips with what had just happened to him on the road, with his former way of life as a Pharisee and the persecutor of the church, and with whatever his life in the future as an apostle would be like. Schaff & Herzog stated, "He was converted in an altogether extraordinary way. No great man ever underwent so violent and sudden a change."[24]

The proud, strong-willed, forceful, commanding Pharisee Paul was suddenly humbled and struck down and stopped in his tracks by the overpowering presence and power and glory of the risen Lord Jesus Christ! Paul had seen the Lord![25] Just that suddenly he was confronted with the blinding, overwhelming, undeniable truth! Jesus was not dead! And his body had not been stolen away by his disciples during the night as the Jewish population had been deceived into believing by the false report that the Jewish high priests had the Roman soldiers spread around the city of Jerusalem and the whole surrounding countryside of Judea. Indeed, that falsehood was still being spread up to the time the apostle Matthew wrote his account of that deception sometime between A.D. 50 to 60 –twenty-seven to thirty-seven years after the conversion of Paul! (ref. Matthew 28:11-15)

Now when Jesus appeared to Paul on the road, Jesus spiritually enlightened Paul with the truth of the gospel. Paul indicated that about eighteen or nineteen years afterwards: "For I make known to you, brothers, that the gospel that was preached by me is not according to man; for indeed I neither received it from a man, nor was I taught it, but I received it by revelation of Jesus Christ." (Galatians 1:11, 12)

With those words Paul made it clear that he had not received the gospel from men. Paul had not learned the gospel he preached in the usual manner of having been instructed by others. He did not have to take instructional classes from the other apostles or from other individuals who had seen and heard Jesus' preaching and teaching. No, Paul had received it directly from Jesus himself, just as Jesus had taught the gospel to his original twelve apostles.

Now there have been some different opinions about how Paul received the gospel by revelation from Jesus. Did he receive an understanding of the gospel and spiritual enlightenment while on the road when Jesus appeared to him? Or, did he receive the gospel in two or more revelations at various times? This writer is of the same opinion as Martin Luther[26] that Paul received the gospel by special revelation from Jesus on the road to Damascus. At that time Paul was given the fundamental understanding of the gospel and spiritual enlightenment that converted him from an unbelieving, brutal adversary to Jesus' gospel and church to a believer in Jesus himself. But this writer also grants the possibility that Jesus might have given during Paul's three days of blindness further revelations about himself, his offices as prophet, priest, and king, and facts about his three-year ministry with his teachings to complete Paul's preparation for preaching and teaching his gospel as his bondservant.

It has been thought that during the three days of his sitting alone in his blindness he must have been deeply dejected and depressed. Yes, to a great extent he was. But it must be born in mind that Paul was now a spiritually regenerated believer in Jesus Christ. He had been converted. He had been spiritually enlightened to understand the gospel of God's grace in Christ that he had never understood before. That gospel fosters a peace and joy and hope as nothing else can do, as it would have begun to do in Paul as well upon his conversion. We can expect that during those three days amid his other reflective thoughts he would have begun to experience to some degree the joy and excitement that we see today in a new convert upon his coming to faith in Jesus and seeing the forgiveness and eternal salvation and everlasting blessedness in heaven that are his.

And so, not just dejection and depression are a fitting description of Paul during those three days. Other thoughts and emotions would have been bubbling up within him as well. A better description of Paul during that time may be "bewilderment", especially at first. It would have been natural for him to pass through a stage of self-reflection over his past life and Jewish/Pharisaic religious beliefs. Coupled with his new spiritual enlightenment of the gospel and its promises and hope, Paul was likely to have gone through a state of bewilderment, a chaotic state of his mental forces, in which especially at first can best be described as disordered and jumbled up. Surely thoughts and feelings ebbed and flowed through his mind as he tried to sort everything out and to make sense of it all in the process of coming to the realization of the many falsehoods and failures in his past and what would ultimately be the course of his life as an apostle of Jesus in the future. What Paul had just gone through on the road had happened so fast! He would have needed some time to sort everything out and to put his new life into focus. It is therefore understandable that Paul neither ate nor drank anything during those three days. Mentally and emotionally he could not!

At first the feelings of shock must have struck him down to the very foundations of his soul. The revelation of Jesus would have been so startling and overwhelming. Jesus' appearance was vivid proof of just how wrong he had been. Jesus was not a dead false rabbi; he was the living Lord! The Son of God! The long-awaited Messiah, the Christ! Realizing this fact, Paul's thoughts and emotions would have begun to be taken up with guilt. How wrong he had been in persecuting the name of Jesus. How wrong he had been in attempting to destroy Jesus' Church of believers. Then Paul would have been struck with the enormity of what he had done. The feelings of guilt would have been profound. He had blasphemed the name of Christ, the Son of God himself! He had persecuted, physically beaten and abused, chained and imprisoned, attempted to force to blaspheme the name of Jesus, condemned and executed – innocent men and women who had done no more than to put their faith in the risen Lord Jesus Christ! How could God ever forgive him for all that he had done? In the depths of that guilt were the times especially when Paul would have experienced the emotions of deep dejection and depression. It was a wrongdoing and guilt that would remain within him for the rest of his life. It came out at times, as it did when he wrote thirty years later to Timothy:

> 12 I give thanks to Christ Jesus our Lord who strengthened me, because he considered me faithful, when he appointed me into his service,
>
> 13 even though I was formerly a blasphemer and persecutor and violent *man*. But I was shown mercy, because I acted in unbelief while being ignorant.
>
> 14 And the grace of our Lord was present in great abundance with faith and love, which are in Christ Jesus.
>
> 15 This statement is trustworthy and worthy of full acceptance: Christ Jesus came into the world to save sinners; of whom I myself am foremost.
>
> 16 But I was shown mercy for this reason, that Christ Jesus may demonstrate in me as the foremost all his patience, as an example for those who are going to place their faith upon him for eternal life.
>
> 17 Now to the King eternal, immortal, invisible, the only God, be honor and glory forever and ever. Amen. (1 Timothy 1:12-17)

By the end of those three days of self-reflecting on his despicable deeds of which he was guilty, it was that mercy and grace and love and faith of God in Jesus Christ, of which Paul wrote to Timothy, that carried him through and delivered him from a lifetime of depression and despair.

As Paul stated to Timothy, he had acted in unbelief and ignorance. During those solitary hours of the three days in which he sat, Paul would have come to realize how misguided his zeal for God had been throughout his whole life. Beginning already in his childhood when he was being raised and trained as a Pharisee of Pharisees, he was acquiring a misguided zeal for God. Having had such a personal experience himself, he was later able to say about his fellow Jewish countrymen:

> 1 Brothers, to be sure, my heart's desire and my prayer to God in their behalf is for their salvation.
>
> 2 For I bear witness about them that they have a zeal for God, but not according to precise knowledge;
>
> 3 for while being ignorant of the righteousness of God, and seeking to establish their own righteousness, they did not subject themselves to the righteousness of God;
>
> 4 for Christ is the end of the law for righteousness for everyone who believes. (Romans 10:1-4)

During those three days of quiet self-reflection, while in the process of mentally sorting out his past life and Pharisaic beliefs in the light of Christ's gospel, Paul would have come to realize his failure to properly understand who Jesus of Nazareth really was. From the Mosaic Law in Deuteronomy 21:23 Paul had known that whoever was hung on a tree was under God's curse. Paul knew, very likely as an eyewitness as explained previously, Jesus of Nazareth had been hung on a tree and crucified to death. Therefore, as Paul would have reasoned, Jesus of Nazareth was under the curse of God and could not possibly have been the blessed Messiah, the anointed One of God. Therefore, Paul had also thought prior to his conversion that Jesus of Nazareth had to have been a blasphemer who had equated himself with God and declared himself to be the Son of God. For this reason, Paul had hated and persecuted the name of Jesus by persecuting Jesus' followers who confessed him to be the Son of God and in the process of his doing so had blasphemed God himself!

But on the road when Paul saw Jesus of Nazareth risen from the dead, it became clear to Paul that Jesus of Nazareth was not under

God's curse. But how could that be? The law was clear and could not be mistaken. Jesus had been hung on a tree and was therefore under God's curse. When Jesus revealed the gospel of God's grace to him, however, then this matter was cleared up for him. Then Paul came to understand that God made Jesus, who was guilty of no sin, to be sin for everyone else, as Paul would explain to the Corinthians twenty-three years later (ref. 2 Corinthians 5:21). Having laid the sins of the whole world on Jesus, God put him under his curse in the place of everyone else and condemned him to death, death on the tree of the cross. That innocent, sacrificial death of Jesus satisfied God's justice for the punishment of sin, for which reason God then justified, that is declared righteous, all the sinners on earth. Paul explained this to the Galatians in A.D. 51: "Christ redeemed us from the curse of the law by having become a curse in our place, for it is written, "CURSED IS EVERYONE WHO IS HUNG ON A TREE." (Galatians 3:13)

Once Paul properly understood those things that God had done through Jesus of Nazareth, he was able to start sorting out the other matters concerning the Messiah of God and the Law of Moses. He had been misled about the Messiah by his Pharisaic father, by the teachers in his Jewish school in Tarsus as a boy, by his esteemed professor, the Dr. Gamaliel of the Mosaic Law, and by his fraternity of Pharisees. All had been wrong! All had misled him. The Messiah whom God had promised was not to be a political king of the nation of Israel, who would restore Israel to its former greatness that it had under King David, and who would usher in a millennium of great fortune and abundance. No! The Messiah whom God had promised was to be the King of God's kingdom of grace and of glory, whose kingdom would never end, as God had promised to David in 2 Samuel 7:13. The Messiah was not to come in the pomp and power of an earthly king, but as the lowly, suffering servant foretold in Psalms 22, 69 &118, in Isaiah 9 & 53, and in Zechariah 9:9. How slow of mind and foolish in heart he had been not to have perceived and believed what God had said through his prophets!

What is more, Paul had been misguided about the laws of Moses and the traditions handed down by the rabbis. He had been raised from his infancy as a Pharisee and trained in the Law of Moses. He had been educated in the strictest teachings of the Jewish fathers by Gamaliel. And he had been taught all the traditions of the rabbinical elders. But then, in one swift swoop Paul's whole life's training and religious beliefs as upheld by the self-righteous Pharisees were turned upside down and shown to be false. After Jesus had revealed the gospel to him, and at the same time he had been given the regeneration by the Holy Spirit, the fog of all the falsehoods began to dissipate.

He began to understand that it was not necessary to obey the laws of Moses to obtain eternal life, nor did he have to obey the traditions of the rabbis. As he then came to realize, those traditions were either adiaphora or outright falsehoods. By faith he saw that the gospel of Jesus Christ crucified for sins and raised as proof of God's forgiveness shattered the Pharisaical belief in a righteousness obtained by works of obedience to the laws of Moses and the rabbinical traditions. Eternal life and salvation were not gained by works of obedience but were gifts of God's grace in Christ! Having that understanding, Paul would write about twenty-four years into the future:

> 19 Now we know that whatever the law says, it says to those under the law, so that every mouth may be silenced and all the world become accountable to God;
>
> 20 because as a result of works of law no person will be declared righteous in his presence, for by means of law *comes* a consciousness of sin.
>
> 21 But now a righteousness of God apart from law has been made known, being witnessed by the Law and the Prophets,
>
> 22 that is a righteousness of God by means of faith in Jesus Christ, for all those who believe, for there is no distinction;
>
> 23 for all have sinned and lack the praise of God,
>
> 24 being declared righteous as a gift by his grace through the redemption that is in Christ Jesus; . . .
>
> 28 We are of the opinion, therefore, *that* a person is declared righteous by faith without works of law. (Romans 3:19-24 & 28)

With the preceding realization the elation would have set in. The joy of the gospel, the joy of having had Jesus save him from the guilt of his oh-so-many-sins, the joy of having been given eternal salvation and life, the joy experienced by the new convert who comes to understand and to believe these divine truths – that joy would have begun to fill his soul and to lift up his spirit.

Interspersed between his jumbled feelings of guilt and the realization of his many errors and the assurances of the gospel just revealed to him, Paul would have been praying to God as a penitent sinner for the forgiveness, instructions, guidance, and strength he so desperately needed. Left to himself Paul could not obtain any of these. He was totally helpless and dependent upon the mercy and kindness of God to hear and answer his pleas. It is not unlikely at times during those three days of his blind darkness when he was driven to his knees that he recalled God's words and promises in such psalms as:

Psalm 50:15:
   Call upon me in the day of trouble; I will deliver you, and you will honor me.
   Psalm 5:2 & 3:
   2 Pay attention to the sound of my cry for help, my King and my God; because unto you do I pray.
   3 In the morning, O Lord, you will hear my voice; In the morning I will direct my prayer to you, and I will wait expectantly.
   Psalm 25:11
   For the sake of your name, O Lord, Forgive my iniquity, because it is great.
   Psalm 32:1-6
   1 Blessed is he whose transgression is forgiven, whose sin is covered.
   2 Blessed is the man whom the Lord does not charge with iniquity, and in whose spirit there is no deceit.
   3 When I kept silent about my sin, my body wasted away With my roaring all the day long.

4 For day and night your hand was heavy upon me; My vitality ebbed away as in the heat of summer.

5 I acknowledged my sin to you, And the guilt of my sin I did not cover up; I said, "I will confess my transgressions to the Lord," And you, you pardoned the guilt of my sin.

6 Therefore, let everyone who is pious pray to you at this time when you may be found.

By the end of the three days the Lord Jesus had sufficiently humbled Paul and prepared him for the apostolic service to which he had called him. Both Luke in Acts 9:10-19 and Paul in Acts 22:12-16 give accounts of what happened to Paul at the end of those three days. Piecing their two accounts together, we are informed:

Now there was a disciple in Damascus named Ananias, a devout man in accordance with the law, favorably spoken of by all the Jews who were living there. And the Lord said to him in a vision, "Ananias!"

And he said, "Here I am, Lord."

And the Lord said to him, "Get up! Go to the narrow street that is called Straight and in the house of Judas ask for a man from Tarsus named Saul. For behold he is praying, and he saw a man in a vision named Ananias come in and place his hands on him in order that he might regain his sight."

And Ananias replied, "Lord! I have heard from many persons about this man, how many harmful things he has done to your saints in Jerusalem; and here he has authority from the chief priests to bind in chains all who call upon your name."

But the Lord said to him, "Go! For this man is my chosen instrument to carry my name before both Gentiles and kings, and the sons of Israel. For I will show him how many things he must suffer for the sake of my name."

Then Ananias departed and entered into the house, and when he came to Paul and stood near him, after he placed his hands upon him, he said, "Brother Saul, the Lord – Jesus, who appeared to you on the road on which you were coming – has sent me, in order that you may regain your sight and be filled with the Holy Spirit."

And immediately something like scales fell from his eyes, and he regained his sight, and Paul became able to look up to him.

Then Ananias said, "The God of our fathers has selected you to come to know his will and to see the Righteous One and to hear a solemn declaration from his mouth, because you will be a witness to him to all mankind of the things that you have seen and heard. And now why do you delay? Get up, get yourself baptized and get your sins washed away, calling on his name."

And Paul got up and was baptized. And after he received food, he regained his strength.

Following Jesus' command, Ananias went to the house of Judas on Straight Street. Upon his arrival there Ananias addressed Paul as "Brother Saul". Ananias was then recognizing that Paul was a fellow believer in the gospel of Jesus. Paul needed no additional instructions from Ananias, since Jesus had fully instructed him in the gospel. Paul only needed to receive his sight by Ananias placing his hands on him. When Ananias did lay his hands upon Paul, Paul not only had his eyesight restored, he was also filled with the Holy Spirit. When Jesus revealed the gospel to Paul on the road, Paul was converted and received the gift of the Holy Spirit and the spiritual regeneration to faith in Jesus. Now in this instance when Ananias placed his hands upon Paul, Paul was filled with the Holy Spirit who gave Paul the special gifts and powers that would enable him to perform miracles and carry out his apostolic ministry. Minutes afterwards Paul was baptized with the Trinitarian baptism as a sign and seal of the forgiveness of all his sins that he received and of the membership in the Christian Church that he received as well.

Paul was then able to eat and to drink. The three days of his sincere, heartfelt repentance were completed. Luke reports in Acts 9:19: "Then he was with the disciples in Damascus for some days." Ananias was most likely the one who introduced Paul to those disciples of Jesus. The men and women whom Paul had come to Damascus to arrest, bind in chains, and force march to Jerusalem were now the same men and women whom Paul joined in Christian fellowship and called his brothers and sisters in Christ. Most assuredly those initial minutes after Ananias introduced Paul must have been strained and quietly restrained. Conversation would have been limited, for those present, like Ananias, surely had heard that Paul had authority from the chief priests to persecute and arrest them. Now they were suddenly confronted with the very man whose name aroused fear and dread within them. Those men and women must have looked at Paul with suspicions, doubts, and disbelief.

Beyond a doubt those initial minutes must have been strained and tense for Paul as well. What should he say? What could he say to undo the agony and fears that his very presence aroused within those men and women? His first words were likely to have been awkward as Paul searched within himself for the appropriate words to say. Being the Christian, Spirit-filled man that he was then, he probably began by confessing the wrongs he had done and asking for their forgiveness as God for Jesus' sake forgave him. Once the "ice was broken", so to speak, the icy relationship in the air would have begun to melt. In the course of the days that Paul spent with them, as they came to realize more and more that they had nothing to fear from him, they would have genuinely received him into their midst. What really would have allayed their fears was hearing that at once he began preaching the gospel of Jesus in the synagogues of Damascus.

Through his conversion, as explained in this chapter, Paul became a changed man. Motivated by the gospel of Jesus Christ and elated with the joy it gave to him, Paul was now a man filled with a desire to honor, love, and serve God to thank God for all that he had done for him in and through Jesus Christ. Paul had been called to serve as an apostle, so serve Paul would do – most gladly, and to his dying breath, as it did turn out! And so, without realizing it or consciously thinking of it, Paul had become what he would later call himself – Paul, an apostle, a bondservant of the Lord Jesus Christ!

---

1. Kittel, Gerhard, editor; Theological Dictionary Of The New Testament, Volume IV; Wm. B. Eerdmans publishing Company; Grand Rapids, Michigan; reprinted 1973; p. 476, 477. 478
2. Moulton, W. F and Geden, A. S.; A Concordance of the Greek Testament; Printed in Great Britain by Morrison and Gibb Limited for T. & T. Clark, Edinburgh; Fourth Edition Reprinted 1970; p. 618
3. John 5:1-18; This text says "the Jews", not the Pharisees. In John 1:19 John also used the designation "the Jews", but then explained in John 1:24 those Jews were the Pharisees. So in the text of John 5:1-18 "the Jews" can also be understood to refer to the Pharisees, as well as to the other rulers of the Jews.
4. Matthew 15:1-20; Mark 7:1-5
5. Luke 5:17-26; Mark 2:1-10
6. Matthew 12:38-45, 16:1
7. Matthew 9:11-3; Mark 2:15-17; Luke 18:9-14
8. Matthew 12:1-8; Matthew 12:9-14
9. Luke 5:17-26; Mark 2:1-10
10. Matthew 12:22-37)
11. Matthew 23:1-35
12. Acts 26:9
13. Acts 6:8-15; 7:51-60; 8:1
14. Romans 8:28; Ephesians 1:22
15. Kretzmann, Paul E.; Popular Commentary of the Bible, New Testament Volume I; Concordia Publishing House; St. Louis, Missouri; p. 576
16. Acts 9:11
17. Davis, John D.; A Dictionary of the Bible, Fourth Revised Edition; Baker Book House; Grand Rapids, Michigan; Seventeenth Printing, 1969; p. 159, 160
18. Aharoni,Yohanan & Avi-Yonah, Michael; The MacMillian Bible Atlas, MacMillan-Publishing Co., Inc.; New York; p. 153
19. Josephus, Flavius; The Wars Of The Jews; 2.20.2; Josephus – Complete Works; Kregel Publications; Grand Rapids, Michigan; Twelfth Printing, 1974; p. 497
20. Matthew 17:1, 2; Mark 9:2m 3; Luke 9:28, 29
21. Acts 22:17-21
22. Acts 18:9, 10
23. Acts 23:11
24. Jackson, Samuel Macauley, Editor-in-Chief; The New Schaff-Herzog Encyclopedia of Religious Knowledge, Volume VIII; Baker Book House; Grand Rapids, Michigan; Reprinted 1977; p. 406
25. Paul would testify to this fact in 1 Corinthians 9:1.
26. Martin Luther; A Commentary on St. Paul's Epistle to the Galatians; Zondervan Publishing House; Grand Rapids, Michigan; p.35

6

PAUL'S CHARACTERISTICS AFTER HIS CONVERSION

In This Chapter: The Source Of Information About The Man Paul; Paul's Conversion Made Him A Changed Man; Notable Aspects Of The Man Paul – Spiritual, Emotional; Mental; Physical; His Lifestyle; His Ministry

---

The Source Of Information About The Man Paul

To begin this chapter on the man Paul himself after his conversion a word is in order on the source from which the information in this chapter is drawn. The source is all -important, for two thousand years have passed since Paul lived, labored, and was martyred. So after such a long period of time, how can we know anything for sure about him? What we know about the Christian man Paul comes from the most reliable source of all – the New Testament Scriptures, namely the Pauline Letters and the Book of Acts. What makes this source of information so reliable is the fact that it is the inspired, inerrant Word of God. Therefore, what the New Testament Scriptures tell us about Paul is absolutely trustworthy, reliable, true, and without error.

Paul's Conversion Made Him A Changed Man

When the risen Lord Jesus appeared to Paul to reveal to him God's gospel of forgiveness and eternal salvation, Paul became a Christian believer in Jesus. His conversion was the turning point in his life. He would never again be what he had formerly been, and he would forever after be a changed man – a Christian man and bondservant of Christ Jesus.

Rather than present in bits and pieces throughout this biographical commentary what can be known about Paul as a Christian man, all that personal information will be presented in this one chapter. Then the reader can come to see Paul at as the whole person that he was and better understand what lay behind the life and ministry of Paul as he reads about it. This chapter will therefore explore these notable aspects of the man Paul: his spiritual, emotional, mental, and physical aspects as well as the aspects of his lifestyle and ministry.

Spiritual Aspects
  a. Paul, A Bondservant Of Christ Jesus

Through his conversion Paul became a bondservant of Christ Jesus, which he stated he was in Romans 1:1, Philippians 1:1, Titus 1:1, and in Galatians 1:10.

As explained in the opening paragraphs of this biographical commentary, a bondservant was literally a slave, a man in bonds and servitude to someone else. This describes Paul's relationship to Christ Jesus. From Galatians 1:10 we learn that as a bondservant Paul was not intent upon pleasing men to win their favor; rather, his goal and his commitment was to be pleasing to Christ and to do what was Christ's will for him.

Acts 26:16 further clarifies what the nature of Paul's relationship to Christ was as a bondservant. In that verse the glorified Lord Jesus Christ told Paul, "I appeared to you to appoint you a minister and a witness . . ." The word "minister" is a Greek term that meant an under rower, a subordinate rower. And it then meant anyone who served with his hands, a servant. The term was used to designate attendants and officers in the service of magistrates and kings. It was used to denote anyone who rendered a service and aided another in some work.[1] The term "minister", then, tells us that Paul was to be an underling, an attendant, a helper. Jesus appointed him to be under him as his helper in preaching the gospel and carrying out Jesus' directives and orders. Paul was to do what Jesus told him to do. Paul was, then, a bondservant in the very sense of its meaning of a slave, a man in bonds who was in servitude to someone else – in Paul's case to Christ Jesus.

In 2 Timothy 2:24-26 Paul stated what a bondservant should be like. The qualifications that Paul listed tell us much about what he himself was like. He was not quarrelsome, but gentle, and was able to teach. He bore the evil misdeeds of those who were against him without feelings of resentment. He gently corrected his opponents, not only to keep the commandment of his Lord Jesus in Matthew 5:38-41, but also for the sake of the gospel ministry to save souls that they might be delivered from the devil's stronghold to understand precisely the truth of the gospel for their salvation.

b. *Paul As A Christian Man*

As a Christian man Paul possessed a love and an appreciation of the gospel. He held the gospel of Jesus Christ as most dear to him. That gospel of God's grace in the crucified and resurrected Lord Jesus Christ became so precious to Paul that he gladly gave up everything that he had formerly considered of value and benefit to him. He told the Philippians:

> 7 But whatever things were to my credit, these I have considered a loss for the sake of Christ.
>
> 8 More than that, I indeed continue to consider all things to be loss on account of the surpassing greatness of knowing Christ Jesus my Lord, for the sake of whom I have suffered the loss of all things, and I continue to consider *them* rubbish in order that I may gain Christ

> 9 and be found in him, not having my own righteousness that comes from the law but that which is through faith in Christ – the righteousness from God on the basis of faith, ... (Philippians 3:7-9)

Before his conversion Paul had hated the name of Jesus of Nazareth. He did all in his power to stamp out the gospel of Jesus Christ and to persecute with imprisonment and death every Jewish believer in Jesus. But after his conversion Paul was anything but antagonistic towards Jesus' gospel and ashamed of it. Paul embraced it wholeheartedly and wrote these oh-so-memorable words:

> 16 I am not ashamed of the gospel, for it is the power of God for salvation for everyone who believes, first of all not only to the Jew but also to the Greek;
>
> 17 for the righteousness of God is revealed in it from faith to faith, as it is written, "BUT THE RIGHTEOUS WILL LIVE BY FAITH." (Romans 1:16, 17)

To Paul, and as he expounded it, the gospel was the power of God for salvation for everyone who believed it. The Greek word for "power" that Paul used in verse 16 above is the word from which the English word "dynamite" is derived. Yes, the gospel of Jesus Christ contains and unleashes such power that it can and does blow away the spiritual darkness of unbelief and opens the sinner's eyes to see that Jesus died on the cross to pay for his sins and save him from the eternal punishment in hell that he deserves. That gospel's power blasted open Paul's hard, unbelieving heart and brought him to faith. That occurred at his conversion when he saw for himself the crucified Lord Jesus risen from the dead and living.

After that Paul was never again ashamed of the gospel; it was the very basis of his faith and the only source of his hope. The gospel was God's message of reconciliation in Christ Jesus, as Paul stated in 2 Corinthians 5:19 & 21. Through his conversion Paul was enabled to see that the reconciliation of sinners included himself. Christ died on the cross for **his** sins and was raised to life for **his** forgiveness. Jesus had been delivered up on the cross for **his** sins and was raised from the dead as God's declaration of **his** forgiveness.[2] Through faith in Jesus he was declared righteous and justified.[3]

It was the power of that gospel working within his heart that upheld Paul through all his persecutions and imprisonments and sufferings up to his dying breath. And so, he wrote to Timothy in 2 Timothy 1:12 a short time before his martyrdom:

> For this reason I indeed suffer these things, but I am not ashamed, for I know whom I have believed, and I am convinced that he is able to guard what I have entrusted *to him* for that day.

Having such power to save souls for eternal life in heaven, that gospel was of the foremost importance above all else to Paul in his preaching and teaching. Accordingly he wrote in 1 Corinthians 15:3, 4:

> For I handed down to you of foremost importance, what I also received, that Christ died for our sins in accordance with the Scriptures, and that he was buried, and that he has been raised on the third day in accordance with the Scriptures.

And it was that power of the gospel through which the Holy Spirit was working mightily in Paul that fueled the ministerial fire that flamed within Paul. That ministerial fire within Paul can be observed throughout this biographical commentary of Paul's life.

Paul was the Christian man that he became because he was filled with the fruit of the spirit. The fruit of the Christian's converted spirit that is given by the Holy Spirit is really one package holding all the various fruits. Paul stated in what that fruit package of the spirit consisted in Galatians 5:22, 23: "The fruit of the spirit is love, joy, peace, patience, kindness, goodness, faithfulness, gentleness, self-control." As a Christian man Paul exhibited those traits of his regenerated spirit starting with his conversion. Those traits were evident in him as can be seen in his letters and ministry that shall be discussed in this biographical commentary.

When a Christian conducts himself in accord with those various traits, he will live righteously in his relationship with others. Love, the very first fruit of the converted spirit, motivates the Christian to live according to the commandments of God and do what is right to and for others. Paul was filled with this fruit of love, as will be discussed in some following paragraphs. That fruit of love moved him to carry out the commandments of God and to live righteously as he described in Romans 13:8-14.

Committed to living righteously, Paul said in 1 Corinthians 6:12 that he would not be mastered and enslaved by anything. Having that determination, Paul said in 1 Corinthians 9:24-27 that he beat his body and made it his slave to do what would please God and so he would not forfeit God's gift of eternal life in Jesus Christ.

Through living righteously and not letting any kind of sin be a master over him, Paul lived his life and served in his apostolic ministry with a clear conscience. He admitted to maintaining a clear conscience a number of times in 1 Corinthians 4:4, 2 Corinthians 1:12, Acts 23:1, Acts 24:16.

And Paul was not a hypocrite who did not practice what he preached. What he taught others in his letters about Christian living he lived himself. He and his life were examples for the first century Jewish and Gentile Christians. So many of them were formerly pagans, who especially needed a firsthand example of what a Christian was like so they had a model they could pattern themselves after. Paul understood well that as an apostle and bondservant of the Lord he was to serve as an example for Christians to follow. He urged those Christians repeatedly, as he did in 1 Corinthians 4:16 & 11:1 and in Philippians 3:17 & 4:9, to be imitators of him.

Paul remains that example even for us to this day. Thus all the instructions that Paul gave in his thirteen letters provide us with an insight into what Paul as a Christian man was like himself. For he applied those instructions to himself as well as to his readers, which is very evident in the sections of his letters in which he used the first person singular and plural to include himself in what he was teaching to his Christian readers. Here are some references to substantiate this point: Romans 5:1-11; 6; 7; 8; 13:11-14; 1 Corinthians 6:12-15; 8; 10; Philippians 3; 1 Thessalonians 5:1-11; 2 Thessalonians 3:1-15.

Paul was an example. But was he perfect? No. And he admitted such, which also shows that he was a truly penitent sinner. He confessed that he was a sinner in Romans 7:14-25:

14 For we know that the law is spiritual; but I belong to the realm of the flesh, having been sold as a slave to sin.

15 For I do not approve what I do; for what I desire *to do*, this I do not do, but what I hate, this I do.

16 Now if I do not desire *to do* what I do, I agree with the law that it is morally good.

17 And as a matter of fact I myself am no longer doing it but the sin dwelling in me does it.

18 For I know that nothing good dwells in me, that is in my flesh; for the desiring is present in me, but doing the morally good is not;

19 for the good that I desire *to do* I do not do, but the evil that I do not desire *to do* this I do.

20 Now if I do what I do not desire to do, it is no longer I myself doing it but the sin dwelling in me.

21 So I find this trait that when I desire to do what is morally good the evil is present in me;

22 for I joyfully agree with the law of God in my inner man,

23 but I see another trait in the members of my body waging war with the ruling activity of my mind and making me captive in the ruling activity of sin that is in the members of my body.

24 *Oh*, I am a wretched man! Who will deliver me from this body of death?

25 Thanks be to God *who will deliver me* by means of Jesus Christ our Lord! Consequently, on the one hand I myself with my mind am a slave to the law of God, but on the other hand with my flesh *I am a slave* to the ruling activity of sin.

Paul was a sinner. He had his weaknesses. Paul's statement in Galatians 1:14 that he formerly had kept advancing in Judaism over and above many of his contemporaries is an indication that he had a weakness of pride. His dispute with Barnabas over John Mark may be cited as an instance of weakness as well.[4] And at times he exhibited a fiery temperament. That shall be discussed later in this chapter.

In spite of Paul's being an imperfect sinner who had some weaknesses, from the Christian instructions he gave to others we can observe what kind of a Christian man he was himself. But we must grant that he was an imperfect sinner who at times failed to hit the mark of perfection that God's law demanded. Fail as he did at times, he kept pressing ahead to gain perfection – the perfection that God would grant to him in eternal glory. He stated this in Philippians 3:12-14:

> 12 Not that I have already taken hold *of these things* or have already been made perfect, but I keep pressing on if I might indeed lay hold of *that* for which I was taken hold of by Christ Jesus.
>
> 13 Brothers, as for me, I do not consider myself to have taken hold of *it*; but one thing *I do*, while forgetting the things that lie behind and continuing to strain for the things that lie ahead,
>
> 14 I keep pressing on toward the goal for the prize of the upward calling of God in Christ Jesus.

c. Paul Was A Man Of Prayer

Paul was a man who believed in the power of prayer. This is evident from his words in Ephesians 3:20, 21:

> Now to him who is able to do infinitely more than all we ask or think according to the power that is working in us, to him *be* the glory in the church and in Christ Jesus to all generations forever and ever. Amen.

Paul prayed for the churches that he founded and for the individual Christians as well. Except for his Second Letter to the Corinthians and his Letter to the Galatians he began his letters with a prayer or with a giving of thanks for the congregation or the individual to whom his letter was written.[5]

Having the confidence that God did indeed answer the prayers brought to him by his Christian people, Paul also sought the prayers of those churches to whom he wrote. He asked them to pray for his gospel ministry. In Romans 15:30-32 he asked the Romans to pray for his safety and for the success of his delivering the collection for the saints in Jerusalem. In Ephesians 6:19, 20 Paul asked the Ephesians to pray that the Lord would give him the words to speak the gospel of Jesus Christ boldly as he ought to speak it during his trial in Rome. In Colossians 2:2-4 Paul asked the Colossians to pray that God would give to him and his fellow workers the opportunity to spread the gospel of Christ as well as speak it clearly. And in 2 Thessalonians 3:1, 2 he asked the Thessalonians to pray that the word of the Lord would keep spreading and that he and his fellow workers would be delivered from wicked and evil men.

d. *Paul was not an "Enthusiast"*

Paul was not an enthusiast as the Lutheran dogmaticians[6] [7] defined the term as meaning the power of the Holy Spirit works apart from and without the Holy Scriptures, and that the Holy Scriptures, the Sacrament of Holy Baptism, and the Sacrament of Holy Communion are not God's divine means of grace through which God offers and conveys the forgiveness of sins, eternal life and everlasting salvation. In this discussion this writer is not using the term "enthusiast" in the sense of those meanings.

Rather, with the term "enthusiast" this writer means that Paul did not expect, or call upon, God to use his divine miraculous power to alleviate Pail's own problems and tribulations or those of his coworkers and friends.[8] For the sake of the advancement of the gospel God at times used the hands of Paul to perform miracles. But Paul did not call upon God to use his almighty power to miraculously alleviate Paul's own discomforts, inconveniences, sufferings or hardships. Yes, Paul surely prayed and called upon God, as all of us Christians do, for God to help him according to his particular needs, as Paul did when he prayed three times that his thorn in the flesh would depart from him. But when God's answer was "No", because it was better for Paul to suffer that thorn in the flesh to keep him from falling into the sin of pride and conceit, Paul accepted God's answer as good for him and a blessing to keep him humble.

Paul learned from the Lord at the same time that God's grace was sufficient for him to carry him through his life's tribulations and troubles (ref. 2 Corinthians 12:7-10). In Christ Jesus, his Savior, Paul had the gracious promise of God's forgiveness and gifts of eternal life and salvation to bolster his faith to accept what was God's will for him and to endure whatever sufferings and hardships that might include, such as the ongoing pain of his thorn in the flesh. And so, Paul lived his Christian life in the same way that all of us Christians need to do – by faith and in patience endurance as his life's situations required – whether in tribulations, calamities, extreme afflictions, beatings, imprisonments, riots, toils, sleeplessness, hunger (ref. 2 Corinthians 6:4 & 5), or being thirsty, poorly clothed, physically and verbally abused, or homeless (ref. 1 Corinthians 4:11 & 12). Paul had no special privileges or divine powers at his disposal, any more than we Christians have today, that he could use any time it suited him to alleviate his own hardships. Having that grace of God in Christ Jesus to which he could cling in every situation of his life, Paul learned to be content in whatever his circumstances might be. That grace of God in Jesus Christ was always his source of strength that enabled him to persevere through every kind of situation (ref. Philippians 4:10-13).

What is more, Paul came to know that the Lord God Almighty wants his Christian people to use the natural means that they have at their disposal, when such means are available, rather than look to God to perform a miraculous deliverance to aid them or to alleviate their tribulations and troubles.[9] For this reason, Paul did not call upon God to send an angel to bring him the cloak that he left with Crispus in Troas but asked Timothy to bring the cloak along when Timothy would come to him (ref. 2 Timothy 4:13). Furthermore, when his beloved son in the faith Timothy was plagued with a stomach problem and frequent illnesses, Paul did not call upon God to miraculously heal Timothy's ailing stomach. Instead, Paul urged Timothy to use the natural, medicinally beneficial means of drinking a little wine as a remedy for his stomach ailments rather than drinking only water (ref. 1 Timothy 5:23).

Paul certainly was not an enthusiast. He lived his life as a Christian man in the same way God calls on all of us Christians to live each day – by faith in God's grace and in patient endurance until God chooses to call us home to himself in heaven.

e. Paul's Faith, Hope, And Love

The Holy Spirit blessed Paul with a strong faith to face and accept the trials and troubles that came up in his life and ministry. On his first missionary journey after having likely gone through the dangers of mountain and river crossings and dangers from bandits and then indeed the hardships of persecutions even to the extent of having been stoned and left for dead, by faith Paul returned encouraging the Christians of the churches he had founded. He encouraged them, saying, "Through many tribulations we must enter into the kingdom of God."[10] Indeed, Paul knew firsthand about having many tribulations. Yet he accepted and endured them, for by faith he knew this divine truth that he taught to the Romans, "We know that all things work together for good for those who love God, for those who are called according to *his* purpose."[11] In the process of going through the great many tribulations and rigors of his life and ministry, Paul's trust in God enabled him to learn to be content without grumbling and complaining in whatever dangers and hardships and sufferings that came upon him. And so he could truthfully tell the Philippians, "Indeed I have learned to be content in whatever circumstances I find myself."[12] Having great confidence in God's plan of eternal life and salvation, Paul was able to boldly declare, "If God *is* for us, who *can be* against us? As a matter of fact he who did not spare his own Son but delivered him up for us all, how will he not also with him freely give us all things?"[13] On the basis of God's promises in the Savior Jesus Christ Paul had absolutely no fear of his final judgment one day or of condemnation in hell. He confessed that faith of his in his memorable words:

There is now no condemnation for those *who are* in Christ Jesus. (Romans 8:1)

For I am convinced that neither death nor life nor angels nor demons nor things present nor things to come nor powers nor height nor depth nor any created thing will be able to separate us from the love God that is in Christ Jesus our Lord (Romans 8:38, 39).

Now Paul was a human being like we all are. Being such he knew by experience the emotion of fear, as we all experience at times. In addition to the dangers and persecutions mentioned in the preceding paragraph, which surely must have given rise to fears for his body and life, we have his own written attestation to the fears that he and his fellow workers experienced during the riot of the silversmiths in Ephesus:

8 For I do not want you to be ignorant, brothers, concerning our tribulation that happened in Asia, because we had been oppressed to an extraordinary degree above and beyond *our ability*, so that we despaired of even living.

9 Yes, we ourselves had within ourselves the sentence of death, in order that we may not have come to put confidence in ourselves but in God who raises the dead,

10 who rescued us from so great a death and will *always* rescue us, in whom we have put hope that he will even yet rescue us. (2 Corinthians 1:8-10)

In those words describing his fear of death Paul also confessed his faith in God to deliver him. That faith enabled him to face death squarely in the eye. This, indeed, Paul did, for he experienced a martyr's death by beheading at the hand of Emperor Nero. And with that martyr's death he glorified God and his Lord Jesus Christ right through his dying breath. His faith in the face of death can be seen in his following words:

For this reason I indeed suffer these things, but I am not ashamed, for

I know in whom I have believed, and I am convinced that he is able to guard what I have entrusted *to him* for that day. (2 Timothy 1:12)

6 For I myself am already being poured out as a drink-offering, and the time for my departure has come.

7 I have fought the good fight, I have finished the course, I have kept the faith;

8 from now on a crown of righteousness is reserved for me, which the Lord, the righteous judge, will give to me on that day, moreover not to me only but also to all who have loved his appearing. (2 Timothy 4:6-8)

That strong faith gave Paul a great hope, that is, a confident waiting upon God to grant him deliverance from his life of suffering and death into a new eternal kingdom of righteous, blessedness, and life forevermore. Paul expressed this hope in his following words:

16 For this reason we do not lose heart, but even though our outer man is being destroyed, yet our inner man is being renewed day by day.

17 For our momentary light affliction is producing for us an eternal weight in glory far beyond all measure and proportion,

18 while we do not keep our eyes on the things that are seen but on the things that are not seen, for the things that are seen are temporary, but the things that are not seen are eternal. (2 Corinthians 4:16-18)

1 For we know that if our earthly tent-house is torn down, we have a building from God, an eternal house made without hands in the heavens. (2 Corinthians 5:1)

What is more, Paul was filled with the first fruit of his converted spirit, which was love. The fruit of the spirit was mentioned above. In Paul's discussion of the gifts of the Spirit in 1 Corinthians 12-14, Paul used himself as an example and spoke of the greatest gift of the converted spirit – love, without which Paul said he was nothing! In 1 Corinthians 13:1-10 & 13 Paul wrote those immortal words of God on the meaning of agape love that have echoed down through the millennia and which also reveal the agape love that flowed from Paul's heart and soul:

> 1 If I speak with the tongues of men and angels, but I do not have love, I have become a brass gong ringing out or a clashing cymbal.
>
> 2 And if I have *the gift of* prophecy and know all the mysteries and all the knowledge, and if I have all the faith so as to move mountains from one place to another, but I do not have love, I am nothing.
>
> 3 And if I give all my possessions to feed the poor, and if I hand over my body to be burned, and I do not have love, I benefit nothing.
>
> 4 Love is patient, love is kind. It is not jealous, does not boast, is not conceited.
>
> 5 *Love* does not behave disgracefully, does not seek things for itself, does not become angry, does not take into account the wrong done.
>
> 6 It does not rejoice in wickedness, but rejoices with the truth.
>
> 7 It covers all things, believes all things, hopes all things, endures all things.
>
> 8 Love never fails. But *if there are* prophecies, they will pass away; *if there are* tongues, they will cease; if there is knowledge, it will pass away.
>
> 9 For we know in part and we prophesy in part;
>
> 10 but whenever perfection may come, the imperfect will pass away.
>
> 13 But now remain faith, hope, love – these three; but the greatest of these is love.

We see an example of Paul's love in his Letter to Philemon. He showed his love to help and to do what was best for both Philemon and Onesimus. He offered to pay for any damages or indebtedness for which Onesimus owed Philemon. Paul wrote to Philemon, "But if he (Onesimus) has caused you any loss or is indebted to you, charge this to my account. I, Paul, *write this* in my *own* hand – I myself will pay the damages." (Philemon 18, 19a) Furthermore, Paul exhibited and confessed his love and compassion for his fellow Christians and workers as he did in Philippians 2:25-30.

Indeed, Christian love is giving and doing what is right and best for the other person and putting that other person even before oneself. This is a definition for the agape love spoken of in the Gospels and the Epistles of the New Testament. Paul described how that agape love shows itself toward others when he told the Philippians:

> (Do) nothing out of selfish ambition or empty pride, rather in humility considering one another as being better than yourselves, not by each one of you looking out for your own interests but by each one of you *looking out for* the interests of others (Philippians 2:3, 4).

Paul exhibited this selfless agape love in putting the other person first before himself. He would forego using or indulging in a liberty that he rightfully could use and do for the sake of a fellow Christian whose saving faith and soul were at stake. In Paul's day and place the eating of meat that came from an animal that had been sacrificed to an idol was something that a Christian could do. However, for the Christians who were formerly pagan worshippers of that idol, the eating of that meat was considered wrong, something to be avoided. There was a chance that if those former pagans saw another Christian eating such meat, they could be encouraged to eat it also even though their conscience thought it was wrong. In their case, if they ate that meat they sinned against their conscience and in the process against God. Paul knew in good conscience that it was permissible to eat that meat and that he could do so without sinning. But he also knew that if he ate that meat in front of another Christian whose conscience thought that it was wrong to eat it, he might cause that other Christian to fall into sin. That Paul would not do. So he wrote in 1 Corinthians 8:13, "For this reason if food causes my brother to fall into sin, I will absolutely not eat meat ever again, in order that I may not cause my brother to fall into sin."

While gratefulness is not the same virtue as Christian love, gratefulness does express an appreciation for another person and what he has done. Paul was also surely grateful. This virtue is evident from what he wrote to the Philippians in 4:14-18. Time and again they had sent him supplies to support him in his work of spreading the gospel of Jesus in other cities. For doing so he thanked them and informed them of what a truly God-pleasing sacrifice that was.

Mental Aspects
  a. Intellect

Paul was observant, absorbing what he saw in things and people and then applying those observations in his teaching of God's word. Three examples of this should suffice.

First example: In Acts 17:16 he noticed that the city of Athens was full of idols. This observation led him to see that the people of Athens were a very religious people,[14] who had been sadly misled by the devil and needed to hear the truth of the gospel. Paul then very aptly applied these observations about the Athenians in the introduction of his address to the men in the Areopagus in Acts 17:22, 23.

Second example: This example comes from Ephesians 6:10-17. The Book of Ephesians is one of Paul's prison letters. Up to the time that Paul wrote the Book of Ephesians he had been imprisoned in Caesarea for two years, under Roman guard during his voyage from Caesarea to Rome that lasted about nine months, and then under house arrest in Rome. Throughout those years of being under the watchful eye of a Roman soldier or chained to one, he had plenty of time to observe the military dress and armor of the Roman soldier. Paul then applied those observations to instructing Christians on how to be armed to fight the battle against Satan and his evil schemes.

Third example: This third example is from 1 Corinthians 7:32-34. During his apostolic ministry Paul had been observing husbands and wives in their relationship with one another. He had observed a difference between unmarried Christian men and women and married Christian men and women. In response to questions about marriage from the Corinthian congregation he applied his observations to his instructions about marriage and being Christians. He wrote:

> 32 Now I want you to be free of concern. The unmarried man is concerned about the things of the Lord, how he may please the Lord;
>
> 33 but the married man is concerned about the things of the world, how he may please his wife,
>
> 34 and he is divided. And the unmarried woman and the virgin is concerned about the things of the Lord, that she may be holy both in body and in spirit; but the married woman is concerned about the things of the world, how she may please her husband.

Paul also used his observations for his own benefit when it was to his advantage to do so, as he did when Tribune Claudius Lysias conducted a hearing of Paul before the Jewish Sanhedrin. On that occasion Paul used his observation to divide and conquer his Jewish adversaries and to turn them against one another. Luke informs us of this in Acts 23:6-10.

Not only was Paul observant, he was a man of great learning as well, as even governor (procurator) Festus of Judea acknowledged when according to Acts 26:24 he said in a loud voice, "You are out of your mind Paul! Your great leaning is driving you mad!" As stated in Chapter 4 Paul studied under the renowned Pharisee and teacher of the Law, Gamaliel. Conybeare and Howson said this about the influence that Gamaliel had upon the mind of Paul:

> If we were briefly to specify the three effects which the teaching and example of Gamaliel may be supposed to have produced on the mind of St. Paul, they would be as follows: – candour and honesty in judgment, – a willingness to study and make use of Greek authors, – and a keen and watchful enthusiasm for the Jewish law.[15]

Paul's superior intelligence was a natural gift of God. Having been so mentally gifted, Paul was very logical in his teaching the truths of God. He had a keen mind. It was quick to sense and anticipate the arguments and objections of would-be detractors who opposed the word of God and the gospel of Jesus Christ that he taught. Paul's anticipating the objections and arguments of his opponents is especially seen in his Letter to the Romans and his letters to the Corinthians.

A very good example of how he anticipated a potential argument is seen in 1 Corinthians 1:13-16. There Paul wrote:

> 13 ... you were not baptized in the name of Paul, were you?
>
> 14 I thank God that I baptized none of you except Crispus and Gaiius,
>
> 15 lest anyone say that you were baptized in my name.
>
> 16 Now I did also baptize the household of Stephanas; beyond that I do not know if I baptized anyone else.

It had slipped Paul's mind when he wrote the above verses that he had also baptized the household of Stephanas. He then remembered he had baptized Stephanas' household and quickly wrote verse 16 to correct his oversight, because he knew well that someone in the Corinthian congregation, if not Stephanas himself, would remember that he had baptized the household of Stephanas. Realizing that the objection would certainly be raised, he added verse 16 to nullify the objection before it could even be made. This instance also exemplifies the genuine humanness of Paul. Like us all, his mind too could slip and forget some fact or detail.

Romans 6:1 provides yet one more example that is easy to see. In the latter part of Romans 5 Paul explained that while sin in the world increased and abounded God's grace in Christ Jesus for the forgiveness of sins abounded even more. In response to that Paul anticipated that the gainsaying unbelievers would assert that then people could sin all the more in order that God's grace may abound all the more. They would argue that Paul's gospel of salvation by God's grace in Christ Jesus was in effect a license to sin all the more. In response to that erroneous argument Paul asked in Romans 6:1, "What shall we say then? Shall we go on persisting in the sin, in order that the grace might be present in abundance? God forbid!" Paul then explained in Romans 6 that the response of the believer in Jesus Christ to God's grace is not a life of living in sin but a life of putting off sin to live righteously in the sight of God.

Galatians 4:21-31 provides a good example of how Paul reasoned with his opponents and with those who did not understand and accept the gospel that he preached. From this example we gain an insight into in the verses of Acts that tell us that Paul reasoned with the Jews and the Gentiles. It enables us to better understand how Paul reasoned with them.

> 21 Tell me, those *of you* who desire to be under law, do you not understand the law?
>
> 22 For it is written that Abraham had two sons, one by the slave woman and one by the free woman.
>
> 23 But the one by the slave woman has been born by natural means, the other by the free woman by means of a promise.
>
> 24 Things of such a nature are spoken allegorically; for these are two covenants, one from Mount Sinai, bearing children into slavery, which is Hagar.
>
> 25 Now Hagar is Mount Sinai in Arabia, and she corresponds to the present Jerusalem, for she is a slave with her children.
>
> 26 But the Jerusalem above is free, which is our mother;
>
> 27 for it is written,
>
> "REJOICE, BARREN WOMAN WHO DOES NOT GIVE BIRTH;
>
> BREAK FORTH AND CALL OUT, YOU WHO DO NOT SUFFER BIRTH PAINS;
>
> FOR THE MANY CHILDREN OF THE ABANDONED *WOMAN* ARE MORE THAN *THE CHILDREN* OF HER WHO HAS A HUSBAND."
>
> 28 And as for you, brothers, like Isaac, you are children of promise.
>
> 29 But just as at that time the one who was born by natural means kept persecuting the one who was born by the Spirit, so it is even now.
>
> 30 But what does the Scripture say? "DRIVE OUT THE SLAVE WOMAN AND HER SON, FOR THE SON OF THE SLAVE

WOMAN SHALL ABSOLUTELY NOT BE AN HEIR WITH THE SON" of the free woman.

31 Therefore, brothers, we are not children of a slave woman but of the free woman.

b. Paul's Mannerisms

The Book of Acts and the Pauline letters do not reveal that Paul had any mannerisms that were unique to him and were outstanding. One mannerism that Paul had was a hand gesture. Paul used this gesture at the start of an address he was about to make to a crowd or an audience.[16] The gesture with the hand was simply a signal to the assembly or the crowd to be silent so he could address them. This hand signal was typical of men who were about to make a public speech.[17]

Another mannerism that has been attributed to Paul is a look with his eyes that was intended to exert power upon others. The Greek term Luke uses is atenizo, which means to fix one's eyes on, to look intently, and to gaze at. Luke uses the term in a number of verses in the Book of Acts and in his gospel. Paul uses it twice in writing to the Corinthians. In none of the verses is the term used for fixing one's eyes on someone to exert power over him.[18] Paul would not have resorted to such a mannerism as a means of exerting power over his hearers and influencing them. The power on which Paul relied was the gospel of Jesus Christ that was the power of God for the salvation of all who believed. The claim, then, that Paul fixed his eyes on someone to exert power over them is clearly false. In the instance of Acts 13:9 Paul's fixed eyes and glare was not an exertion of power but merely an indication of his holy indignation with Elymas for opposing the gospel that Paul was sharing with the proconsul of Cyprus.

Although it was not a mannerism as we usually understand the term, Paul had one outstanding characteristic that did set him apart from others – the manner in which he wrote. He wrote with large Greek letters that were larger than usual. In Galatians 6:11 he stated, "See with what large letters I have written to you in my own hand."

And in 2 Thessalonians 3:17 he informed his readers, "I, Paul, write *this* greeting with my own hand, which is a sign in every letter; *this is* the way I write." As a sign of his letter's authenticity, he wrote to the Corinthians and to the Colossians, "This greeting is in my own hand, Paul's."[19]

Physical Aspects
   a. *Paul's Appearance*

The super-apostles, who will be described in connection with Paul's Letters To The Corinthians, complained that Paul presented himself as being weighty and strong in his letters, but his physical appearance was weak and unimpressive. What is more, they said his manner of speaking was contemptible, for he was a poor, untrained orator and speaker.[20]

Those false super-apostles insulted Paul's physical appearance. There is no description of Paul's facial and physical appearance in the New Testament. There is a description of Paul that comes from a legendary, apocryphal source entitled the Acts Of Paul And Thecla. At its beginning it describes Paul as:

> little in stature, bald-headed, bow-legged, well built (vigorous), with knitted eye-brows, rather long-nosed, full of grace, appearing now as a man, and now having the face of an angel[21]

Conybeare & Howson also published a description of Paul's appearance that was based upon the description given by John Malalas (a Greek chronicler who lived c. 491-578) and Nicephorus (a Greek Orthodox Patriarch from 1084-1090). This description was written over 400 years after Paul's martyrdom, so Malalas obviously did not have firsthand knowledge of Paul's facial and physical features. What was Malalas' source of information at that late date is unknown to this writer. But the description does tell us how Paul looked according to early tradition. And as with the preceding description of Paul, so this description also aids our imagination in seeing the man Paul as he might have been. And so Conybeare & Howson stated:

> "St. Paul is set before us as having the strongly marked and prominent features of a Jew, yet without some of the finer lines indicative of Greek thought. His stature was diminutive, and his body disfigured by some lameness or distortion, which may have provoked the contemptuous expressions of his enemies. His beard was long and thin. His head bald. The characteristics of his face were, a transparent complexion, which visibly betrayed the quick changes of his feelings, a bright gray eye under thickly overhanging united eyebrows, a cheerful and winning expression of countenance, which invited the approach and inspired the confidence of strangers."[22]

Paul himself told us one feature about his physical appearance. He wrote to the Galatians, "In the future let no one cause trouble for me, for I myself bear the marks of Jesus on my body."[23] The beatings and the whippings and the stoning that he endured for his preaching the gospel of Jesus had all left their physical marks and scars on Paul's body and disfigured him by A.D. 51 when he wrote his Letter to the Galatians.

b. Paul's Physical Health

When Jesus called Paul to be his chosen instrument to carry his name to Gentiles and kings and the Israelites, Jesus said, "I will show him how many things he must suffer for the sake of my name."[24] Those words of Jesus foretold in A.D. 33 that Paul's apostolic ministry would be characterized by much suffering. And it was for the next 35 years until his martyrdom.

It is not surprising, therefore, that from very early times in the history of the Church as a result of all that Paul went through his health has been the subject of much discussion and conjecture. There are two groups of verses that Paul himself wrote that make statements about his health. We will look at them after first mentioning briefly Second Corinthians 4:7-5:10.

The verses of Second Corinthians 4:7-5:10 have been thought to be about the frailty of Paul's physical health, but that is not the case.[25] These verses are not about the frailty of Paul's bodily health but about the frailty of Paul and his coworkers as mere men who were preaching the gospel of God's grace in Christ Jesus in the face of oppressive persecution. Notice that Paul wrote "we have this treasure in clay vessels, . . ." Paul was not speaking of just himself and his own health. And he surely was not writing about the poor health of all the men in his party, namely of himself and his coworkers. Paul used a metaphor and said they all were clay vessels. Clay jars and vessels were simply common, inexpensive, fragile, containers lacking great strength and value that were sure to be broken and discarded. Such containers were Paul and his coworkers, as are all of God's pastors and teachers and missionaries. By comparison to them God's gospel of Jesus Christ that gives God's grace, peace, and gift of eternal life and salvation is immensely precious and powerful. One would therefore think that God would put that gospel in the strongest and costliest containers as would befit it. But God did not do so. He placed that gospel in the hearts and souls of mere human men who were like those inexpensive, fragile clay jars and vessels. God did so, Paul said, "in order that the extraordinary greatness of the power may be of God and not from us."[26]

Now that was a valuable, humbling lesson that Paul learned from the thorn in the flesh that God gave to him, which will be discussed in the following paragraphs. From that thorn in the flesh Paul had learned that the success of the gospel preaching that he and his coworkers did was not due to themselves but to the extraordinary greatness of the power of God. And from 2 Corinthians 4:8 Paul makes it clear that even if their lowly, weak bodies were destroyed by the enemies of their gospel preaching, their suffering and being put to death would result in their eternal life and glorification. Such is the case and comfort for all of God's servants who preach and teach the gospel of Jesus Christ in this world that opposes them.

Now the two pertinent sections that discuss Paul's bodily health are 2 Corinthians 12:2-9 and Galatians 4:13, 14.

In 2 Corinthians 12:2-9 Paul wrote:

2 I know a man in Christ who fourteen years ago – whether in *his* body I do not know, or outside of *his* body I do not know, God knows – such a man as this was snatched away up to the third heaven.

3 And I know such a man as this – whether in *his* body or apart from his body I do not know, God knows –

4 that he was snatched away to paradise and heard utterances *that are* too sacred to tell, which *utterances* are not permissible for a man to speak.

5 I will boast about such a man as this, but I will not boast about myself except in my weaknesses.

6 For if I shall *someday* wish to boast, I shall not be a fool, because I shall speak *the* truth; but I refrain *from doing so*, lest anyone consider me *to be* more than what he sees me *to be* or what he hears from me.

7 So, in order that I may not lift myself up *with pride*, because of the extraordinary nature of the revelations, there was given to me a thorn in the flesh, a messenger of Satan, in order to keep afflicting me, in order that I may not lift myself up *with pride*.

8 Concerning this I pleaded three times with the Lord that it might depart from me;

9 and he said to me, "My grace is sufficient for you; for its power is brought to the end *of its work* in weakness." Most gladly, therefore, I will rather boast in my weaknesses, in order that the power of Christ may rest upon me.

According to Paul God gave him a thorn in the flesh that was a messenger of Satan to keep afflicting him. There are in these words of Paul two figures of speech and a personification. How are we to understand them? The first figure of speech is the thorn in the flesh. God gave Paul some kind of an affliction that was like a thorn in the flesh. It inflicted a sharp, piercing pain. The second figure of speech is in the Greek phrase of the words translated "to keep afflicting me." Literally the Greek word means "to keep beating with the fist." So whatever the affliction was, it pounded Paul and hurt him. The present tense of that Greek verb tells us that the action of being beaten up was a continuous assault without interruption and intermittent periods of relief. Then there is the personification: the affliction itself was a messenger of Satan. Apparently, as in the case of Job, God allowed Satan to afflict Paul. Satan afflicted Paul with the evil intention of making him miserable to destroy his faith and to turn him against God. God, on the other hand, was allowing the affliction for Paul's good in accordance with Romans 8:28. God's good intention and purpose was to keep Paul from falling into the sin of being puffed up with pride because of the extraordinary revelation of having seen the glory of heaven and having heard what no one else was permitted to hear. Paul had an evil, sinful nature like everyone else, as he himself admitted in Romans 7:13-25. Therefore, there was the danger that that sinful nature would lead him into the sin of pride. To prevent that from happening, God gave Paul that thorn in the flesh as a painful reminder to keep him humble. When God gave Paul that thorn in the flesh cannot be determined. Paul said he was given that revelation of God in paradise fourteen years earlier, in A.D. 42, long before he wrote the above verses in late A.D. 56. How soon or how long after Paul had that revelation the incessant pain started is unknown. Once it did start Paul prayed that God would take it away from him, so he could better carry out his apostolic ministry of preaching the gospel. In fact he prayed three times that God would take it away, because God did not grant his request. After the third time of asking, God told him, "My grace is sufficient for you; for its power is brought to the end *of its work* in weakness."

The other pertinent text regarding Paul's health is in Galatians 4:13, 14. There Paul wrote:

13 You know that because of an illness I preached the gospel to you the first time

14 and my illness that was a trial for you, you did not utterly despise nor detest, but you received me as an angel of God, *indeed* as Christ Jesus.

The reason for Paul's preaching the gospel to the Galatians the first time about A.D. 46 to 47 was a physical illness of some kind. Literally the word "illness" in the Greek text is "a weakness of the flesh." That phrase "weakness of the flesh" has been understood to mean an illness, as Professor J. P. Koehler and other commentators have understood it. Koehler thought that illness might possibly have had some connection with the thorn in the flesh mentioned in 2 Corinthians 12. Based on what Paul wrote in the above verses Koehler thought that on Paul's body there was something repulsive that caused a feeling of loathing to come over the Galatians that tempted them to despise Paul and to turn away from him in disgust. But they resisted that temptation and received Paul as an angel of God.[27]

At this point an observation needs to be made about correlating Paul's thorn in the flesh with his illness in Galatia. Various commentators have equated the two. Paul's illness in Galatia, however, was not necessarily a flare up and another incidence of his thorn in the flesh. The repulsive disfigurements of Paul's illness in Galatia were not necessarily symptoms of his thorn in the flesh. The two may have been the same bodily affliction and disease, but this cannot be proven and said for certain. It was very possible that the thorn in the flesh was some kind of a physical malady that did not have the symptom of the bodily disfigurement that Paul suffered in Galatia. And we do not know that the illness Paul suffered in Galatia reoccurred from time to time. Perhaps Paul suffered that Galatian illness only once and was never bothered by it again. Commentators who have equated the two diseases have then made up their lists of what they thought were the combined symptoms of the two diseases. But there is no conclusive evidence in Acts or in the Pauline epistles that the illness Paul suffered in Galatia was the thorn in the flesh that Paul described in Second Corinthians 12. If one equates the two, then one must say the thorn in the flesh that Paul endured throughout the length of his life was always marked by the symptom of the repulsive disfigurement of the Galatian illness.

Now considering that Paul's thorn in the flesh constantly pierced him with pain from sometime around or after A.D. 42 to his martyrdom in A.D. 68, Paul in his letters never even hinted that he was suffering such nagging pain day in and day out. Rather he continued to conduct his apostolic ministry of preaching, teaching, evangelizing, looking after all the congregations that had been started, writing letters of encouragement and instructions, and coordinating the assignments of where and when his coworkers were to go next. All this he did year after year without so much as a whimper or an instance of self-pity that surfaced in any of his letters or was reported by his physician Luke in the Book of Acts. This is remarkable! It shows just how great of a bondservant he was for his Lord Jesus Christ, a bondservant who put his apostolic ministry before all things, even before himself, and suffered and endured much to carry it out. What an example he was for all Christians of all ages!

The above two texts in Paul's letters lead us to ask: What was Paul's "thorn in the flesh" and his "weakness of the flesh/illness" that he suffered in Galatia? Over the millennia since Paul's martyrdom many answers have been given. Let us look at the kinds of explanations that commentators and Christian tradition have made.

Professor Joh. P. Meyer wrote regarding Paul's thorn in the flesh:

> This is, of course, metaphorical language, pointing to some very painful physical condition. Paul considered it a 'gift' of God. It did not come to him by accident. It was not a natural result of his labors and of his enforced mode of living. It was directly imposed by God."[28]

J. B. Lightfoot in 1865 in his Epistle Of St. Paul To The Galatians[29] put in a rough chronological list five classifications of the many conjectures of subjective opinions that had been ventured about Paul's thorn in the flesh. First, early tradition said it was a bodily illness – a headache. Among the early churchmen who held this opinion were Tertullian (the first great writer of Latin Christianity who lived c. A.D. 155-230), Jerome (an ecclesiastical author who died September 30, 420), and Pelagius (a teacher in the church who was born in the fourth century and undermined the teaching of divine grace). Second, the commentators who followed thought

Paul's thorn was the opposition Paul encountered and the persecution he suffered from his enemies. Chrysostom (c. A.D. 349-407) was of this opinion, as were the Greek Church fathers. Third, later, especially after the sixth century into the middle ages, monks and ascetics believed Paul's thorn in the flesh was carnal, sexual thoughts. Fourth was Martin Luther's opinion, which Lightfoot labeled spiritual trials. The thorn in the flesh was not carnal longing or a bodily malady. Luther inclined more and more to spiritual trials, as faintheartedness in his ministerial duties, temptations to despair or to doubt, or to blasphemous suggestions of the devil. Then fifth, and lastly, the opinion about Paul's thorn in the flesh came full circle and returned to the initial opinion of a bodily illness and malady of some kind.

In his description of Luther's opinion Lightfoot noted what Luther had said in his commentary on Paul's Letter to the Galatians. So let us see what Martin Luther himself said in his lectures of 1531:

> When Paul speaks of the infirmity of the flesh he does not mean some physical defect or carnal lust, but sufferings and afflictions which he endured in his body. What these infirmities were he himself explains in II Corinthians 12:9 10: "Most gladly therefore will I rather glory in my infirmities, that the power of Christ may rest upon me. Therefore I take pleasure in infirmities, in reproaches, in necessities, in persecutions, in distresses for Christ's sake: for when I am weak, then I am strong." And in the eleventh chapter of the same Epistle the Apostle writes: "In labors more abundant, in stripes above measure, in prisons more frequent, in deaths oft. Of the Jews five times received I forty stripes save one. Thrice was I beaten with rods, once was I stoned, thrice I suffered shipwreck," etc. (II Corinthians 11:23-25) By the infirmity of his flesh Paul meant these afflictions and not some chronic disease. He reminds the Galatians how he was always in peril at the hands of the Jews, Gentiles, and false brethren, how he suffered hunger and want.[30]

Conybeare & Howson discussed Paul's thorn in the flesh and ill health several times in their biography of Paul. Regarding Paul's illness in Galatia they stated,

> We cannot say what this sickness was, or with absolute certainty identify it with that 'thorn in the flesh' to which he feelingly alludes in his Epistles, as a discipline which God had laid on him.[31]

Conybeare and Howson furthermore asserted that the chronic malady under which Paul suffered, referring to his thorn in the flesh, continually impeded his efforts and shackled his energy.[32] Yes, he daily had to battle against the pain that his thorn in flesh caused him, but there is no indication from the Book of Acts or in Paul's letters that his efforts were impeded or his energy shackled or that he labored under a continual depression. The Book of Acts and Paul's letters indicate just the opposite, that he was a robust man filled with energy and possessing a constant drive few other men could have kept up with.

Ramsay also had a theory as to what was Paul's "thorn in the flesh." He wrote:

> Now it is a probable and generally accepted view that the 'physical weakness,' which was the occasion why Paul preached to the Galatians, was the same malady which tormented him at frequent intervals. I have suggested that this malady was a species of chronic malaria fever; and, in view of criticisms, it is necessary to dwell on this point; for I have incurred the blame, of exaggerating an ephemeral attack.[33]

Ramsay then dwells for three pages on the subject in defense of his case for chronic malaria with its accompanying headache. He asserts that, "...the oldest tradition of the subject, quoted by Tertullian and others, explains the 'stake (thorn) in the flesh' as headache."[34] The stories of illness and headache that he propounded in the course of those three pages, however, in no way prove that Paul's "thorn in the flesh" was chronic malaria. Furthermore, the fact that Paul's thorn in the flesh was an ongoing, continual, sharp piercing pain eliminates the possibility of intermittent flare-ups of malaria.

Schaff-Herzog took a different tact. They stated that Paul's thorn in the flesh was "possibly ... some nervous disease."[35]

Having looked at the preceding explanations, we turn once again to J. B. Lightfoot for his brief analysis.

> These passages (2 Corinthians 12:7 & Galatians 4:13, 14) so closely resemble each other that it is not unnatural to suppose the allusion to be the same in both. If so, the subject seems to have been especially present to St. Paul's thoughts at the season when these two epistles were written; for they were written about the same time.
>
> What then was this 'stake (thorn) in the flesh,' this 'infirmity (weakness) of the flesh,' which made so deep an impression on his (Paul's) mind?
>
> Diverse answers have been given to this question, shaped in many instances by the circumstances of the interpreters themselves, who saw in the Apostle's temptation a more or less perfect reflection of the trials which beset their own lives.[36]

How far such subjective feelings did influence the progress of interpretation was shown above in Lightfoot's chronological list of conjectures.

Lenski expressed a very negative opinion of all the different conjectures that have been given over the millennia about Paul's thorn in the flesh. This writer tends to agree with Lenski's assessment of those conjectures even though Lenski's analogy is a bit strong.

> The question is constantly asked as to just what this figurative language (in 2 Corinthians 12:7) means literally. Paul's letters as well as the Acts are searched for clues. The result is that no man knows.... It is really a question of forming a diagnosis. The data on which to base it are wholly insufficient.... Yet the theologians, who are laymen in the field of medicine and disease, proceed to diagnose the case like the most expert medics and insist on the correctness of their findings.

These theologians are acting the part of quacks. To allow them to do so is to condone their quackery. To accept any diagnosis thus made is to honor quackery... A few good medical men have examined our passage. Still fewer have ventured an opinion, and an opinion is about all that could be offered[37]

Lenski then went on to list the diagnoses that commentaries and books had made up to his time of writing – seventeen of them!

So the truth is: As far as what Paul's thorn in the flesh was only the Lord now knows.

c. *Paul's Aging*

When Paul wrote his Letter to Philemon at the same time of writing his Letters to the Ephesians and to the Colossians, he referred to himself as "Paul an old man."[38] He wrote that when he was sixty to sixty-one years old. When he wrote his Pastoral Letters of First Timothy and Titus, he was sixty-three years old and was sixty-seven when he wrote Second Timothy. According to Conybeare & Howson about the time Paul wrote his Pastoral Letters (1 & 2 Timothy and Titus), he may have "lost some of his former energy."[39] They attribute his possible loss of energy to his age and the many years of laboring under physical hardships. They claim, furthermore, that his health had been broken by his affliction of the thorn in the flesh. They then hold out a lengthy laundry list of negative experiences that must "have preyed upon the mental energy of the man." Thus, they say, in his older age "he might well be worn out both in body and mind. And this will account for the comparative want of vigor and energy which has been attributed to the Pastoral Epistles, if there be any such deficiency." Furthermore, they assert, such a lack of energy was responsible for Paul's leaving Timothy and Titus to take charge of matters in Ephesus and Crete rather than attending to those matters himself.[40] Conybeare and Howson do not come out plainly and assert these things to be their conclusion and opinion, rather they only leave the door open to the possibility that these things were the case. In essence they are at the same time both "for" and "against", in agreement with and yet not so certain of, those things they stated.

There is, however, no evidence that Paul's aging sapped his energy, slowed and curtailed his ministerial activities, or in any way adversely affected his writing of his Pastoral Letters. Lenski holds the same opinion. He writes:

Do these three letters (referring to First & Second Timothy and Titus) show that Paul is aging? Do they lack the virility of the other letters or the perfection of Philemon in particular? Are they less well arranged? To give an affirmative answer to these questions is in our judgment going too far. The purpose and the subjects treated are different; the mastery with which they are handled is the same as we find in the other letters. Paul's mental powers are undiminished. His last letter (Second Timothy) has been well called his 'swan song."[41]

We can, then, discount any charges that Paul's age adversely affected the later years of his correspondence and his missionary drive.

Emotional Aspects

a. Paul's Emotional Health

Paul's emotional state was tied to what was happening in the churches and in his apostolic ministry at the time. The Pauline Letters provide ample evidence of this, as can be seen in the following verses. While Paul was waiting for Titus to come with his report on the Corinthian congregation, Paul was worried about the congregation and felt dejected. But those feelings immediately passed away upon Titus' arrival with good news from Corinth. Then at once he was joyful and comforted. He wrote in 2 Corinthians 7:5-7:

> 5 For indeed since we came into Macedonia our flesh had no relief; on the contrary, we were afflicted in every way – conflicts from without and fears from within.
>
> 6 But God, who comforts the depressed, comforted us with the arrival of Titus;
>
> 7 moreover, not only with his arrival but also with the comfort

with which he had been comforted on the basis of you, reporting to us your longing, your mourning, your zeal for me, so that I rejoiced even more.

Paul rejoiced at the coming of Stephanas, Fortunatus, and Achaicus from Corinth.[42] Paul rejoiced in the Corinthians' repentance.[43] Paul was joyful over the Philippians' fellowship in the gospel.[44] Paul continued rejoicing because in every way Christ was being preached.[45] Paul rejoiced that through his imprisonment Christ would be glorified in his body.[46] Paul was glad and rejoiced with the Philippians.[47] Paul said he would have a cheerful spirit when he found out how the Philippians were getting along.[48] Paul wrote to the Romans, "Your obedience has become known to all; therefore I rejoice over you, . . ."[49] And he told the Thessalonians, "You are our glory and joy! . . . What thanksgiving can we give to God for you in return for all the joy with which we are rejoicing in the presence of God because of you . . ."[50]

In spite of all the joy Paul expressed in the preceding verses, it has been asserted that Paul's thorn in the flesh was responsible for Paul feeling dejected and gloomy and suffering from depression.[51] But there is no evidence to support the hypothesis that Paul's daily piercing pain caused him to continue suffering a chronic depression. What is more, it has been suggested that Paul's daily piercing pain was the cause for his feeling dejected and gloomy and sad while waiting and looking for Titus first in Troas and then in Macedonia. Referring to how he felt in Troas Paul said, "I had no rest in my spirit."[52] And writing of his condition in Macedonia he said, ". . . our flesh had no relief."[53] The supposition of Paul's feeling dejected and gloomy also ties Paul's thorn in the flesh to his emotional health. Those two comments of Paul quoted above hardly make sufficient grounds to diagnose Paul as having an emotional health problem and suffering from chronic depression. What is more, in the 2 Corinthians 7:5 verse Paul did not speak of just himself but also of those fellow workers who were accompanying him. Are we to believe that they all were suffering from chronic depression at the same time because of Paul's thorn in the flesh? Contrary to such conjectures Paul considered his thorn in the flesh a gift and blessing of God to him for his good. Far from sounding like a man suffering a bad case of depression Paul wrote in 2 Corinthians 12:7-10:

> 7 So, in order that I may not lift myself up *with pride*, because of the extraordinary nature of the revelations, there was given to me a thorn in the flesh, a messenger of Satan, in order to keep afflicting me, in order that I may not lift myself up *with pride*.
>
> 8 Concerning this I pleaded three times with the Lord that it might depart from me;
>
> 9 and he said to me, "My grace is sufficient for you; for its power is brought to the end *of its work* in weakness." Most gladly, therefore, I will rather boast in my weaknesses, in order that the power of Christ may rest upon me.
>
> 10 Accordingly I take pleasure in weaknesses, in insults, in calamities, in persecutions and extreme afflictions for Christ's sake; for whenever I am weak, then I am strong.

As stated in the first paragraph in this section on Paul's emotional health, Paul's emotions were tied to what was going on in the congregations he founded and served. In the case of the Corinthian congregation it was riddled with problems and on the verge of falling away from Christ and his gospel. Paul had done everything he could do to resolve the problems and to salvage his apostolic ministry in the Corinthian congregation. He had written a letter to the congregation and sent Titus as his representative to talk with its leaders and members. He was anxiously waiting word on how his letter to the congregation was received and whether it moved the members to resolve their problems. He was like a mother anxiously waiting to hear news about a troubled child of hers. So Paul's feeling low, being disquieted, gloomy, dejected, and worried were indeed natural, human emotions. Such natural emotions were certainly not symptomatic of his suffering chronic depression! The very suggestion and hypothesis of such a depression is both demeaning and insulting to the Christian man and bondservant of the Lord who repeatedly, one could almost say routinely, endured and suffered all the persecutions and hardships that he endured and suffered!

Far from suffering chronic depression Paul actually had a cheerful disposition in his life. The reason for his being so cheerful was God's gracious gift of eternal life in God's blessed kingdom of glory and righteousness. As evidence of this cheerful disposition Paul wrote in 2 Corinthians 5:6-8:

> 6 Consequently, always being of good cheer and knowing that while we are at home in the body we are away from home with the Lord,
>
> 7 for we live by faith not by sight –
>
> 8 and indeed we are of good cheer and choose rather to be away from the body and at home with the Lord.

Do the words "always being of good cheer" describe a Christian who was plagued by chronic depression? Would a man with a bad case of depression write, "Finally, my brothers, always rejoice in the Lord. . . Keep rejoicing in the Lord always, again I will say, keep rejoicing"? (Philippians 3:1; 4:4)

Now, to drop that ill suggestion of Paul being depressed and to go on with the discussion on Paul's overall emotional health, Paul did not dwell on the past matters of his life. He looked forward not backward. This is clear from his words in Philippians 3:12-15, which were quoted previously. In those verses Paul said that he forgot about the things in the past. That tells us a lot about him as a man. He had a lot in his past. First, he had all the despicable deeds that he had committed about twenty-eight years earlier while persecuting the church. As bad as those things had been, he did not let them dwell on his mind. They were past; they were done; they were forgiven for the sake of Christ's purifying blood.[54] The same was true for whatever other wrongdoings and faults lay in his past. Second, he had the successes that he could have dwelt on, particularly the successes he had had up to that time in preaching and teaching the gospel. He did not dwell on those either. They likewise were past, done, and really owed their credit to God who had been working through the power of the gospel that Paul had preached. So forgetting about his past sins and successes, Paul pressed on in his life toward the heavenly goal for which God had called him to faith in Christ Jesus. That goal was the important matter that Paul's mind and emotions dwelt upon.

Aspects Of Paul's Lifestyle
  a. Paul's Perspective On His Life In And Under Christ

On the basis of Paul's statements in his New Testament letters this writer was able to piece together what seems to have been Paul's perspective on his life in and under Christ Jesus his Master and Savior. Paul's perspective began with what Christ had done for him. And so, Paul saw himself as a Christian man whom Christ had bought for the price of his own blood.[55] This being true, Paul saw that his body and life were not his own.[56] He therefore belonged to the Lord, as he wrote in Romans 14:7, 8:

> 7 For not one of us lives for himself, and not one of us dies for himself;
>   8 for not only if we live, we live for the Lord, but also if we die, we die for the Lord. So not only if we live but also if we die, we belong to the Lord.

As a Christian man whose faith rested solidly on the gospel of Jesus Christ, Paul also saw that when the day came that he would die, he would be with the Lord in heaven and have a resurrected body and eternal life.[57] In that case dying was much better than living. But if he did not die and he lived, then as an apostle and bondservant of the Lord Jesus Christ, living would mean fruitful labor for him. He said choosing between the two – living or dying, was a difficult choice for him. To die and to be with Christ was much better for him, but to live and have fruitful labor in preaching the gospel was much better for all the Christians to whom he was ministering.[58]

Belonging to the Lord, whether he lived or whether he died, he said that he had learned to be content in whatever his circumstances were at any given time. If that circumstance meant having an abundance of food, drink, clothing, and the necessities of life, well and good. But if that circumstance meant his being in need, hungry and thirsty and poorly clothed and cold, that was all right too. And if the circumstance meant persecution and hardship and suffering for Christ and the spreading of Christ's gospel to save others, that was fine as well, for that was a part of his calling as an apostle and bondservant of the Lord.[59] Thus he said he could do all things through his Lord and God who strengthened him[60]

Understanding that he belonged to the Lord and that he was the Lord's bondservant to serve him, Paul did not concern himself with earthly and political matters. For by faith he knew that his citizenship was in heaven.[61] He therefore lived himself as he taught the Christians in the churches under his care to live. Since his citizenship was in heaven, he kept "seeking the things above, where Christ is sitting at the right hand of God," and he kept "setting his mind on the things above, not on the things upon the earth."[62] Accordingly, he did not live for the earthly pleasures that the worldly-minded people all around him lived for, as did all too many people who considered themselves Christians but whose lifestyles showed them to be otherwise. And so he urged the Philippians in Philippians 3:17-19 to follow this example of his on how to live in the world, writing to them:

> 17 Always be fellow imitators of me, brothers, and keep noticing those who are conducting themselves in the same way as you have us for an example.
> 18 For many are conducting themselves, of whom I often told you, and now I say even weeping, as enemies of the cross of Christ,
> 19 whose end is eternal destruction, whose God is their belly, *whose* glory is their shame, who set their minds on the earthly things.

Having been bought and redeemed by the blood of Christ, in his day-to-day living Paul saw that he was not his own to do as he pleased to use the members of his body as instruments for sin. No, he could not let sin reign in his mortal body; on the contrary, he must present himself to God as one who used the members of his body only for righteous living.[63] Paul could not let sin reign in his mortal body, for his body was a temple of God the Holy Spirit![64] This being true, he was intent upon using that temple of God to glorify God, as he also taught the Corinthians, and now us, to do: "For you have been bought for a price; by all means, then, glorify God in your body."[65]

b. Paul As A Christian Citizen

Paul was a law-abiding Christian man who obeyed the government, even the pagan Roman government. Not only did he obey it, he also taught Christians to obey it.[66] He obeyed the government even when the government officials mistreated him. He was beaten and jailed without a proper trial in Philippi.[67] He was kept imprisoned unjustly for up to two years because Felix, the governor of Judea, wanted Paul to pay him a bribe for his freedom. Then when Felix was removed from his office, he left Paul in prison because he wished to grant a favor to the Jews.[68]

Paul was both a citizen of Tarsus and a citizen of Rome as well, which was discussed in Chapter 4. At times he declared his Roman citizenship to the various authorities. How Paul was able to substantiate his Roman citizenship on those occasions is unknown. F. F. Bruce had an interesting, though not convincing, hypothesis of how Paul might have been able to prove his Roman citizenship.[69] He explained that a child born of Roman parentage had to be registered shortly after birth. The child's name was then kept on record in the official register of the particular Roman province. The father or agent for the child was given a certified copy of a diptych, which consisted of folding tablets. That certificate was then legal evidence of Roman citizenship. F. F. Bruce then speculated that it was possible that Paul might have produced this certificate of folding tablets to prove his citizenship when he appealed to his rights as a Roman citizen. This information, based on his source F. Schulz, provides interesting historical background on the certification of a child's Roman citizenship, but given Paul's life of travels and river crossings and shipwrecks, it does not seem likely that such folding tablets would have long survived. To this writer the matter of how Paul verified his Roman citizenship is still an unsolved mystery.

Whether Paul had to provide proof of his citizenship or his verbal claim of citizenship was accepted until such time as the authorities could verify his claim, Paul did assert and stand on his Roman citizenship and made use of his rights that it provided. He stood on his Roman citizenship because it guaranteed to him a fair trial and protection from punishment by scourging and crucifixion. In Philippi he protested that his rights as a Roman citizen were denied to him when he was publicly beaten with a rod and imprisoned and put in stocks without having been given a fair trial.[70] And Paul twice stood on his rights in Palestine as a Roman citizen. The first time was when he was taken into Roman custody in Jerusalem and Tribune Claudius Lysias ordered that Paul be examined by scourging.[71] The second time was when Paul was in Caesarea during his trial before Porcius Festus. On that occasion he appealed his case to the imperial court of Caesar.[72] Then, when Paul had been transferred to Rome for trial, because he was a Roman citizen he was allowed to live under house arrest rather than being locked up in a dungeon until his case was heard and his trial was completed.

There is no evidence in the Book of Acts or in Paul's letters that he involved himself in any way in the politics of Rome and its provinces. In fact Paul's own words to Timothy in 2 Timothy 2:3 & 4 indicate just the opposite would have been true. Christ Jesus had enlisted Paul to be his apostle to the Gentiles. His being in that service of Christ as his bondservant left him no time to be entangling himself in everyday worldly affairs, which also would have included what was going on in the politics of the Roman Empire. He wrote to Timothy, "Suffer hardship with me as an excellent soldier of Christ Jesus. No one who serves as a soldier becomes entangled in the affairs of everyday life, in order that he may strive to please the one who enlisted him." Paul knew that in Christ Jesus his citizenship was in heaven, not in a worldly kingdom such as Rome was. To that citizenship in heaven above all Paul clung, as he wrote in Philippians 3:20, "For our citizenship is in heaven, from which we also are eagerly awaiting a Savior, the Lord Jesus Christ."

c. Paul's Manner Of Living

The life of Paul was anything but easy. He described in 1 Corinthians 4:11-13 the kind of life that he lived as an apostle up to the time he wrote his First Letter to the Corinthians in early A.D. 56:

> 11 Until this present hour we are customarily both hungry and thirsty and poorly clothed and physically abused and homeless
>
> 12 and labor by working with our own hands; when we are verbally abused, we bless *in return*; when we are persecuted, we endure it;
>
> 13 when we are slandered, we speak kindly; until now we have become as the scum of the earth, the filth of all people.

Paul also wrote in 2 Corinthians 11:27, 28:

> 27 *I have been* in toil and hardship, without sleep frequently, in hunger and thirst, often in involuntary fastings, in the cold without sufficient clothing;
>
> 28 apart from *these* secondary matters *there is* the pressure on me everyday, *namely*, the worry about all the churches!

In 2 Corinthians 6:4, 5 Paul said:

> 4 ... *we are* commending ourselves as ministers of God in everything, in much patient endurance, in tribulations, in calamities, in extreme afflictions,
>
> 5 in beatings, in prisons, in riots, in toils, in sleeplessness, in hunger, ...

In 1 Thessalonians 2:9 Paul stated:

> Surely you remember, brothers, our work and hard and difficult labor,

that while working night and day in order to not be a burden to anyone, we preached the gospel of God to you.

And in 2 Corinthians 4:8-11 Paul wrote:

8 We are being pressed hard on every side but not being crushed, not knowing what to do but not being utterly at a loss,

9 being persecuted but not being forsaken, being struck down but not being destroyed,

10 always carrying about in the body the dying of Jesus, in order that the life of Jesus may also be revealed in our body.

11 For we who are living are constantly being handed over into death because of Jesus, in order that the life of Jesus may also be revealed in our mortal flesh.

Paul said that his life was a theater of exhibitions for the whole world:

For, it seems to me, that God has displayed us, the apostles, as the least of all, as men sentenced to die, because we have been made a theater of exhibitions for the world, both for angels and for people. (1 Corinthians 4:9)

There were some times in his life that were a little better and easier to bear. Whatever his circumstances were, he learned to be content with the kind of life that he had at the time, as he said in Philippians 4:1-13. And as one last comment on Paul's manner of living: his working hard to support himself and his refusing to be a lazy, gossipy busybody was an example for the Christians of his day and of all ages on how to live a sanctified, God-pleasing life.[73]

Aspects Of Paul's Ministry
   a. Characteristics Of Paul In His Ministry

Accolades of praise have been heaped upon Paul over time for his outstanding mission efforts and achievements. He was surely a man of outstanding, unique qualifications. But as talented as Paul was, his competency as a successful apostolic missionary was not of his own doing. Paul himself placed the credit where the credit was properly due. He said, "Not that we are competent of ourselves to claim anything as from ourselves; on the contrary, our capability is from God, who made us capable ministers of a new covenant – not of *the* letter but of the Spirit; . . ."[74]

What Paul said was so true. By the providence of God Paul was born and raised in Tarsus, which was "no insignificant city" as he told Tribune Claudius Lysias upon his arrest in Jerusalem. Thus Paul was given the opportunity to grow up and study as a boy in a cultural city that rivaled Athens and Alexandria as a center of Greek philosophy and literature. By the providence of God he also was able to study under Gamaliel, the renowned Pharisaic doctor of the Law of Moses. And by the creative powers of God Paul was given the natural abilities and mental powers that made him so intellectually sharp and insightful. And above all else God blessed him with the Holy Spirit and his divine gifts, without which Paul would have remained in his ignorant state of spiritual darkness and unbelief such as he had been in before his conversion by the Holy Spirit.

And so, Paul had nothing to boast about as far as who and what he was and his competency for the ministry. All of that was God's doing, as he readily admitted in 2 Corinthians 5:6 above. Nor did he boast about his apostolic ministry and the souls that were brought to faith in Jesus for eternal life through it. Paul remained a humble bondservant of the Lord Jesus in this regard also. As proof of this he wrote to the Romans, "I will not presume to say anything except what Christ accomplished through me by word and deed for the obedience of the Gentiles . . ."[75]

Paul was an apostle and a minister of the gospel not because of anything he was or had done but solely by the grace of God. Paul said this in Ephesians 3:7-9:

7 ... of which (gospel) I was made a minister by virtue of the gift of the grace of God that was given to me according to the working of his power.

8 This grace was given to me, the very least of all the saints, to preach the gospel to the Gentiles, the inexhaustible riches of Christ,

9 and to bring to light to everyone what is the administration of the mystery that has been hidden from the earliest times in God who created all things, ...

Before looking into the particular characteristics of Paul in his apostolic ministry as a bondservant of Jesus Christ, we should look at the manner in which he conducted his ministry in the congregations he founded. First Thessalonians 2:1-12 gives us a good example of how he worked in the congregations and also trained his fellow workers to conduct themselves. In those verses Paul tells us that he was repeatedly the target of intense persecution. In spite of the persecution that was inflicted upon him, however, God gave him the courage to speak the gospel of Jesus Christ without drawing back. In his sharing the gospel with the people his persuasive instructions were not cloaked in impurity or deceitfulness. He did not try to gain friends and influence people by pleasing them by what he said and by flattering his listeners. He did not seek any personal gain for himself or people's praise. While among them he did not assert his apostolic authority; rather he was gentle with tender love and affections. He not only shared the gospel with the people, but he even shared his very own life. He worked hard and labored day and night in order to preach the gospel with them. He continually lived and conducted himself in a holy, blameless manner. And as a father treated his own children, he urged and encouraged the Christian converts to conduct themselves in a God-pleasing manner.

In his ministry Paul took an evangelical approach to addressing issues that called for some kind of action. Paul's evangelical approach was to call upon congregations and individuals to exercise their Christian faith on their own to do what was God's will rather than command them to do it. Three examples of this will be sufficient to establish this point.

The first example is from 1 Corinthians 14. The Corinthians' worship services were disorderly as a result of their not using their spiritual gifts in an orderly, proper manner. In 1 Corinthians 14:26-40 Paul undertook the task of correcting those problems and teaching the Corinthians how their spiritual gifts were to be used in their worship services. Paul wrote to the Corinthians:

> 26 What does it come down to, then, brothers? When you come together, each one has a psalm, *each* one has a teaching, *each one* has a revelation, *each one* has a tongue, *each one* has an interpretation. **Let all things be done for edification.**
>
> 27 If anyone speaks in a tongue, **let it be done by two or at the most three, and one after the other, and let one man interpret.**
>
> 28 But if there is no interpreter, **let the tongue speaker remain silent in church, and let him speak to himself and to God.**
>
> 29 **Let two or three prophets speak, and let the others pass judgment;**
>
> 30 but if a revelation is revealed to another who is seated, **let the first prophet be silent.**
>
> 31 For you all can prophesy one at a time, in order that all may learn and all may be encouraged,
>
> 32 and the spirits of prophets are subject to *the* prophets;
>
> 33 for God is not *a God* of disorder but of peace.
>
> ¶ As in all the churches of the saints,
>
> 34 **let the women be silent in the churches,** for they are not allowed to speak; on the contrary, **let them be in subjection,** just as the law says.
>
> 35 And if they wish to learn something, **let them ask their own husbands at home,** for it is disgraceful for a woman to speak in church.
>
> 36 Or was it from you that the word of God went out, or did it come to you only?
>
> ¶ 37 If someone thinks he is a prophet or spiritually gifted, **let him**

know for certain the things which I am writing to you are the Lord's command;

38 and if someone does not acknowledge *this*, he himself is not acknowledged.

39 So then, my brothers, always eagerly desire prophesying, and yet do not forbid the speaking in tongues.

40 **Let all things be done decently and in accordance with good order.**

Notice all the emboldened clauses in the above verses in which Paul says "let" this or that be done. He does not say that the congregation "should" tell the men or women in the worship services what they are to do or not to do. Rather, Paul encourages the congregation to implement the particular action on their own as the best God-pleasing action to take. Nor does Paul tell the individuals themselves what they "should" or "must" do. Rather he calls on them to exercise their faith and of their own Christian will do what is the God-pleasing thing for them to do as a fruit of their faith. It is unfortunate that English translations of the above emboldened clauses often translate the Greek present imperative tenses as "must" or "should" rather than with the permissive force of "let", for those translations lose Paul's evangelical approach to addressing the issues and turn those verses into legalistic commands, which Paul did not make.

The second example of Paul's evangelical approach to resolving issues is found in 1 Timothy 2:11. There Paul wrote to Timothy: "Let a woman learn in silence in all submission." Here again notice the "let" of permissiveness rather than a stern command of "must" or "should". Here, too, Paul called on the women to exercise their faith in doing what was God's will for them in the public assemblies of the church where men were present and involved. And, what is more, Paul did not tell Timothy what he should be commanding the women to do. What was said above about the mistranslation of the Greek present imperative holds true in this verse as well.

The third example of Paul's evangelical manner of addressing matters is found in Philemon 8-17. In these verses Paul was writing to

Philemon about how to treat his runaway slave Onesimus, whom Paul had sent back to him. Paul gave no commands to Philemon about the treatment of Onesimus; Paul only appealed to Philemon as to what he could do of his own free will in exercising his faith toward his runaway slave who had become his Christian brother. Paul went so far as to even offer to pay Philemon for any financial losses that Onesimus may have caused him!

While working among the congregations Paul preached the gospel free of charge without taking any pay or honorarium.[76] He did so because he was willing to do it for Christ his Lord and Master. Paul had the right under God to receive a living from his preaching of the gospel, as he himself taught the congregations that he did in Galatians 6:6 where he said, "Now let the one who is taught the word give a share of all good things to his teacher." In defense of his apostolic ministry he wrote to the Corinthians in 1 Corinthians 9:3-9:

> 3 This is my defense to those who examine me:
>
> 4 Do we not have the right to eat and drink?
>
> 5 Do we not have the right to take a believing wife along, like the rest of the apostles and the brothers of the Lord and Cephas?
>
> 6 Or do only Barnabas and I not have the right to refrain from working?
>
> 7 Who ever serves as a soldier by providing his own rations? Who plants a vineyard and does not eat its fruit? Or who tends sheep and does not drink some of the milk of the flock?
>
> 8 I am not saying these things in accordance with a human principle, am I? Or does the law not say these things?
>
> 9 For in the law of Moses it is written, "YOU SHALL NOT MUZZLE THE OX WHILE IT IS THRESHING." God is not concerned about oxen, is he?

Being a bondservant of the Lord Jesus Christ who called him to serve as an apostle, Paul was under an obligation to all people to preach the gospel that they may believe in Jesus and be saved. He said this in Romans 1:14, 15: "I am under obligation to both Greeks and barbarians, to both wise and foolish; in the same way I am eager to preach the gospel also to you who are in Rome." Having such a calling from the Lord Jesus Christ and being under such an obligation, Paul stated, "For if I preach the gospel, it is not a reason for boasting for me; for a necessity lies upon me; for woe is me if I do not preach the gospel."[77]

Paul was obligated to preach the gospel to all people. That included the Jews as well as the Gentiles. He was called by the Lord to be an apostle to the Gentiles, but the Lord Jesus said he was also to carry his name to the Jews.[78] In compliance with his Lord Jesus' directive, Paul did so. And he never lost his love for his fellow countrymen – the Jews.[79] And so, Paul's custom when he entered a new city was to go the synagogue to share the gospel with the Jews first. It was after the Jews had rejected the gospel that he preached that he turned to the Gentiles.

Paul was driven by a sense of urgency to spread the gospel. It seems clear that he felt he had no time to waste, and in fact he did not waste any time. Three examples from his ministry exemplify this work ethic of Paul.

The first example is from Acts 17:14-18:4. After the brothers in Berea escorted Paul away from the Jewish persecution there to safety in Athens, Paul was to wait in Athens for Silas and Timothy to join him. But Paul did not sit around doing nothing. Seeing the city of Athens full of idols kept irritating Paul, for the idols were visible evidence of to what extent the devil had blinded the minds of the Athenian people and led them into the worship of what was actually demons.[80] In this way those people were being led straight to hell. Their souls were being lost. The truth of God's word and the message of Jesus Christ needed to be proclaimed to them as soon as possible for the sake of their salvation. And so, Paul wasted no time in starting to do just that. He quickly began reasoning with the Jews and the proselytes in the synagogue and proclaiming the gospel of Jesus Christ to them. From there he then went into the marketplace everyday and shared the gospel with whoever was there. He then began conversing with the Epicurean and Stoic philosophers, telling them about Jesus Christ and his resurrection from the dead. They in turn took him to the Areopagus where he preached the word of God and that God was going to judge the world by the man Jesus whom he had raised from the dead. Some of the men believed and became followers of Paul. Paul then left Athens alone without waiting for Silas and Timothy. He pushed on ahead to Corinth where he began reasoning in the synagogue every Sabbath, trying to persuade the Jews and Greeks.

The second example that Paul did not waste time but went right to work preaching the gospel is from Acts 18:18-20. At the end of his second missionary journey when he was traveling back to Jerusalem and Antioch in Syria, Paul had a layover in Ephesus. He then went into the synagogue in Ephesus and reasoned with the Jews, who then began asking him to remain longer with them.

And the third such example is from Acts 28:16 & 17 when Paul arrived in Rome to begin his first Roman imprisonment. It was after only three days of being in Rome and in his own rented quarters that he summoned the Jewish leaders in Rome. He then met with them, and on the day that they appointed he taught the gospel of Jesus Christ to them from Moses and the prophets.

Paul had more than just a sense of urgency for his ministry; he also had a high degree of education and intelligence to aid him in his ministry. But in his ministry, he did not try to impress people with a persuasive oratory or with a superior knowledge and wisdom. He simply concentrated on preaching the gospel of Christ, which, as he said in Romans 1:16, 17, was the power of God for salvation. So he did nothing but preach the gospel and let the power of that gospel work on and in the hearts of his listeners, so that the people's faith would rest solidly on the power of the Spirit of God and not on any oratory or wisdom of his own. Paul made this clear when he wrote:

> 1 When I came to you, brothers, I did not come with a persuasive oratory or a superiority of wisdom, proclaiming to you the mystery of God.

2 For I did not intend to know anything among you except Jesus Christ and him crucified...

4 ... and my message and my preaching *were* not in persuasive words of wisdom but with a demonstration of the Spirit and power,

5 in order that your faith may not stand on the wisdom of men but on the power of God. (1 Corinthians 2:1, 2, 4, 5)

Paul was indeed highly educated and intelligent for service in the gospel ministry, which was all to the credit of God as stated previously. Yet Paul was a human being of living flesh and blood as we all are. And like all of us human beings he too had his times when he felt he was inadequate and not up to the job of the ministry facing him in spite of the education and intelligence he had. He admitted this in 1 Corinthians 2:3, where he wrote, "And in weakness and in fear and with much trembling I came to you."

Paul served God wholeheartedly with his spirit in his gospel ministry. He stated this in Romans 1:9: "For God, whom I serve with my spirit in the gospel of his Son, ..." His whole life was dedicated to serving and working for Christ. He plainly stated this was his purpose for living in Philippians 1:21-26, which verses were referred to previously.

Paul's motivation for carrying out his apostolic ministry was the love of Christ who died for him, indeed for all. Having been reconciled to God by Christ's redeeming sacrifice, he labored as an ambassador of Christ urging others to be reconciled to God through Christ Jesus their Savior. Paul wrote:

14 For the love of Christ drives us, because we have come to conclude this, that one died for all; so, then they all died;

15 and he died for all in order that those who are living no longer keep living for themselves but for him who died for them and was raised again.

18 Now all these things *are* from God, who reconciled us to himself through Christ and gave us the ministry of reconciliation,

19 that is, God was in Christ reconciling the world to himself, not

counting people's sins against them, and established among us the word of reconciliation.

20 Therefore we are working as ambassadors in Christ's behalf, as though God is appealing to you through us; we beg you in Christ's behalf, be reconciled to God.

21 God made him who knew no sin *to be* sin in place of us, in order that we might become the righteousness of God in him. (2 Corinthians 5:14, 15, 18-21)

As a bondservant Paul was dedicated to his Lord and Master Jesus Christ. When the prophet Agabus told Paul that he would be bound and imprisoned in Jerusalem, and Paul's traveling companions and fellow Christians were pleading with him not to go to Jerusalem, Paul responded, "What are you doing, sobbing and breaking my heart? As for me, I am prepared not only to be tied up but to die in Jerusalem for the name of the Lord Jesus!"[81] And throughout his ministry, as he specifically told the Corinthians, he wanted to know nothing among the people and churches but "Jesus Christ and him crucified."[82]

During his apostolic ministry Paul harbored no jealousy over others preaching the gospel of Jesus Christ. He exhibited no jealousy with regard to the ministrations of Apollos in Corinth; rather he valued Apollos as his fellow worker laboring for the same end result, namely the saving of souls.[83] And he showed no hint of jealousy whatsoever when he wrote about others preaching the gospel. Indeed, he said, some were preaching the gospel out of jealousy to cause him strife. He wrote in Philippians 1:12-18a:

12 Now I want you to come to know, brothers, that the things concerning me *here* have worked for the greater advancement of the gospel,

13 so that my imprisonment on account of Christ has become known in the whole palace guard and to all the rest *of the people*,

14 and most of the brothers in the Lord have become confident because of my imprisonment to have much more courage to speak the word without fear.

15 Some are indeed preaching Christ out of jealousy and strife, but some are indeed preaching Christ out of good will.

16 The latter do so out of love, because they know that I am appointed for the defense of the gospel;

17 the former are proclaiming Christ out of selfish ambition, not *out of* sincerity, thinking to cause trouble *for me* in my imprisonment.

18a What then? In any case, in every way, whether in pretense or truthfulness, Christ is proclaimed, and in this I continue rejoicing.

When the truth of the gospel was being attacked and threatened, when the church of Christ and the salvation of souls hung in the balance, when Christ's true gospel ministry was under siege – Paul was a fighter and a defender of the faith, at which times that fiery temperament of his flashed and burned profusely. This can be observed in his dealing with the Corinthians who did not reject the false super-apostles in Corinth and his dealing with the Galatians who were turning from the true gospel to follow the lead of the Judaizers. In such cases Paul did not mince words. He was blunt. He said what he knew had to be said in no uncertain terms. But he did so in love for the spiritual benefit of those misguided Christians to direct them in the ways of God. He told the Corinthians in no uncertain terms in 2 Corinthians 11:19, 20:

19 For you, being so intelligent, gladly put up with fools!

20 For you put up with it if someone reduces you to slavery, if someone devours you, if someone takes *possession of* you, if someone exalts himself over you, if someone slaps you in the face!

He told the Galatians straight out in Galatians 3:1-4:

1 You senseless Galatians! Who bewitched you? You before whose eyes Jesus Christ was portrayed openly as having been crucified!

2 This is the only thing I want to find out from you: Did you receive the Spirit as a result of works of law or as a result of the preaching of faith?

> 3 Are you so senseless? Having begun with spirit are you now finishing yourselves up with flesh?
>
> 4 Have you experienced so much in vain? If indeed it was in vain?

He did not spare those false super-apostles in the Corinthian congregation either when he wrote in 2 Corinthians 11:13-15:

> 13 For such kind of men are false apostles, deceitful workmen, masquerading as apostles of Christ.
>
> 14 And no wonder, for Satan himself masquerades as an angel of light;
>
> 15 it is no great thing, then, if his servants also masquerade as ministers of righteousness, whose end will be according to their deeds.

And his stern rebuke of the circumcising Judaizers must have hit them like a knockout uppercut when he wrote to the Galatians,[84] "O how I wish that those who are upsetting you would even have themselves castrated!"

What is more, being much concerned about the Judaizers who were troubling the Philippians, Paul warned the Philippians about them, saying, "Beware of the dogs! Beware of the evil workers! Beware of the mutilation!"[85]

That fiery temperament and indignation at times revealed that his standard of judgment was the Word and commands of God. At such times his impatience became apparent with those who should have been adhering to the Word of God but were not doing so. A case in point is found in Acts 23:1-5 where Paul stood before the Jewish Sanhedrin at the hearing held by Tribune Claudius Lysias. Luke reports for us:

> 1 And when Paul had looked steadily at the Sanhedrin, he said, "Men, brothers, I have led my life in all good consciousness before God until this day."
>
> 2 And the high priest Ananias ordered those standing beside him to strike his mouth.

> 3 At that time Paul said to him, "God is about to strike you, you whitewashed wall! And do you sit judging me according to the law, and yet acting contrary to the law you order me to be struck?"
> 4 But those standing beside *him* said, "Do you *dare to* berate God's high priest?"
> 5 And Paul replied, "I did not know, brothers, that he is *the* high priest. For it is written, 'You shall not speak evilly about a ruler of your people.'"

Yes, Paul at times exhibited his fiery temperament, but he was also a Christian man and bondservant of Jesus Christ who displayed moments of intense fondness, compassion, love, and tenderness. 2 Corinthians 2:4 is one example:

> For out of severe affliction and anguish of heart I wrote to you with many tears, not in order that you might be made sorrowful, but in order that you might realize the love that I have especially for you.

To the Philippians Paul wrote:

> 7 It is right for me to think this in behalf of you all, because I have you in my heart both in my imprisonment and in my defense and confirmation of the gospel – you who are my fellow sharers of God's grace.
> 8 For God is my witness, that I am longing for all of you with the affection of Christ Jesus. (Philippians 1:7, 8)

In Philippians 2:12 he addressed the Christians in Philippi as his "beloved". His tenderness and compassion were also evident in his concern over Epaphroditus' being deathly ill, which caused Paul so much grief.[86] And in Philippians 4:1 Paul wrote, "Therefore, my beloved brothers, whom I long for, my joy and my crown, in this manner go on standing firm in the Lord, dear friends." An expression of his tender concern for the Galatians is found in Galatians 4:19, 20:

19 My children, with whom I am again undergoing birth pains until Christ is formed in you,

    20 I was just wishing to be present with you now, and to alter my voice, for I am puzzled about you.

Paul had a heart filled with a love for souls. He did not want to see a single person lost and condemned. He himself would forego indulging in a Christian liberty if his indulging endangered the soul of another person, as already stated above in connection with the discussion on Paul's agape love. What us more, he would do all that he could, everything in his human power and control, to reach out to a precious soul to save him or her. This love of Paul to save souls is evident in his words of 1 Corinthians 9:1-22:

19 For although I am free from all *people*, I made myself a slave to all *people*, in order that I may gain the greater number *of people*;

    20 indeed to the Jews I became like a Jew, in order that I may gain Jews; to those under law I became like a man under law, although I myself am not under law, in order that I may gain those under law;

    21 to those without law I became like *a man* without law, although I am not without the law of God but in the law of Christ, in order that I may gain those without law;

    22 to the weak I became weak, in order that I may gain the weak; I have become all things to all *people*, in order that by all means I might save some.

Now in the course of his performing his apostolic ministry Paul performed miracles. In 2 Corinthians 12:12 he wrote, "To be sure, the signs of an apostle, not only miraculous signs but also wonders and deeds of power, were performed among you with all perseverance." In the Book of Acts Luke reported instances of Paul's performing miracles. In Philippi he cast out the demon from the girl who had a spirit of divination. In Iconium the Lord testified to Paul's preaching by the miraculous signs and wonders he enabled Paul to perform.[87] In Lystra Paul healed a man who had been crippled from his mother's womb.[88]

After being shipwrecked on the island of Malta, Paul was healing those who were sick.[89]

Luke furthermore reports in Acts 19:11 that God kept performing extraordinary miracles in Ephesus through Paul's hands. By means of those amazing miracles God was testifying in favor of the gospel that Paul was preaching. For the sake of the Ephesian people God was putting his stamp of approval on that gospel. Through those miracles God was declaring to the Ephesians that the gospel of free forgiveness and eternal life through faith in Jesus Christ was his word and message. Luke says that the miracles were so extraordinary that even handkerchiefs and aprons from Paul were carried to the sick and their diseases departed from them and evil spirits were cast out of them.[90]

Because of his love for souls and his high regard for the gospel ministry in which he served, Paul gave no occasion for anyone to take offense from anything he said or did. He wanted to be sure that the Lord's gospel ministry could not be faulted, which would result in an individual being turned away. For this reason he commended himself as a minister of Christ in everything.[91]

In his ministry Paul had an ambition that he desired to achieve. That ambition was to preach the gospel of Jesus Christ where it had not been preached before. He wrote in Romans 15:20, "And in the same way I have as my ambition to be preaching the gospel where Christ has not been known, in order that I may not be building upon another man's foundation." Then in Romans 15:23, 24 he went on to say his ambition was to go to Spain and preach the gospel there: ". . . but now no longer having a place *for a field of work* in these regions, and having a desire to come to you for many years when I proceed to Spain."

b. The Teachings Of Paul

To write a biographical commentary on the life of Paul one must include a discussion of what he taught. But to explore and to expound all the doctrines that Paul taught in his ministry is beyond the scope of this biographical commentary, for to cover that subject thoroughly one must write a dogmatics book. But some comments on some of the matters that Paul addressed in his apostolic teaching are possible and needed.

What Paul taught was the inspired Word of God. In his ministry he taught what the Lord revealed to him. Paul's teachings were the teachings of his Lord and Master Jesus Christ and what the Holy Spirit taught him to say. Paul did not invent new teachings of his own. As he told the Thessalonians,

> When you received the word of God that you heard from us, you received it not as the word of men but just as it actually is – the word of God, which indeed is at work in you who believe. (1 Thessalonians 2:13)

Being filled with the Spirit of God as an apostle, he did on occasion comment on what he thought was right under God but did not have a direct command from God on which he could base what he taught. In those cases Paul was giving his advice, which could or could not be taken.[92] We can see that Paul conducted his teaching ministry on this basis in the following verses that he wrote:

> If someone thinks he is a prophet or spiritually gifted, let him know for certain the things which I am writing to you are the Lord's command. (1 Corinthians 14:37)
>
> Do not deprive one another, unless by agreement for a time that you may devote yourselves to prayer, and *then* come together again so that Satan may not begin to entice you to sin because of your lack of self-control. I say this as a concession, not a command. (1 Corinthians 7:5, 6)
>
> Now to those who have gotten married I give this command, not I but the Lord, . . . (1 Corinthians 7:10)
>
> Now to the rest I myself say, not the Lord, . . . (1 Corinthians 7:12)
>
> Now concerning the virgins I do not have a command of the Lord, but I am giving an opinion as one who has been shown mercy by the Lord to be trustworthy (1 Corinthians 7:25)

But in my own judgment she is more blessed if she remains as she is, and I do believe I have the Spirit of God. (1 Corinthians 7:40)

It needs to be pointed out that even when Paul stated that what he was saying was not a direct command of the Lord, he was giving his advice and what he wrote as an apostle was still the inspired word of the Holy Spirit.[93]

In his ministry Paul taught that there was no difference between Jews and Gentiles in God's kingdom of grace. Paul taught this, for example, in Galatians 3:27, 28:

27 For as many of you as were baptized in Christ, allowed yourselves to be clothed in Christ;

28 there is neither Jew nor Greek, there is neither slave nor free, there is not a male and a female, for you believers, you are all one in Christ Jesus.

Paul specifically states that this understanding that the Gentile believers in Christ Jesus were equal to and equal with the Jewish believers in Christ was made known to him by a revelation from God. The Gentiles were fellow heirs and fellow members and fellow sharers in the gospel of Christ together with the Jews. That knowledge Paul called a mystery, for it was an unknown divine truth to the people of the world in previous generations. Paul explained how he came to understand this divine truth in Ephesians 3:1-6:

1 For this reason, I, Paul, the prisoner of Christ Jesus for the sake of you Gentiles –

2 If, indeed, you have heard of the office of administrator of the grace of God that was entrusted to me for you,

3 that by revelation there was made known to me the mystery, as I have briefly written before,

4 by which you are able when you read it to understand my insight into the mystery of Christ,

5 which *mystery* was not made known to the sons of men in other

generations as it has now been revealed by the Spirit to his holy apostles and prophets,

6 *that* the Gentiles are fellow heirs *with the Israelites* and fellow members and fellow sharers of the promise in Christ Jesus through the gospel, ...

Now in his ministry Paul taught the law, that is the holy moral will and commandments of God. He taught the law to show people like us our sins and the punishment of God that we deserve,[94] to curb the evil deeds of our sinful nature and hold it in check,[95] and to guide us in how to live a God-pleasing life.[96] Paul taught all the moral commandments of God, but throughout his ministry he had to teach the first commandment that forbids idolatry time and again in place after place. For in the cities to which he went he was constantly confronted with the idols of the Greeks and the Romans and the pagan citizens who worshipped them. Just outside the city of Antioch, Syria, for example, was the temple of Apollo. Athens had so many idolatrous altars that it even contained one dedicated to "The Unknown God". Ephesus was the location of the temple of the Great Artemis of the Ephesians. Corinth had twelve heathen temples. And the city of Rome was filled with places of idolatrous worship for its pagan citizens. And very often in connection with the idols' temples was temple prostitution. Outside of Antioch was the Daphne Groves that held the temple of Apollo and was notorious as the sin-sick city of the East for its immorality. In Corinth, the sin-sick city of the West, there were more than one thousand temple prostitutes offering their sexual services. So in his ministry Paul was compelled to teach and to warn against the sin of idolatry as he did in 1 Corinthians 8:1-13 & 10:14-22, as well as the sins of sexual immorality, as he did in 1 Corinthians 6:9-20 and Galatians 5:19 & 20a.

Throughout his ministry, as shall be observed in the following biographical commentary, Paul was required to repeatedly address the false teaching of the Judaizers. They were false Christians who acknowledged the name of Jesus Christ but denied the sufficiency of his redeeming sacrifice for salvation. In many cases they were former

Pharisees[97] who insisted the Mosaic Law must be obeyed and that the rite of circumcision must be administered. To combat the spread and acceptance of their false teaching, Paul emphasized the doctrine of justification by grace and faith alone without the works of the law. Paul's Letter to the Galatians was a doctrinal masterpiece on the subject of justification by grace and by faith. Likewise Romans 3 & 4 were other key presentations on this subject. And throughout his other letters he upheld God's grace and the Christian's faith as the way to be saved, as he did in the beautiful words the Holy Spirit inspired him to write in Ephesians 2:8, 9: "For by this grace you have been saved through faith, and this not from yourselves, it is the gift of God, not as a result of works, so that no one may boast."

On commenting briefly on the teachings of Paul this writer dare not overlook his teachings on the pastoral ministry within the Christian Church. In his letters Paul laid down the principles for the public ministry of the Church. He did so especially in his three pastoral letters to Timothy and to Titus. In them he listed what are the qualifications needed to serve in the Church's public ministry. First Corinthians 14:33b-38 is also an important section regarding who can serve in that ministry. The principles that Paul laid down are timeless and make up the foundation for much of what is called Pastoral Theology today. Pastoral Theology is a study used to prepare men to serve as pastors. The men learn what is involved in being a pastor of a Christian congregation, what the qualifications for the ministry are, and what the work and problems of the ministry are. The Church indeed needs to give thanks to God for the pastoral principles that he had his apostle and bondservant Paul put in writing for the ages.

As Paul taught important principles for the pastoral ministry of the Church, Paul also taught key truths about the Church itself. Paul, regarded as the greatest of missionaries in the history of the Church, was the apostle and the bondservant of the Lord Jesus Christ through whom the Lord gathered his infant Church in what is now Turkey, Greece, Italy, and Spain, and started raising it up to be what it was supposed to be in its maturity. Being such a missionary, and having been taught by the Lord himself, who could have expounded the Lord's principles on the Church better than Paul?

One very important principle that the Holy Spirit moved Paul to emphasize and uphold in his ministry was the unity of the Church. As an example of this Paul wrote to the Ephesians:

> 3 (Make) every effort to be keeping the unity of the Spirit in the bond of peace;
>
> 4 one body and one spirit, just as you were also called in one hope of your calling;
>
> 5 one Lord, one faith, one baptism;
>
> 6 one God and Father of all, who is over all and through all and in all. (Ephesians 4:3-6)

Since the Christians in the Church were to keep the unity of the Spirit in the bond of peace, in his ministry Paul taught them that there was to be no divisions in the Church. Paul made this clear in his First Letter to the Corinthians:

> Now I urge you, brothers, by reminding you of the name of our Lord Jesus Christ, that you all speak the same thing, and that there may be no divisions among you, but that you may go on being made complete in the same mind and in the same judgment. (1 Corinthians 1:10)

So that there may be no divisions in the Church, all its members were to be united in the same faith and teachings. The various congregations in Christian liberty could have differing opinions on adiaphora that were neither commanded nor forbidden by God, such as whether women had to wear a veil in the worship services as was the custom in the Corinthian congregation but not in other congregations elsewhere.[98] But within the Church of Christ there were not to be differing beliefs and differing teachings on the doctrines that God himself had plainly taught. On those teachings the Church was to be united. Accordingly Paul issued the following instructions:

> Now I urge you, brothers, to keep looking out for those who go on making divisions and snares into error contrary to the doctrine you indeed have learned, and keep turning away from them. (Romans 16:17)
>
> Customarily reject a heretical person after a first and second warning, knowing that such a person is perverted and is sinning, while being self-condemned. (Titus 3:10, 11)

According to Paul's divinely inspired statements, if false teachers arose in the Church who were speaking doctrines contrary to the doctrines of God that we now have in his Holy Scriptures, the members of the Church were to take note of who they were, and after properly instructing them in what God himself taught, if the false teachers persisted spreading their heresies, the Church members should turn away from them and exclude them from the Church. In this way the unity of the Church in its faith, doctrines, and practices would be preserved.

This writer can only wonder what Paul would say today about all the falsehoods and heresies that have been promulgated and are now being not only tolerated but have been accepted within the visible church on earth! He quite possibly would say: "I am not surprised! For the Holy Spirit had me tell you this would happen. He inspired me to say:

> For the time will come when people will not put up with correct doctrine, but because of having an itch to have their ears tickled, they will heap up teachers according to their own desires,
>   and on the one hand they will turn their ears away from the truth, and on the other hand will turn aside to myths.' (2 Timothy 4:3, 4)

During his ministry Paul undertook a significant charitable collection among the Gentile churches he founded to benefit the poor Christians of the Jewish mother church in Jerusalem. He undertook this collection, not just to aid the poor Jewish Christians in Jerusalem, but also to build up the unity of the Church, to join the Gentile element of the young Church with the Jewish element into one truly united body. Paul's aim was to bring about within the Church the understanding and the bond that whether the members were Gentile or Jewish they were all one in Christ.[99] More will be said about this collection in the following biographical commentary on Paul's third missionary journey.

In addition to Paul's emphasizing the unity of the Church he emphasized that the Church was one body made up of many different members. The imparting of this information about the Church with its many members was so important that the Holy Spirit moved Paul to write three significant sections on this subject. They are found in his Letters to the Ephesians and to the Corinthians and to the Romans – to three different local churches in three different inspired letters, yet all espousing the same truth. And in those three sections Paul taught that each member was an important part of the Church and had his particular gift(s) to use in the training and building up of the Church. Paul wrote in 1 Corinthians 12:12: "For even as the body is one and it has many members, and all the members of the body, although they are many, are one body, so also is Christ." Regarding all those many members Paul taught and wrote:

> 7 Now to each one of us grace has been given according to the measure of the gift of Christ....
>
> 11 And he himself gave some *to be* apostles, some *to be* prophets, some *to be* evangelists, some *to be* pastors and teachers,
>
> 12 for the purpose of training the saints for service work, for building up the body of Christ,
>
> 13 until we all arrive at the unity of the faith and the precise knowledge of the Son of God, *and arrive* at a full-grown man, at a mature measure of the fullness of Christ, ... (Ephesians 4:7 & 11-13)

Paul explained in further detail the differing functions of the many members in 1 Corinthians 12:4-11:

> 4 Now there are different kinds of gifts, but the same Spirit;

5 and there are different kinds of ministries, and yet the same Lord;

6 and there are different kinds of works done, but the same God, who works all things in all believers.

7 Now to each one is given the disclosure of the Spirit for that which profits *the church of believers*.

8 For to one the teaching of wisdom is given by means of the Spirit, to another the teaching of knowledge by virtue of the same Spirit,

9 to another faith by the same Spirit, to another gifts of healings by the one Spirit,

10 and to another the working of miracles, to another prophecy, to another the distinguishing of spirits, to another different kinds of tongues, and to another the interpretation of tongues;

11 the one and the same Spirit works all these gifts, distributing to each person individually just as he intends.

Elaborating further on the diversity of gifts and functions among the many members, Paul wrote in Romans 12:3-8:

3 For I say by the grace given to me to everyone among you not to think too highly of yourselves beyond what you ought to think, but to think sensibly of yourselves, as God has bestowed to each one a measure of faith.

4 For just as we have many members in one body, and the many members do not have the same function,

5 in the same way we, who are many, are one body in Christ, and every one members of one another.

6 And having different gifts according to the grace given to us *let us use them* accordingly: if it is prophecy, *let it be done* in agreement with the Christian faith;

7 if it is ministry, *be active* in ministry; if it *is being* one who teaches, *be active* in teaching;

8 if *it is being* one who encourages, *be active* in encouraging; the one who shares *of what he has, share* in a singleness of purpose; the one who

presides over *some matter, lead* with diligence; the one who shows mercy, *show it* with cheerfulness.

Seeing that the many members were given different gifts and abilities by the Holy Spirit, Paul taught that the Christians should not be divided by petty jealousies over those differing gifts. Rather they should honor and rejoice in one another and their differences. Paul made this clear in 1 Corinthians 12:12-26:

> 12 For even as the body is one and it has many members, and all the members of the body, although they are many, are one body, so also is Christ.
>
> 13 For by one Spirit we all also were baptized into one body, whether Jew or Greek, whether slaves or free, and we all were given one Spirit to drink.
>
> 14 For the body also is not one member but many *members*.
>
> 15 If the foot says, "Because I am not a hand, I am not a part of the body," *it would* not for this reason not be a part of the body;
>
> 16 and if the ear says, "Because I am not an eye, I am not a part of the body," *it would* not for this reason not be a part of the body.
>
> 17 If the whole body were an eye, where *would* the hearing *be*? If *the* whole body *were* hearing, where *would* the sense of smell *be*?
>
> 18 But, as a matter of fact, God arranged the members in the body, each one of them, just as he wanted *them to be*.
>
> 19 Now if they all were one member, where *would* the body *be*?
>
> 20 But now, to be sure, there are many members, but only one body.
>
> 21 Now the eye cannot tell the hand, "I have no need of you," or again, the head *cannot tell* the feet, "I have no need of you."
>
> 22 On the contrary, the members of the body that seem to be inferior are much more necessary,
>
> 23 and the members of the body that we think are more dishonorable, on these we place greater honor, and our private parts are given greater modesty,
>
> 24 and our presentable members have no need *for it*. But God has

blended *the members of* the body, and has given greater honor to the member lacking *honor*,

25 in order that there may be no division in the body, but that the members have the same concern for one another.

26 And if one member suffers, all the members suffer together with it; if one member is honored, all the members rejoice with it.

Having established the fact that the Church was one body of many differing members, Paul taught that it was to this body of believers in Christ that the ministry of reconciliation was given. The ministry of preaching and teaching the gospel of Jesus Christ was not given just to Paul, or to Peter, or just to the apostles. It was given to the Church to proclaim, which it does publicly through its properly called pastors and teachers. Paul taught this in his ministry, as he did in 2 Corinthians 5:18-21, which were quoted above.

The Holy Spirit enabled Paul to understand on what the future of the Church's growth depended – future servants and members of the Church proclaiming and sharing the good news about Jesus to others outside of the Church. This principle of servants and members proclaiming and sharing the gospel was based on the Lord Jesus' own mission directives:

Go and make disciples of all nations, baptizing them in the name of the Father and the Son and the Holy Spirit, teaching them to observe everything I have commanded you. (Matthew 28:19, 20)

Go into all the world and preach the gospel to all creation. (Mark 16:16:15)

The principle was that through the Church's called servants and individual members evangelizing outsiders, new individuals would be brought to faith in Jesus and added to the Church. Paul saw this very phenomenon throughout the years of his own ministry. And he saw an excellent example of this during his early work in Antioch, Syria, in A.D.43 & 44. There, Jewish Christian men had begun speaking to Greek pagans and sharing the gospel of Jesus with them. The result was large numbers of Greek pagans were brought to faith in Jesus and added to the Church. Understanding that the future growth of the Church depended upon Christians sharing the gospel with others, Paul instructed Timothy, "The teachings that you heard from me in the presence of many witnesses, these entrust to faithful men, such ones as will be competent to also teach others." (2 Timothy 2:2). For this reason also Paul stated that a qualification to serve in the public ministry of the Church was that a man must be able to teach.[100]

And so, led by the Spirit, Paul understood and taught that the Church was one united body in faith and doctrine, was made up of many members who were entrusted with the ministry of reconciliation for the building up of the Church, and being such they would march forward as one gigantic army proclaiming the gospel of Christ Jesus. The spirit of this Church militant in action was caught by the hymn writer Sabine Baring-Gould in 1864 in his hymn <u>Onward, Christian Soldiers.</u>

> Like a mighty army Moves the Church of God;
> > Brothers, we are treading Where the saints have trod.
> > We are not divided, All one body we,
> > One in hope and doctrine, One in charity.
> > Onward, Christian soldiers, Marching as to war,
> > With the cross of Jesus Going on before.

Now, in the following chapters on Paul's missionary journeys and imprisonments, we will see both the preceding personal characteristics of the Lord's bondservant Paul and how he began this marching forward to the Gentiles with the banner of Jesus' gospel "going on before."

---

1. Thayer, Joseph Henry, PhD.; Greek-English Lexicon of the New Testament; Zondervan Publishing House; Grand Rapids, Michigan; p. 641, 642
2. Romans 4:25
3. Romans 3:28
4. Acts 15:37-40

5. Romans 1:8-10; 1 Corinthians 1:4; Ephesians 1:15-19; Philippians 1:3-5 & 9; Colossians 1:3-14; 1 Thessalonians 1:2-5; 2 Thessalonians 1:3, 4; 2 Timothy 1:3, 4; Philemon 4-6
6. Luecker, Erwin, L., editor; Lutheran Cyclopedia; Concordia Publishing House; St. Louis, MO. Revised Edition, 1975; p, 271
7. Mueller, John Theodore; Christian Dogmatics; Concordia Publishing House; St. Louis, MO.; 1934; p. 651
8. Pieoer, Francis: Christian Dogmatics, Vol I; Concordia Publishing House; St. Louis, MO.; 1950; fourth printing 1965; p. 252, 253
9. Ibid.
10. Acts 14:22
11. Romans 8:28
12. Philippians 4:11
13. Romans 8:31, 32
14. Acts 17:22
15. Conybeare, W. J. & Howson, J. S.; The Life And Epistles of St. Paul; Wm. B. Eerdmans Publishing Company; Grand Rapids, Michigan; p. 48
16. Acts 13:16, 21:40
17. Acts 12:17, 19:33
18. Acts 1:10, 3:4, 3:12, 6:15, 7:55, 10:4, 11:6; Luke 4:20, 22:56; 2 Corinthians 3:7, 13
19. 1 Corinthians 16:21; Colossians 4:18
20. 2 Corinthians 10:10 & 11:6
21. Schaff, Philip; History of the Christian Church, Vol.1, W.B. Eerdmans Publishing Company, Grand Rapids, MI; 1910, p. 282; Photolithoprinted, 1971
22. Conybeare, W. J. & Howson, J. S.; The Life And Epistles of St. Paul; Wm. B. Eerdmans Publishing Company; Grand Rapids, Michigan; p. 178, 179
23. Galatians 6:17
24. Acts 9:16
25. Conybeare, W. J. & Howson, J. S.; The Life And Epistles of St. Paul; Wm. B. Eerdmans Publishing Company; Grand Rapids, Michigan; p. 437
26. 2 Corinthians 4:7
27. Koehler, J. P.; The Epistle Of Paul to the Galatians; Northwestern Publishing House, Milwaukee, Wisconsin, 1957; p. 116, 117
28. Meyer, Joh. P.; Ministers of Christ – A Commentary on the Second Epistle of Paul to the Corinthians; Northwestern Publishing House, Milwaukee, WI; 1963; p. 293)
29. Lightfoot, J. B.; Epistle Of St. Paul To The Galatians; Zondervan Publishing House; Grad Rapids, Michigan; Thirteenth Zondervan Printing, 1975; p. 186-189
30. Luther, Martin; A Commentary on St. Paul's Epistle to the Galatians; Theodore Graebner, translator; Second Edition; Zondervan Publishing House; Grand Rapids, Michigan; no date indicated; p. 176
31. Conybeare, W. J. & Howson, J. S.; The Life And Epistles of St. Paul; Wm. B. Eerdmans Publishing Company; Grand Rapids, Michigan; p. 210
32. Ibid., p. 437
33. Ramsay, W. M.; St. Paul The Traveler And Roman Citizen; Baker Book House; Grand Rapids, Michigan; p. 94
34. Ibid., p. 97
35. The New Schaff-Herzog Encyclopedia of Religious Knowledge, Vol. VIII; "Paul,

The Apostle"; Jackson, Samuel Macauley, editor-in-chief; Baker Book House; Grand Rapids, Michigan; p. 406
36. Lightfoot, J. B.; The Epistle of St. Paul To The Galatians; Zondervan Publishing House, Grand Rapids, Michigan; Thirteenth Printing, 1975; p. 186
37. Lenski, R. C. H.; *The Interpretation of* St. Paul's First and Second Epistles to the Corinthians; Augsburg Publishing House; Minneapolis, Minnesota; Copyright 1937 and 1963; p. 1301, 1302
38. Philemon 9
39. Conybeare, W. J. & Howson, J. S.; The Life And Epistles of St. Paul; Wm. B. Eerdmans Publishing Company; Grand Rapids, Michigan; p. 746
40. Ibid., p. 747
41. Lenski, R. C. H., *The Interpretation of* St. Paul's Epistles to the Colossians, to the Thessalonians, to Timothy, to Titus, and to Philemon; Augsburg Publishing House, Minneapolis, Minnesota; p. 480 & 481
42. 1 Corinthians 16:17
43. 2 Corinthians 7:9
44. Philippians 1:3-5
45. Philippians 1:18
46. Philippians 1:18-20
47. Philippians 2:17, 18
48. Philippians 2:19
49. Romans 16:19
50. 1 Thessalonians 2:20; 3:9
51. Conybeare, W. J. & Howson, J. S.; The Life And Epistles of St. Paul; Wm. B. Eerdmans Publishing Company; Grand Rapids, Michigan; p. 437
52. 2 Corinthians 2:13
53. 2 Corinthians 7:5
54. 1 John 1:7
55. 1 Corinthians 6:20
56. 1 Corinthians 6:19
57. 1 Corinthians 15:35-58 & 2 Corinthians 5:1-8
58. Philippians 1:21-24
59. Acts 9:15, 16
60. Philippians 4:10-13
61. Philippians 3:20
62. Colossians 3:1, 2
63. Romans 6:1-4 &12-14
64. 1 Corinthians 6:19
65. 1 Corinthians 6:20
66. Romans 13:1-7
67. Acts 16:20-24 & 35-37
68. Acts 24:26, 27
69. Bruce, F. F.; New Testament History; Doubleday; New York, London, Toronto, Sydney, Auckland; p. 235
70. Acts 16:37,38
71. Acts 22:25-29
72. Acts 25:11 & 12
73. 2 Thessalonians 3:6-13

74. 2 Corinthians 3:5, 6
75. Romans 15:18
76. 2 Corinthians 11:7
77. 1 Corinthians 9:16
78. Acts 9:15
79. Romans 9:1-4a
80. 1 Corinthians 10:20
81. Acts 21:13
82. 1 Corinthians 2:2
83. 1 Corinthians 3:5-9
84. Galatians 5:12
85. Philippians 3:2
86. Philippians 2:27
87. Acts 14:3
88. Acts 14:8-10
89. Acts 28:8, 9
90. Acts 19:11, 12
91. 2 Corinthians 6:3, 4
92. Pieoer, Francis: Christian Dogmatics, Vol. I; Concordia Publishing House; St. Louis, MO.; 1950; fourth printing 1965; p. 260
93. Ibid.; p. 261
94. Romans 3:20
95. 1 Timothy 1:9, 10
96. Romans 7:7, 16, 21 & 22
97. Acts 15:1, 5
98. 1 Corinthians 11:1-16
99. See Ephesians 2:11-22 for Paul's explanation that in Christ the Gentiles and the Jews were brought together into one body. See also Galatians 3:26-27
100. 1 Timothy 3:2; Titus 1:9

III
THE INITIAL YEARS OF PAUL'S SERVICE

Paul's Age: 33-45
Date: A.D. 33-45

7

PAUL IN DAMASCUS AND ARABIA; PAUL'S FIRST VISIT TO JERUSALEM

PAUL'S AGE: 33-35 DATE: A.D. 33-35

Paul's Ministry In Damascus And Visit To Arabia

After Paul had sat in the darkness of his blindness and in repentance for three days, and Ananias had then come to restore his sight, Luke informs us in Acts 9:19 & 20:

> 19 Then he was with the disciples in Damascus for some days.
> 20 And at once he began proclaiming Jesus in the synagogues, that this man is the Son of God.

After Paul's conversion and he had had his sight restored, he spent some days with the members of the church in Damascus. How long of a period of time that was Luke does not tell us. It was probably not long, for Luke does tell us that at once he began proclaiming in the synagogues that the man Jesus was the Son of God. As a result of Jesus' revelation to him and the Holy Spirit's filling him with the gifts and powers for his apostolic ministry, Paul was consumed with a new zeal. Paul's old misguided zeal for God had been turned around, straightened out, and put on its proper course. He was now zealous for God to preach the gospel of Jesus Christ for the saving of not only Jews but also the Gentiles to whom Jesus was sending him. Accordingly, and to begin his new apostolic ministry, Paul at once began proclaiming the good news about Jesus in the synagogues. By the time he began doing so he had already cast aside the commission of the high priest in Jerusalem to go and persecute the followers of Jesus in Damascus. Paul now had a new, higher high priest, the Lord Jesus Christ, who was his Master who was giving him his orders for service. And as a bondservant of Jesus Christ Paul was intent upon following Jesus' commission to go as an apostle and preach the gospel beginning with the Jews in Damascus.

There was more than one synagogue in the city of Damascus to accommodate its large Jewish population. Paul at once began making a trip to each of them at least once. On each occasion he proclaimed the gospel of Jesus Christ, declaring to the Jews present that the man Jesus was truly the Son of God. We can picture Paul proclaiming that Jesus was the long-awaited Messiah foretold by the prophets of old. And there in Damascus he began his apostolic ministry by proclaiming what he would go on to proclaim throughout the years ahead in every city to which he went. This is certain, for he told King Agrippa II twenty-six years later:

> 19 For which reason King Agrippa, I was not disobedient to the heavenly vision,
> 20 but I continued to proclaim first to those in Damascus and Jerusalem, and throughout all the country of Judea, and then to the Gentiles, to repent and to turn to God, doing works worthy of repentance. (Acts 26:19, 20)

Paul's message would have indeed stirred up the Jews in the synagogues. Those Jews, like Ananias and the Christian disciples in Damascus, must also have heard that Paul had come there with authority from the chief priests to persecute and arrest every Jew who confessed faith in the name of Jesus. But then, surely in shocked disbelief, those Jews in the synagogues were hearing Paul preaching the very name of Jesus whom he was supposed to be persecuting and eradicating. And in all the synagogues where Paul went to preach Luke reports,

> And all who heard *him* kept being astounded and were saying, "Is this man not the man who destroyed those who called upon this name in Jerusalem, and who had come here for this, that after he had bound them *in chains*, he might take them along to the chief priests?" (Acts 9:21)

For just how long Paul continued to go around to the synagogues preaching the message of Jesus Luke does not tell us. It probably was not very long. But during that time the Holy Spirit was working in Paul and pouring out his gifts upon him, for Luke reports,

> "Saul continued to receive more power and to confound the Jews who were living in Damascus, proving that this man is the Christ." (Acts 9:22)

It appears that it was after that short period of beginning to preach the gospel of Christ in Damascus that Paul traveled to Arabia. The reason for his departure from Damascus to go to Arabia is not told to us. The reason may possibly have been that the Jews in the synagogues of Damascus had begun rejecting Paul's gospel and were starting to vocally oppose him. To avert a possible uprising at the time, Paul may have decided it was best to withdraw from Damascus for a while. If this had been Paul's reason, he did not do anything that Jesus himself had not done, for Jesus during his three-year ministry also withdrew from the Jews at times.

Luke in his brief style, which we will observe repeatedly in the course of this biographical commentary, does not mention Paul's trip to Arabia. We only know about it because Paul mentioned it in his Letter to the Galatians. Writing about his activities after Jesus called him to be an apostle, Paul stated in Galatians 1:16b-18a:

> 16b . . . I did not immediately consult with flesh and blood,

> 17 nor did I go up to Jerusalem to those who were apostles before me; on the contrary, I went away into Arabia, and returned once more to Damascus.
>
> 18 Then after three years I went up to Jerusalem to visit Cephas, . .

The events that occurred over the three years that Paul recorded in Galatians 1:16b-17 fit into Luke's account between the end of Acts 9:22, which says, "Saul continued to receive more power and to confound the Jews who were living in Damascus, proving that this man is the Christ." and the beginning of Acts 9:23, which says, "Now after many days had passed, the Jews plotted to kill him." In Luke's account the three years are stipulated as "after many days had passed." The three years according to the Jewish manner of keeping time could have been three full years or one full year plus a part of the preceding year and a part of the following year. The latter seems the more probable.

Paul said that he left Damascus to travel to Arabia. No other information about Paul's trip to Arabia is told to us. We have no idea just where Paul might have gone in that vast domain of Arabia, nor do we know what he did while he was there. Several opinions have been given about Paul's time in Arabia. Martin Luther thought that since Jesus had called Paul to be an apostle to the Gentiles, Paul must have gone to Arabia to start preaching to the Gentiles there without delay.[1] Another opinion has been that Paul went to Arabia for a quiet time of meditation and communion with God. And it has also been stated that Paul went to Arabia to wait until God made it clear that the time had come for him to begin his apostolic ministry. All that can be said for certain is we know nothing about Paul's trip to Arabia or for how long he was in Arabia itself.

Luke's report of Paul's activities then picks up where Paul left off in Galatians 1:17 by saying that he returned to Damascus. Luke informs us in Acts 9: 23, "Now after many days had passed, the Jews plotted to kill him." Based on these words of Luke it seems apparent that after Paul returned to Damascus, he resumed going to the synagogues in the city and was again preaching that the man Jesus was the Messiah, the Christ. And as he had done before going to Arabia, he was again proving from the Old Testament Scriptures that Jesus was the Son of God. The Jews surely must have remembered his preaching to them previously. And once again they were unable to refute what he was proving to them from the Scriptures. Instead of believing the gospel, however, they hardened their hearts against it and developed a growing hatred of Paul. They therefore wanted to stop Paul's teaching by doing away with him. So the Jews of the various synagogues formed a plot to kill Paul. This opposition to Paul's teaching and this plot to kill him was just the first of this kind of opposition and conspiracy and murderous plot that Paul would have to face throughout his apostolic career. In fact this was just the first of the many different kinds of fulfillments of Jesus' words that Paul would have to endure, for Jesus had said, "I will show him how many things he must suffer for the sake of my name."[2]

Luke's account in Acts 9:24, 25 then tells us:

> 24 But their plot became known to Saul. And they even kept watching the gates, not only by day but also by night, in order that they might kill him.
> 25 Then his disciples took him at night and let him down through a window in the city wall by lowering him in a reed basket.

In 2 Corinthians 11:32, 33 Paul adds some details of his own about his escape:

> 32 In Damascus the governor of King Aretas was guarding the city of the Damascenes to arrest me,
> 33 and through a window in a basket made of ropes I was let down through the city wall and escaped from his hands.

Luke's and Paul's reports complement one another. The Jews who formed the plot to kill Paul had also enlisted the assistance of the governor of Damascus to help them in apprehending Paul. Who the governor was is unknown. One opinion has been that he was an Arabian Sheikh. He ruled over Damascus at that time in behalf of King Aretas. Aretas was king of Petra, the mercantile metropolis in the desert of that part of Arabia known as Stony Arabia. It seems that the Jews must have convinced the governor that Paul was some sort of an agitator and troublemaker who was stirring up civil unrest among the many Jewish inhabitants of the city. For the sake of law and order they insisted Paul must be arrested. The governor then had the city gates watched day and night to prevent Paul's escape. The Jewish plotters eagerly joined in watching those city gates.

But as Luke reported, Paul somehow became aware of the plot against him. Disciples of Paul's, who must have been Jewish converts who had believed the gospel of Jesus that Paul was preaching, came to Paul's aid. Piecing Luke's and Paul's accounts together, it is apparent that Paul's disciples made ropes out of reeds that they twisted together, with which they wove a basket and a sturdy rope long enough to lower Paul down out of the window to the ground below. The window in that part of the wall was obviously left unguarded, either because the window was so high up that no one thought it could be used as an escape route, or because no one thought of guarding it. So it was that the proud, strong-willed, forceful, commanding Paul, who had come to Damascus to persecute the disciples of Jesus, was humbled to fleeing from Damascus in the dark to escape being persecuted himself and killed as a disciple of Jesus. This was the first of the numerous experiences he would have of which he wrote in 2 Corinthians 11:26: ". . . in dangers from my countrymen, in dangers from Gentiles, in dangers in the city, . . ." In great strength he had come to Damascus, now in great weakness he had to leave it. Of such a weakness he would later write as a bondservant of Jesus Christ about twenty-one years later:

> 9 Most gladly, therefore, I will boast in my weaknesses, in order that the power of Christ may rest upon me.
>
> 10 Accordingly I take pleasure in weaknesses, in insults, in

calamities, in persecutions and extreme afflictions for Christ's sake; for whenever I am weak, then I am strong. (2 Corinthians 12:9, 10)

Paul's First Visit To Jerusalem After His Conversion Paul's Age: 35 Date: About Late A.D. 35

Once outside the Damascus' wall Paul fled on foot. He had not gone to Jerusalem since he had left it three years earlier. Now he set his mind upon going aback, not as the persecutor of Jesus' name and Church that he had been but as the preacher of Jesus' name that he was then. He was alone, on foot, and a fugitive from the local authority. He had about one hundred and forty miles to walk. It would have taken him about seven days to walk that distance. We can only wonder if he had managed to bring enough food and water with him to sustain him for the journey, or, if he had been able to buy provisions in towns along the way. Nothing is told to us about how he survived for nearly a week.

Paul's escape from Damascus and his flight to Jerusalem took place about the latter part of A.D. 35. Luke then informs us in Acts 9:26 & 27:

> 26 Now when Paul arrived in Jerusalem, he began to try to associate with the disciples, but they all continued to be afraid of him, because they did not believe he was a disciple.
>
> 27 Then Barnabas took hold of him and brought him to the apostles, and related to them how he had seen the Lord on the road and that the Lord had spoken to him, and how in Damascus he had spoken fearlessly in the name of Jesus.

Upon his arrival in Jerusalem Paul attempted to associate with the disciples of Jesus in the church of Jerusalem, but to no avail. They were afraid of him. Either they had not heard any bits of news about Paul's conversion in Damascus and his following activities of preaching the gospel of Jesus, or if they had heard them, they had refused to believe them. The memories of his persecution of the Church and the atrocities he had carried out against the Jewish Christians in Jerusalem still lived vividly in their memories. And so, Paul was being shut out from associating with the Jewish Christians in Jerusalem, because they did not believe he had become a disciple of Jesus. They remained afraid that he was merely trying to spy out who currently were the believers in Jesus, so he might then persecute, arrest, and execute them also.

Paul continued to experience such a cold reception and rejection until Barnabas saw what Paul was experiencing. Then Barnabas brought him to the apostles who were present at the time in Jerusalem and introduced him to them. Luke had previously introduced the man Barnabas in Acts 4:36, 37 because of the important part Barnabas played in establishing the infant apostolic Church of Christ Jesus, and because Barnabas became Paul's fellow worker in Antioch and on Paul's first missionary journey. In Acts 4:36, 37 Barnabas was introduced as an example of the charitable giving that was being done in that early Apostolic Church in Jerusalem. In that introduction Luke provides us with the following details about Barnabas:

> 36 Now Joseph, a Levite, and a Cyprian by nationality, who was called Barnabas by the apostles (which when translated means 'Son of Encouragement,')
>
> 37 who owned a field, sold it, and brought the money and placed it at the feet of the apostles.

Barnabas' Jewish name was Joseph, but the apostles gave him the name Barnabas, which meant "Son of Encouragement", because that was what he did so well. Among the Jewish Christians he was an encourager. He was born in Cyprus of a Jewish family of the priestly tribe of Levi. He was clearly a man of some wealth amid all the very poor Jewish Christians in Jerusalem and its surrounding area. This is evident from the fact that he had owned a field that he sold in order to give the funds from the sale to the apostles for the care of the poor. In this way he became well known to the apostles and became highly respected in the early church of Jerusalem.

Luke informs us, "Then Barnabas took hold of him and brought him to the apostles."[3] When Barnabas brought Paul to the apostles and introduced him to them, they were therefore willing to listen to what Barnabas had to say. He related to them that Paul had seen the Lord Jesus on the road to Damascus, at that time Jesus had spoken to him, and afterwards Paul had been speaking fearlessly in the name of Jesus and preaching the gospel. Now how Barnabas had come into possession of all this detailed information about Paul is unknown. Being respected among the apostles as he was, he surely would not have told them this information about Paul unless he knew for a fact that what he was telling them was the truth.

Since the communication of information coming from Damascus to Jerusalem at that time seems to have been quite sketchy and sparse, and since the information Barnabas related to the apostles was so detailed by comparison, this writer tends to think that perhaps Barnabas was in Damascus himself at the time of Paul's conversion, that he was then present with the disciples of Damascus when Ananias introduced Paul to them and Paul then spent some days with them, and that Barnabas was in Damascus when Paul had begun preaching the name of Jesus to the Jews in the city's synagogues. It seems that Barnabas' having been an eyewitness to the facts he presented to the apostles must be held as a possible explanation for how he came into possession of the details he told to the apostles. But then this explanation raises another question that begs for an explanation: Why didn't Barnabas report this information to the apostles and to the church in Jerusalem previously? Maybe he did not report it before because he himself had only recently returned to Jerusalem from Damascus. That is a possibility.

Paul himself provides us with a few more details about this first visit of his to Jerusalem after his conversion and which of the apostles he then saw. In Galatians 1:18, 19 he wrote:

18 Then after three years I went up to Jerusalem to visit Cephas, and I remained with him for fifteen days;

19 but I did not see another one of the apostles, only James the brother of the Lord.

Paul's flight from Damascus to Jerusalem took place three years after he had left Jerusalem and proceeded to Damascus to persecute the disciples of Jesus. When he returned to Jerusalem for the first time after his conversion, he remained there only fifteen days. During that time the two apostles Peter and Paul met for the first time, and Peter welcomed Paul as his houseguest. What a blessing it would have been, and how enlightening it would have been, to have been able to stand off to the side and just listen to Peter and Paul, who had just met and were becoming acquainted, talk. What interesting and spiritually uplifting things they may have discussed about the crucified, risen, and ascended Lord Jesus Christ and his Church! And surely their conversation would have come around to Paul's experience of seeing Jesus on the road outside of Damascus three years earlier and his resulting conversion. In that context the subject of Paul's persecution of the church would surely have come up. There was Paul talking, who had been the chief persecutor of the followers of Jesus in Jerusalem, and there was Peter listening, who was one of those followers of Jesus who had to live through the terror and the arrests and the executions of his fellow believers at the hands of Paul who was sitting across from him. Peter had once asked Jesus how many times he should forgive a brother who sinned against him – seven times? And Peter had heard Jesus tell him as many as – seventy-seven times! There, while sitting and listening to Paul talk about his misguided madness and crimes against Christians, Peter had the opportunity to practice what Jesus had preached to him – to forgive from the heart.[4] And Peter could see that the Lord Jesus Christ himself had forgiven Paul, so surely he should do likewise.

While Paul stayed and saw Peter, none of the other apostles were present in Jerusalem at the time. They all were most likely away from the city doing mission work in various places as Jesus' witnesses. The only other man of distinction and reputation whom Paul saw on this visit was James, who was the half-brother of the Lord Jesus. James was the head of the church in Jerusalem, which is evident in Acts 15 that reports the Apostolic Council Meeting in Jerusalem.

At first glance it looks like there is a contradiction between Luke's statement in Acts 9:27 that Barnabas brought Paul to the apostles and Paul's statement in Galatians 1:19 that while in Jerusalem outside of Cephas he saw none of the other apostles but only James, the brother of the Lord. If Paul said he saw only the apostle Peter and James, who was not one of Jesus' twelve apostles, how could Luke say that Barnabas brought Paul to the apostles, a plural meaning more than one. Though this may seem like a contradiction, it is not. The reason it is not is that the Greek word for "apostle" has a broad and a narrow meaning. In its broadest sense "apostle" means a delegate and a messenger, who has been commissioned and sent out as such. In its narrowest sense "apostle" means one of the Twelve whom Jesus called to be an apostle and Paul whom Jesus called later on the road to Damascus. In Acts 9:27 Luke used the term "apostle" in its broadest sense to include James, who was the head of the church in Jerusalem and its delegate and messenger, as well as the apostle Peter. Other verses can be found in which "apostle" is used in this broadest sense also: Acts 14:14 names Barnabas as an apostle with Paul; Philippians 2:25 names Epaphroditus as an "apostle" in the Greek text which is translated "messenger"; and in 2 Corinthians 8:23 the brothers are called in the Greek text "apostles" which is translated "delegates".

After Barnabas introduced Paul to the apostles, meaning Peter and James, they then vouched for Paul among the Christians in Jerusalem that he was truly a disciple and an apostle of Jesus Christ. Luke then reports in Acts 9:28-30:

> 28 And (Paul) was with them, going in and out among them in Jerusalem, while speaking fearlessly in the name of the Lord.
>
> 29 And he not only kept speaking but also kept debating with the Greek-speaking Jews. Then they began attempting to kill him.

30 But when the brothers learned of this, they brought him down to Caesarea and sent him away to Tarsus.

Once the apostles Peter and James had vouched for Paul, he was able to mingle with the Christians in Jerusalem. While doing so he also was speaking fearlessly in the name of the Lord Jesus. He obviously would have been doing so among the Jewish Christians. But it is apparent that he must have also started going around speaking fearlessly to the Jews in the city at their synagogues. There in Jerusalem the Greek-speaking, Hellenistic Jews refused to accept what Paul was saying about Jesus. They objected to his gospel message and argued with him. Paul did not back down. He debated with them on the basis of what the Old Testament Scriptures stated. They could not refute Paul's words of wisdom from the Scriptures nor the Holy Spirit who was speaking through him. Frustrated that they could not out-debate Paul and persuade him to abandon his teaching about Jesus, they turned to violence as a means to put an end to Paul's speaking. They began attempting to kill him. As Paul himself had done in his misguided zeal for God while persecuting the church, they were now fulfilling the words of Jesus and Paul was on the receiving end of their misguided zeal. Paul found himself experiencing, as he had previously in Damascus, the truth of what his Lord Jesus had said: "They will expel you from the synagogue; why, an hour is coming when everyone who kills you shall think he is offering a religious service to God!"[5]

Twenty-two years into the future about June 1st A.D. 57 when addressing the Jewish rioters who had mobbed him, Paul himself related what happened next:

17 Now it happened to me when I returned to Jerusalem and while I was praying in the temple that I fell into a trance

18 and saw (Jesus) saying to me, "Hurry and come out of Jerusalem quickly, because they will not accept your testimony about me!"

19 And I said, "Lord, they themselves know that in one synagogue

after another I indeed used to imprison and beat those who were believing in you.

20 And when the blood of your witness Stephen was being shed, indeed I myself was standing by and giving my approval and guarding the garments of those who were killing him."

21 And he said to me, "Go, because I will send you far away to the Gentiles." (Acts 22:17-21)

After Jesus' ordering him to get out of Jerusalem immediately, Paul probably recalled how three years earlier frustrated Jewish men had plotted against Stephen for speaking fearlessly about Jesus, and Stephen ended up being stoned to death. Paul would have recalled that, because he himself had been an accomplice to Stephen's murder. Now the table had been turned; he himself was the man who had been speaking fearlessly in the name of Jesus, and he was the one in danger of being killed.

Now when Paul's fellow Christians in Jerusalem came to know about the plot of those Jews to kill Paul, they brought him down to Caesarea and sent him away to Tarsus where he would be safe. In Caesarea he might have boarded a ship and traveled by sea to Tarsus rather than walking on the road that followed the shoreline around the northeastern tip of the Mediterranean Sea.

Now all of what has just been described – Barnabas' introducing Paul to Peter and James, Paul's then meeting Peter for the first time and staying with him, Paul's mingling with the Christians in Jerusalem, Paul's speaking in the synagogues and debating with the Hellenistic Jews, their attempting to kill him – all of this happened within just the short space of fifteen days.

---

1. Luther, Martin; A Commentary on St. Paul's Epistle to the Galatians; Theodore Graebner, translator; Second Edition; Zondervan Publishing House; Grand Rapids, Michigan; no date indicated; p. 42
2. Acts 9:16
3. Acts 9:27
4. Matthew 18:21, 22, 35
5. John 16:2

8

PAUL IN TARSUS, SYRIA, AND CILICIA; PAUL'S VISION OF HEAVEN

PAUL'S AGE: 35-43 DATE: LATE A.D. 35 TO THE FALL OF A.D. 43

In This Chapter: Report On The Church In Judea, Galilee, And Samaria; The Uncertainties Of Paul's Ministry In Tarsus, Syria, And Cilicia; The Dating Of Paul's Ministry In Tarsus, Syria, And Cilicia; Geography And Historical Background Of The Province of Cilicia; Historical Background Of The City Of Tarsus; Paul's Mission Field In Syria And Cilicia; Paul's Mission Methodology In Cilicia And How The Gospel Was Received; Paul's Vision Of Heaven

---

A Report On The Church In Judea, Galilee, And Samaria

Both Paul and Luke provide short reports about the state of the Church in Judea, Galilee, and Samaria after Paul left Jerusalem and fled to Tarsus. Paul reports in Galatians 1:22-24:

> 22 And I continued to be unknown in person to the churches of Judea which were in Christ,
>
> 23 and they only kept hearing, "The man who was formerly persecuting us is now preaching the good news about the faith that he was formerly trying to destroy!"

24 And they continued praising God because of me.

Luke also reports in Acts 9:31

Consequently the church throughout all of Judea and Galilee and Samaria continued to have peace. While being built up and proceeding in the fear of the Lord and in the comfort of the Holy Spirit, the church kept increasing.

The Uncertainties Of Paul's Ministry In Tarsus, Syria, And Cilicia

When Paul fell into the trance in the temple and Jesus spoke to him, Jesus said he was sending Paul far away to the Gentiles.[1] And Acts 9:30 says that Paul's fellow Christians then sent him off to Tarsus. So it is apparent that Jesus used Paul's fellow Christians to send Paul where he wanted Paul to go – far from Jerusalem to the Gentiles in Tarsus. That is where the Lord Jesus intended his bondservant Paul to start preaching the gospel. Jesus ordained that Paul's service as an apostle would not be in Jerusalem but among the Gentile cities and provinces of Rome starting in Syria and Cilicia.

Now Tarsus was in Cilicia. Cilicia's eastern border lay next to Syria and not very far from the Syrian city of Antioch. So Luke's report in Acts 9:30 that Paul was sent to Tarsus agrees with Paul's statement in Galatians 1:21 that when he left Jerusalem, he "went into the regions of Syria and Cilicia," which were located at the northeastern tip of the Mediterranean Sea.

Like Paul's trip to Arabia, this mission outreach to the city of Tarsus and the regions of Syria and Cilicia is shrouded in uncertainty. Neither its exact length of time nor the specific areas of Syria and Cilicia in which Paul worked are specified in Acts or in the Pauline letters. We do know with certainty, however, that Paul did mission work during this time and in these places. This is a known fact for three reasons. First, Jesus sent him to the Gentiles in Syria and Cilicia for one purpose – to preach the gospel to them. Second, the letter that the Apostolic Council would later send to resolve the issue of whether the Gentiles had to be circumcised and obey the Law of Moses was sent to the Gentiles in Syria and Cilicia as well as to the church in Antioch, Syria, where the controversy arose. It is obvious, then, that Paul had founded churches in Syria and Cilicia. Third, when Paul took Silas and began his second missionary journey, Acts 15:41 states, "And he went through Syria and Cilicia strengthening the churches." This statement, too, makes it very clear that Paul did mission work and founded new churches in Syria and Cilicia during this time of A.D. 35-43.

This evangelization of the city of Tarsus and the regions of Syria and Cilicia was the longest mission endeavor of Paul's apostolic ministry. It lasted eight years, as compared to about the three years of his first missionary journey to Galatia, the three years of his second missionary journey through Galatia into Greece, and the three years of his third missionary journey in Ephesus. For eight years Paul worked in Syria and Cilicia and yet Luke does not even mention it. We know of it only because of Paul's brief report of it in just ten words in the Greek text of Galatians 1:21, which are translated, "Afterwards I went into the regions of Syria and Cilicia."

This should not trouble us, however. To put this into its proper perspective, we should realize that if the Holy Spirit had not inspired Luke and Paul to write what they did, we would never have heard of or known anything about such Roman provinces as Galatia, Asia, Macedonia and Achaia either, or about such cities as Lystra, Iconium, Philippi, Thessalonica, Berea, and Ephesus. It was just not according to the Holy Spirit's wisdom to provide us with the details of these eight years of Paul's labor in Syria and Cilicia, just as the Holy Spirit did not choose to record the ministries of Thomas or the other original apostles except for what is written about Peter in the Book of Acts and his first letter.

The Dating Of Paul's Ministry In Tarsus, Syria, And Cilicia

Since the length of Paul's evangelization of Syria and Cilicia is not specifically stated by Luke or Paul, its length is a conjectural conclusion for all biographers, including this writer. This is due to a lack of a reference by Luke or Paul to a definite event or place or person in this period of Paul's life that can be tied to a specific historical date. The only historical person mentioned that could be considered as a possible link to dating this time of Paul's life and ministry in Syria and Cilicia is Aretas, king of Arabia Petra. He reigned from 9 B.C. to A.D.39 when he died, a span of 48 years. Paul mentioned him in 2 Corinthians 11:32 in connection with his escape from Damascus. Aretas was the father-in-law of Herod the Tetrach. When Herod decided to divorce Aretas' daughter in order to marry his brother Philip's wife Herodias, Aretas declared war on Herod and defeated Herod's army in A.D. 36. It has been supposed that Aretas might then have held Damascus for a brief period of time. But just when Aretas held Damascus is uncertain. And Paul's escape from Damascus cannot be tied with certainty to Aretas' defeat of Herod's army in A.D. 36 either. These things being the case, all that can be said for certain is that Paul's escape from Damascus had to have happened before A.D. 39 while Aretas was still alive.

Yet Conybeare and Howson in their Pauline biography considered the year A.D. 36 a key date. They did say, however,

> "Any attempt to make this (Paul's) escape from Damascus a fixed point of absolute chronology will be unsuccessful; but, from what has been said, it may fairly be collected, that Saul's journey from Jerusalem to Damascus took place not far from that year which saw the death of Tiberias and the accession of Caligula" (which year was A.D. 37).[2]

The reader may wonder why the above date of A.D. 36 as the date when Aretas was in control of Damascus after defeating Herod's army had been considered so important to Conybeare and Howson. The reason is this: then the date of Paul's conversion could be dated as about A.D. 36, and his return to Jerusalem after three years could be dated around A.D. 39, and likewise Paul's being sent off to Tarsus to begin his mission work in Syria and Cilicia could then be said to have started about A.D. 39. And his mission work with his headquarters in Tarsus could then be said to have extended from A.D. 39-44 (the year of Herod's death), at which time Conybeare and Howson said Barnabas then went to Tarsus to get Paul and bring him to work in Antioch. In this manner they set the date and length of five years for Paul's work in Syria and Cilicia.

In support of that above dating Conybeare and Howson also calculated the year of A.D. 36 as the year for Paul's conversion. Now they calculated the year of A.D. 36 as the year of Paul's conversion by figuring that according to Galatians 2:1 the Apostolic Council of A.D. 50 convened fourteen years after Paul's conversion, and that that period of fourteen years included the three years from Paul's conversion to his first return to Jerusalem for fifteen days.[3] This writer disagrees with their date of A.D. 36, however, as the year of Paul's conversion. As explained near the end of Chapter 2, the information attributed to Chrysostom and the information provided by Paul both indicate that Paul's conversion occurred in A.D. 33. The date of A.D. 33, then, sets the date for Paul's escape from Damascus as A.D. 35, using the Judaic method of keeping time that part of a year is counted as a whole year.

Having explained all the preceding information regarding the dating of Paul's conversion in A.D. 33 and his escape from Damascus in A.D. 35, it can now be said that Paul's first visit to Jerusalem for fifteen days clearly happened in A.D. 35, after which he was immediately sent off to Tarsus in the regions of Syria and Cilicia to begin his apostolic ministry there. So, his period of mission work in those places lasted for eight years from late A.D. 35 to when Barnabas came to get him to work for a year in Antioch starting in the fall of A.D. 43. And this period of eight years is definitely the longest period of Paul's work in any one area. Those eight years consists of the seven full years of A.D. 36 to 42 plus the last few months of A.D. 35 and the first eight months of A.D. 43, which together make up the eighth year.

The Geography And Historical background Of The Province of Cilicia

Paul stated that he went into the regions of Syria and Cilicia. Going back to the time of the Persians, due to the Taurus mountain range Cilicia was considered to have a geographical affinity with Syria to its east more so than with Asia Minor to its west and north. Syria and Cilicia were looked upon as a political unit and the names "Syria and Cilicia" in the order of their importance had become a geographical term for that region.[4] At the time of Paul Cilicia was a part of the united Roman province of Syria-Cilicia.[5]

Cilicia was surrounded by a fortress of natural barriers with the Taurus Mountains to its north and the Mediterranean Sea to the south. Through those mountains was the Cilician Gate, a pass that connected the flat plain of Cilicia with Cappadocia in the north.

Geographically Cilicia consisted of two unlike regions. The inaccessible western region was called "Rough Cilicia" that was also known as Cilicia Tracheia.[6] It consisted of branches of Mount Taurus that extended down to the Mediterranean Sea. Inland its inhabitants were notorious robbers and bandits. The eastern region was called "Flat Cilicia" that was also known as Cilicia Pedias.[7] It was a highly fertile plain dominated by three rivers – the Cydnus, the Sarus, and the Pyramis.[8]

In the second millennium B.C. the two regions of Cilicia were known as Kizzuwatna, which was a part of the Hittite Empire,[9] [10] and ruled by a prince from the Hittite family, who was called "priest". Hittite records state the two main cities on the plain of Flat Cilicia were Tarsa (Tarsus) and Adanija (Adana).[11] After the fall of the Hittite Empire around 1,190 B.C., Cilicia was a part of a Neo-Hittite kingdom named Tarhuntassa that had its capital in Pamphylia. The Assyrians discovered the region in the ninth century B.C., which was near the time of the ministries of Elijah and Elisha in the Divided Kingdom of Israel. The Assyrians called the flat plain "Qu'e" and the western rough region Hilakku, from which the name Cilicia was first derived. After the demise of the Assyrians, a new Greek kingdom arose with its capital at Tarsus and the name given to the region was Cilicia. Then around 545 B.C. Cyrus the Great of Persia annexed Cilicia. That was six years before Cyrus issued his decree in 539 B.C. to allow the first exiles from Judah in the Babylonian captivity to return to Jerusalem. In 333 B.C. Alexander the Great defeated the Persians and gained control of Cilicia for the Greeks. After the death of Alexander the Great in 323 B.C. two of his generals divided Cilicia; Ptolemy I Soter who ruled Egypt took control of the coastal region and Seleucus I Nicator who ruled Syria took possession of the interior. But by around 110 B.C. the power of the Seleucids over the interior of Rough Cilicia was weakening. The inhabitants of Rough Cilicia then began their pirating activities. The Mediterranean coastline was full of hiding places for the pirates.[12] Both the Seleucids and the Romans took some indecisive actions against them but nothing more, for both the economies of the Seleucids and the Romans needed the slaves that the Rough Cilician pirates were selling to them.[13] [14]The pirates dominated the area from about 133-67 B.C. until Pompey the Great defeated them[15] and settled those whom he thought were worthy of being saved in Soli, which he renamed after himself Pompeiopolis.[16] The pirates' seafaring presence has been substantiated by the archaeological findings of moorings, buildings, stairs, defensive walls, fortresses, submerged columns, the remains of anchors, and shipping jars.[17] Cilicia came under Roman rule in 64 B.C.[18] The Roman general Mark Anthony in 36 B.C. gave Cleopatra VII Cilicia as a gift.[19] [20] [21]

As for exports Cilicia was known for its abundance of grains raised in its fertile plains, as well as for its iron and silver ores.[22] From around 1990 reports have been made about Turkey's ancient mining industries of copper and tin that were the essential metals needed to produce bronze during the Bronze Age.[23] Sixty miles north of Tarsus in the Taurus Mountains an ancient tin mine dating back to 2,870 B.C.[24] [25] was discovered. Another important product of Cilicia was its goats-hair cloth, called Cilicium, which was used to make tents. Paul would have used that cloth in his trade as a tent-maker.[26]

The Historical Background Of The City Of Tarsus

The city of Tarsus was located in Flat Cilicia, also known as Cilicia Pedias, near the western portion of the plain where the cold, swift waters of the Cydnus River[27] flowed down to the sea from the melting snows up in the Taurus Mountains. The river flowed through the middle of the city near a gymnasium in which the young men worked out.[28] The city was located about twelve miles upstream from the shores of the Mediterranean Sea. The river was navigable for shallow craft up to Tarsus. About six miles downstream from Tarsus the river broadened out into a good-sized lake called Rhegma. The lake provided safe anchorage for ships and was partly fringed with quays and dockyards.[29] The ancient geographer and historian Strabo (born c. 63 B.C.; died 23 A.D.) also stated that at that lake were ancient arsenals and that it was a naval base for Tarsus.[30]

Tarsus was a crossroads for trade by sea and by land that made the city an important, prosperous center of commerce. The River Cydnus connected it to its seaport to the south, as did a road. That road from the port then connected with the two main roads that intersected at Tarsus. The one road followed along the shoreline of the Mediterranean and through such cities to the east of Tarsus as Mopsuetia and Adana, then around the northeastern tip of the Mediterranean and south to Antioch, Syria, then down to Jerusalem and into Egypt. That same road went southwest from Tarsus along the Mediterranean to Corycus, Cilician Seleucia, cities in Pamphylia, and on into western Asia Minor. The second intersecting main road at Tarsus proceeded north through the valleys that made up the Cilician Gates to roads branching northeast into Cappadocia or northwest through northern Galatia and then Bithynia to Byzantium in Thrace and southern Europe. Or, there were branches of that second main road to the north that turned eastward into Armenia. This information is based on David H. French's Itinerarium Butdalenise east and west maps.[31]

The ancient history of Tarsus parallels that of the province of Cilicia noted above. A devastating tragedy in the city's history occurred in the twelfth century B.C. when the Sea Peoples destroyed it. The Sea Peoples were a rather mysterious people as far as their origins. They comprised a confederacy of naval raiders who attacked the coastal cities of the Mediterranean.[32] Some centuries after Tarsus had been destroyed the Greeks resettled the city.[33]

According to ancient Greek legend the city of Tarsus was founded by Perseus. The Assyrian king Shalmaneser III captured the city in 833 B.C. and later king Sennacrerib of Assyria recaptured it in 698 B.C. After the Persians took control of the city it was the capital of their client kingdom of Cilicia. Then came Alexander the Great in 333 B.C. and saved the city from being set ablaze by the Persians. The Greek Seleucid kings who succeeded Alexander renamed the city "Antioch-on-the-Cydnus" according to coins dated as 1171 B.C.[34] at the time of Antiochus Epiphanes IV. About 170 B.C. he gave Tarsus a reorganized constitution as a free city.[35] In 83 B.C. the city came under the control of Tigranes I, king of Armenia, but as a result of Pompey the Great's victories the city became subject to Roman rule in 64 B.C. The Romans made it a free city.[36] Tarsus was given that status as a reward for its support and sacrifices during the Roman civil wars. As a free city Tarsus could have its own laws, customs, and officials. And it was free from the occupation of Roman forces and being under their constant guard.[37] Augustus also gave Tarsus an exemption from imperial taxation. He entrusted the administration of Tarsus to his former instructor Athenodorus, a Stoic philosopher and native of Tarsus by birth.[38]

Besides being the capital of the Roman province of Cilicia, it was also an important center of philosophy and literature that rivaled the cities of Athens and Alexandria. Strabo said that the residents of Tarsus devoted themselves eagerly both to philosophy and education in general so that they surpassed Athens and Alexandria and any other place that could be named that had schools and lectures of philosophers. Strabo also stated that Tarsus had many schools of rhetoric. Furthermore, what was so different about the university at Tarsus was that its student body was made up only of residents of Tarsus. The university had no foreign students. But when the resident students of Tarsus completed their education there, they then moved away to other cities and few ever returned.[39] Tarsus was a Greek city in character where Greek was spoken and Greek literature was cultivated. It had previously been the home of some famous Stoic philosophers in the Roman Empire, namely Antipater, Archedemus, Athenodorus who had tutored Augustus, and Nestor, who tutored Marcellus the nephew of Augustus.[40] As far as the paganism of the city, its chief deity was Sandon throughout most of its established history up to the third century A.D. and the beginning of the Christian era.[41]

In the course of the city's history the footsteps of some very famous, powerful, historical personages crossed its path and walked its streets. Cicero resided in Tarsus while serving as the proconsul of Cilicia in 51-50 B.C. Julius Caesar visited the city in 47 B.C. Mark Antony resided there for a time when he governed Rome's eastern provinces after 42 B.C.[42] Cleopatra then also came to Tarsus of Cilicia.[43] And the "Sea Gate" of Tarsus, that is also known as "The Gate Of Cleopatra", has her name because Cleopatra VII, Queen of Egypt, walked through it.[44] Plutarch, the first century A.D. Greek biographer, described the spectacle that Cleopatra put on in 41 B.C. when she came to Mark Antony in Tarsus to face charges for having financed Cassius in Cassius' and Brutus' civil war against Mark Antony and Octavian.[45] Plutarch reported that Cleopatra sailed up the Cydnus River dressed as the pagan goddess Aphrodite (Venus) in a barge with a golden poop deck, was powered by rowers with silver oars, and was rigged with purple sails. The sound of the music of a flute accompanied with pipes and flutes was heard while Cleopatra reclined beneath a canopy spangled with gold and had boys fanning her. Nearby the fairest maidens attired as the mythological sea nymphs and the daughters of Zeus were stationed at the rudder-sweeps and reefing-ropes. To add to this spectacle the fragrance of countless offerings of incense drifted from the barge and floated over both riverbanks, filling the nostrils of the spectators who were following along on each side of the river.[46] Upon her arrival she walked through the Sea Gate where she met Mark Antony.[47] [48] During the time that followed Tarsus then became the scene of their famous feasts[49] and romance.

And then came the Lord Jesus Christ's bondservant who graced the streets of Tarsus – the apostle Paul. Tarsus was his hometown in which he maintained his Tarsian citizenship throughout his life.[50] After he returned home to Tarsus and to its familiar structures and surroundings in late A.D. 35, he surely began the work for which his Master Jesus had sent him there – to preach the gospel, especially to the Gentiles. And it was that work that Paul did as the bondservant of the Lord Jesus Christ that far surpassed in lasting importance the accomplishments of those famous, powerful personages mentioned above. Unbeknown to them the One True God of heaven and earth, Paul's God whom he served, had used them to help bring about the favorable conditions and time for the coming of Jesus Christ and his bondservant Paul. But when the accomplishments of those famed personages had served that divine purpose, they themselves and the glory of their kingdoms waned and faded into history. But the achievements and the writings of the apostle Paul in and for the kingdom of Christ still endure and will endure for all eternity. Truly the apostle Paul was the most important, famous personage to have crossed the path of Tarsus and to have walked its streets.

Paul's Mission Field In Syria And Cilicia

Paul had a rich mission field in the regions of Syria and Cilicia. He maintained Tarsus as the headquarters for his mission outreach. It appears that he limited his field of endeavor to the extreme northern area of Syria, north of the city of Antioch. He did not go as far south as Antioch in northern Syria. We know this from the fact that Antioch was evangelized by others, as Luke reports in Acts 11:19-22, which will be discussed in Chapter 9.

There was a Jewish population in the province of Cilicia. How big of a Jewish population is unknown. Paul's hometown of Tarsus was one example of such a population in Cilicia. Until 2012, however, no ancient synagogues had ever been located or excavated in Cilicia. Then in the July/August issue of the <u>Biblical Archaeology Review</u> the article "Turkey's Unexcavated Synagogues" was published. It stated two unexcavated synagogues had been found in Cilicia; one at the ancient coastal harbor city of Korykos, or Corycus, about seventy-five miles southwest of Tarsus, and the other at the site now known only by its modern name of Catioren. Its ancient name is still unknown.[51] These Jewish settlements as well as others that no doubt existed in Cilicia comprised one part of Paul's mission field in that province.

Within the region of Cilicia were a number of Greek/Roman Gentile cities to which Paul could have carried the gospel during the course of his eight years of work there. For example, traveling from the east of Cilicia to its west, one comes first to the city of Issus. It was almost on the border of Cilicia and Syria up at the northeastern most tip of the Mediterranean Sea. It was located on a strategic bottleneck of coastal plain between the inland mountains and the sea. It was the location of the Battle of Issus in 333 B.C. at which Alexander the Great defeated the Persian army of Darius II. The remains of a Roman aqueduct are still visible near the city. Moving to the west about sixty miles was the city of Adana. It was brought under Roman rule by Pompey the Great. About thirty miles further west was the city of Tarsus, which was the metropolis and capital of Cilicia. Then about thirty miles southwest of Tarsus was the port city of Pompeiopolis that was formerly called Soli. It dates back to about 1,000 B.C. In it archaeologists have unearthed various gods of its pagan inhabitants.[52] Strabo names quite a few towns and cities in his geographical discussion of Cilicia.[53] What is more, David H. French's provincial map of the Roman road-network of Asia Minor shows numerous cities to which Paul could have traveled in Cilicia on a number of Roman roads surely to have been earthen "trackways".[54] In an address to the Jews King Herod Agrippa II remarked around A.D. 55 and twelve years after Paul completed his work in Cilicia that there were five hundred cities in Asia.[55] About thirty-five to forty years after the time of Paul's mission work in Cilicia, it has been said that forty-seven cities were in existence in Cilicia when Vespasian united the province in A.D. 72.[56] So there were plenty of cities in Cilicia where Paul could have preached the gospel of Christ.

In addition to the field of Jews and Gentiles in Cilicia Paul also had a mission field in the philosophical and educational center in Tarsus. There he would have been able to sow the seed of God's word among the heathen philosophers. He could have debated with them and witnessed to them. We do not know for certain that he did so, but since he readily did so in Athens in A.D. 51, it is not unreasonable to think that he would have done so in Tarsus as well.

Paul's Mission Methodology In Cilicia And How The Gospel Was Received

It is likely that Paul started his mission work in Cilicia as he had done in Damascus and Jerusalem – by going to the Jews in their synagogues. He is likely to have done that in his own home city of Tarsus first before going to other cities. He would have gone to the synagogue in Tarsus where he had attended services and school throughout his childhood. The Jewish members would have recognized him as the local boy who had gone off to Jerusalem to go to school, had grown up, and had come home. To those Jewish townspeople present, and to his own Pharisaic parents if they were still alive and to his sister if she was still living in Tarsus, he would have proclaimed that Jesus of Nazareth was the Christ who had been promised to come. But that experience for him was probably disappointing, because he and his message would not have been well received. For one thing he was the local boy who had just come home. As Jesus said to his own townspeople when he went home to Nazareth and they rejected him, "A prophet is not without honor except in his own hometown and household." Those words would have been true for Paul in his day as they are to this day. As Jesus' townspeople rejected him and went so far as to attempt to kill him by throwing him off the cliff, so Paul's townspeople were likely to have rejected him as well.

It is quite likely that throughout all the cities of Cilicia to which Paul went he gained a hearing from the Jews in Cilicia like he gained from the Jews in Damascus and Jerusalem. After hearing the gospel of God's grace and that Jesus was the promised Christ and Son of God, however, most of them were likely to have hardened their hearts against that message and wanted to silence the messenger. And when Paul turned to the Gentiles to share the gospel of Jesus with them, the Jews very likely stirred up the Gentiles to turn them against him. This no doubt happened to Paul in Cilicia as it repeatedly happened to him on all three of his later missionary journeys (ref. Acts 14:2, 5 &19; 17:5 & 13; 18:12; 19:18, 19).

A further reason to think Paul was opposed and resisted in Cilicia is because of what Paul would later write about himself in A.D. 56 to the Corinthians:

> ... in labors much harder, ... in floggings beyond measure, in danger of death often; five times I received at the hands of the Jews forty lashes minus one, ... I have been on journeys frequently, in dangers from rivers, in dangers from bandits, in dangers from my countrymen, in dangers from Gentiles, in dangers in the city...[57]

While Paul's saying he had been in hard labor was true of his three later missionary journeys, that hard labor could also be said to have been very true of Paul's eight years in Cilicia as well. To the best of this writer's knowledge during those years he was completely alone and on his own without even at least one traveling companion as he had on his later missionary journeys. Being on his own without support from anyone, he would have had to do mission work by day and labor by night to support himself – a very trying and tiring time to say the least! As for the dangers of rivers and bandits that he wrote about, western Cilicia was known as Rough Cilicia, rough in geography and rough in character because of the robbers and rebellious inhabitants who dwelled in that region. What especially suggests that Paul's eight years in Cilicia were dangerous and life threatening were the floggings beyond measure and the five whippings at the hands of the Jews. Those floggings and whippings do not fit into the time Paul spent in Damascus and then in Jerusalem for fifteen days, nor in any of Paul's three missionary journeys, nor in his being mobbed by angry Jews in Jerusalem at Pentecost, nor in the years of his imprisonments.

Indeed, his being mobbed in Jerusalem and his years of imprisonment did not occur until after Paul had written his Second Letter to the Corinthians in which he mentioned the floggings and whippings. So those occasions definitely are eliminated from consideration. The only remaining time and place, then, that those floggings and whippings can be fit into Paul's life is in his eight years of missionary work in Cilicia. All of these preceding things just mentioned would have made for a most difficult and dangerous time of carrying the gospel of Jesus to the Jews and the Gentiles in Cilicia, not to mention Syria.

Having experienced such times, it is reasonable to think that during those years in Cilicia and Syria Paul developed the missionary strategy that he would follow and implement in all of his three later missionary journeys. Paul saw first in Damascus and then during his brief visit to Jerusalem how the Jews had hardened their hearts against the gospel that he preached and plotted to kill him. But Paul would have continued to go to the synagogues to proclaim the gospel to the Jews in Cilicia because it was Jesus' will that he deliver the gospel to the Jews,[58] and because they were his brothers and fellow countrymen according to the flesh who were so dear to his heart.[59] The Jews, however, for the most part being the stiff-necked and uncircumcised in hearts and ears people that Stephen called them,[60] who always resisted the Holy Spirit, Paul surely saw very quickly in Cilicia also how they rejected the gospel of Jesus and turned against him. What, then, was he to do? What Jesus had appointed and called him to do – go to the Gentiles! And so Paul then did. In this way his missionary strategy was developed in obedience to Jesus' will to witness to the Jews, out of love for his fellow Jews, in accordance with Jesus' command that he go to the Gentiles, and through the school of rejection and hard knocks. Starting, then, in Cilicia, he would have gone to a synagogue in a city where he then would have preached the gospel of Jesus Christ. Some converts were likely to have been won over by the working of the Holy Spirit in that gospel he preached. But when the unbelieving Jews in the synagogue rejected the gospel and started speaking against it and himself, he would have taken the Jews who did believe with him and leave the synagogue to go elsewhere.

Then he would have turned to the Gentiles in the city, among whom the gospel would have won a favorable hearing and numerous converts. Then as happened later and elsewhere, upon seeing the success of Paul's preaching, the unbelieving Jews were provoked to jealousy and did everything they could to stir up the Gentiles against him and initiate a persecution against him. That persecution in Cilicia would have included the floggings and whippings mentioned above. Then he would have been forced to move on to the next city. But in this way a church had been founded, which he would continue to check on and to nourish and to build up as best as he could as often as he could. So, it came about that by the end of the eight years of hard work and sufferings in Cilicia a number of churches had been founded. How many is impossible to even guess.

Paul's Vision Of Heaven

Now it is possible that because of the intense opposition and persecution that Paul had been suffering beginning in Damascus and Jerusalem and continuing for years in Cilicia, and with much more still to come for years, that God stepped in to comfort and encourage his bondservant Paul. For in the year of A.D. 42 God gave Paul a vision he would never forget. Paul wrote about this vision in his Second Letter to the Corinthians in late A.D. 56. In 2 Corinthians 12:2-5 Paul wrote:

> 2 I know a man in Christ who fourteen years ago – whether in his body I do not know, or outside of his body I do not know, God knows – such a man as this was snatched away up to the third heaven.
>
> 3 And I know such a man as this – whether in his body or apart from his body I do not know, God knows –
>
> 4 that he was snatched away to paradise and heard unspeakable words, which are not lawful for a man to speak.
>
> 5 I will boast about such a man as this, but I will not boast about myself except in my weaknesses.

Paul felt compelled to write about this vision to silence the boasts of the so-called super apostles in Corinth who were discrediting his apostleship and ministry there. Much more will be said about this in connection with the discussion on Paul's third missionary journey. In describing this vision Paul spoke of himself in the third person, as though he were writing about someone other than himself. His having written of himself in this fashion reveals his humility that would not permit him to boast about himself as the false super apostles were accustomed to doing. From what Paul wrote in the above verses, fourteen years afterwards Paul still did not know whether his vision of heaven was an in-body or out-of-body experience. He still could not say whether he was taken bodily into heaven or just his spirit without his body entered into heaven. Such knowledge was beyond his human understanding. As Paul stated, only God knows. Whatever his state of being was at the time, he suddenly and unexpectedly was snatched away into heaven. Paul said it was the third heaven. By that expression "the third heaven" he meant it was not that heaven where the birds fly and the clouds float, nor the heaven from which the stars shine, but the heaven in which the all mighty and majestic God sits on his glorious throne and the holy angels worship him without end and the souls of the believers bask in the brilliance of God's presence. It was "paradise" as Paul also called it. "Paradise" was a Greek term for a beautiful garden. It came to mean "heaven" as a description taken from the Garden of Eden. God gave Paul a foretaste of what was awaiting him and all who believed the gospel of Jesus Christ.

In relating his vision of heaven Paul says nothing about what he saw but only about what he heard. What he heard were literally in the Greek text "unutterable utterances". Paul heard real words he could understand. But they were unspeakable words that he could not speak to others. In the last part of verse 4 above Paul explained the reason he could not speak those words to others. His explanation can be translated in two different ways, depending upon how the translator understands the Greek term "exon". The term has two meanings: lawful, or permissible, and possible, or to be able.[61] [62] One rendering of the verse, then, could be that Paul was not permitted or allowed to repeat to others the words that he heard. The other rendering could be that it was not humanly possible for Paul to repeat the words. This second rendering conveys the meaning that the words Paul heard and understood were heavenly, celestial words that were impossible to reproduce and speak in an earthly tongue.[63] [64] The words were spoken in a divine language that could not be expressed in human terms. Either way, the words that were spoken were intended only for Paul's encouragement, comfort, and understanding. That having been the case, nothing more can be said mow about what Paul heard.

---

1. Acts 22:21
2. Conybeare, W. J. & Howson, J. S.; The Life And Epistles of St. Paul; Wm. B. Eerdmans Publishing Company; Grand Rapids, Michigan; p. 68
3. Ibid., p. 835, Note "B"
4. Ibid., p. 87
5. Bruce, F. F.; The Acts Of The Apostles; William B. Eerdmans Publishing Company; Grand Rapids, Michigan; Third Revised And Enlarged Edition; 1990; p. 244
6. Ancient History Encyclopedia; Cilicia; https://www.ancient.eu/Cilicia
7. Ibid.
8. Livius.org; Articles on Ancient History – Cilicia;https://www.livius.org/articles/place/cilicia/
9. Livius.org; Articles on Ancient History – Cilicia; https://www.livius.org/articles/place/cilicia/
10. Bruce, F. F.; The Acts Of The Apostles; William B. Eerdmans Publishing Company; Grand Rapids, Michigan; Third Revised And Enlarged Edition; 1990; p. 244
11. Livius.org; Articles on Ancient History – Cilicia; https://www.livius.org/articles/place/cilicia/
12. Strabo; The Geography Of Strabo; Book XIV, Chapter 5, paragraph 6 on the webpage; published in Vol. V of the Loeb Classical Library edition, 1928;http://penelope.uchicago.edu/Thayer/E/Roman/Texts/Strabo/14E*.html http://penelope.uchicago.edu/Thayer/E/Roman/Texts/Strabo/14E*.html
13. Livius.org; Articles on Ancient History – Cilicia; https://www.livius.org/articles/place/cilicia/
14. Strabo; The Geography Of Strabo; Book XIV, Chapter 5, paragraph 2 on the webpage; published in Vol. V of the Loeb Classical Library edition, 1928; http://penelope.uchicago.edu/Thayer/E/Roman/Texts/Strabo/14E*.html*.html
15. Ancient History Encyclopedia; Cilicia; https://www.ancient.eu/Cilicia
16. Strabo; The Geography Of Strabo; Book XIV, Chapter 5, paragraph 8 on the webpage; published in Vol. V of the Loeb Classical Library edition, 1928; http://penelope.uchicago.edu/Thayer/E/Roman/Texts/Strabo/14E*.html
17. Ancient History Encyclopedia; Cilicia; https://www.ancient.eu/Cilicia
18. Livius.org; Articles on Ancient History – Cilicia; https://www.livius.org/articles/place/cilicia/

19. Ancient History Encyclopedia; Cilicia; https://www.ancient.eu/Cilicia
20. Wikipedia; Cilicia; https://en.wikipedia.org/wiki/cilicia (Roman province)
21. Antony, being so captivated by Cleopatra, likely gave her Cilicia because she had been pressuring him to do so, as she repeatedly pressured him to give her the dominions belonging to other rulers. She was a covetous woman who was never satisfied with what she had but was always demanding more. She even murdered her own brother to prevent his becoming king of Egypt and got Antony to kill her sister Arsinoe. See Josephus Antiquities 15.4.1
22. Ancient History Encyclopedia; Cilicia; https://www.ancient.eu/Cilicia
23. Kaptan, Ergun; Findings Related To The History Of Mining In Turkey; http://citeseerx.ist.psu.edu/viewdoc/download;jsessionid=3C8FC26699BFBA76A3A6BC0351F2F9B8?doi=10.1.1.535.6413&rep=rep1&type=pdf
24. New York Times, the Science page; Enduring Mystery Solved As Tin Is Found In Turkey; https://www.nytimes.com/1994/01/04/science/enduring-mystery-solved-as-tin-is-found-in-turkey.html
25. The University of Chicago Chronicle, January 6, 1994, Vol. 13. No. 9; Bronze Age Source Of Tin Discovered; chronicle.uchicage.edu/940106/tin.html
26. Wikipedia; Cilicia; https://en.wikipedia.org/wiki/cilicia
27. Strabo; The Geography Of Strabo; Book XIV, Chapter 5, paragraph 12 on the webpage; published in Vol. V of the Loeb Classical Library edition, 1928; http://penelope.uchicago.edu/Thayer/E/Roman/Texts/Strabo/14E*.html
28. Ibid.; paragraphs 10 & 12 on the webpage
29. Bible Hub; Tarsus; http://bibleatlas.org/tarsus.htm
30. Strabo; The Geography Of Strabo; Book XIV, Chapter 5, paragraph 10 on the webpage; published in Vol. V of the Loeb Classical Library edition, 1928; http://penelope.uchicago.edu/Thayer/E/Roman/Texts/Strabo/14E*.html
31. French, David H.; Roman Roads & Milestones Of Asia Minor Vol.4;http://biaa.ac.uk/ckeditor/filemanager/userfiles/electronic_publications/Vol.%204%20The%20Roads-Fasc.%204.1.pdf.16 & 17 http://biaa.ac.uk/ckeditor/filemanager/userfiles/electronic_publications/Vol.%204%20The%20Roads-Fasc.%204.1.pdf
32. Ancient History Encyclopedia; Sea Peoples; https://www.ancient.eu/Sea_Peoples/
33. Bruce, F. F.; The Acts Of The Apostles; William B. Eerdmans Publishing Company; Grand Rapids, Michigan; Third Revised And Enlarged Edition; 1990; p. 244
34. Ibid.; p. 244
35. Bruce, F. F.; New Testament History; Doubleday; New York, London, Toronto, Sydney, Auckland; 1969; p. 235
36. Bruce, F. F.; The Acts Of The Apostles; William B. Eerdmans Publishing Company; Grand Rapids, Michigan; Third Revised And Enlarged Edition; 1990; p. 245
37. Ancient Pages; Biblical City Of Tarsus: Excavations Reveal Its Secrets From Paul The Apostle's Times; http://www.ancientpages.com/2016/01/04/biblical-city-of-taurus-excavations-reveal-its-secrets-from-paul-the-apostles-times/
38. Bruce, F. F.; The Acts Of The Apostles; William B. Eerdmans Publishing Company; Grand Rapids, Michigan; Third Revised And Enlarged Edition; 1990; p. 245
39. Strabo; The Geography Of Strabo; Book XIV, Chapter 5, paragraph 13 on the webpage; published in Vol. V of the Loeb Classical Library edition, 1928; http://penelope.uchicago.edu/Thayer/E/Roman/Texts/Strabo/14E*.html
40. Strabo; The Geography Of Strabo; Book XIV, Chapter 5, paragraph 14 on the

webpage; published in Vol. V of the Loeb Classical Library edition, 1928; http://penelope.uchicago.edu/Thayer/E/Roman/Texts/Strabo/14E*.html

41. GraecoMuse; Archaeological Sites of Cilicia, Anatolia; Part 1; An Archaeological Blog, May 2012; https://graecomuse.wordpress.com/2012/05/08/ancient-sites-of-cilicia-anatolia-part-1/
42. Ancient History Encyclopedia, Mark Antony; https://www.ancient.eu/Mark_Antony/
43. Josephus Antiquities 14.13.1; Also Encyclopedia of World Biography, Mark Antony Biography; https://www.notablebiographies.com/Lo-Ma/Mark-Antony.html
44. Ancient Pages; Biblical City Of Tarsus: Excavations Reveal Its Secrets From Paul The Apostle's Times; http://www.ancientpages.com/2016/01/04/biblical-city-of-taurus-excavations-reveal-its-secrets-from-paul-the-apostles-times/
45. Plutarch; The Parallel Lives, paragraph 25; Published in Vol. IX of the Loeb Classical Library edition 1920; http://penelope.uchicago.edu/Thayer/e/roman/texts/plutarch/lives/antony*.html
46. Plutarch; The Parallel Lives, paragraph 26; Published in Vol. IX of the Loeb Classical Library edition 1920; http://penelope.uchicago.edu/Thayer/e/roman/texts/plutarch/lives/antony*.html
47. Ancient Pages; Biblical City Of Tarsus: Excavations Reveal Its Secrets From Paul The Apostle's Times; http://www.ancientpages.com/2016/01/04/biblical-city-of-taurus-excavations-reveal-its-secrets-from-paul-the-apostles-times/
48. Turkish Archaeological News; Cleopatra's Gate In Tarsus; https://turkisharchaeonews.net/object/cleopatras-gate-tarsus
49. Wikipedia; Tarsus, Mersin; https://en.wikipedia.org/wiki/Tarsus,_Mersin
50. Acts 22:3
51. Biblical archaeology Society, The Bible History Daily website; The Lost Sites Of Ancient Cilicia; https://www.biblicalarchaeology.org/daily/biblical-sites-places/biblical-archaeology-sites/the-lost-sites-of-ancient-cilicia/
52. Information about these four cities is readily available on the Internet, so no further documentation is required here.
53. Strabo; The Geography Of Strabo; Book XIV, Chapter 5; published in Vol.www.example.com V of the Loeb Classical Library edition, 1928; http://penelope.uchicago.edu/Thayer/E/Roman/Texts/Strabo/14E*.html
54. French, David H.; Roman Roads & Milestones Of Asia Minor Vol.4;www.example.com p. 83 http://biaa.ac.uk/ckeditor/filemanager/userfiles/electronic_publications/Vol.%204%20The%20Roads-Fasc.%204.1.pdf
55. Josephus, Flavius; Wars Of The Jews II.16.4; Josephus – Complete Works; Kregel Publications; Grand Rapids, Michigan; Twelfth Printing, 1974; p. 488
56. https://en.Wikipedia.org/wiki/Cilicia; article "Cilicia", Roman and Byzantine Cilicia; August 2017. How reliable the source for this information is this writer cannot say. But even allowing for some discrepancy, it still verifies that there were a considerable number of cities in Cilicia to which Paul could have carried the gospel of Jesus Christ.
57. 2 Corinthians 11:23, 24, 26
58. Acts 9:15
59. Romans 9:2, 3
60. Acts 7:51
61. Kittel, Gerhard, editor; Theological Dictionary Of The New Testament, Volume II;

Wm. B. Eerdmans publishing Company; Grand Rapids, Michigan; reprinted February 1973; p. 560
62. Arndt, William F. and Gingrich, F. Wilbur; Greek-English Lexicon of the New Testament and Other Early Christian Literature; The University Of Chicago Press; limited edition licensed to Zondervan Publishing House; 1957; p. 274
63. Meyer, Joh. P.; Ministers of Christ – A Commentary on the Second Epistle of Paul to the Corinthians; Northwestern Publishing House, Milwaukee, WI; 1963; p. 291
64. Pieoer, Francis: Christian Dogmatics Vol. I; Concordia Publishing House; St. Louis, MO.; 1950; fourth printing 1965; p. 234

9

THE CITY OF ANTIOCH, SYRIA; KING HEROD & HIS DEATH; THE FAMINE IN JERUSALEM

PAUL'S AGE: 43-45 DATE: THE FALL OF A.D. 43-45

In This Chapter: Historical Information About The City Of Antioch; The Evangelization Of The Jews And Pagan Greeks In Antioch; Barnabas Sent To Antioch; Paul Begins Work In Antioch In The Fall Of A.D.43; Paul's Ministry With Barnabas In Antioch For A Year; Believers In Jesus Are First Called Christians In Antioch; Presence Of Luke In Antioch; Agabus Foretells The Great Famine In Judea; King Herod Agrippa I's Persecution Of Christians In Jerusalem And His Death; The Dating And Work Of Paul And Barnabas In Famine Relief A.D. 45 & Early 46

Historical Information About The City Of Antioch

Near the end of the years of Paul's work in Syria and Cilicia God the Holy Spirit began opening a new mission opportunity in the nearby city of Antioch, Syria. It is evident from the Book of Acts that after A.D. 43 Antioch became an important center of Christianity. The church in Antioch commissioned and supported Paul's three missionary journeys. The city was located on the south side of the Orontes River about fifteen to twenty miles inland from the Mediterranean Sea, with mountains to the south and the west with a valley in front of it that was around five miles wide.

After the death of Alexander the Great his empire was divided up among his top generals. A general of Alexander's in the Asiatic campaign was Seleucus I Nicator (assassinated in 281 B.C.). He did not receive a portion of the divided empire in its first distribution, but after the Second Battle of Issus in 301 B.C., he gained the control of Syria.[1] He became the first in a dynasty of Greek kings to rule Syria. About 300 B.C. he founded the city of Antioch, which he named after his father Antiochus.[2] At the time he founded Antioch he also made the Jews, who had been dispersed there, citizens with the same privileges as the city's Greek inhabitants.[3] In 64 B.C. Pompey the Great made Syria a Roman province, and Antioch then came under the rule of the Romans.

By the first century of the Christian era Antioch was the third leading city of the Roman Empire in population and prosperity, ranking only behind Rome and Alexandria.[4] The article "Antioch" on Wikipedia stated its population at the time of Caesar Augustus was 500,000, but no substantiating source was cited. Antioch was the capital and metropolis of Syria, which it was at the time of Paul's apostolic ministry. The city was important militarily and commercially. It was on the trade routes that came through there and brought spices and silk to the city.

Four to five miles from the city was the Daphne groves of bay trees. The Daphne groves were a pleasure resort for the citizens of Antioch, which contained the temple of Apollo. Seleucus I Nicator laid out the grove and built the temple. The Daphne grove became a reputed center of ill repute for immorality and extraordinary excesses of pleasure. Conybeare and Howson described the population of Antioch as being for the most part a "worthless rabble of Greeks and Orientals."[5] Of the many Greek cities whose populations had given themselves over to illicit sexual abandonment, vice, and depravity, Antioch was considered the greatest and the worst. It was the pagan, immoral metropolis of the East that rivaled the pagan, immoral city of Corinth in the West.

The main thoroughfare of Antioch ran through the entire length of the city, a distance of about four miles, which was lined with four rows of parallel columns. The road in the center of the columns was open to the sky above, but on each side of the road the columns were covered to make a portico walkway. As beautiful as the landscape to the groves of Daphne and the buildings and the street of Antioch were, they were often subjected to the damage done by repeated earthquakes that struck the area. One terrible earthquake struck the area in A.D. 37. The damage caused by the earthquake was so extensive that emperor Claudius sent two Roman senators to assess the damage done to the city of Antioch.[6] Paul would have been working in nearby Tarsus and northern Syria and Cilicia at the time that earthquake occurred. Over the centuries that followed earthquakes and Muslim/Christian wars ultimately destroyed the beautiful city.

The Evangelization Of The Jews And Pagan Greeks In Antioch
Luke reports in Acts 11:19-22 how God the Holy Spirit began opening the new mission opportunity in Antioch.

> 19 Consequently those who were scattered by the oppression that arose in connection with Stephen traveled as far as Phoenicia and Cyprus and Antioch, speaking the word to no one except to Jews alone.
>
> 20 But some of them were men from Cyprus and Cyrene, who when they came to Antioch began speaking to the Greeks also, proclaiming the good news of the Lord Jesus.
>
> 21 And the hand of the Lord continued to be with them, and a large number who believed turned to the Lord.
>
> 22 And this news[7] about them was heard by the church[8] that was in Jerusalem, and they sent Barnabas out from *Jerusalem* to travel as far as Antioch.

Verse 19 above is a flashback to Acts 8:4. There Luke stated that beginning with the persecution of Jesus' followers that erupted in Jerusalem in A.D. 32 when Stephen was stoned, many Jewish Christians in Jerusalem fled and went from place to place preaching the word of God. Here in Acts 11:19 Luke provides us with more details of what happened. Some of those Jewish Christians fled to Phoenicia, which was a narrow strip of land along the eastern shore of the Mediterranean Sea, the southern tip of which was north of Galilee. Others boarded ships and sailed to the island of Cyprus in the northeastern portion of the Mediterranean Sea. Still others fled overland or by sea to Antioch in northern Syria. When they fled to those places, they spoke the message about Jesus Christ only to their fellow Jews. In this way the Holy Spirit was spreading the gospel of Jesus and founding Jewish Christian congregations in those places.

Some comments about how the date of the evangelization of the Jews and pagan Greeks in Antioch was arrived at are now needed. Luke's chronology in the Book of Acts is very reliable in recounting the many historical events in the order in which they occurred. Often, however, in his brief style of recounting the spread of the gospel and the consequent growth of the Church, he fails to provide the details that would enable us to date those historical events and to then see the passage of time in between them. Such is the case here. The impression the reader is given in verses 19 and 20 above is that the bringing of the gospel to the Jews in Antioch by Jewish Christians who fled from Jerusalem occurred about the same time that Jewish Christian men from Cyprus and Cyrene started sharing the gospel with Greek pagans in Antioch. Actually those two events were separated by a space of five to eight years.

The reason for this separation in time in Luke's account is this: Verse 19 about the Jewish Christians' flight from Jerusalem to Antioch is a flashback to A.D. 32 and Acts 8:4. With that flashback Luke picks up the thread of his historical narrative about the gospel of Jesus Christ being spread outside of Jerusalem and beyond Judea into foreign countries and cities. Wedged in between the bringing of the gospel to the Jews in Antioch in verse 19 and the evangelization of the Greek pagans in Antioch in verse 20 is a period of five to eight years during which time Luke reports important events in Peter's apostolic ministry. During that five to eight-year gap between verses 19 and 20 Peter was spreading the gospel of Jesus in Lydda and Joppa of Judea and afterwards preaching the gospel in Caesarea of Samaria to the Gentile Roman Centurion Cornelius, who was a convert to Judaism.[9] Luke reports those events in Peter's ministry starting with Acts 9:32 and ending with Acts 11:18.

Now, Luke reports that those years of Peter's apostolic ministry started after Paul's short visit in Jerusalem for fifteen days. As explained previously, Paul visited and left Jerusalem in A.D. 35. So the first year of those five to eight years of Peter's ministry would have been in or after A.D. 35. When Luke concludes those years of Peter's apostolic ministry, he then takes up Barnabas bringing Paul to Antioch, which occurred in the fall of A.D. 43. So the last year of those five to eight years of Peter's ministry was in or before A.D. 43.

The words Peter spoke at the Apostolic Council in A.D. 50 provide some support to Peter's having preached the gospel to Cornelius in or before A.D. 43. Luke reports in Acts 15:7 that Peter said, "Men, brothers, you yourselves understand that **some time ago** God made a choice for himself among you, that the Gentiles hear by my mouth the word of the gospel and believe." Note that Peter said his witnessing the gospel to Cornelius occurred "some time ago," which would have been some length of time before A.D. 50. In the context of Luke's chronology that Peter witnessed the gospel to Cornelius before Barnabas called Paul to Antioch indicates that Peter preached the gospel to Cornelius about the same time or not too long before Barnabas called Paul to Antioch in A.D. 43. That time of in or before the year A.D. 43 harmonizes well with Peter's words in A.D. 50 that it had been "some time ago" that he had preached the gospel to Cornelius. Looking backward from A.D. 50 as Peter was doing when he said "some time ago", A.D. 43 or before would have indeed been "some time ago."

Having gone into the details of when the evangelization of the Jews and pagan Greeks in Antioch took place, we can now proceed to the details of how the gospel was brought to those pagan Greeks. That was indeed a momentous occasion! For the first time Jewish laymen were speaking to and reaching out to pagan Greeks! That was unheard of! In A.D. 42 to 43, as now understood from the preceding comments, some Jewish Christian laymen from Cyprus and Cyrene came to Antioch. They were Hellenists, which means they were Jews who had been living under the influence of the Greek culture and customs in Cyprus and Cyrene. Hellenistic Jews tended to be more liberal in their views than the Aramaic Jews of Jerusalem and Judea. Those Hellenistic Jewish Christians began speaking to Greeks and proclaiming the good news of the gospel to them. Luke informs us that the hand of the Lord continued to be with those Jewish Christians in their proclaiming the gospel to those decadent, pagan Greeks of Antioch. "The hand of the Lord" is a figure of speech called an anthropomorphism. It stands for the power of the Lord. The power of the Lord God was working mightily in and through the message of the gospel the laymen were speaking. That gospel was then bringing many Greeks to faith in the Lord Jesus Christ. As Luke reports, a large number of them were turning away from their idols like Apollo and turning to the Lord as their God.

Now this news was soon heard in the church in Jerusalem. This news was indeed new and revolutionary! What was so new and revolutionary at that time in the history of the Christian Church was this: Jewish Christian men had set aside the Jewish teaching that Jews could not associate and speak with non-Jews and Gentiles, and they were proclaiming the gospel to pagan Greeks who began believing in large numbers. Up to the time that Peter went and spoke the gospel to the Gentile Cornelius, Peter himself had been under the strong influence of that Jewish teaching and tradition. Being so influenced, Peter told Cornelius, "You understand that it is unlawful for a Jewish man to associate closely with, or to approach one of, another nation. And yet God has explained to me to say no person is unclean or impure."[10] God made that clear to Peter, that no Gentile person was unclean and to be avoided, when God gave Peter the vision of the unclean creatures that God said Peter should get up and eat. When Peter objected on the basis of the Mosaic Law, God told Peter, "What God has made clean, you stop making unclean!" The blood of Jesus that took away the sins of the world and cleansed the Jews from their sins[11] was the same blood that made all the Gentiles in the world forgiven and clean at the same time. Therefore, there was no reason for Peter not to associate with and speak to Gentiles like Cornelius and those with him. This realization finally penetrated Peter's head and straightened out his narrow-minded thinking. But this did not happen until twelve to thirteen years after Jesus' ascension into heaven and the outpouring of the Holy Spirit on Pentecost! Now just one or two years after Peter's witnessing to Cornelius, the revolutionary news was heard in the mother church of Jerusalem that Jewish Christian laymen had overcome and tossed aside that restraining Jewish teaching and were actively engaging and speaking to pagan Greeks, not even Greeks who had been Jewish proselytes like Cornelius! Those Jewish Christians were speaking the gospel to pagan Greeks, and the power of God the Holy Spirit was working in those Greek pagans, converting them, and bringing them to faith in Jesus in large numbers. What those Jewish Christian laymen had begun doing was according to the will of God for the universality of his Christian Church, not only at that time but for all times.

Barnabas Sent To Antioch

Luke informs us in Acts 11:22 quoted above that when the church in Jerusalem heard the news that Jewish Christians were witnessing to the pagan Greeks, it sent Barnabas from Jerusalem to Antioch. The purpose for his mission was obvious, to go and see for himself if the news that they had heard was in fact true. Luke does not mention the apostles but only the church. It would be safe to assume, then, that the apostles were away from Jerusalem at the time to witness the gospel elsewhere. This assumption gains support from the fact that the church in Jerusalem, not any of the apostles, made the decision to send Barnabas, and that the church sent Barnabas not one or two of the apostles.

Luke then tells us in Acts 11:23-26:

> 23 When Barnabas arrived[12] and saw the grace of God, he rejoiced and began to urge everyone to continue in the Lord with all their heart,[13]
>
> 24 because he was a good man and full of the Holy Spirit and faith. And a large crowd was added to the Lord.
>
> 25 Then he went out to Tarsus to search for Saul,
>
> 26 and when he found *him,* he brought *him* to Antioch. Then it happened for them that for a whole year they gathered together with the church and taught a large crowd. And the disciples were first called Christians in Antioch.

When Barnabas arrived, he at once saw "the grace of God". The grace of God is an invisible disposition of God's undeserved love and favor toward sinners that resides within God himself. Barnabas was seeing the physical, tangible results of that grace of God in the persons of the large number of pagan Greeks who had been converted by the power of the gospel that brought them to faith in Jesus Christ. Seeing all those converted souls was a most heartwarming experience for Barnabas. The sight lifted him up and caused him to rejoice in what a marvelous manner God was building up his church by gathering in all those Gentile converts! With much gladness of heart Barnabas began living up to the name "Barnabas" that the apostles had given to him.[14] The name meant "Son of Encouragement." That is exactly what Luke reports Barnabas began doing; he began encouraging all of those Greek converts "to continue in the Lord with all their heart." By the power of the gospel and the Holy Spirit's working faith in them through that gospel they had turned away from their former idols to turn to the Lord. Now they needed to continue walking by faith with the One true God of heaven and earth. For those who are saved are not those who temporarily believe in the Lord but then turn away from him later, but those who are saved are those who believe in the Lord and continue in that faith to the end of their life on earth. Jesus said in Matthew 24:13, "The one who endures to the end, this one shall be saved." And in Revelation 2:10 he says, "Be faithful until death, and I will give you the crown of life."

Paul's Mission Work In Tarsus, Syria, And Cilicia Ends When Barnabas Brings Paul To Antioch In The Fall Of A.D. 43

For how long Barnabas continued encouraging and working among the Greek converts is unknown. But probably not too long after his arrival in Antioch he realized that he needed help because of the large mass of Greek converts. They needed a lot of teaching for their growth to spiritual maturity in their knowledge of God's teachings and for their living sanctified lives apart from the decadent, pagan ways of their past. To enlist that help he turned to the one man of the Lord at that time whom Barnabas had known went out to work among the Gentiles – Paul, the man Christ Jesus had called to be his apostle to the Gentiles. Jewish Christians witnessing the gospel to Greek Gentiles was new and revolutionary to those in the mother church at Jerusalem; but witnessing to Greek pagans was not new or revolutionary to the apostle Paul. He had already been doing that for eight years!

So Barnabas went out to Tarsus to search for Paul. It had been eight years since he had introduced Paul to the apostles in Jerusalem. How after eight years he knew where Paul was and what Paul was doing at the time is unknown. This writer thinks that because the regions of Syria and Cilicia where Paul had been working were only about one hundred miles overland around the northeastern tip of the Mediterranean Sea, some Jewish Christians or Greek converts who knew about Paul and his ministry may have informed Barnabas about Paul. However Barnabas came to know about Paul's whereabouts and work, Barnabas left Antioch in search of Paul. How he managed to find him is also a mystery. When he did find him in Tarsus, Barnabas obviously must have told Paul about the revolutionary news that had been taking place in Antioch. He surely must have encouraged Paul to return with him to assist in all the teaching that needed to be done there. No doubt Paul saw the hand of God in the conversion of those large numbers of pagan Greeks in Antioch. Paul then readily agreed. As he would do in his future missionary journeys, Paul must have left the churches that the Lord had enabled him to found in Syria and Cilicia in the hands of God to watch over.[15]

Paul's Ministry With Barnabas In Antioch For A Year Beginning In The Fall Of A.D. 43

So Barnabas brought Paul to Antioch. When Paul entered what had previously been the beautiful city of Antioch, he is likely to have seen the remains of the destruction caused by the powerful earthquake that had struck only six years earlier. It is doubtful that by the time Paul came to Antioch all the collapsed buildings and houses and various kinds of structures had been cleaned up and all the buildings and decorative columns had been reconstructed and restored to what they had been before. For it must be kept in mind that Antioch prior to the earthquake had been the third largest and most prosperous city in the Roman Empire with a population approximating 500,000, and the damage to the city was so extensive that Claudius had commissioned two senators to go and assess the damage and rubble.

Upon Paul's arrival in Antioch Luke tells us in Acts 11:26, "Then it happened for (Paul and Barnabas) that for a whole year they gathered together with the church and taught a large crowd." In Antioch Paul and Barnabas worked together as a team teaching the word of God to the Greek converts and indoctrinating them in the Christian teachings. Since to the best of this writer's knowledge Paul had been working alone from the first days of Damascus to the end of his ministry in Cilicia, this would have been the first time Paul had someone to work with him. Together Paul and Barnabas became a team that lasted for about seven years through their work together in Antioch and Paul's first missionary journey.

The Believers In Jesus Are First Called Christians In Antioch

Luke informs us in Acts 11:26, "And the disciples were first called

Christians in Antioch." While Paul was working with Barnabas in Antioch the believers in Jesus came to be called Christians for the first time. As W. M. Ramsay asserted,[16] the term Christians attested to the fact that the believers in Antioch became a familiar subject of talk, probably gossip and slander, in the city. The name "Christian" must have originated outside the circle of believers in Jesus. The followers of Christ Jesus were talked about in the popular society of Antioch as ones who were connected with "Christos". "Christos" is the Greek name for "Christ", and it was the title for "the Anointed One, the Messiah" who had been promised in the Old Testament (Psalm 2:2 is one example). The title of "Christ" would not have originated among the unbelieving Jews who rejected Jesus of Nazareth as 'the Christ', for the title of "Christ" was sacred to them. They would never have profaned that title by assigning it to Jesus of Nazareth whom they hated and crucified. The name "Christos", then, must have been the manner in which the Greek converts explained to their pagan neighbors who it was in whom they believed to be the very Son of God who saved them from sin and death and gave to them eternal life. The pagan neighbors, of course, had no idea of whom that "Christos" was. Some of those pagans probably took "Christos" to be a strange god whom the followers of Christ worshipped, as did the Athenian men who are reported in Acts 17:18; while other pagans likely assumed "Christos" to be the leader of Christ's followers. In any case the name likely belonged to popular slang, and the strange term "Christos" was modified to "Chrestos", which the pagans would have thought as a more suitable and natural name for a leader or a god since it meant "good, useful". 'Chrestians" was the form in which the name was often used and occurred in inscriptions. Tertullian (c. A.D. 165-240) is also reported to have said that non-Christians pronounced it "Chrestianos" as a word associated with the Greek term "chrestos".[17]

The Presence Of Luke In Antioch

It is very probable that during the time Paul and Barnabas were working in Antioch Luke himself was present and one of the Greek converts they were teaching. The Overview Of The Gospel Of Luke in the Vivid English Translation Of The New Testament discusses in detail the probability of Luke's being in the congregation of Antioch at this time.[18] If Luke's presence was indeed a fact, as seems quite possible that it was at this time in Paul's life and ministry that Paul became acquainted with Luke and his friend. The Overview Of The Gospel of Luke states:

> Luke was a Gentile, probably a Greek. This appears to have been the case, because Paul distinguished him from his Jewish co-workers who were "from the circumcision" (see Colossians 4:10-14). Luke had taken up residence in Antioch, Syria. Acts 11:28 in the Greek manuscript known as the Codex Bezae has an insertion that makes Luke present at the meeting of the church in Antioch when the prophet Agabus foretold there would be a great famine. Paul and Barnabas were there as well. While there is some question that this version of Acts 11:28 was original, it indicates that by the fourth century the opinion was held that Luke lived in Antioch and by the early A.D. 40s had become a Christian and member of the church in Antioch. Acts 6:5 also gives some incidental evidence to Luke's having lived in Antioch and to his having been a member of the church there. In Acts 6:5 Luke stated who were the first deacons chosen by the church in Jerusalem. He stated that one of them, Nicolas, had been a convert to Judaism from Antioch. Luke apparently knew this from his personal knowledge of the members of the church in Antioch, where he had also been a member.
>
> Ancient tradition supports that Luke was an Antiochian. The Anti-Marcionite Prologue, dated between A.D. 160 and 180, states, "Luke was an Antiochian of Syria, a physician by profession." This statement also appears in Eusebius' Church History (about A.D. 323) and in Jerome's De Viris Illustribus (A.D. 392). Origen is also quoted in Eusebius' Church History as saying that Luke was an Antiochian by descent and a physician by profession.
>
> Luke was a physician (see Colossians 4:14). Thus Antioch is a

credible place for Luke to have lived. For Antioch was the location of a famous ancient medical school. There Luke was likely to have studied medicine.

Accepting as true that by December of A.D. 43, according to this chronology, Luke was a member of the church in Antioch who attended the meeting at which Agabus spoke of a great famine, Acts 11:19-21 quoted above gives us an insight into how Luke become a Christian. When the Jewish Christians of Cyprus and Cyrene cane to Antioch and began preaching the gospel of Jesus to the Greek pagans there, Luke must have been among those Greeks who listened and believed the gospel of Jesus. In this manner Luke was converted from Greek paganism to Christianity. After Barnabas brought Paul to Antioch, Luke would surely have been one of those Greeks who listened to them expounding the teachings of God. Later Luke was chosen to become the Holy Spirit's inspired writer of twenty-five percent of the New Testament. Of all the men whom the Holy Spirit employed to write the New Testament Luke was the only Gentile writer among them.

Agabus Foretells The Great Famine In Judea
In Acts 11:27-30 Luke tells us:

27 Now in these days prophets came down from Jerusalem to Antioch.

28 And one of them named Agabus got up and foretold by means of the Spirit *that* a great famine was about to come[19] upon the whole inhabited earth; it would come during *the reign* of Claudius.

29 Then the disciples, each one according to his financial ability, determined to send aid to the brothers living in Judea,

30 which they also did by sending *their gift* to the elders by the hand of Barnabas and Saul.

"These days" of which Luke wrote in verse 27 above was that

period of time when Paul and Barnabas were busy teaching in the church of Antioch during the last months of A.D. 43. During that time in what might have been the month of December some prophets came down from Jerusalem to Antioch. These prophets were Christians who had been given the gift of foretelling the future by the Holy Spirit.[20] Paul himself became an eminent prophet who foretold the future as well as taught the truths of God's Word. Two examples of this were Paul's having taught and wrote about the great Antichrist in 2 Thessalonians 2:1-12 and about the terrible times to come in the last days in 2 Timothy 3:1-13, the fulfillment of which matters we are seeing even now.

Luke mentions by name only one of the prophets who came to Antioch, Agabus. Luke mentions Agabus once again in Acts 21:10 as foretelling Paul's imminent imprisonment. For what purpose Agabus and the other prophets came to Antioch Luke does not say. It seems that they may have come for the very purpose of delivering the message that Agabus delivered. He foretold by the power of the Holy Spirit that a great famine was about to come upon the whole inhabited earth during the reign of Claudius. This prophecy of Agabus was fulfilled but not in the sense that "the whole inhabited earth" meant everywhere around the world at the same time. The Greek term for "inhabited earth" in this verse meant the Roman Empire, as Luke also used the Greek term in Acts 24:5. Now no famine occurred throughout the whole Roman Empire during the reign of Claudius. But at different times for different reasons in different places of the empire there were famines during Claudius' reign. Dion Cassius reported a famine in Rome during the reign of Claudius.[21] Tacitus also reported a famine in Rome at the time of Claudius.[22] Tacitus stated that Claudius was even surrounded by a frenzied mob of Roman citizens and had to be rescued by Roman soldiers when the populace learned there was no more than a fifteen-day supply of food for the whole city of Rome. Tacitus did not blame the food shortage on infertile soil in Italy however, but on the hazards of shipping the needed grain from Africa and Egypt. Eusebius was also said to have written that a famine occurred in

Greece while Claudius was emperor.[23] And then there was the great famine in Judea, upon which we want to concentrate our attention now.

Upon hearing that a famine was coming, the newly converted Greek Christians of the church of Antioch, and no doubt the Jewish Christian members as well, promptly decided upon a course of action to help their Jewish Christian brothers and sisters in Judea survive that famine. Each member of the church in Antioch determined that he would give aid according to his individual financial ability. The church in Antioch then started to take up a collection for that charitable purpose. In making that determination those newly converted Christians were exhibiting the exuberance of their newfound faith in Christ Jesus and the joy that exhilarated their hearts and "their first love"[24] prompted by the gospel. Those same kinds of characteristics can be seen to this day in new adult converts who are brought to faith in Jesus and enter the local congregation. Oh that those Spirit-engendered characteristics would only continue undiminished over time in all members of the Church!

Luke in his brief style of historical reporting did not elaborate on the details that went into making the collection and then carrying out the relief mission in Judea. Luke described the entire collection and relief mission in but just three verses – Acts 11:29, 30 quoted above and 12:25 which brought the famine relief mission to a close. Luke wrote. "Now Barnabas and Saul returned from Jerusalem after having completed their mission, taking along with them John, who was also called Mark."

It is evident that the collection in the church of Antioch was started before the famine began. It most likely was taken over some period of time on a weekly basis, such as Paul would do years later among the Gentile churches in Greece and Galatia.[25] More will be said about the relief mission in Judea after the following brief discussion on King Herod Agrippa I.

King Herod Agrippa I's Persecution Of Christians In Jerusalem And His Death

Now while the Christians in Antioch were starting to gather their collection, and while Paul and Barnabas were continuing their working together for a year teaching the Greeks in Antioch, some very important events were taking place first in Jerusalem and then in Caesarea. For there was a period of fifteen months between Acts 11:29's mentioning the congregation's decision to take the collection and Acts 11:30's stating Paul and Barnabas took the congregation's collection to Jerusalem. Luke explains in Acts 12:1-23 what those events were that occurred during those fifteen months. We need to know about those intervening events, because they provide vital details that make it possible to date the next portion of Paul's life that he spent working on famine relief. And since those events are about King Herod Agrippa I for the most part, we should also become familiar with a few details about him and his life.

King Herod Agrippa I should not be confused with Herod the Tetrach of Galilee who divorced his wife, the daughter of King Aretas, to marry Herodias the wife of his brother Philip, and who later beheaded John the Baptist. Agrippa I, as he was also called to distinguish him from his son Agrippa II, was a grandson of Herod the Great who slaughtered the babes of Bethlehem at the time of Jesus' birth. King Herod Agrippa I was also the brother of Herodias who divorced Philip to marry Herod the Tetrarch. So king Herod Agrippa I was the brother-in-law of Herod the Tetrach. King Herod Agrippa I was educated in Rome with Drusus, the son of emperor Tiberias, and with Claudius, who was emperor at the time of the great famine in Judea. Herod Agrippa I, then, had high political connections in Rome, which he used as much as possible to curry favor for himself and to further his own political ends and power. He was self-serving, power-hungry, unscrupulous, treacherous, murderous, and extremely extravagant.[26] By the time of his death the dominions of his kingdom equaled those of his grandfather Herod the Great.

To begin Luke's report of what events occurred between Acts 11:29 & 30 Luke informs us in Acts 12:1-5:

1 Now about that time Herod the king laid his hands upon some of those belonging to the church in order to persecute *them*.

2 Then he had James the brother of John put to death with a sword.

3 And when he saw that it was pleasing to the Jews, he proceeded to seize Peter also. (Now this was *done* during the days of the Feast of Unleavened Bread.)

4 And after he arrested him, he put him in prison, handing him over to four squads of four soldiers each to guard him, *and* planning to bring him before the people after the Passover.

5 So, to be sure, Peter continued to be kept under guard in the prison, but a prayer was constantly being made by the church to God for him.

About the time that Agabus came to Antioch in December of A.D. 43 and foretold the forthcoming famine, Luke says King Herod Agrippa I initiated a persecution of some Jewish Christians in Jerusalem. His motivation for doing so was to gain further favor for himself among the Jews and to increase his popularity among them. He also arrested the apostle James and beheaded him, which showed just how far he intended to proceed in persecuting the church. When Herod saw how much his beheading of James pleased the Jewish population, he then seized and imprisoned Peter as well.

Luke states that Herod arrested Peter during the days of the Feast of Unleavened Bread, which began on the Friday after the sacrificing of the Passover lamb and the eating of the Passover the Thursday evening before (ref. Leviticus 23:6). Herod kept Peter under heavy military guard with the intention of putting Peter on trial before the people after the festival of the Passover and the Feast of Unleavened Bread was over. He would then sentence him to death and have him executed. The Passover falls between late March and mid-April. This information that Luke provides enables us to date Herod's persecution of Christians from around the beginning of January to late February A.D. 44 and his murder of James around late February to early March. Herod's arrest of Peter would have occurred around late March to mid-April.

Luke reports what happened next in Acts 12:6-17:

6. Now when Herod was about to bring him out, that night before[27] Peter was sleeping between two soldiers, having been bound with two chains, and *there were* guards in front of the door keeping watch over the prison.

7 And behold, an angel of the Lord stood nearby, and light shone in the cell. And when he struck Peter's side, he woke him up, saying, "Get up quickly!" And the chains fell off of his hands.

8 Then the angel said to him, "Bind your shirt around your waist[28] and put on your sandals!" And he did so. And the angel[29] says to him, "Throw your robe around you and follow me!"

9 And when he went out, he followed him, and yet he did not know that what was being done by the angel was really happening,[30] rather he kept thinking he was seeing a vision.

10 And when they had passed by the first and second guard, they came to the iron-gate leading into the city, which opened for them by itself. And after they went out, they proceeded up one narrow street, and at once the angel departed from him.

11 And when Peter came to his senses, he said, "Now I truly know that the Lord sent forth his angel and rescued me out of the hand of Herod and from all *that* the Jewish people were expecting."[31]

12 And when he became aware *of this*, he went to the house of Mary, the mother of John who is also called Mark, where many had been brought together and were praying.

13 Then when he knocked at the door of the gate, a servant-girl named Rhoda came to answer the door.

14 And when she recognized Peter's voice, because of her[32] joy she did not open the gate; rather she ran in and reported *that* Peter was standing in front of the gate.

15 But they said to her, "You are out of your mind!" But she kept insisting it was so. Then they began to say, "It is his angel!"

16 But Peter continued to remain *in front of the gate* knocking *at the door*. And when they opened it, they saw him and became astounded.

17 And after he signaled to them with his hand to be silent, he

related to them how the Lord had brought him out of the prison, and he said, "Report these things to James and to the brothers." And when he went out, he proceeded to another place.

King Herod had his intentions and plans to murder Peter after the Passover celebration and to persecute Christ's church, but the Lord was on his throne in heaven laughing at Herod and scoffing at Herod's vain plans.[33] For try as Herod might with all his royal authority and earthly powers to overthrow the Lord's Christ and his church, he was helpless against the Lord's almighty powers and the power of all the prayers of the Church being offered up to God in Peter's behalf. For this reason the night before Herod was to try and execute Peter, the Lord's angel came into the prison where Peter was being held and led him out safely to freedom. The military guards were powerless to stop it.

Luke tells us in Acts 12:18-23 what happened the next day and in the following months:

18 Then when it became day, there was no small mental agitation among the soldiers as to what had become of Peter.[34]

19 And after Herod searched for him and did not find him, he examined the guards and ordered them to be led away *to their execution*. And when he went down from Judea to Caesarea, he continued to stay there.

20 Now he continued to be extremely angry with the people of Tyre and Sidon. And with one purpose they had come to him, and after winning over Blastus, the king's chamberlain, they repeatedly asked for peace, because their country was being supplied with food from the king's country.[35]

21 Then on the appointed day Herod, having dressed in royal clothing and having sat down on his speaker's platform, began to deliver an address to them.

22 Then the crowd started crying out loudly, "The voice of a god and not of a man!"

23 And at once an angel of the Lord struck him, because he did not give glory to God. And he breathed his last and was eaten by worms.

Having had his intentions and plans to murder Peter thwarted by the Lord, Herod withdrew from Jerusalem and continued to stay in Caesarea. Josephus wrote that then on a certain day:

> ... (Herod) exhibited shows in honour of Caesar, upon being informed that there was a certain festival to make vows for his (Caesar's) safety. At which festival, a great multitude was gotten together of the principal persons, and such as were of dignity through his province. On the second day of which shows he put on a garment made wholly of silver, and of a contexture truly wonderful, and came into the theatre early in the morning; at which time the silver of his garment being illuminated by the fresh reflection of the sun's rays upon it, shone out after a surprising manner, and was so resplendent as to spread a horror over those that looked intently upon him: and presently his flatterers cried out, one from one place and another from another ... that he was a god: and they added, – "Be merciful to us; for although we have hitherto reverenced thee only as a man, yet shall we henceforth own thee as superior to mortal nature." Upon this the king did neither rebuke them, nor reject their impious flattery.[36]

Herod used the festival for his own aggrandizement, and when the crowd was proclaiming him to be a god and not a man, and he was wallowing in all the attention and adulation being heaped upon him, the Lord's angel – as Luke stated – struck him because he did not give glory to God. He died and was eaten by worms. Josephus' accounts are not on a par with the inspired Scriptures, in this instance the Book of Acts. And Josephus gave a detailed account of Herod's death after the above quotation, which this writer considers an untrustworthy exaggeration of Herod's humble public acceptance of his death. It is interesting to note, however, that Josephus' above account does corroborate the truthfulness and accuracy of Luke's scriptural account in the Book Of Acts. This indeed is interesting because Josephus was a Jew, not a Christian, who wrote his history of the Jews for a secular Roman audience, not for a Christian readership.

The Dating And Work Of Paul And Barnabas In Famine Relief
  Paul's Age: 45-46 Date: A.D. 45 To Early 46

Figuring that Herod left Jerusalem in April shortly after Peter's miraculous release from prison, and figuring on the basis of Luke's statement that Herod continued to stay in Caesarea up until his death, a date of August 1st A.D. 44 for his death is a reasonable estimate.

Upon Herod's death a message would then have been sent to emperor Claudius to inform him about Herod's death and the lack of an authorized Roman official to govern those domains of Rome's empire that had been under Herod's jurisdiction. Allowing time for the courier to travel by ship from Caesarea to Rome before the weather turned bad and while the shipping season was still open, the message might have reached Claudius around mid-September. If this were the case, it is possible that Claudius would not have appointed a man to fill the vacancy until around October 1st A.D. 44. When he did make the appointment, he appointed Fadus Cuspius procurator of Judea. Fadus then governed Judea from A.D. 44 into the year 46. In A.D. 46 Claudius appointed Tiberias Alexander to succeed him. Tiberias ruled over Judea during the years of A.D. 46-48.

The preceding are important dates for dating the time Paul served with Barnabas in Jerusalem on a mission of famine relief, for Josephus stated in his Antiquities 20.5.2 that the great famine in Judea happened during the reigns of Fadus Cuspius and Tiberias Alexander as procurators of Judea. Based on the dates that Fadus and Tiberias were procurators of Judea, the Judean famine apparently began with the spring harvest of March to June A.D. 45 when the barley and wheat crops would have been harvested. And the famine would have then continued into the summer and fall harvests of the fruit crops of grapes, figs, and olives, which should have been harvested from July to November of the same year. With these crop failures the Jewish

Christians in Judea would have begun experiencing the shortage of vital foodstuffs. It has been reported that the grain crops made up more than fifty percent of the average Israelite's daily consumption of calories. Fruits, especially figs, together with olive oil were the next most important foods in the Israelite's diet.[37]

While the preceding events regarding Herod, the appointment of Fadus, and the onset of the famine were taking place, the church in Antioch had been busy taking its collection to aid the Christian famine victims in Judea. At the same time Paul and Barnabas were working together to evangelize and teach the Greeks in Antioch for a whole year. After that year of work and the members' of the congregation taking of the collection, it is probable that the church in Antioch met around the end of A.D. 44 and decided to have Paul and Barnabas hand carry its collection to the elders of the church in Jerusalem.[38]

The members of the church in Antioch were likely to have had two reasons for selecting Paul and Barnabas to hand carry their collection to the church in Jerusalem. First, Paul and Barnabas were recognized among them as being outstanding leaders in the congregation. Second, the membership of the church of Antioch was for the most part made up of the many Gentile Greeks who had been converted by the gospel. That heavy majority of Greek Christians understood they were sending their collection to the church of Jerusalem, which consisted of Jewish Christians with Jewish customs and elders of which they as Gentiles had little understanding. They therefore probably thought it would be best to have men represent their church of Antioch who were thoroughly familiar with the Jewish church in Jerusalem and with its Jewish elders, members, and customs. Paul and Barnabas met those requirements perfectly. What is more, Paul and Barnabas were well known and trusted by the leaders of the church in Jerusalem. The members of the congregation of Antioch knew, therefore, that they could trust Paul and Barnabas to represent them knowledgeably and properly and better than anyone else among them.

So, after having chosen Paul and Barnabas to carry their collection, the congregation likely waited to the beginning of the failing harvest season in March to send Paul and Barnabas to Jerusalem. When they arrived in Jerusalem, they gave the collection of money to the elders of the church there. Giving the funds to the elders of the church would have been in keeping with the decision of the apostles and the Jerusalem church years before. At that time the decision had been made that the apostles would devote themselves particularly to prayer and the ministry of the word.[39] The elders would attend to the administration of the congregation, such as overseeing the waiting on of tables done by the deacons.[40] Together the apostles and elders oversaw the doctrine and practice of the church, which was made evident at the Apostolic Council as Luke noted in Acts 15:6.

With the money that Paul and Barnabas brought from Antioch, the elders in Jerusalem could then purchase food for the hungry Christians in Jerusalem and Judea. The elders of the church were not the only ones to have bought food supplies. Josephus also reports that during the great Judean famine Queen Helena of Adiabene, a proselyte to Judaism, sent her servants and had them buy a great quantity of grain in Egypt at a great expense. She also sent other servants to Cyprus who brought a cargo of dried figs. Queen Helena then had these foodstuffs brought to Jerusalem and distributed to those in need. Josephus further reports that many people died for a lack of funds to buy food for themselves.[41] This information from Josephus gives us an insight into what the elders in Jerusalem most likely did as well to help the hungry Christians. And it can be assumed that Paul and Barnabas also helped to oversee the purchase of grain and figs and olive oil from Egypt and Cyprus. After the food supplies had been shipped to Jerusalem, they might have assisted also with the distribution of the food in Jerusalem and its surrounding areas in Judea. It is not unlikely that Paul and Barnabas remained in Jerusalem to help with the famine relief throughout the year of A.D. 45 and did not return to Antioch until early 46. Luke reports in Acts 12:30 that upon completing their relief mission, they returned to Antioch with John who was also called Mark.

In the manner reported and proposed in Chapters 7-9 the Lord's bondservant Paul completed the beginning of his apostolic ministry. He had been transformed by the Lord Jesus from a Church destroyer into a Church builder. These opening years of his ministry in his Lord Jesus' service had already been filled with much traveling, opposition, danger, and success – and this was only the beginning! There was so much more to come, as shall be shown starting in Part IV describing his first missionary journey.

---

1. The New Schaff-Herzog Encyclopedia of Religious Knowledge, Vol. X; "Seleucidae"; Jackson, Samuel Macauley, editor-in-chief; Baker Book House; Grand Rapids, Michigan; p. 339
2. Davis, John D.; A Dictionary of The Bible; Baker Book House; Grand Rapids, Michigan; Seventeenth Printing, June 1969. p. 39
3. Josephus, Flavius; The Antiquities Of The News, 12.3.1; Josephus – Complete Works; Kregel Publications; Grand Rapids, Michigan; Twelfth Printing, 1974; p. 251
4. Josephus, Flavius; The Wars Of The Jews, 3.2.4 Josephus – Complete Works; Kregel Publications; Grand Rapids, Michigan; Twelfth Printing, 1974; p. 503
5. Conybeare, W. J. & Howson, J. S.; The Life And Epistles of St. Paul; Wm. B. Eerdmans Publishing Company; Grand Rapids, Michigan; Reprinted March 1974; p. 103
6. 1902 Encyclopedia; https://www.1902encyclopedia.com/A/ANT/antioch.html
7. Lit. the word
8. Lit. in the ears of the church
9. Acts 9:32-11:18
10. Acts 10:28
11. 1 John 1:7
12. Lit. who when arriving
13. Lit. with the resolve, or purpose, of the heart
14. Acts 4:36
15. Acts 20:32
16. Ramsay, W. M.; St. Paul The Traveler And Roman Citizen; Baker Book House; Grand Rapids, Michigan; Preface p. 47, 48
17. The New Schaff-Herzog Encyclopedia of Religious Knowledge, Vol. III; "Seleucidae"; Jackson, Samuel Macauley, editor-in-chief; Baker Book House; Grand Rapids, Michigan; p. 39
18. This can currently be viewed on Christian Inconnect; http://www.christianinconnect.com/gospel-of-luke.html
19. Lit. about to be
20. 1 Corinthians 12:10 lists prophecy as one of the gifts of the Holy Spirit at the time of Paul
21. Dion Cassius, LX.11; http://penelope.uchicago.edu/Thayer/E/Roman/Texts/Cassius_Dio/60*.html

22. Tacitus; The Annals of Imperial Rome, XII, Penguin Books, Reprinted with revised bibliography, 1996; p. 271
23. Conybeare, W. J. & Howson, J. S.; The Life And Epistles of St. Paul; Wm. B. Eerdmans Publishing Company; Grand Rapids, Michigan; Reprinted March 1974; p. 104, footnote 3
24. Revelation 2:4
25. 1 Corinthians 16:1-4
26. Josephus 19.8.2
27. Lit. on that night
28. Lit. gird yourself
29. Lit. he
30. Lit was true
31. Lit. from all the expectation of the people of the Jews
32. Lit. the
33. Psalm 2:1-4
34. Lit. what consequently had become of Peter
35. Lit. from the royal, or kingly, or belonging to a king
36. Josephus, Flavius; Antiquities Of The Jews, 19:8:2; Josephus – Complete Works; Kregel Publications; Grand Rapids, Michigan; Twelfth Printing, 1974; 412
37. "Harvest Seasons of Ancient Israel"; https://archive.gci.org/articles/harvest-seasons-of-ancient-israel/
38. Acts 11:30
39. Acts 6:4
40. Acts 6:2-5
41. Josephus, Flavius; Antiquities Of The Jews, 20.2.5 & 20.5.2; Josephus – Complete Works; Kregel Publications; Grand Rapids, Michigan; Twelfth Printing, 1974; p. 416, 418 & 419

IV
PAUL'S FIRST MISSIONARY JOURNEY

Paul's Age: 46-49
Date: A.D. 46-49

10

PAUL'S DIVINE CALL THROUGH THE CHURCH; HIS MISSION WORK ON CYPRUS

In This Chapter: Paul Was Christ's Instrument To Carry The Gospel Into Gentile Lands; Paul's Divine Call Through The Church; Paul's Mission Work On Cyprus

---

Paul Was Christ's Instrument To Carry The Gospel Into Gentile Lands

After appearing to Paul on the road to Damascus, Jesus said about Paul, "This man is my chosen instrument to carry my name before both Gentiles and kings, and the sons of Israel."[1] As explained in preceding chapters Paul was a Jew like the Twelve apostles whom Jesus had originally chosen. But unlike those Twelve, whose backgrounds were in the land of Palestine, Paul's background was not limited to Jewish lands. Much of his background was in the Greek city of Tarsus in the Roman province of Cilicia. Having come from that background Paul was not only familiar with the Jewish culture and language, he was also familiar with that of the Greek. God gave Paul his Jewish upbringing in the Greek city of Tarsus to prepare Paul for his life's work as a bondservant of Christ Jesus. What is more, God had Paul taking his gospel to Greeks and Gentiles in Syria and Cilicia for eight years. His background and those years of experience especially suited him for the call to be Christ Jesus' apostle to the Gentiles as well as to the Jews in the Gentile lands of what is now Turkey, Greece, and Italy, not to mention Spain as a real possibility as well. For these reasons, aside from whatever other reasons laid within God's hidden will of which we know nothing, Paul was Christ's instrument, the tool Christ would use, to carry his gospel of forgiveness, salvation, and eternal life to the Gentiles as well as to his natural countrymen, the Jews, in the Gentile lands.

This chapter on Paul's life and ministry begins in the year A.D. 46. Claudius was the Roman Emperor.

Paul's Divine Call Through The Church

We learn from Luke in Acts 13:1-3:

> 1. Now throughout the present[2] church in Antioch there were prophets and teachers: not only Barnabas and Simeon who was called Niger, and Lucius of Cyrene, but also Manaen (who had been brought up with Herod the tetrarch) and Saul.
>
> 2 And while they were performing a religious service to the Lord and fasting, the Holy Spirit said, "By all means set apart for me Barnabas and Saul for the work to which I have called them."
>
> 3 Then after fasting and praying and laying their hands upon them, they sent them away.

When Paul and Barnabas returned to Antioch in the early part of A.D. 46 from their mission of famine relief in Jerusalem, they very likely resumed their work of teaching the Jewish and Greek converts in the church of Antioch. They probably did so for a short period of time until the time of the events that Luke recorded in the above verses.

Luke tells us that at that time there were prophets and teachers in the church of Antioch. He then lists the names of five men and splits them up into two groups – one was a group of three and the other a group of two. They were all men of Jewish descent whom the congregation held in high esteem and who held important positions in the ministry of the church at Antioch. Luke lists their names and gives an identifying detail about each of them. The first name in Luke's list is Barnabas, of whom Luke has already told us much. The second man is Simeon, which was his Hebrew name. It was not uncommon that Jewish men had a second name, such as John who was called Mark and Saul who was called Paul. Accordingly, since there were a lot of Hebrew men by the name of Simeon, Luke tells us this Simeon in the Antioch congregation also had a Latin surname of Niger to distinguish him from all the other Jewish men by the name of Simeon. His Latin name of Niger meant "dark or black". It is therefore possible that he was a man of dark complexion from Africa.[3] The third man in Luke's list is Lucius of Cyrene. Since Lucius was from Cyrene, some commentators have suggested that he might have been one of the original Jewish men from Cyrene who started sharing the gospel with the Greek pagans in Antioch.[4] The next man that Luke mentions is Manaen. Luke identifies him as a man who had been brought up with Herod Antipas. Herod Antipas became the ruler of Galilee and Perea when the province of Judea was divided into four governmental sections. During his reign he beheaded John the Baptist. Josephus provides some interesting information about the early life of Herod Antipas that helps us to understand Manaen's background.[5] Herod Antipas and his brother Archelaus were the sons of Herod the Great and were born of the same mother, a Samaritan woman named Malthace. Herod Antipas and Archelaus were then brought up and educated in Rome by a private citizen.[6] This information, together with the information that Luke provides, tells us that Manaen must have come from an aristocratic family himself and was brought up and educated in Rome with the two princes, Herod Antipas and Archelaus. It has even been suggested that Manaen was a foster brother to Herod Antipas. Finally, the last name in Luke's list was the apostle Paul.

How Luke knew these personal names and details about these men is not known. His knowledge of these details, in addition to the details about Luke reported in the previous chapter, indicate rather strongly that Luke was indeed a member of the church in Antioch during the year that Paul and Barnabas were teaching there. Luke's being in the congregation was apparently how he knew the details about the men in his list.

There have been various opinions about Luke's list of five prophets and teachers. One opinion has been that Luke put the names in the order of their ages thereby designating Barnabas as the oldest and Paul as the youngest.[7] That opinion seems unlikely because Paul at the time that the five men were in the church of Antioch was forty-six years of age and Manaen who was named before Paul would have been about sixty-six years of age.[8] Are we to believe that Barnabas was in his seventies before making the missionary journey with Paul and

afterwards making a second missionary journey to Cyprus? Another opinion has been that Luke listed the men in the order in which they were converted or the time when they entered the church of Antioch.[9] The thought behind this opinion may have been that Luke was careful to put things in the order in which they happened. Another opinion has been that Luke arranged the names in the order of their importance in the church of Antioch.[10] Barnabas was listed first as the most important because he was sent from the mother church in Jerusalem to investigate the preaching of the gospel to the Greek pagans and became the principal man in leading the church with his encouragement from God's Word. This opinion has some merit because in the second half of the Book of Acts Luke lists Paul first as the leader of the missionary efforts and journeys. The weakness with this opinion, however, is that since Paul was listed last, he would have been considered the least important of the five men. That does not seem likely in as much as Paul was an apostle. Furthermore, he, as well as Barnabas, was selected to represent the church in Antioch and hand carry the congregation's collection to help the Christian famine victims in

Jerusalem. Regarding all such explanations for the order of the list of names the simple truth is this: We really do not know why Luke listed the names in the order that he did.

In the Greek text of Acts 13:1 Luke did divide the five names into two groups of men. The Vivid English Translation Of The New Testament preserved Luke's groupings by noting the first group with the introductory words "not only" and the second group with the words "but also". The first group consists of the three names of Barnabas, Simeon, and Lucius. The second group consists of Manaen's and Paul's names. Since Luke introduced the list of five names by saying there were prophets and teachers in the church of Antioch, some commentators have theorized that the first group of three names must have been the names of the prophets and the second group must have been the names of the teachers. According to that explanation Barnabas was classified as a prophet and Paul was classified as a teacher. But since Luke himself did not specify which of the men were prophets and which of them were teachers, in all truthfulness neither can we. Furthermore, we cannot assert for certain that Barnabas, Simeon, and Lucius were the prophets while Manaen and Paul were the teachers, for there is another possibility that must be considered, namely that all five men could have served as both prophets and teachers.[11] Finally, it needs to be said that since Luke did not tell us why he divided the men into two groups, we really cannot know why the five names are divided as they are. That remains an unsolved mystery.

Acts 13:1 introduces us to the term 'prophet" for the first time, except in the case of Agabus who was mentioned in the preceding chapter. We therefore should look into the scriptural meaning of that term now. Doing so will help us to understand how Luke might have meant it in Acts 13:1.

Thayer in his Greek – English Lexicon defined the meaning of a prophet as a man who was moved by the Holy Spirit to be a spokesman for God and who then declared to others what was revealed to him by divine inspiration, especially future events and in particular such future events as they related to the kingdom of God and human salvation.[12] The title of "prophet" was given to God's Old Testament spokesmen, such as David, Isaiah, Jeremiah, and many others. The title was also applied to John the Baptist and to Jesus as the Messiah.

At the time of the apostle Paul the term "prophet" designated a man like Agabus to whom upon occasion the Holy Spirit revealed a future event for him to proclaim. Such a Spirit-inspired revelation of a future event Paul called "prophecy" in 1 Corinthians 12:9 & 10 where he listed it among the other Spirit-given supernatural gifts of healings, miracles, distinguishing of spirits, speaking in tongues, and interpreting tongues. But Paul especially encouraged and praised in Chapters 12-14 of 1 Corinthians the Spirit-given gift of prophecy. The man to whom the Spirit gave this gift had a thorough knowledge and understanding of the truths of God and the ability to proclaim them clearly and well for the benefit of others, as Paul stated in 1 Corinthians 14:3: "The one who prophesies speaks to people for *their* edification and encouragement and comfort." So at the time of Paul the term "prophet" was used in a double sense: a revealer or future events and an expounder of divine truths. Today we call the expounder of divine truths a preacher of God's Word.

Luke's use of the term "prophet" in Acts 13:1, then, could be understood in two ways. First, it could be understood to mean a man who by the revelation of the Spirit upon occasion revealed a future event. Second, it could mean a Spirit-filled man who was especially knowledgeable in the truths of God and preached them for the purpose of instructing, correcting, and encouraging others.

In Acts 13:1 a prophet who was a revealer of a future event describes Agabus very well. A prophet as a preacher pairs up well with the other term "teacher" in Acts 13:1, and it also describes Barnabas, "The Son Of Encouragement", very well. But, what is more, a prophet in Acts 13:1 could have been a Spirit-filled man who was both a revealer of direct revelations from God as well as a preacher of God's Word. Such a man as this describes the apostle Paul extremely well, for he received direct revelations and communications from God and as an apostle was at the same time an outstanding expounder and preacher of God's Word. Since the term "prophet" can be properly understood in all three of these ways, the reader should be aware that the term "prophet" in Acts 13:1 cannot definitely be said to mean a revealer of the future or a preacher of God's Word, as if it were an "either/or situation". There is no way that anyone now can know for certain which of the above three possibilities was the correct one and only one that Luke had in mind. The best way to understand the term "prophet" in Acts 13:1 is that it could mean all three kinds of prophets. With the single term "prophet" Luke could have meant that at least one of the five men on occasion was a revealer of a future event, at least one of the men was a preacher of God's Word, and at least one of the men – the apostle Paul for sure – was both a revealer of divine revelations and communications and a preacher of God's Word. Furthermore, the reader should bear in mind that in addition to being prophets, all five men could also have been teachers, such as Luke also mentioned in Acts 13:1.

Luke informs us in Acts 13:2 & 3 above about what happened on one certain day in the church of Antioch. Simeon, Lucius, and Manaen together with Paul and Barnabas were performing a religious service to the Lord with the congregation. It was a solemn type of service, for the five men performed it in connection with a fast that they in Christian liberty imposed upon themselves. Their fasting was not an act of obedience to any Mosaic law, for the Law commanded a day of fasting only on the Day of Atonement. But pious Jews of their own free will did fast at times. The five men brought over from their Jewish religious background this custom of fasting in connection with a solemn, divine worship service. It is interesting to see the men following this Jewish custom of fasting together with worship, for the church of Antioch was largely a Gentile congregation of Greek converts. Yet on this occasion the Jewish tradition of fasting was still followed by the five Jewish men.[13]

While the men were leading the congregation in worship and the preaching of the Word of God and in prayer, the Holy Spirit revealed what he wanted the congregation to do. Luke does not tell us how the Holy Spirit revealed what the congregation was to do. It is quite possible that the Holy Spirit gave a revelation to Simeon, or Lucius, or Manaen, the prophets in the congregation besides Paul and Barnabas.

The Holy Spirit said to the congregation, "By all means set apart for me Barnabas and Saul for the work to which I have called them." Here the Holy Spirit informed the church of Antioch that he wanted Paul and Barnabas to be released from their ministry in the church of Antioch and set apart for a special ministry to the Gentiles in other lands.

There are a number of important points to note from this verse. First, the Holy Spirit took the initiative, not Paul and Barnabas. Second, out of the whole church of Antioch the Holy Spirit chose which men he wanted; Paul and Barnabas did not step forward and offer themselves to serve. Third, the Holy Spirit had planned what work was to be done for the benefit of his kingdom by spreading the gospel to the Gentiles; Paul and Barnabas did not say what work they wanted to do. Fourth, the Holy Spirit directed the church to set Paul and Barnabas apart for the work he had planned for them; Paul and Barnabas did not tell the church what work they had decided they would do. Fifth, the Holy Spirit called Paul and Barnabas through the church to do the work to be done; he did not issue the call directly to Paul and Barnabas apart from any involvement of the church. Sixth, Paul and Barnabas did not by their own authority take the work upon themselves and tell the church they were going to do it.

What is said in this inspired verse teaches us numerous important truths about the ministry in Christ's church for all ages. The Holy Spirit decides whom he wants to serve, in what capacity, and when. He then calls the man through the church to do the work that he has planned for him to do. Since the Holy Spirit is the one who does the choosing and the calling through the church, the call that the church then extends to the man is said to be a divine call. The call comes from the Lord through the church to the man. It never happens the other way around – from the man to the church for the Lord. There is no inner calling and self-ordination on the part of the man apart from the church.

Having heard that the Holy Spirit wanted the congregation to set

Paul and Barnabas apart for the mission work that he had called them to do, Luke tells us in Acts 13:3, "Then after fasting and praying and laying their hands upon them, they sent them away."

Luke in his brief style does not indicate whether the original worship service to the Lord was extended or whether a second, separate service was conducted later. Since Luke says in verse 3 that the laying on of hands occurred after a fast, it seems best to understand that after the congregation had been told what the will of the Holy Spirit was, the congregation disbanded. Then on the next day the members observed a period of fasting, after which they reassembled for the second solemn service.

The church of Antioch followed the example and the precedent that the apostles and the church in Jerusalem set in the installation service for the seven deacons. In that installation service the seven men selected to serve as deacons stood before the apostles who led the assembly in prayer and then laid hands on the seven men.[14] The church in Antioch followed that example with the addition of a fast before the service. The service itself most likely included some instruction and encouragement from God's Word as well. The prayers would have then asked for God's blessings on the men, for their safekeeping from harm and danger, and that the Lord would prosper their spreading of the gospel. The service then included the laying on of hands. The laying on of hands was another Jewish religious practice[15] that the early apostolic church freely adopted. The rite of the laying on of hands was a symbolical act of conferring the particular ministry with its duties and privileges to the man being set apart. We do not know who in the church of Antioch performed the rite of the laying on of hands – Simeon, or Lucius, or Manaen, or the elders of the church, or a combination of them all.

The solemn service that the church of Antioch conducted was not an ordination service as we would call it today, in which the church sets apart a man for service in the public ministry of that church. It was not an ordination service because Paul and Barnabas were already prophets and teachers in the service of the Lord in the public ministry of the church of Antioch. Rather, the service was a commissioning service, as we would call it today. A commissioning service is similar to an ordination service but different in that a man who is already in the public ministry is set apart for service in a mission field. Such a commissioning service was appropriate for Paul and Barnabas because they were already in the public ministry of the church of Antioch. They were being released from the ministry in which they were already serving and being set apart for the special work of carrying the gospel to the Gentiles in other lands.

To this day the church has no divine command to conduct ordination or commissioning services. The church today in its Christian liberty chooses to follow the example set by the apostles and the ancient church. Accordingly, today we conduct similar worship services that include the Word of God for instruction and encouragement, prayer that asks for the Lord's blessings upon the man and his ministrations, and the symbolic laying on of hands to confer the particular ministry to the man being ordained or commissioned.

Upon the completion of the commissioning service for Paul and Barnabas Luke tells us the church of Antioch "sent them away." The Greek word in verse 3 for "send away" also means "release" and "set free". It is also the Greek word used for breaking off a marriage relationship and for divorce in Matthew 5:31-32 & 19:1-9 and in Mark 10:1-11. These meanings being true, verse 3 could also be understood to mean that with the commissioning of Paul and Barnabas the church of Antioch also released and set them free from their previous ministry of preaching and teaching in the congregation. Then, having been commissioned and sent by the church, when Paul and Barnabas departed to begin their missionary journey, they did so as the delegates and representatives of the church of Antioch and all its members. The mission work that they were embarking upon was not their personal mission work but that of the church of Antioch. And so it is to this day. The missionaries are representatives carrying out the work of the church body that commissioned them.

Paul's Mission Work On Cyprus

Luke reported Paul's mission work on the island of Cyprus in Chapter 13 of his Book of Acts. Chapter 13 has been considered the beginning of the second half of Luke's book. Starting with that chapter Luke presents Paul as the leading man in the transmission of the gospel to the end of the earth, namely Rome.[16] The reader should be aware, then, that in Chapter 13 Luke changes what name he uses for Paul and in what order he places the names of Paul and Barnabas.

If the reader looks in his Book of Acts, he will note that when Luke referred to Paul for the first time in Acts 7:58, he used the Hebrew name Saul. Luke then continued using the name Saul up through his account of Elymas the false Jewish teacher/magician and the Roman proconsul Sergius Paulus in Acts 13:8. But then in Acts 13:9 Luke stopped using the name Saul and introduced and switched to the Greek name "Paulos", which is "Paul" in English. It appears that Luke realized that in his narrative the Greek name of Paul would be more suitable than the Hebrew name Saul as he, Luke, would report Paul's missionary work among the Greek Gentiles.

The reader will also note in his Book of Acts that starting with Acts 11:30 regarding the famine relief mission up through Acts 13:7 regarding the witnessing to Sergius Paulus Luke put Barnabas' name before the name of Saul. Then starting with Acts 13:9 when Paul chastised Elymas and witnessed to Sergius Paulus Luke presented Paul as the leader of the mission team. From then on Paul's name was stated first and Paul was treated as the more important of the two men.

As this writer promised previously, throughout his comments he would use the name of Paul, not Saul, and put Paul's name first. He would do so to avoid arousing confusion. And now that the reader has been made aware of the preceding, we can move on to Paul's mission work on the island of Cyprus.

After reporting that the church of Antioch commissioned Paul and Barnabas and then sent them away, Luke informs us in Acts 13:4 & 5:

> 4 So, to be sure, having been sent out by the Holy Spirit, they went down to Seleucia, and from there they sailed away to Cyprus.

> 5 And when they arrived in Salamis, they began to proclaim the word of God in the synagogues of the Jews; and they also had John as their helper.

Paul and Barnabas left the city of Antioch behind them and proceeded on what was to be Paul's first missionary journey to the Gentiles as the representative of the church in Antioch. Accompanying them was Barnabas' cousin John Mark.[17] The Greek term that Luke used for the English word "helper" in the above verse is the same word Luke used for Paul in Acts 26:16, where Jesus told Paul what his function would be in Jesus' service as a minister of Christ. This was discussed in detail in Chapter 6. As explained there the Greek term meant an under rower, a subordinate rower. And it then was used to denote anyone who aided another in some work. This meaning of the Greek term tells us that John Mark was to be an underling, an attendant, a helper, to Paul and Barnabas. He was to do whatever tasks they instructed him to do to help them accomplish their mission work. We should not infer from John Mark's serving as an underling and helper, as Conybeare and Howson did, that it was his hands that performed the menial task of baptizing the Jews and Gentiles who were brought to faith by Paul's and Barnabas' preaching.[18] That opinion is unreasonable because the Sacrament of Holy Baptism is not a menial task to be relegated to an underling but is an important part of the gospel ministry in administering the Means of Grace that Christ Jesus gave to his Church for the saving of souls.

When the three men left Antioch, they could have traveled overland by the main road. Overland the distance was about sixteen miles[19] to Seleucia, which was on the northeastern shores of the Mediterranean Sea. However, they could also have sailed downstream on the Orontes River to Seleucia. It was navigable. Its waters flowed all year around and were deep and rapid. Boats of some size were able to sail up and down the river transporting passengers and carrying cargos. The Orontes wound around the bases of high cliffs that made the trip by boat much longer than the overland route,[20] but the distance could still be sailed in about one day.[21].

Seleucia was known as Seleucia Pieria and also as Seleucia By The Sea to avoid confusing it with other cities of the same name. It was the port city of Antioch.[22] Seleucus I Nicator built the city and a fortress in 300 B.C., which he named after himself. Information about him was presented in the previous chapter in connection with the founding of the city of Antioch. The city of Seleucia was built slightly north of the mouth of the Orontes River between small rivers on the western slopes of Coryphaeus, which was one of the southern summits of the Amanus Mountains.[23] Seleucia was one of four cities that made up the "Syrian Tetrapolis" that consisted of Seleucia, Antioch, Apamea, and Laodicea.[24] Because of the topography of the land where Seleucia was built, it was divided into an Upper City that was higher up on the slope of the mountain and a Lower City. The two cities were divided by steep rocks of the mountain and were connected by stairs carved into the steep slope that were wide enough for about six or seven people to walk abreast.[25] The two cities were encircled by a wall, traces of which remain to this day. The ruins of the city show evidence of a necropolis, an amphitheater, a citadel, pagan temples, some irrigation works, and some fortifications.[26] The harbor of Seleucia actually consisted of an inner and an outer harbor. The original stone piers of the outer harbor could still be seen under water according to Conybeare and Howson, whose first edition of Paul's biography was dated in 1852.[27] During the Ptolemaic-Seleucid Wars of the third century B.C. Seleucia was fought over because of its political, military, and economic importance. Seleucia came under the influence of Rome when General Pompey the Great gained control of Asia Minor and Syria in 64 B.C. In 63 B.C. Rome made Seleucia a free city. Two years after Paul's martyrdom Seleucia became a Roman naval base in A.D. 70.[28] Over the centuries Seleucia, together with its surrounding area including Antioch, has been struck by earthquakes. One of them was mentioned in the previous chapter.[29]

At the seaport of Seleucia Paul, Barnabas, and John Mark would have been able to find with relative ease a ship to ferry them over to Cyprus, for ships regularly sailed there. Cyprus was not far away. On a clear day it could be seen from the Syrian mainland. Their ship would take them to the harbor city of Salamis on the east coast of the island. With a fair wind the crossing to Salamis would have taken only a few hours.[30]

Cyprus is rich in history. While making the crossing Paul and his companions sailed through waters off the eastern coast of Salamis that was the site of one of the greatest ancient sea battles. The naval battle took place in 306 B.C. Over 200 ships were involved in the engagement between the fleets of Ptolemy I, the Greek ruler of Egypt, who also after the death of Alexander the Great ruled the island of Cyprus, and Demetrius I of Macedon in Greece. Demetrius and his Greek naval fleet won the battle and he then captured the island of Cyprus.[31]

Paul was sailing to an island that had changed hands a number of times in its long history. In extremely ancient times the Assyrians exerted their power over Cyprus. The city-states of Cyprus "were so well established by 673 B.C. that they were listed on an inscription in Assyria in order to pay tribute to King Esahraddon,"[32] who reigned from 681-669 B.C. It has also been reported that Sargon II collected tribute from the city-kings of Cyprus in 708 B.C.[33] Next, in 525 B.C. the Persians took control of Cyprus and the city of Salamis.[34] It was then fought over by the Persians and the Greeks. There was a great land and sea battle between the Persians and the Greeks in 450 B.C. The Greek forces won that battle and drove the Persians out of Cyprus. The Greeks then took possession of the island. After Alexander the Great died in 323 B.C. Cyprus was ruled by the Greek general Ptolemy I who established his dynasty in Egypt. After the naval battle in 306 B.C., that was mentioned above, Demetrius of Macedon in Greece took control of Cyprus. And centuries later in 58 B.C. Salamis and Cyprus came under the control of Rome.[35][36] Cyprus was made a part of the Roman province of Cilicia in 55 B.C.[37] The island was made a Roman senatorial province in 22 B.C. that was ruled by a proconsul, which it still was at the time of Paul's mission work on Cyprus in A.D. 46.[38]

There are two accounts of how the city of Salamis was founded. The Greek legendary account says Teucher, an archer who fought in the Trojan War, founded the city after that war ended. But it has been reported that inhabitants of Cyprus known as Enkomi founded the city after an earthquake of around 1075 B.C.[39] Salamis became the capital of Cyprus around that time.[40]

Salamis at the time of Paul was a large city.[41] It was the largest city on Cyprus during the Roman period of rule.[42] The city lay in a low, flat plain that extended into the heart of the island between the island's two mountain ranges. It had a good harbor and therefore Paul would have found it a thriving seaport with ships coming in from every part of the Mediterranean Sea that brought goods of every kind.[43] As a result the city was a very wealthy city. One of the outstanding features of the city that Paul would have seen was its large amphitheater. It was built in the beginning of the 1st century A.D. during the earlier part of his life. It had over 50 rows of seats that were laid out in a semi-circle. The theater would seat 15,000 spectators,[44] which indicates, according to archaeologists' method of calculating an ancient city's population, that the city of Salamis had a population of about 150,000 at the time Paul visited it.

Having been born and raised for years in that part of the Mediterranean world, Paul would have known that earthquakes occurred all too often in the countries located there. We know today that they also struck Salamis as well as Antioch and Seleucia in Syria, as was noted before. The recurring earthquakes over time were responsible for a cumulative damage done to the city,[45] of which Paul might have seen some evidence while he was there. Long after Paul's martyrdom the city would be rebuilt by emperor Constantius II who reigned from A. D. 337-361. Ultimately, however, the city would be destroyed by Arab invasions in A.D. 648 and the city would then be abandoned altogether.[46] Not far from its ruins stands the modern city of Famagusta.

When Paul, together with Barnabas and John Mark, crossed the island of Cyprus, the majority of the island was a rugged mountainous terrain with fertile valleys and wide beaches. The Greek Cypriot poet Leonidas Malenis described Cyprus as a "golden-green leaf thrown into the sea" and a land of "wild weather and volcanoes."[47] The island was the third largest island in the Mediterranean Sea. It was shaped like an elongated saucepan. From the eastern most tip of its handle to the extreme western end of its saucepan it was about 125 miles in length. Across the widest points of its saucepan it was 58 miles wide. Cyprus had about 400 miles of coastline.[48] The largest river was the Pediaeus (Pedueos) River that flowed eastward to Salamis, which was located just north of the river. The other rivers on Cyprus were fed by the winter rains that flowed down from the mountain ranges, but those rivers dried up in the hot summer season.[49]

Cyprus at the time of Paul had twelve cities that were scattered throughout the island. Those cities were: Paphos, Kition, Ledrai, and Kyrenia, all of which are thriving cities today; Lapithos, Tamasos, Chytroi (now Kythraia), and Isalion, which are now sleepy villages; Kurion, Anathus, Marion, and Salamis, which now lie in ruins.[50]

The natural inhabitants of those cities were pagans who had a history of worshipping the various gods of Phoenicia – Anat, Baal, Eshmun, Reshef, Mikal, and Melkart, as well as the gods of Egypt – Hathor, Thoth, Bes, and Ptah. The chief deity on the island, however, was the Great Goddess Aphrodite, who was also known by a variety of names. Aphrodite was her Greek name.[51] More will be said about this Greek goddess of love in connection with the following discussion on the city of Paphos.

In addition to the pagan inhabitants of Cyprus there was a large population of Jews. Some may have migrated from Lydia and Phrygia of Asia Minor where Antiochus the Great (reigned 222-187 B.B.C.) had relocated two thousand Jewish families.[52] Some of the Jews on Cyprus might have come there in connection with Herod the Great's mining of the copper mines on Cyprus.[53] The chief export of Cyprus was copper, which gave the island its name of "Cyprus".[54] We know there was a large number of Jews living in Salamis because Luke informs us in Acts 13:5 that was quoted above that there were two or more synagogues in that city.

Paul and Barnabas began their mission work in the city of Salamis in the Jewish synagogues. Being knowledgeable teachers of the Old Testament Scriptures, they would likely have been invited to address the assemblies of the Jews in the synagogues in Salamis. As an example of this Luke tells us in Acts 13:15 that they were given such an invitation in Pisidian Antioch. Upon being given the invitation to speak, they would have likely begun with God's calling of Abraham or of Moses and then proceeding through the history of the Jewish nation[55]. In the course of their address they would have been pointing out God's promises in the Old Testament Scriptures about the coming Messiah (Christ). Then on the basis of those divine promises they would have been teaching the assembled Jews that the man Jesus of Nazareth was that Messiah who was the Son of David and the Son of God. Their address would surely have recounted Jesus' suffering and sacrificial death as the payment for sins, and his having been raised from the dead as God's declaration that sins had been paid for.

Having been called by the Holy Spirit and set apart for this mission work they were beginning to do, it was only fitting that Paul and Barnabas should begin their mission work in the synagogues of the Jews, for it was Jesus' will that Paul be his witness to the Jews as well as to the Gentiles.[56] What is more, the Jews were God's chosen people to whom the divine Scriptures had been given, to whom the covenants and the promises had been given, from whom the Messiah had descended according to the flesh, and among whom God had that Messiah Jesus Christ accomplish mankind's salvation. Furthermore, Jesus had commanded that disciples should be made of all nations[57] of whom the Jews were a part. And as Paul would later write to Timothy that it was God's will that all people come to a knowledge of the truth and be saved,[58] so the Jews should be given that opportunity as well.

The Holy Spirit might have had an additional reason for Paul and Barnabas to begin their witnessing in the synagogues: in those synagogues there would likely have been God-fearing Greeks who worshipped with the Jews. Converts could possibly be made from among them as well. And being Greek people, they would have had Greek friends, relatives, fellow workers, and neighbors to whom they could introduce Paul and Barnabas. Through networking with those God-fearing Greeks more Greek people might be reached with the gospel and converted, Greek people whom Paul and Barnabas might not otherwise have been able to reach.

Luke does not tell us what the outcome of Paul and Barnabas' preaching and teaching in Salamis was. Since the purpose of his Book of Acts was to recount the spreading of the gospel of Jesus Christ and the growth of the Church, for the most part Luke informs us of what were the results of the preaching of the gospel. Because he does not do so in the case of Salamis, we should not think that the preaching and the teaching of God's Word in the synagogues there were a failure and without effect, for God's Word always brings about an effect – either it converts hearts or hardens them. God himself tells us this about his Word in Isaiah 55:10 & 11:

> 10 For as the rain and the snow come down from heaven, and does not return there unless it waters the earth and makes it bring forth and sprout, so that it gives seed to the sower and bread to the eater –
>
> 11 so will my word be that goes forth from my mouth. It will not return to me empty, but rather will accomplish what I desire and make what I sent it for succeed.

But we should also remember that the results are not always immediate. The results may not become evident for a period of time, for Jesus tells us that the Word of God is like seed that is planted in the ground.[59] And like seed the Word of God does not necessarily sprout and grow immediately; it may take a while. So we should not conclude Paul and Barnabas' work in Salamis was a definite failure. Rather, we should conclude that God the Holy Spirit accomplished whatever his purpose was through the preaching of Paul and Barnabas.

Then Luke says in Acts 13:6, "And they traveled through the whole island as far as Paphos." When they had finished proclaiming that gospel in the synagogues of the Jews in Salamis, they began their walk through the island. In his brief style Luke does not provide us with the details of what route they took or what happened on the way or how long it took them to walk to Paphos. If one looks at the map of ancient Cyprus, one can see that except for a valley between the mountain range along the northern coast and the mountains covering about eighty-five percent of the southern part of the island, the interior of the island is mostly mountainous terrain.

Paul's traveling with Barnabas through the whole island as far as Paphos can be understood in two ways. First, it could mean they literally walked through the whole island, criss-crossing back and forth from city to city and north to south while gradually working their way westward until they reached Paphos at the far southwestern end of the island. Such a trek would have been long and at times possibly treacherous. Or, secondly, their traveling through the whole island could mean they walked directly from Salamis in the east to Paphos in the southwest. This writer tends to think the latter was the case, and that they did not travel to all twelve cities on the island. The direct route seems more likely because when Paul and Barnabas separated four years later, Barnabas returned to Cyrus with John Mark.[60] His purpose for returning might have been to complete the mission work that had been left undone before.

Assuming that Paul and Barnabas did travel directly to Paphos from Salamis, the easiest and the most direct route would have been along the southern coastline. If they followed that route, the distance would have been less than one hundred miles. They could have walked that in about five days. In the process they would have passed through the cities of Kition, Anathus, and Kurion before reaching Paphos. But Luke says nothing about their working in those three cities just as he says nothing about their working in the other seven cities on the island.

When Paul and his coworkers reached the southwestern coast of Cyprus, they would have found not just one city of Paphos but two – the old and the new. What is more, they would have come to the most famous place in the ancient Mediterranean world for the worship of Aphrodite.[61] The old city of Paphos is now known as the site of Kouklia. It has been said that the Phoenicians founded the city.[62] But there are different legends and opinions on how the worship of Aphrodite started at Paphos. In any case it appears that her worship there goes back to very ancient times. The United Nations Educational, Scientific and Cultural Organization's website says the temple of Aphrodite in the Old Paphos was erected by the Myceneans from ancient Greece in the 12th century B.C."[63] UNESCO has placed the old city of Paphos on its list of cultural and natural treasures of the world's heritage because of its age and connection with the legend of Aphrodite. The remains of the large sanctuary of Aphrodite can still be seen. Its circumference is marked by huge foundation walls.[64] The worship of Aphrodite was also widespread through the island of Cyprus. It is well known that in ancient times intercourse with the priestesses of Aphrodite was practiced as a method of worshipping the goddess.[65] Such ritual prostitution was also practiced on Cyprus.[66] The cult of Aphrodite continued until the late A.D. 300s of the Christian era.[67]

The new city of Paphos was built about seven miles from the Old Paphos [68] It was built by the sea on a small promontory[69] near a good harbor.[70] The New Paphos was founded by Nikokles, the king of the city-state of Paphos around 320 B.C. He abandoned the old city of Paphos without abandoning its temple of Aphrodite as the center for her worship. Nikokles thought the building of a new city was necessary because the old city did not have a suitable harbor to accommodate the trade that had developed during that 4th century.[71] The New Paphos then grew into an important cultural, financial and administrative center.

Then Ptolemy I Soter, former general under Alexander the Great who had become the ruler of Egypt (reigned from 323-306 B.C.), gained control of Cyprus during the coalition war of 315-311 B.C.[72] When he took over the island of Cyprus, he made Paphos the capital of the island.[73] One reason he did so was that the temple of Aphrodite continued to attract worshippers from all parts of the Mediterranean world. His government collected money from that religious traffic. A second, strategic, reason was that Paphos was near Ptolemy's capital in Alexandria, Egypt. Communication with Paphos was easier than with any other city on Cyprus. What is more, Paphos had an abundant supply of forests for the building of his warships.[74]

During the Roman period of rule the Romans also made Paphos the capital of the island. It was the administrative seat of the Roman proconsul, the most famous of whom was Cicero, the great orator.[75]

THE APOSTLE PAUL, A BONDSERVANT OF CHRIST JESUS   259

When Paul visited New Paphos, he would have seen its large, flourishing theater. The ruins of the theater are still preserved in the northeast part of the city on a hillside called Fabrika.[76] It is the oldest theater on Cyprus. It was used for dramatic performances and spectacles from about 300 B.C. until its final destruction by an earthquake in A.D. 365.[77] When it was at its largest size in the 2nd century A.D., it could seat 8, 500 spectators.[78] That seating capacity indicates that in the 2nd century Paphos had a population possibly as large as 85,000.

It happened that fifteen years before the birth of Jesus Christ, which would have been 19 B.C., a strong earthquake struck the old and the new cities of Paphos and turned them into rubble. Caesar Augustus had the new city of Paphos rebuilt. It was called Augusta; apparently it was named after the emperor himself. The rebuilt city grew rapidly and about the time Paul visited this rebuilt city of New Paphos its population was about 30,000.[79]

Luke continues his narrative by telling us in Acts 13:6b-8 that after Paul and Barnabas had arrived in Paphos,

> 6b . . . they found a Jewish magician and false prophet, whose name was Bar-Jesus,
>
> 7 who was with the proconsul Sergius Paulus, an intelligent man. When this man summoned Barnabas and Saul, he wished to hear the word of God.
>
> 8. But Elymas the magician, for so his name is translated, opposed them, seeking to turn the proconsul away from the faith.

Luke makes no mention of Paul and Barnabas going to a synagogue in Paphos, which they were likely to have done. He states only that they went to the residence of the proconsul Sergius Paulus and appeared before him and probably his retinue as well. Luke was absolutely correct in using the title of "proconsul" for Sergius Paulus. In 58 B.C Rome annexed Cyprus. At the time that Cyprus was under the direct control of the emperor, his appointed "imperial legate" over the island was called by the Roman imperial title of "Propraetor". But then in 22 B.C. the status of Cyprus was changed to a Roman province and its control was transferred from the emperor to the Roman Senate. The Senate then appointed its official to rule over Cyprus, whose title was "Proconsul".[80] So once again the accuracy of Luke's knowledge and narrative is proven to be correct.

Luke informs us that among the retinue of Sergius Paulus Paul and Barnabas found a Jewish magician and false prophet, whose name was Bar-Jesus. The name Bar-Jesus means "son of Jesus", or, "son of Joshua". The Greek wording of Luke's in verse 8 has caused a bit of a linguistic problem that has led to some discussion among the New Testament Greek scholars as to the meaning of the name "Elymas". This is not the place for a lengthy discussion of the Greek and Aramaic names and words in Luke's text. Let it suffice here to say it seems best to understand "Elymas" to be a surname for a "magician, a sorcerer".

Elymas, Luke says, was a Jewish magician and false prophet. As far as his Jewish heritage he was a Jew by birth but nothing more. He had forsaken his Jewish religious and spiritual roots. He had turned from the truths of the Old Testament Jewish Scriptures to spin his own teachings. Just how far he had turned from the Old Testament Scriptures that God had given to the Jews is made extremely evident by the fact that he had turned to magic and sorcery, which were an abomination in the sight of God. For God had told his Jewish people in Deuteronomy 8:10-12:

> 10 Let there not be found among you anyone who causes his son or his daughter to pass through fire, who practices divination, who practices sorcery, or who interprets omens, or practices witchcraft,
>
> 1 or who casts a spell, or who is a medium, or who is a spiritist, or who consults the dead,
>
> 12 because all who do these things are detestable to the Lord, and because of these detestable things the Lord your God will drive them out from your presence.

Some commentators have labeled Elymas as an imposter[81] and a charlatan.[82] They may be right, for fakes and frauds in the field of magic and sorcery have been all too commonplace. But one should not be too quick to write off the possibility that the devil can exert his diabolic powers through someone to work the unexplainable and dastardly deeds if and when God allows him to do so. This word of caution is said for good reason. Among Luke's inspired accounts of Paul's missionary journeys Luke writes in Acts 16:16-18 about the slave girl who had a demonic spirit of divination for fortune-telling. And Paul himself acknowledged that the power of Satan would be at work "in all power and miraculous signs and lying wonders" in connection with the coming of the great Antichrist.[83] Unfortunately, the devil is still alive and powerful, seeking whom he may destroy. So while Elymas might very well have been an imposter and a fraud, since Luke does not label him as such, this writer must allow the possibility that Elymas might have had some diabolic magical powers by which he did influence and control the mind and thoughts of the proconsul Sergius Paulus.

Luke's report that Elymas, a Jewish magician, was practicing his sorcery on the island of Cyprus is not the only such report from the first century. The Roman historian Pliny the Elder, who lived at the time of Paul from A.D. 23 to August 25th, 79, also wrote that in his time there were Jews adept in the art of magic who were cultivating a branch of magic on the island of Cyprus.[84] So the reliability of Luke's report of a Jewish magician at work on Cyprus receives support from a secular Roman writer of the first century. Furthermore, Josephus, who also wrote from around A.D. 75 - 100, wrote of a Jew who was born on Cyprus who pretended to be a magician and who was a friend of Felix the procurator of Judea between A.D. 52-59.[85] That date was only 6 to 13 years after Paul was at Paphos on Cyprus.

Luke informs us that the Roman proconsul was named Sergius Paulus. Some have thought he was the Quintus Sergius Paullus who was named in an inscription at Chytroi (Kythraia) in northern Cyprus. This is uncertain, however, because the inscription does not conclusively indicate the years during which the mentioned Quintus Sergius Paullus served as a proconsul on Cyprus. It is not certain, therefore, that his time in office was at the same time as when Paul and Barnabas were in Paphos. In 1912 Ramsay found at Pisidian Antioch a memorial stone on which was engraved the name "Lucius Sergius Paulus, the younger." He had been the representative of Quirinius, the governor of Syria, and became the Roman governor of Galatia at the time and had a sister named Sergia Paula. Ramsay concluded that this Sergius Paulus, Jr. and his sister were the son and the daughter of the proconsul Sergius Paulus at Paphos, Cyprus.[86]

The Sergius Paulus whom Luke mentions was an intelligent man. The Greek word translated "intelligent" in verse 7 above could also be translated "wise", "having good sense",[87] "having understanding and being learned".[88] We may wonder why such an intelligent Roman man with good common sense and an education, a Roman aristocrat no less, would have a magician like Elymas in his entourage. The answer is: While Sergius Paulus was an intelligent Roman, he was also a Roman of his times. And at his time magic and superstition abounded in the lives of Romans, and clearly in the life of Sergius Paulus as well, which was why Elymas was in his company.

Ingrid De Haas, a Ph.d in ancient Roman history, has written a very informative article about magic among the ancient Romans.[89] She states that every Roman, rich or poor, free or slave, needed or wanted to use magic at one point or another. According to her, "Many Romans frequently visited . . . a neighborhood magician who set up shop outside one of Rome's many temples. There, they paid a small fee for a love potion, charm, spell, or amulet." The Roman government considered magic dangerous and many of its magicians frauds. Therefore the Roman government often tried, but always unsuccessfully, to forbid the use, and even the knowledge, of magic. Throughout the history of the Republic (510 – 27 B.C.) and the Empire (27 B.C. – A.D. 476) laws were made that forbid magic. Under Roman law the practitioners and users of magic were prosecuted and punished. "But the many amulets and books of spells that archaeologists have found all demonstrate that this crackdown did not work. Magic didn't disappear from Rome."

De Haas gave numerous examples of in what ways Romans resorted to magic. If a Roman wanted someone murdered, he could hire a magician. The magical instructions told the practitioner to get a piece of lead, shape it into a thin, flat rectangle, and inscribe the would-be victim's name on it with the request to the spirits of the netherworld to destroy the individual. Then the magician was to pierce the lead tablet with an iron nail, take it to a graveyard, dig a hole in someone's, anyone's, grave and bury the lead tablet. If the magician did all of these things, the intended victim would die. If a Roman had to stop the marital infidelity of a spouse or make his dreams of a love affair with someone a reality, he or she could hire a magician. If a Roman wanted to win a legal case, or fix the outcome of a chariot race to win a bet, he could pay a magician to inscribe a lead tablet with an appropriate message. Since there were no modern medicines to cure illnesses or contraceptives to prevent pregnancy, a Roman man or woman could employ a magician to affect a magical cure or prevent a pregnancy. According to De Haas Romans in general were plagued with a fear of supernatural powers and forces that they believed in but did not understand. So they purchased amulets from magicians to protect them from spells, from spirits and demons, and from evil in the world.

Tacitus, possibly the greatest of the ancient Roman historians, who lived from A.D. 58 to 120, described an instance where magical practices and incantations were employed to kill the Roman General Germanicus, who died on October 10th, A.D. 19, which was just twenty-seven years before Paul stood before Sergius Paullus. Tacitus wrote:

> On leaving Egypt Germanicus learnt that all his orders to divisional commanders and cities had been cancelled or reversed. Between him and Piso there were violent reciprocal denunciations. Then Piso decided to leave to go to Syria. But Germanicus fell ill, and so Piso stayed on. When news came that the prince was better and vows offered for his recovery were being paid, Piso sent his attendants to disperse the rejoicing crowds of Antioch, with their sacrificial victims and apparatus. Then he left for Seleucia Pieria, to await the outcome of Germanicus' illness. He had a relapse – aggravated by his belief that

Piso had poisoned him. Examination of the floor and walls of his bedroom revealed the remains of human bodies, spells, curses, lead tablets inscribed with the patient's name, charred and bloody ashes, and other malignant objects which are supposed to consign souls to the powers of the tomb. At the same time agents of Piso were accused of spying on the sickbed.[90]

This writer also found in Tacitus' <u>The Annals Of Imperial Rome</u> nine separate accounts[91] involving Roman aristocrats in accusations against them of having resorted to astrologers, magicians, or interpreters of dreams in violation of the Roman law. For their breaking the law forbidding the use of such practitioners they were tried, and there were instances of acquittal and instances of being found guilty. The sentence was death. Among those accounts Tacitus reports that the Roman Senate had passed decrees to expel astrologers and magicians from Italy. One, Lucius Pituanius, was thrown to his death from the Tarpeian Rock, another, Publius Marcius, was executed by the consuls in the traditional manner at the sound of the bugle outside the Equiline Gate.[92] Tacitus also related the account of a daughter named Servilla of an aristocratic father. Her father was facing political charges that could destroy him and their family. Servilla was charged with giving large sums of money to magicians for magical rites that would help her father. She was accused of having sold her bridal gifts and necklace to raise the money to pay the magicians.[93] This account, besides showing another incidence of the Romans resorting to magicians, shows that the magicians' services were not free but could be rather expensive.

Further evidence of the presence of magic among the ancient Romans comes from Pliny, who has been quoted as saying about Roman culture,

> We certainly have formulas to charm away hail, various diseases, and burns, some actually treated by experience, but I am very shy of quoting them, because of the widely different feeling they arouse.[94]

Lead tablets such as De Hass described and Tacitus mentioned have been found in the Village of Kent, England, and throughout Europe. In the Village of Kent a third century A.D. Roman lead tablet was found inscribed with a curse. It measured 2.3 by 3.9 inches.[95]

The Romans of the ancient past are an example of what happens when people adrift in the spiritual darkness of their unbelief and ungodliness with no divine truths to which to cling follow the lead of their sinful natures to go down the path of dabbling with and then wallowing in the diabolical depths of the occult looking for some power to turn to in their times of need for help and hope. Such, it appears, was the case of the Roman proconsul Sergius Paulus as well, for he kept a Jewish magician in his entourage close to his side. Sergius as a Roman senatorial legate was supposed to uphold and enforce the laws of Rome. Yet there he was in Paphos violating the Roman law forbidding the use of magicians. It seems apparent that Sergius was Elymas' patron in the sense that Sergius was a powerful, influential, wealthy Roman aristocrat who was supporting Elymas in return for Elymas' magical services. Like the magicians in Rome described above Elymas' magical services would not have been free either, but would have come at a price. Sergius seems to have been paying the price for his daily services by keeping him in his entourage.

It was into that setting of a Jewish magician practicing his magic for a Roman proconsul who was looking for magical guidance for conducting his official duties that Paul and Barnabas walked when they obeyed the summons to appear before Sergius Paulus.

In Luke's brief historical style he omits the details of Paul and Barnabas' arrival in Paphos, saying nothing about when they arrived there, for how long they were there, or about what they did when they arrived there. It is most likely that they did in Paphos what they did in Salamis – they went to the synagogue. There they preached the Word of God and the gospel of Jesus Christ. Within a short time their teaching became known in the city of Paphos. It must have been then that a report was brought to the proconsul Sergius Paulus that there were some new itinerant teachers in the city who were claiming to be teaching the word and message of God.

It is likely that upon hearing this news the proconsul's curiosity was pricked. He was a man of understanding and good sense. As the proconsul of Cyprus he was responsible for maintaining law and order. His good sense was telling him that he needed to know more about these new itinerant teachers. Who were they? What were they doing there? What were they teaching the populace of Paphos and Cyprus? Was their teaching subversive and dangerous to the authority of Caesar and Rome? Were they troublemakers who were stirring up the people? Having such kinds of questions, he would have wanted answers. Furthermore, he himself was probably curious to know what was that word of God that they were teaching? And what God? There were all sorts of gods. The mythological pantheon of the pagans was full of them. And if those men were really teaching the word of God, what did that God have to say? And so Luke reports in Acts 13:7, "When this man summoned Barnabas and Saul, he wished to hear the word of God."

The summons was likely to have been delivered by a residential guard of the proconsul. He then would have escorted them to the residence and court of the proconsul. Once in the proconsul's presence, Sergius would have questioned them and indicated that he wanted to know what they were teaching the people that was supposedly the word of God. Paul and Barnabas would then have begun witnessing the spiritual life-giving gospel of Jesus Christ, through which the power of the Holy Spirit was at work to create faith in the man Sergius Paulus. For the first time the Roman proconsul was hearing about the One true God of heaven and earth and about his Son Jesus Christ who lived a sinless life, gave that innocent life as the payment for all sins, and was raised to life again as God's declaration that sins were forgiven.

But when Paul and Barnabas were sharing that word and message of God with the proconsul, Luke tells us, "Elymas the magician, for so his name is translated, opposed them, seeking to turn the proconsul away from the faith" (Acts 13:8). Being a magician, Elymas no doubt had demonstrated some powers of the black arts that the proconsul and those in his court had seen. But he was also a Jewish false prophet who taught doctrines contrary to the word of God. In this case Elymas was opposing the gospel of God's grace in Jesus Christ. Elymas was making assertions that the gospel of Jesus Christ that Paul and Barnabas were expounding was false and should not be believed. Elymas was arguing that the gospel was a falsehood in order to prevent the proconsul from believing the truth of the gospel and the Christian faith. Through his opposing Paul and Barnabas Elymas was perverting the righteous way of God to deliver the proconsul from the devil's power to save the proconsul's soul. And it is likely that Elymas had an ulterior motive for trying to turn the proconsul against the Christian faith – Elymas' own livelihood in the court of the proconsul was at stake. If the proconsul were to become a Christian, he would stop listening to Elymas and Elymas would lose his lucrative, pleasurable lifestyle in the proconsul's court.

After Elymas had been opposing Paul and Barnabas for a while, the Holy Spirit filled Paul, who then glared at Elymas in a righteous anger. Moved by the Holy Spirit to chastise Elymas in order to lead him to repent of his ungodly magical arts and teachings, Paul sternly rebuked Elymas,

> 10 "O you son of the devil! Full of every kind of treachery and wickedness! You enemy of all righteousness! Will you never stop making crooked the straight ways of the Lord?
>
> 11 And now, behold, the hand of the Lord is against you! And you will be blind, unable to see the sun for a period of time" (Acts 13:10 & 11).

Luke then tells us:

> 11. And immediately a mist and darkness fell upon him. And while going around blindly, he kept searching for individuals to lead him by the hand.
>
> 12 Then, when the proconsul saw what had happened, he believed, being struck with astonishment at the teaching of the Lord. (Acts 13:11, 12).

The words Paul spoke by the authority of the Holy Spirit had an immediate effect. A mist and darkness, perhaps like a sudden descending cloud, came down upon Elymas. It struck him blind. He could not see a thing or the light of day. He began stumbling around, desperately searching for someone who could take him by the hand to lead him. That sudden miraculous chastisement of God the Holy Spirit inflicted by the hand of Paul greatly impressed the proconsul. He was probably shocked to see the power of Paul's words so quickly carry out the chastisement of blindness that Paul had declared would happen. The proconsul could not deny the reality of what he had just seen happen. At once he realized that the divine power of Paul was much greater than the demonic magical power of Elymas. The proconsul just as quickly grasped the truth that Paul truly spoke the word of God about the Lord and Savior Jesus Christ. What Paul had told him was true! And so the proconsul believed and was struck with amazement over the word of God that Paul had taught him.

This true account from the missionary life of Paul is a graphic instance of the battle for the minds of mankind that the devil wages against God and his Word. In this account of Luke's one can see the devil at work behind the false teaching and magic of Elymas in an effort to maintain his control over the mind of the proconsul Sergius Paulus. The proconsul's mind was bound up in the devil's domain of spiritual darkness, unbelief, magic, and sin. The devil had the proconsul's mind and soul and he was not about to give the proconsul up without a fight. The devil was a "strong man" holding what was his in his iron grip. The proconsul needed to be released from the devil's strong hold and set free. There was only one way that could happen. Jesus tells us how it is done. He says, "How can anyone enter into the house of the strong man and carry off his possessions unless he first ties up the strong man? And then he will plunder his house!"[96] First the devil must be tied up; then the minds and souls that belong to him can be carried off. What ties up the devil is the gospel of Jesus Christ that frees those souls held in his possession. Paul had taught the proconsul the gospel of Jesus Christ, and that gospel freed the proconsul's mind to believe in Jesus and to turn away from the devil and the devil's lies. In this way the battle for the minds of mankind is fought one man or woman or child at a time. This was the kind of battle Paul would be engaged in throughout his apostolic ministry as a bondservant of the Lord Jesus – binding up the devil by the power of the gospel and setting people free to believe in Jesus Christ to be saved for eternal life. And throughout his apostolic ministry Paul continued to encounter the devil's opposition as shall be seen in this biographical commentary.

It was there while in the attendance with the proconsul that the leadership of Paul came into the forefront according to Luke's historical narrative. The Holy Spirit came upon Paul and Paul was the one who then did the talking and performed the miraculous chastisement. So, starting at this point in Luke's narrative it is Paul's name that is given the prominence as the most important man on the mission team. Starting at the next verse of Acts 13:13 the reader can note that the missionary expedition became known as "Paul and his companions". The role of leadership had passed from Barnabas to Paul. And it was also at this point that Luke ceased to use the name of Saul and began to use the name of Paul.

---

1. Acts 9:15
2. Lit. throughout the existing, or being, church
3. Balge, Richard D.; The People's Bible, Acts; Northwestern Publishing House, Milwaukee, Wisconsin; 1988; p. 135
4. Acts 11:20
5. Josephus, Flavius; "Wars of the Jews" 1.28.4; Josephus – Complete Works; Kregel Publications; Grand Rapids, Michigan; Twelfth Printing, 1974; p. 463
6. Josephus, Flavius; "Antiquities of the Jews" 17.1.3; Josephus – Complete Works; Kregel Publications; Grand Rapids, Michigan; Twelfth Printing, 1974; p. 357
7. Smith, Robert H.; Concordia Commentary, Acts; Concordia Publishing House; St. Louis, Missouri; 1970; p. 198
8. Manaen's estimated age of 66 is based upon the fact that he was brought up with Herod Antipas who was born in 20 B.C. and the date when Manaen and Paul were in the church of Antioch together was in A.D. 46.
9. Lenski, R. C. H.; The Interpretation of The Book of Acts; Lutheran Book Concern, 1934; Assigned to The Wartburg Press, 1944; Assigned to Augsburg Publishing House, 1961; p. 492
10. Kretzmann, Paul E.; Popular Commentary of the Bible, New Testament, Volume I; Concordia Publishing House; St. Louis, Missouri; p. 595

11. Balge, Richard D.; The People's Bible, Acts; Northwestern Publishing House, Milwaukee, Wisconsin; 1988; p. 135
12. Thayer, Joseph Henry; Greek-English Lexicon of the New Testament; Zondervan Publishing House; Grand Rapids, Michigan; p. 553
13. Joel 1:14 & 2:15 are examples
14. Acts 6:6
15. Numbers 27:18 & Deuteronomy 34:9
16. Acts 1:8
17. Colossians 4:10
18. Conybeare, W. J. & Howson, J. S.; The Life And Epistles of St. Paul; Wm. B. Eerdmans Publishing Company; Grand Rapids, Michigan; Reprinted March 1974; p. 115
19. Conybeare, W. J. & Howson, J. S.; The Life And Epistles of St. Paul; Wm. B. Eerdmans Publishing Company; Grand Rapids, Michigan; Reprinted March 1974; note 5, p. 111
20. Ibid.; note 5, p. 111
21. Ibid.; p. 111
22. Davis, John D.; A Dictionary of the Bible, Fourth Revised Edition; Baker Book House; Grand Rapids, Michigan; Seventeenth Printing, 1969; p. 692
23. Seleucia Pieria; Wikipedia; https://en.wikipedia.org/wiki/Seleucia_Pieria
24. Seleucia in Pieria; Livius.org.; https://www.livius.org/articles/place/seleucia-in-pieria/
25. The Hellenistic Era: Seleucia Pieria; a historical document by an author whose work shows a firsthand knowledge of the ancient city and its history; http://www.angelfire.com/sd/scevko/history2.html
26. Seleucia Pieria; Wikipedia; https://en.wikipedia.org/wiki/Seleucia_Pieria
27. Conybeare, W. J. & Howson, J. S.; The Life And Epistles of St. Paul; Wm. B. Eerdmans Publishing Company; Grand Rapids, Michigan; Reprinted March 1974; p. 112
28. Seleucia, Syria; BiblePlaces.com; https://www.bibleplaces.com/seleucia/
29. The Hellenistic Era: Seleucia Pieria; a historical document by an author whose work shows a firsthand knowledge of the ancient city and its history; http://www.angelfire.com/sd/scevko/history2.html
30. Conybeare, W. J. & Howson, J. S.; The Life And Epistles of St. Paul; Wm. B. Eerdmans Publishing Company; Grand Rapids, Michigan; Reprinted March 1974; p. 113
31. Military History Encyclopedia On The Web; historyofwar.org; Battle of Salamis of Cyprus, 306 B.C.; http://www.historyofwar.org/articles/battles_salamis_306.html
32. Ring of Christ; Ancient Cities of Cyprus; http://ringofchrist.com/ancient-cities-cyprus
33. Wikipedia; Salamis; Wikipedia; https://en.wikipedia.org/wiki/Salamis,_Cyprus
34. Ancient Origins; The Ancient Ruins of Salamis, the Once Thriving Port City of Cyprus; https://www.ancient-origins.net/ancient-places-europe/ancient-ruins-salamis-once-thriving-port-city-cyprus-002870
35. Bruce, F. F.; The Acts Of The Apostles; William B. Eerdmans Publishing Company; Grand Rapids, Michigan; Third Revised And Enlarged Edition; 1990; p. 295
36. Cyprus Department of Antiquities dates Roman control as 58 B.C.; Republic of Cyprus; Department of Antiquities; Nea Oafos;

http://www.mcw.gov.cy/mcw/da/da.nsf/All/
59FFC9310818070EC225719B003A2EB8?OpenDocument
37. Bruce, F. F.; The Acts Of The Apostles; William B. Eerdmans Publishing Company; Grand Rapids, Michigan; Third Revised And Enlarged Edition; 1990; p. 295
38. Acts 13:7
39. AMCIENT HISTORY ET CETERA; etc.ancient.eu/travel/colonnade-of-the-gymnasium-of salamis-cyprus; http://etc.ancient.eu/travel/colonnade-of-the-gymnasium-of-salamis-cyprus/
40. Ancient Origins; The Ancient Ruins of Salamis, the Once Thriving Port City of Cyprus; https://www.ancient-origins.net/ancient-places-europe/ancient-ruins-salamis-once-thriving-port-city-cyprus-002870
41. Ancient Origins.; The Ancient Ruins of Salamis, the Once Thriving Port City of Cyprus; https://www.ancient-origins.net/ancient-places-europe/ancient-ruins-salamis-once-thriving-port-city-cyprus-002870
42. Ibid.
43. Ibid.
44. Ibid.
45. Ibid.
46. Ibid.
47. Encyclopedia Britannica; Geography of Cyprus; https://www.britannica.com/place/Cyprus
48. Google statistics for the size of Cyprus
49. Encyclopedia Britannica; Geography of Cyprus; https://www.britannica.com/place/Cyprus
50. Ring of Christ; Ancient Cities of Cyprus; http://ringofchrist.com/ancient-cities-cyprus/
51. Wikipedia; Ancient History of Cyprus; https://en.wikipedia.org/wiki/ancient_history_of_cyprus
52. Conybeare, W. J. & Howson, J. S.; The Life And Epistles of St. Paul; Wm. B. Eerdmans Publishing Company; Grand Rapids, Michigan; Reprinted March 1974; p. 14
53. Conybeare, W. J. & Howson, J. S.; The Life And Epistles of St. Paul; Wm. B. Eerdmans Publishing Company; Grand Rapids, Michigan; Reprinted March 1974; note 2 on p. 14
54. Bruce, F. F.; The Acts Of The Apostles; William B. Eerdmans Publishing Company; Grand Rapids, Michigan; Third Revised And Enlarged Edition; 1990; p. 295
55. Examples of this kind of an address can be seen in Stephen's address in Acts 7:1f and in Paul's address in Pisidian Antioch in Acts 13:16f
56. Acts 9:15
57. Matthew 28:19
58. 1 Timothy 2:3, 4
59. Matthew 13:1-9 & 18-23; Mark 4:1-9 & 13-20; Luke 8:4-15
60. Acts 15:39
61. Wikipedia; Paphos; https://en.wikipedia.org/wiki/Paphos
62. Bruce, F. F.; The Acts Of The Apostles; William B. Eerdmans Publishing Company; Grand Rapids, Michigan; Third Revised And Enlarged Edition; 1990
63. UNESCO; Paphos; http://whc.unesco.org/en/list/79
64. Wikipedia; Paphos; https://en.wikipedia.org/wiki/Paphos
65. Ibid.

66. Ibid.
67. Wikipedia; Aphrodite; https://en.wikipedia.org/wiki/Aphrodite#Worship
68. Wikipedia: Paphos; https://en.wikipedia.org/wiki/Paphos
69. Republic of Cyprus; Department of Antiquities; Nea Pafos; http://www.mcw.gov.cy/mcw/da/da.nsf/All/59FFC9310818070EC225719B003A2EB8?OpenDocument
70. Paphos Municipality; Paphos Through Time; http://www.pafos.org.cy/en/page/pafos-through-time
71. Paphos Municipality; Paphos Through Time; http://www.pafos.org.cy/en/page/pafos-through-time
72. Encyclopedia Britannica; Ptolemy I – Soter; https://www.britannica.com/biography/Ptolemy-I-Soter
73. Republic of Cyprus; Department of Antiquities; Nea Pafos; http://www.mcw.gov.cy/mcw/da/da.nsf/All/59FFC9310818070EC225719B003A2EB8?OpenDocument
74. Paphos Municipality; Paphos Through Time; http://www.pafos.org.cy/en/page/pafos-through-time
75. Ibid.
76. Paphos Municipality; Paphos Through Time; http://www.pafos.org.cy/en/page/pafos-through-time
77. Republic of Cyprus; Department of Antiquities; Nea Pafos; http://www.mcw.gov.cy/mcw/da/da.nsf/All/59FFC9310818070EC225719B003A2EB8?OpenDocument
78. University of Sydney; Archaeologists uncover Roman roads from ancient Cyprus; https://sydney.edu.au/news-opinion/news/2015/11/09/archaeologists-uncover-roman-roads-from-ancient-cyprus--.html
79. Paphos Municipality; Paphos Through Time; http://www.pafos.org.cy/en/page/pafos-through-time
80. Bible Archaeology; Cyprus, Sorcerers, and Sergius; https://biblearchaeology.org/research/new-testament-era/3902-cypriots-sorcerers-and-sergius?highlight=WyJzb3JjZXJlcnMiLCJnc29yY2VyZXJzJyIsInNlcmdpdXMiLCJnc2VyZ2l1cyIsImN5cHJ1cyJd
81. Conybeare, W. J. & Howson, J. S.; The Life And Epistles of St. Paul; Wm. B. Eerdmans Publishing Company; Grand Rapids, Michigan; Reprinted March 1974; p. 118
82. Lenski, R. C. H.; The Interpretation o of The Book of Acts; Lutheran Book Concern, 1934; Assigned to The Wartburg Press, 1944; Assigned to Augsburg Publishing House, 1961; p. 499, 500
83. 2 Thessalonians 2:9
84. Perseus Digital Library; Gregory R. Crane, Editor-In-Chief; Tufts University, see section 5425; http://perseus.uchicago.edu/perseus-cgi/citequery3.pl?dbname=PerseusLatinTexts&getid=1&query=Plin.%20Nat.%2030.2
85. Josephus, Flavius; Josephus – Complete Works; Antiquities 20:7:1; Kregel Publications; Grand Rapids, Michigan; Twelfth Printing, 1974
86. Cobern, Camden M.; The New Archaeological Discoveries; Funk & Wagnalls Company; New York & London; 1917; see p. 538-540; Google the following: "PDF Cobern, Camden M.; The New Archaeological Discoveries; Funk & Wagnalls Company; New York & London; 1917"
87. Gingrich, F. Wilbur; Shorter Lexicon of the Greek New Testament; The University of Chicago Press; Chicago and London; Fourth Impression 1973; p. 209

88. Thayer, Joseph Henry; Greek-English Lexicon of the New Testament; Zondervan Publishing House; Grand Rapids, Michigan; p. 604
89. The Ultimate History Project; Roman Magic: Control In An Uncertain World; http://ultimatehistoryproject.com/roman-magic-amulets-bullae-lunulae.html
90. Tacitus; The Annals of Imperial Rome, 2.69; Penguin Books, Reprinted with revised bibliography, 1996; p. 111, 112
91. See Tacitus' The Annals of Imperial Rome, Book II c. 27, 31; Book IV.21; Book VI. c. 30; Book XII. c. 21 & 38 & 65; Book XVI. c. 30/
92. Tacitus; The Annals of Imperial Rome, Book II.31; Penguin Books, Reprinted with revised bibliography, 1996
93. Tacitus; The Annals of Imperial Rome, Book XVI. c. 30-31; Penguin Books, Reprinted with revised bibliography, 1996
94. Wikispaces Classroom; https://hum111.wikispaces.com/Magic+in+Ancient+Rome; unfortunately since this quotation was cited in the manuscript for this book, this website has been taken down. The reader may also consult "Pliny and Magic" found at: https://www.jstor.org/stable/pdf/287886.pdf;

   The reader can also see what Pliny wrote about magicians, their practices and remedies in his Book 30 that can be found at: http://www.perseus.tufts.edu/hopper/text?doc=Perseus%3Atext%3A1999.02.0137%3Abook%3D30%3Achapter%3D1
95. Live Science; Ancient Roman Tablet Holds 'Black Magic' Curse; https://www.metanexus.net/ancient-roman-tablet-holds-black-magic-curses/
96. Matthew 12:29

11

PAUL'S MISSION WORK IN SOUTHERN GALATIA

In This Chapter: Paul's Work In Pisidian Antioch; Iconium; Lystra; Derbe; Conclusion Of Paul's First Missionary Journey & Return To Antioch, Syria

---

Pisidian Antioch

Luke informs us in Acts 13:13: "Now when Paul and his companions set sail from Paphos, they came to Perga, *a city* of Pamphylia." Paul together with Barnabas was in the process of doing the work the Holy Spirit had called him to do.[1] And going to Perga of Pamphylia was the next leg of his missionary journey. Whether the Holy Spirit indicated this to Paul by a revelation or a simple mental prompting we do not know. However the Holy Spirit directed Paul, from a purely human standpoint when one looks at the rest of Paul's first missionary journey that Luke reports in Acts 13 & 14, one can quickly understand why Paul set sail for Perga. Beginning at Perga was the "Via Sebaste" road, also known as the "Imperial Road", which would take Paul into the interior of Asia Minor. Caesar Augustus had commanded that road be built in 6 B.C.[2] He had the road built to move Roman troops quickly throughout the region to hem in the mountain tribes who continued to attack and plunder that region and to connect together the recently established Roman settlements and colonies in the southern part of Galatia. The road was also intended to connect those cities to a port on the Mediterranean Sea for the purpose of bringing in military reinforcements and supplies and to facilitate commerce. The Via Sebaste started at Perga as a part of the Roman road going northwest to Ephesus[3] that had been built during the time of the Roman Republic prior to 27 B.C.[4] The Via Sebaste branched off the Republican road a short distance out of Perga and turned up on a more northerly course to Comama and then to Apollonia, headed northwest and then looped around to the northeast to Pisidian Antioch. From Pisidian Antioch it then extended southeast to Iconium, Lystra, and Derbe.[5] [6]Paul's missionary journey into southern Galatia simply followed that Roman road to those Galatian cities and back again to Perga in Pamphylia. The road gave him a way through the rugged, mountainous terrain and through the marauding mountain tribesmen as safely as possible.

The voyage from Paphos to the coastline of Pamphylia was about 160 miles. Paul and his companions would have sailed across a gulf that was called the Sea of Pamphylia.[7] [8] [9] Up until about 110 years earlier those waters had been infested with pirates. The waters were not safe to sail through until Pompey the Great finally rooted the pirates out and put an end to their plundering, murderous activities. Pompey's conquering and subjugating the pirates was a part of God's plan and providence for preparing the sea for safe travel for Paul and the other apostles that they might take the gospel of Jesus Christ to the ends of the earth.

Paul and his party would have likely reached the mainland of Pamphylia in about two days. The name Pamphylia comes from a compound Greek word that can be literally translated as having the "characteristic of every kind of tribe or nation". Davis said the Greeks popularly interpreted the name to mean an assemblage of mingled tribes.[10] The name gives us an insight into the nature of Pamphylia from the start of its inhabitation. It was made up of people of various kinds of ancestry.

As they approached land Paul would no doubt have looked from the railing of the ship across the expanse of water that was the Bay of Attaleia[11] to the Pamphylian mainland. Pamphylia was a region of Asia Minor between the Taurus mountain range to the north and the shores of the Mediterranean Sea there in the south. Off to Paul's left he would have been able to see Lycia on the western border of Pamphylia and out of sight to his right lay Cilicia on its eastern border where Paul had labored on his own for 8 years. The province of Pamphylia formed a narrow strip of fertile land that had a coastline of about 75 miles in length. Its width was about 30 miles from north to south.[12] Just three years earlier in A.D. 43 when Paul was completing his work in Syria and Cilicia and beginning to work with Barnabas in Syrian Antioch, Pamphylia was made part of the Roman province of Pamphylia – Lycia. Pamphylia remained such until about the time of Paul's martyrdom in A.D. 68.[13]

Gazing at the coastline of Pamphylia from the deck of the gently rolling ship Paul was looking upon the coast that had together with the coast of Cilicia provided the coves and hiding places for the pirates who had once occupied them. Beyond that coastline was a land that had a long history. It had once been occupied by Hittites around 1,500 B.C.[14] That was about sixty years before the Lord had Moses lead the nation of Israel out of slavery in Egypt to freedom in the Promised Land of Canaan. The Hittites' name for the Pamphylian city of Perga was "Partha". The Great King Tudhaliya IV of the Hittites signed a peace treaty at the end of the 13th century B.C. with his vassal King Kurunta of Tarhuntassa, who had been waging war with Partha (Perga).[15] [16] The treaty set the western border of King Tarhuntassa's domain as the city of Perga and the River Cestrus.[17]

Greeks colonized Pamphylia and its city of Perga from the latter part of the Mycenaean age and the Bronze Age,[18] which was 1,600 – 1,100 B.C.[19] Mycenaean settlements appeared on the coast of Asia Minor[20] about the time of the reigns of King Saul and King David in Israel. In 546 B.C., 40 years after the fall of Jerusalem when the

Israelites were carried off into captivity in Babylon, Cyrus the Great of Persia defeated Croesus king of Lydia of western Asia Minor. The region of Pamphylia then came under the control of Persia. Around 465 B.C. the Athenians defeated the Persians and ruled the region until close to 400 B.C. when the Persians then regained Pamphylia. In 333 B.C. Alexander the Great marched into the area, defeated the Persian king Darius III, and Pamphylia was once again under the control of the Greeks.[21] The Greeks then thoroughly Hellenized the region. After Alexander died and his empire was divided among his generals, the region was ruled by the Greek dynasty of the Seleucids that began with Seleucus I Nicator. When the Romans defeated the Seleucid King Antiochus III in 190 B.C., the Romans included Pamphylia among the provinces annexed to the dominions of Eumenes of Pergamum. Not long afterwards the inhabitants of Pamphylia joined with those of Pisidia and Cilicia in pirate raids,[22] and the Pamphylian city of Slide became their slave market. In 188 B.C. Pamphylia came under the control of the Romans. Most of the ruins of the city of Perga are from the period of Roman domination.[23] Pamphylia was at first a part of the Roman province of Cilicia. In 43 B.C. it was later added to the province of Asia. In 31 B.C. the Roman general Octavian (who in 27 B.C. became Caesar Augustus) made Pamphylia a part of the region of Galatia.[24] It was then included in the kingdom of Galatia ruled by Amyntas, the king. [25]After he was killed, it became a Roman province in 25 B.C.

Pamphylia was the most important, major producer of olive oil in the region of the Mediterranean. The production center was connected with the city of Perga. Artifacts from it date back to the 1st century B.C.[26]

The population of Pamphylia and its city of Perga would have had a heavy concentration of Greek inhabitants. There were Jews in the province of Pamphylia also, for Jews from Pamphylia were present in Jerusalem on the day of Pentecost according to Acts 2:10.

Paul's ship would have sailed through the Bay of Attaleia to the mouth of the River Cestrus. The river was still navigable then. Paul's ship would have been able to sail the seven miles up the river to the landing port of Perga.²⁷ In the following centuries up through the late Roman period the Cestrus River silted up and became unnavigable.²⁸ It has since been diverted to irrigate the fields in the area.²⁹ When Paul, Barnabas, and John Mark had sailed up the river to the landing port of Perga and stepped off the ship, the city of Perga would have been about 3 miles east of the river port.³⁰

Perga, which is now the Turkish village of Martina or Murtana,³¹ was situated on the fertile plains of Pamphylia between the Cestrus (Aksu today) River and the Catarrhactes (now the Duden Nehri) River.³² It was located about thirteen miles east of modern Antalya³³

The name Perga indicates that the history of the city predates the time of the Greeks.³⁴ As a result of a clay tablet that was found in the ancient Hittite capital of Hattusa, some scholars identify Perga with the Hittite city of Partha that was already noted.³⁵ The Greeks colonized the city in the latter part of the Mycenaean age.³⁶ Its following centuries of history coincided with that of its province of Pamphylia, which was given above. Alexander the Great and a part of his army once occupied the city of Perga.³⁷ From the time of Alexander onward the city was Hellenized.³⁸

Excavations of the city show that it was built in a quadrangular shape.³⁹ It was surrounded with walls that were reinforced by towers.⁴⁰ The walls were built about the 3ʳᵈ century B.C. during the Hellenistic Age,⁴¹ and while Perga was ruled by the Greek Seleucid kings. Long sections of the walls are still standing.⁴²

As Paul approached the city with Barnabas and John Mark, he would have seen an acropolis standing above the lower part of Perga.⁴³ The acropolis had been built for defense. The acropolis dates back to the Bronze Age⁴⁴ and the time of the Mycenaean occupation. It rises up in the north while the main part of the city lies below in the flatland south of the hill.

Perga came under Roman rule in 188 B.C. In 129 B.C. it became part of the Roman province of Asia. After the Roman province of Galatia was created in 25 B.C., the Romans connected Galatia to the coast of the Mediterranean Sea in 6 B.C. by constructing a new road to Perga called the Via Sebaste that was mentioned in a preceding paragraph.[45]

Perga was the capital of the province of Pamphylia.[46] [47]At the time of Paul and into the 2nd century A.D. Perga was one of the most important cities in the province of Pamphylia[48] along with the cities of Sillyon, Aspendos, and Slide.[49]

Today Perga is a large site of ancient ruins in the village of Murtina, or Murtana. The Hellenistic gateway and walls are the only pre-Roman structures. They are dated in the third century B.C. That gateway consists of two round towers and a horseshow-shaped courtyard through which Paul and his companions would have passed into the city.[50] In the 2nd century through about the 4th century A.D. the vast majority of the Roman developments in the city of Perga were built. During that time the theater, the stadium, the colonnaded streets, the water canal or aqueduct in the middle of the street, the bathhouses, the fountains, the gymnasium, the agora or marketplace and shops, the Roman houses and mosaics were constructed.[51] [52] Those structures did not exist when Paul visited Perga.

One impressive structure that did exist at the time Paul visited Perga was the temple of the goddess Artemis. In former ancient times the goddess was called Vanassa Pereiia, or Pergaean Queen. In the Hellenistic era the goddess became Hellenized as Artemis.[53] The city of Perga gained fame as the place of the worship of Artemis. The temple of Artemis stood on a hill outside of the city. In honor of the goddess annual festivals were celebrated.[54] In the 2nd century B.C. Perga minted its own coins with the image of Artemis and her temple.[55] During the Christian era the people associated Artemis with the Virgin Mary and continued to worship her.[56]

The importance of Perga declined with the silting up of the Cestrus River during the Roman period of history.[57] In the 8th century A.D. the city was razed to the ground during the Arab invasions and was never rebuilt.[58] Today the city of Perga is an archaeological site and tourist attraction.

After Paul, Barnabas, and John Mark walked the three miles from the river landing, they passed through the Hellenistic gate into the city of Perga. Once again Luke in his brief narrative style does not tell us where they went, what they did, who they saw, or for how long they stayed. And the fact that Luke did not report that they preached the gospel at this time makes it clear they did not do so. On their return trip to Perga Luke states they preached the gospel. The only matter of importance that Luke does report is: "Then John deserted them and returned to Jerusalem" (Acts 13:13).

Why John Mark deserted Paul and Barnabas Luke does not say, so we do not know. Perhaps there is an element of truth to the reason Conybeare and Howson offered.[59] John looked up the road of the Via Sebaste leading into the rugged mountains that had to be passed through and crossed amid the murderous mountain tribesmen and wild animals and he lost his nerve. His sense of courage and trust in the Lord's divine protection temporarily evaporated. The comforts of home with his mother in Jerusalem looked much more attractive than the dangers up ahead on the Via Sebaste road. Ten years into the future in A.D. 56 Paul would recount the dangers he went through on his missionary journeys and say: "I have been on journeys frequently, in dangers from rivers, in dangers from bandits, ... in dangers from Gentiles, in dangers in the wasteland, . . ."[60] Whatever John's reason for deserting, Paul did not think it was justified. A little less than two years into the future when he was preparing to make his second missionary journey with Barnabas, Paul would make his displeasure with John's desertion clear. More will be said about this in connection with Paul's preparations for his second missionary journey in Chapter 1 of Volume II.

After John Mark left them, Luke informs us in Acts 13:14, "They went on from Perga and came to Pisidian Antioch." The distance from Perga to Pisidian Antioch following the Via Sebaste was about 160 miles.[61] An average person walking on level ground walks at a pace of about 3 miles an hour. Allowing for some break times throughout the day, the hiker will walk about 20 miles in a day. Since Paul and Barnabas would have been gradually walking uphill to the higher elevation of Pisidian Antioch, they might have walked only 18 miles a day. At a rate of 18 to 20 miles a day it would have taken them 7 1/2 to 8 days to reach Pisidian Antioch. Such a hike would have required them to walk all day and sleep out in the elements under the stars at night.

Paul and Barnabas would have had to make preparations for such a long trek through the rugged terrain of the Taurus Mountains. They would have needed to be ancient predecessors to the modern day "back packers", but without the benefit of lightweight materials like waterproofed nylon and prepackaged, non-perishable foodstuffs. Yet they would have "traveled light" with as little baggage as possible to weigh them down and to slow them down. They would have needed at least one pair of sturdy sandals that would last and not wear out quickly, a wide-brimmed hat to protect their heads and faces from the sun and the rain, and food and water. The food that they would have carried with them was likely to have been some bread, parched grain, dried olives, dried figs, and dates[62] that they probably carried in a leather sack, the long strap of which was slung over their neck and hung down on their opposite side by their waist. They were likely to have carried some water in leathern bags used to hold water or wine.[63] Like the food sack, their water bag was likely to have been slung over the same side of their neck to hang down on the same side of their waist as their food sack. They probably depended upon finding some fresh water sources along the way such as springs. They would have passed near a lake and perhaps some streams. Being an experienced traveler, Paul very likely talked to individuals in the city of Perga about what lay ahead of them along the Via Sebaste and where they could find fresh water and places where they could camp at night.

One more thing they would have carried with them was a mat to sleep on. That would have been the sum total of their bedding. The reason for that being the outer garment they would have warn during the day would also have served as their blanket at night to keep them warm. Their outer garment was most likely made of wool or of goat's hair. Such an outer garment would have insulated them from the heat by day and the cold by night. What is more, it would have been waterproof and would protect them from the rain as well.[64] The Lord himself upheld the value of this outer garment when he issued the command that if a lender took a man's outer garment as security for a debt, the lender had to return the garment to its owner by nightfall so he might keep warm and be able to sleep.[65]

In spite of such careful planning and preparations, however, there were some times during Paul's missionary journeys when he did suffer the lack of such basic necessities and provisions. Perhaps this trek through the Taurus Mountains on the Via Sebaste was one of those occasions. In 2 Corinthians 11:27 he wrote, "I have been in toil and hardship, without sleep frequently, in hunger and thirst, often in involuntary fastings, in the cold and without sufficient clothing."

For his uphill journey with Barnabas from sea level to 3,600 feet above sea level[66] [67]Paul would have also needed to be strong and healthy. A modern family tour guide in Turkey tells his prospective tourists that the physical requirements for a hike up a stretch of the ancient Via Sebaste road are "regular exercise and strong health."[68] Such strong, healthy physical requirements cast serious doubts upon William M. Ramsay's theory that Paul was sick and suffering from chronic malaria while in Perga and therefore had to hike up to the higher elevation and climate of Pisidian Antioch to cure his attack of malaria.[69] It is not likely that if Paul would have been as sick and as weak as Ramsay theorized, that Paul or anyone else would have been able to withstand the rigors of a 7 1/2 to 8 day uphill hike by day, sleeping outdoors on the ground in the cool dampness by night, and surviving on only the meager provisions he would have been carrying. It is much more likely to assume that Paul was in good health when he started the journey up the Via Sebaste and at a later time became sick along the way, for which reason he stopped and put that time of his illness to the good use of witnessing the gospel to the Galatian Gentiles.[70]

Having prepared themselves for the hike before them, and dressed in their long outer garments with broad-brimmed hats[71] on their heads and with their food and water bags hanging on their one side and their mats hanging on their other side, they set out on their 160-mile uphill hike to Pisidian Antioch on the Via Sebaste paved highway. Some of the roads in parts of Asia Minor may possibly have been first built five centuries earlier by the Persians, then developed by the Greeks in the Hellenistic age, and afterwards adopted by the Romans. David H. French, a recognized expert on the ancient Roman roads in Asia Minor, noted such a possible history of the roads in western Asia Minor.[72] The earliest Roman roads from the Roman Republican era, which would have been prior to 27 B.C., were earthen roads, "trackways", not paved "highways".[73] There were three kinds of Roman roads: earthen roads that French referred to as trackways that were made by human and animal traffic and wagon wheels; gravel roads also known as quarried roads and roadways; and then paved roads made of stone blocks laid tightly together that were called highways.[74] [75] The Via Sebaste was a paved highway. Alongside the road was a footpath for pedestrians so they would be safe from the passing road traffic. When Paul and Barnabas stepped up to the Via Sebaste, they would have seen the large stones tightly fitted together and stretching out before them into the distance. Except for the Via Sebaste road that they were about to walk along, there were no paved roads in the province of Galatia where they were going until A.D. 79,[76] 11 years after Paul's martyrdom. So all of Paul's future travels in Galatia other than on the Via Sebaste road would have been on earthen roads, "trackways", or gravel roads. In Asia Minor the earliest record of road paving was found on Augustan milestones commemorating the construction of the Via Sebaste in 6 B.C.[77]

Together Paul and Barnabas pressed on up the Via Sebaste from the low coastland of Pamphylia to Pisidian Antioch, a city in the southern region of the Roman province of Galatia in the Taurus mountain range. In the Galatian province to which they were going a Celtic people had migrated from Gaul in 278-277 B.C.[78] They had been driven out from their homeland in Celtica. Those Celtic exiles then mixed with other native tribes and took possession of the region around the city of Ancyra.[79] The name of the Roman province Galatia received its name from that Celtic kingdom.[80] This Celtic kingdom gradually expanded throughout the period of the 2nd and 1st centuries, especially when it became an ally of the Romans. When the Celtic kingdom of Galatia reached its greatest expanse, it included not only the "ethnic Galatia" in the area around Ancyra, but also the areas of the Phrygians, Lycaonians, Anatolians, as well as an area of the Armenians to the east and Hellenized cities to the south. When Amyntas, the last Celtic king, was killed in a battle with the rebellious tribesmen known as the Homonades in 25 B.C., the majority of the kingdom was taken over by Augustus. He added to it the adjacent territory that then came to be the Roman province of Galatia.[81] [82] Paul's mission work with Barnabas concentrated on the Hellenized, non-Celtic cities in what was then the southern region of the Roman province of Galatia.

As Paul hiked up and down the rugged terrain of the Taurus Mountain passages, he would have been noticing houses and villages here and there, for at the time that the region of Pisidia came under the control of the Romans the majority of the people of Pisidia lived on the summits of the Taurus Mountains. Some Pisidians who lived north and above the Pamphylian cities of Side and Aspendus occupied hilly places planted in olive trees.[83] Strabo listed nineteen cities in the region of Pisidia. He said some of the cities were located in the mountains while others were farther south in the lower foothills.[84] Among those people, he said, were those trained in piracy.

On his hike up the highway Paul would have also seen that the region of Pisidia was a very fertile area planted with olive trees and vineyards. The region provided abundant pasturage for cattle of various kinds. Around those fertile land areas Paul would have observed forests that provided different kinds of timber.[85] But Paul had to remain watchful. That mountainous region was full of precipices and ravines. They made natural fortifications for the Pisidian inhabitants, however. Through those mountain ravines the Eurymedon and Cestrus Rivers flowed down to the fertile plains below and into the Pamphylian Sea of the Mediterranean. No doubt Paul was relieved each time he saw a bridge the Romans had built to accommodate travel for travelers like himself, Roman troops, and commercial shipping.[86]

The ancient site of Pisidian Antioch was discovered by F. V, J. Arundell in 1832.[87] Thanks to the labors of archaeologists since then we are able to know something of the civilizations that once occupied the area of Pisidian Antioch. Archaeological excavations in 1924 around the city of Pisidian Antioch indicated that the surrounding mounds date back to the 3rd millennium B.C. If that dating is indeed correct, then there were people who began occupying this area only a few centuries after the Noachian flood that occurred in 2,613 B.C. and about the time of Abraham who lived from 2,185 to 2,010 B.C.[88] In the city of Pisidian Antioch itself there have been no archaeological finds indicating the presence of Hittite, Phrygian, or Lydian civilizations. It has been learned from Hittite records, however, that this region was called "Azawa" and that there were independent communities in this region. Throughout those ancient times the inhabitants of the Pisidian region were able to remain independent communities because of the natural barriers provided by the Taurus Mountains[89].

It is believed that the city of Pisidian Antioch was originally founded in an area where there had been an earlier Greek settlement. The first inhabitants are thought to have been settlers from the ancient Greek city of Magnesia on the Meander in Ionia, which was a central western coastal region of what is now Turkey.[90] Archaeological finds at the Temple of Men Askenos to the northeast of the city date back to the 300s B.C.[91] It has been commonly reported that Pisidian Antioch was founded by Seleucus I Nicator after 300 B.C. and named after his father.[92] But it seems that Pisidian Antioch was likely to have been founded when the area was taken over by the Seleucid Empire and named after one of the Antiochi rulers.[93] It is perhaps best to understand this in the sense that the Antiochi Empire founded the city as a strategic military fortress against the attacks of the Celtic Galatians who had come into the area. The city was not in the region of Pisidia but was near it. The city was actually in the adjoining region of Phrygia Galatica. Because of the city's close proximity to Pisidia, it came to be called Pisidian Antioch to distinguish it from the fifteen other cities the Antiochi rulers named "Antioch".[94] [95] [96] The city came under the control of the Romans in 25 B.C. and was made a part of the Roman province of Galatia. Augustus then made it a Roman colony and a key civil and military center.

The city of Pisidian Antioch was built on a hill for defense. Its acropolis covered 115 acres, which was just under two tenths of a square mile, and was fortified with walls. On its east side a deep ravine fell off to the Anthius River below that flowed into Lake Egirdir. The walls and defense systems of the present visible ruins are dated from the A.D. 300s. That being true, they were built a couple of centuries after the time Paul visited Antioch. Little is known about the previous gates and fortifications of the Hellenistic period that might have existed at the time of Paul. This is the case for two reasons. First, archaeologists have not yet excavated down to them.[97] Only a small percentage of Antioch has been excavated.[98] Second, some time after the city came under control of the Romans, they demolished the ancient Greek buildings and built impressive Roman structures in their place.[99] Today the ruins of Pisidian Antioch lie about six tenths of a mile from the Turkish village of Yalvaç.

On a neighboring hill to the east of the city lie the ruins of the temple of the pagan god Men Askaenos. It was the chief deity of the city. Archaeologists have found inscriptions there that indicate that a strong pagan cult of Men, as the god was known, existed at that site between the 4th century B.C to the 4th century A.D. Men was a lunar god, that the early Greeks who colonized the area brought with them.[100] Ramsay excavated the temple of Men in 1910-1913. He discovered the temple's colossal altar that measured 66 by 41 feet. The temple's area measured 241 by 136 feet and was surrounded by a wall 5 feet thick. The soil above and below the stone floor of the central chamber was full of animal bones and teeth.[101]

When Paul visited Pisidian Antioch the population consisted of native inhabitants, Greeks, Romans, and Jews.[102] The Jews are known to have resided there because Luke tells us in Acts 13:14 that Paul and Barnabas went into their synagogue. How many Jews resided in Pisidian Antioch is unknown. Seleucus I Nicator made the Jews citizens of those cities that he built in Asia and gave them privileges equal to those of the Greeks in those cities. [103] Those privileges continued to the time of Josephus' writing about A.D. 75. At the time of Antiochus III, known as Antiochus the Great,[104] who reigned in the late 200s B.C., there was a revolt among the populace of Phrygia and

Lydia. Antiochus the Great then gave an order to his general Zeuxas that 2,000 Jewish families in Mesopotamia and Babylon were to be moved with all their belongings into Phrygia, which was the region where Pisidian Antioch was located. They were moved there for the purpose of stabilizing the area. Antiochus the Great treated the Jews who made the move very well to insure their support of him and his rule. He let them have their own laws, gave them land on which they could build homes and a farm and grow vineyards, exempted them from paying taxes for ten years, and supplied them with wheat until they could raise their own. What is more, he also decreed that no one was to trouble them.[105] And so, the Jews moved into the area and over a period of more than two hundred years until the time of Paul's visit in A.D. 46 multiplied to make a sizable population in the region of Asia Minor.

There is evidence that the Jews were an important political and social part of the population of Pisidian Antioch. A funeral monument of a Jewish woman from the 1st century A.D. was found. The monument says her name was Debora, the Greek spelling for the Hebrew Deborah. She was an Antiochian who had been given in marriage to a famous man named Pamphylus and that she was a descendant of ancestors who held many offices of state in the Fatherland. This monument's proclamation of her intermarriage to a famous Gentile shows both the prominence of her Jewish family and the breakdown of the Jews' exclusiveness from the Gentiles that had taken place over 2 1/2 centuries of living among the Gentiles. If her Jewish family, particularly the men, had not given in to various heathen practices and idolatry, it would not have enjoyed the political and social acceptance that it had.[106]

As Paul hiked up the Via Sebaste with Barnabas, he would have noticed the temperature was gradually cooling. And the temperature at Pisidian Antioch would have felt much cooler than that at Perga. From his vantage point at the outskirts of Pisidian Antioch he would have seen that the rolling countryside around the city was a fertile soil suitable for growing fruits and for farming. Such a fertile land would have been very favorable for the retired Roman soldiers who had moved to that Roman colony to live.[107] And when Paul came to the gate of the city, he may not have realized that he was standing at the point where the construction of the Via Sebaste had begun. For in accordance with the order of Caesar Augustus, the Roman governor of the province of Galatia, Cornuntus Arrutius Aquila, commenced the construction. The construction program divided the Via Sebaste into two parts. The first part looped around to the southwest and down to Perga.[108] Later, the second part of the highway extended southeast to Iconium, Lystra, and Derbe.[109]

Paul was able to travel on foot as far as the southern part of the province of Galatia when he had to stop because of an illness, literally "a weakness of the flesh". Based on Paul's account in Galatians 4:13, 14 that he preached the gospel for the first time in Galatia because of an illness, one wonders if Paul had intended to travel farther into the northern regions of Galatia before stopping. Whether this was Paul's intention is impossible to say. Now it is possible, and seems likely, that after Paul's hiking for just over a week up the Via Sebaste and sleeping on the ground in the cool dampness of the mountains, that it was at Pisidian Antioch, Paul's first stop in Galatia, where he had to stop because of an illness. Because of that illness, he then preached the gospel to the southern Galatian people. For how long Paul was sick and preached the gospel there is unknown. Luke once again in his brevity does not mention this instance of Paul's illness. But in Galatians 4:14 Paul says that his illness was a trial for the Galatians. It was a trial, first of all, because it apparently made him physically repulsive to look at. It may also have been a trial because his illness may have lasted for a while. If it did last a while, then it is apparent that in spite of his being sick and repulsive looking, Paul kept working right through his illness to continue his mission ministry to the Galatians. It appears he may have done that because Luke tells us in Acts 13:14 & 44-46 that after Paul and Barnabas arrived in Antioch, they went into the synagogue on the Sabbath day and then on the following Sabbath day Paul again spoke the word of the Lord with Barnabas to the crowd that had gathered to hear it. Now whether Paul stayed in Antioch until he was over his illness, or he pressed on while he was still sick to the other Galatian cities cannot be stated with certainty. But since Paul's mission work in Galatia appears to have lasted for about 2 years, it is unlikely that his illness continued throughout that entire period of time. For more information about the nature of Paul's illness, see the section in Chapter 6 about Paul's physical health.

When Paul and Barnabas entered the city, they probably looked for lodging, especially if Paul were sick so he could get out of the elements and rest. As soon as possible they likely walked through the city to become familiar with it and to find the Jewish synagogue. The synagogue would have been easy to find. The city was only 115 acres in size. Furthermore, the ancient Jews made sure their synagogues were located in prominent paces. If possible, they located their synagogue on the highest ground of a town to symbolize that the synagogue was the most important place there. If that was not possible, they located the synagogue on a street corner or at the entrance to the public marketplace. And if a prominent place could not be had, they mounted a pole on the roof of the synagogue that was higher than the tallest structure in town to mark its location.[110]

When they had found the synagogue and its Jewish officials, Paul and Barnabas would likely have told them who they were, what their credentials were – for example that Paul had studied under the great doctor of the Law Gamaliel in Jerusalem and that Barnabas was a Levite, where they were from, and what they were doing – such as visiting the synagogues to share the good news of what God had done among the Israelites. In this way they would have paved the way for the synagogue officials to invite them to address the assembly as visiting rabbis. It was probably not often that the synagogues in Galatia had traveling rabbis come to visit and address their members. The synagogue officials would probably have been eager to invite Paul and Barnabas to speak in order to hear what message they brought.

Over the centuries the synagogue had gradually developed to what it was at the time of Paul. Its origin is now clouded in the obscurity of tradition. There is no hint in the Old Testament Law or the Prophets of synagogue-worship as it was practiced at the time of Paul. The local synagogue did not fit into the tabernacle form of worship that

God established through Moses. But this changed during the Babylonian captivity when the Jews were deprived of the temple. Lacking the temple services, a need arose for some kind of an assembly for instruction, worship, and prayer. The institution of the synagogue then became desirable. The Old Testament Books of Ezra and Nehemiah give the rudimentary beginnings of the synagogue after the return from Babylon.[111] The Jews patterned the furnishings and the parts of the worship service of the synagogue after Ezra's reading of the Law of Moses described in Nehemiah 8:1-8. The synagogue assemblies began for the purpose of instructing those who had returned from Babylon ignorant of the Jewish teachings and tainted by heathenism. Afterwards a further need for the synagogue and its development arose during the time of persecution under the Greek King of Syria, Antiochus Epiphanes, and the uprising of the Maccabees of Israel.[112] The need for the synagogue rose dramatically after the Romans destroyed the temple with the city of Jerusalem in A.D.70.

During those centuries it became clear that the synagogue was established for the main purpose of instructing the Jewish people through the reading of the Law of Moses. Edersheim stated,

> "The main object of the synagogue was the teaching of the people. The very idea of its institution, before and at the time of Ezra, explains and conveys this, and it is confirmed by the testimony of Josephus (Against Apion, ii.17"[113]

This purpose of the synagogue was brought out plainly in the gospels' portrayals of Jesus teaching in the synagogues (see Matthew 4:23; Mark 1:21 & 6:2; Luke 4:15, 6:6 & 13:10; John 6:59 & 18:20).

The word "synagogue" is derived from the Greek word "sunago", which means "gathering together".[114] The synagogues were under the authority of their respective synagogue officials, or rulers, who also exercised discipline.[115] It was a Jewish requirement that in a town or a village there had to be at least 10 men to form a synagogue. Larger towns often had more than one synagogue and large cities usually had a number of synagogues. Based on Luke's statement in Acts 13:14, "... they went into the synagogue on the Sabbath day, ..." it is evident that Pisidian Antioch had but one synagogue.[116] If the membership of a synagogue was small and it could not afford to construct an appropriate building for its use, a large room in a private house was used for its services[117].

Luke informs us in Acts 13:14 that after they went into the synagogue on the Sabbath day, "... they sat down." When Paul had been approaching the synagogue, he would have been able to see not very far away the pagan temple of Men, the chief deity of the city for more than three hundred years. When Paul looked over at that pagan temple, what thoughts might have rushed through his mind about the pagans who worshipped there in the darkness of their spiritual blindness? For he knew those people were lost souls without hope and without God in the world.[118] Being without Christ, those people were heading towards eternal destruction unless by the gospel of Jesus Christ they were brought to faith and made heirs of eternal salvation. Perhaps such thoughts rushed through Paul's mind and reminded him of the seriousness of his work as a bondservant and apostle of the Lord Jesus Christ – people's lives and eternal salvation were dependent upon his doing his job of proclaiming the gospel!

The synagogue of Pisidian Antioch into which Paul went was likely to have been typical of the synagogues of that ancient period. Edersheim has provided us with detailed information about what the structure, interior, furnishings, and worship service of the ancient synagogues in Palestine were like. This writer assumes the synagogues to which Paul went during his apostolic ministry were very much like those in Palestine with perhaps some slight differences.

Those like Paul who worshipped in the synagogue were expected to display a decency and cleanliness in their dress and a quietness and reverence in their demeanor.[119] In Palestine the synagogues were built so that upon entering it the worshippers would be facing towards the city of Jerusalem.[120] Whether that custom was followed in the foreign lands of Asia Minor and Greece this writer does not know, but it seems unlikely. That custom was merely a matter of the orientation of the synagogue and its interior that had no meaning in the Jewish form of worship itself.[121]

Inside the synagogue Paul would have seen the women sitting in a section built just for them with its one access way and a boarded partition with gratings that separated them from the men. That section corresponded to The Court Of The Women in the temple of Jerusalem. The separation of the sexes in the synagogue was strictly observed as it was in the temple. That separation simply followed ancient Eastern customs and manner of thinking,[122] which is observed in some cultures even to this day.

When Paul sat down in the men's section, he would have seen in the front half of the synagogue a raised platform called the "bima". Those who were called up to read ascended by the side of the platform nearest to their seat and then descended on the opposite side. In the middle of the "bima" stood a wooden lectern and a chair. From the lectern the prescribed portions of the Law and of the Prophets were read and addresses were delivered. The reader stood; the preacher sat. Luke reports this custom in Luke 4:20.[123] Prayer was offered standing, except for the solemn litanies when the worshippers prostrated themselves. At the rear of the "bima" stood "the "ark", a chest that symbolically corresponded to the Most Holy Place in the Temple where the Ark of the Covenant had been kept. That front part of the synagogue known as "the ark" was the most important, sacred part of the synagogue, for in it the scrolls of the Law were kept. Sometimes there was a second "ark" in which the scrolls of the Prophets and damaged rolls of the Law were kept. In front of the "ark" that held the scrolls of the Law hung a veil. That veil symbolized the veil that hung before the Holy Place in the Temple. Above the veil was suspended the ever-burning lamp. Near that stood the eight- branched candlestick that was lit during the eight days of the Feast of Dedication of the Temple mentioned in John 10:22. Edersheim cautioned that that custom and other practices were impossible to determine exactly.[124]

Monetary collections in the synagogue were limited to giving aid to the poor or the redeeming of captives.[125] Paul would adopt this custom and apply it in the Gentile churches when he organized a collection for the poor saints in Jerusalem. That will be discussed in Chapters 6 & 7 of Volume II in connection with his third missionary journey.

Paul knew the synagogue service and its parts well from his early childhood in Tarsus and from his youth and early adulthood in Jerusalem. The service begin with the "Shema", "Hear, O Israel, . . ." The "Shema" was a type of a creed that was composed of Deuteronomy 6:4-9, 11:13-21, and Numbers 15:37-41. It, together with its accompanying benedictions,[126] appears to have been read at the lectern. The prayers that followed were spoken by the service leaders in front of the "ark" where the scrolls of the Law were kept.[127] The most important part of the service came next, the reading of Law of Moses. It had been read throughout the history of Israel. Exodus 24:12 says that God told Moses he would give him the law and the commandments that he had written for the instruction of the Israelites. With those words God made it clear already on Mount Sinai that the law was intended to be read for the instruction of his people. Deuteronomy 31:9-13 says that about forty years later, shortly before his death, Moses commanded the priests and elders of Israel that at the Feast of Tabernacles in the year of Jubilee the law was to be read to the people that they might hear and learn it. Nehemiah 8:1-8 also informs us that the Book of the Law of Moses was read to the assembly of the people. At the Apostolic Council Meeting in Jerusalem James, the head of the Church in Jerusalem, told the assembly of apostles and elders, "For Moses from ancient times has those who preach him in every city, and he is read in the synagogues every Sabbath." (Acts 15:21)

In later centuries the Law of Moses was divided into fifty-four selections, or lections, which were read every Sabbath.[128] There were fifty-four to provide extra lections for the Jewish leap year.[129] But in ancient times, particularly the 1st century at the time of Paul, the lectionary of selected readings appears to have been arranged differently with selected readings for three and a half years, which was one half of a Jubilee period. In Palestine, since the original Hebrew had given way to the Aramaic language and many Jews no longer understood the Hebrew, a translator translated the verses of the selected reading.[130] In Pisidian Antioch where Paul was, and in the other Greek cities of Asia Minor as well as in Macedonia and Achaia, Greece, the readings would have been taken from the Greek Septuagint translation for the sake of those Greek-speaking Jews. That Greek Septuagint was also of great benefit for the God-fearing Greeks who were in attendance.

After the reading of the Law, a selection of the Prophets was read. From the time of the Syrian persecution of the Jews around the 2nd century B.C. the selections of the Prophets to be read complemented the selected readings of the Law. It is not known now what that ancient lectionary for the Prophets was. It is apparent that sometimes liberty was given to individual rabbis to select the portion of verses from the Prophets that they would read. Such freedom was given to our Lord Jesus in his hometown synagogue in Nazareth.[131]

In the service sketched above there was a liturgical element that consisted of prayer and the pronouncing of the Aaronic blessing.[132] In Palestine priests who were descendants of Aaron pronounced the blessing. But if none were present, the blessing was spoken by the service leader who led the devotional part of the service.[133] In the Pisidian Antioch synagogue and those in Asia Minor and Greece, the blessing would most likely have been pronounced by the local synagogue's service leader. The speakers of the blessing pronounced it with uplifted hands. There was no element of praise in the services.[134]

After the reading of the Prophets a sermon or address followed for the instruction of the congregation. The service then concluded with that sermon or address.

The synagogue services were pretty well organized and regulated as explained in the preceding paragraphs. The services were elastic, however,[135] with some degree of freedom in them.[136] And as explained above, the purpose of the synagogue was teaching the people. The teaching in the service was done through the combination of a reading of the selection from the Law plus the reading of the selection from the Prophets, which were then followed by the sermon or address.

Now Luke tells us in Acts 13:15,

> Then after the reading of the Law and the Prophets, the synagogue rulers sent *an invitation* to them, saying, "Men, brothers, if you have some message of encouragement for the people, you may speak."

In the above verse Luke summarizes the entire synagogue service with the reading of the Law and the Prophets. The other traditional parts of the service described above would surely have been included as well. But after the reading of the Prophets, the message of encouragement was to be presented. At that time the synagogue rulers sent an invitation to Paul and Barnabas to speak the sermonic message. The Greek text of Acts 13:15 does not contain the words "*an invitation*". The Greek text says they simply "sent" to Paul and Barnabas. What they sent the context makes clear. They sent either a written or an oral message that invited Paul and Barnabas to address the assembly.

Now the purpose of the synagogue, as already stated, was to teach the people. Paul put that purpose to good use repeatedly throughout his apostolic ministry, as he did in Pisidian Antioch. Luke reports in Acts 13:16a, "Then after Paul got up and signaled with his hand, he said, . . ." In spite of his being sick and repulsive looking, as the leader of his two-man mission team Paul got up from his seat to speak. There were some liberties that were allowed in the synagogue services. Paul seems to have employed such a liberty on this occasion. Instead of walking up onto the raised platform at the front of the synagogue to deliver his sermon seated, he remained by his seat standing. His doing so made his sermon more informal than it would have been if he had delivered it up front on the raised platform. Before starting to speak he raised his hand to signal to the assembly for silence. Apparently the synagogue rulers' sending someone back to Paul and Barnabas to invite them to address the assembly stirred up some amount of excitement among the worshippers. We can appropriately imagine the men turning around in their seats to look back at Paul standing to address them and signaling with his hand to silence the chatter that had begun to ripple through the men and the women in their respective segregated sections of the synagogue.

Having gained everyone's attention and silence, Paul began by saying, "Israelite men and those of you who fear God, listen." (Acts 13:16b) As was customary in that age the address was delivered to the men, not the women, although the women were intended to benefit from the sermon as well. Paul's opening words, "Israelite men and those who fear God" was the customary manner of beginning an address to a mixed assembly of Jews and Greek Gentiles who worshipped the one God of Israel. Sometimes the term "brothers" was also used to address the Jewish men.

Paul's opening address of "and those of you who fear God" spoke to the Greek Gentiles who were present who had forsaken their former pagan polytheism. In its place they had embraced the monotheism of the Jews and had started to worship the One true God of Israel with the Jews in the synagogue. They had not taken the step of proselyte conversion, however, that accepted circumcision and obedience to the laws of Moses. If they had taken the step of full proselyte conversion, they would no longer have been put in a separate class apart from the Jews and called Greeks as they were in Acts 14:1, 18:4 & 19:10, or called "those who fear God" or "God-fearing" as they were in Acts 13:16 & 26, 16:14, 17:17 & 18:7, but they would have been called Jews and included with the Jews in Paul's opening address to the Jews. Since they had not become Jews by proselyte conversion, they continued to be considered Greeks who "feared God".[137] In Acts 13:43, which reads: "And after the synagogue *service* had broken up, many of the Jews and of the God-fearing proselytes followed Paul and Barnabas, . . ." Luke clarifies what he meant by his use of the phrase "those who fear God and God-fearing" and his use of the Greek term for proselytes. He coupled the Greek term sebomenoi, which is translated "God-fearing", with the Greek term for proselyte, proselutoi. "God-fearing" modifies the proselytes and describes them as ones who feared and worshipped the One God of the Jews. And proselytes, on the other hand, were simply those who feared God. They were still God-fearing Greeks in a separate class from the full-fledged Jews. They were not full-fledged converts to Judaism.

Now according to Acts 13:50 numbered among the "God-fearing" Greeks were some God-fearing prominent Greek women. Like the prominent Jewish woman Deborah of Pisidian Antioch mentioned in a preceding paragraph, these prominent God-fearing Greek women who came to the synagogue were also surely married to wealthy Greek men of high political and social standing. It is very likely that they too were present in the women's section of the synagogue when Paul delivered his sermonic address.

Luke reports in Acts 13:17-41 what Paul then said to the assembly:

17 The God of this people Israel chose our fathers, and he made the people great during their stay in the land of Egypt, and with an uplifted arm he led them out of it.

18 And for a period of about forty years he put up with them in the wilderness,

19 and after destroying seven nations in the land of Canaan, he gave the land over to them as an inheritance.

20 These things took place over a period of about four hundred and fifty years. And after these things he gave them judges until the time of Samuel the prophet.

21 And then they asked for a king, and God gave them Saul, the son of Kish, a man out of the tribe of Benjamin, for forty years.

22 And after he removed him, he raised up David for them as king, about whom he also testified favorably and said, 'I HAVE FOUND DAVID[138] the son of Jesse, A MAN AFTER MY OWN HEART,[139] who will do all the things that are my will.'

23 From the descendants of this man, according to his promise, God has brought to Israel a Savior, Jesus,

24 after John had been proclaiming before his coming a baptism of repentance to all the people of Israel.

25 And while John was finishing his course of work, he customarily said, 'What do you suppose I am? I myself am not the

Christ! Rather, behold, One is coming after me, the sandals of whose feet I am not worthy to untie.'

¶ 26 Men, brothers, sons descended from Abraham, and those among you who fear God: to us the message of this salvation has been sent out.

27 For those who live in Jerusalem and their rulers, because they did not know this Jesus, indeed fulfilled the words of the prophets that are read every Sabbath by condemning him.

28 And although they did not even find one charge for a death sentence, they demanded Pilate to have him put to death.

29 And when they carried out everything that had been written about him, they took him down from the cross and laid him in a tomb.

30 But God raised him up from the dead.

31 He appeared over a period of many days to those who went up with him from Galilee to Jerusalem, who, to be sure, are now his witnesses to the people.

32 And as for us, we are proclaiming the good news of the promise that had been made to the fathers,

33 that God has completely fulfilled this promise for us, their descendants, by raising up Jesus, as it had also been written in the second Psalm,

'YOU ARE MY SON,

TODAY I HAVE BEGOTTEN YOU.'[140]

34 Moreover, that he raised him up from the dead no longer destined to return to corruption has been spoken of in this manner,

'I WILL GIVE YOU THE HOLY AND TRUSTWORTHY BLESSINGS PROMISED TO DAVID.'[141]

35 Therefore he also says in another Psalm,

'YOU WILL NOT PERMIT YOUR HOLY ONE TO SEE CORRUPTION.'[142]

36 For David, to be sure, after he served the purpose of God in his own generation, fell asleep and was added to his fathers and saw corruption,

37 but the man whom God raised up did not see corruption.

38 Therefore let it be known to you, men, brothers, that through this man forgiveness of sins is being preached to you,

39 By this man everyone who believes is justified from all the things which you were not able to be acquitted by the law of Moses.

40 So be careful that what has been spoken in the prophets does not come upon you:

41 'LOOK, YOU SCOFFERS,

AND MARVEL AND PERISH.

FOR I MYSELF AM CARRYING OUT A WORK IN YOUR DAYS,

a work WHICH YOU SHALL ABSOLUTELY NOT BELIEVE EVEN IF SOMEONE SHOULD TELL YOU IN DETAIL.'[143]

This sermon of Paul's gives us an example of how he addressed the Jews and God-fearing Greeks in the synagogues to present the good news about Jesus Christ the Messiah to them. Paul's sermon is also an example for Christian pastors and preachers of how a good sermon should be constructed homiletically with a theme and parts. Paul's sermon above consisted of three parts, which he noted by the vocative words "Israelite men and those of you who fear God" in verse 16b, "Men, brothers, sons descended from Abraham" in verse 26, and "Men, brothers" in verse 38. The theme of Paul's sermon is found in verse 23. Homiletically Paul's sermon can be outlined with this theme and parts:

God Has Brought To Israel The Savior Jesus:

1. Who Was The Messiah Promised To Come From King David

2. Whom The Scriptures Foretold Would Be Put To Death And Then Raised To Life

3. In Whom We Are Preaching There Is The Forgiveness Of Sins.

Perhaps Paul began his sermon by following the lead of what had been said in the readings of the Law and the Prophets. The content of those readings would have given him a natural lead-in with which the men and women in the synagogue could immediately associate. In the first part of his sermon Paul began with Israel's history that in Egypt God had taken the small number of the Jews' forefathers, seventy in number,[144] and made them into the great nation of Israel, which numbered about two million when they left Egypt in the exodus to Canaan. There in Canaan about four hundred and fifty years later the Jews' forefathers had asked Samuel for a king. God then gave them Saul for a king. When God replaced Saul, God gave the Israelite people David for a king. Having led up to David in his sermon, Paul began to direct the attention of those in the synagogue to the promise God had made to David. God had promised the Messiah would come from David. At that point Paul delivered the theme of his sermon – God had fulfilled his promise to send the Messiah and sent to Israel a Savior. The name of that Savior was Jesus. As proof that that Jesus was the promised Messianic Savior Paul pointed to the testimony of John the Baptist, whom the Jews there in the synagogue with Paul would surely have heard about.

In the second part of his sermon Paul directed everyone's attention to the testimony of the Old Testament Scriptures that foretold the Messiah would come to save the people of Israel. Those Scriptures said the Savior would be put to death but that God would raise him from the dead. At that point in his sermon Paul announced to the assembly the news that all that those Scriptures had foretold had actually come to pass. In ignorance the Jewish people of Jerusalem and their rulers had Pontius Pilate condemn the Savior to death by crucifixion, because they did not really know who he was. After they had done everything to him that had been written in the Scriptures, they took him down from the cross and buried him in a tomb. But afterwards God raised him from the dead! The Savior Jesus was truly alive and living! The people who had walked with the Savior from Galilee to Jerusalem where he was crucified were witnesses that he was alive and living. The Savior appeared to them, not just once, but a number of times over a period of many days. Then Paul declared that he and Barnabas were proclaiming the good news that God had completely fulfilled his promise to them all by raising the Savior from the dead, just as his resurrection had been foretold in the Scriptures.

In the third part of his sermon Paul told the assembly that they should know that the forgiveness of sins was being proclaimed to them. Everyone who believed in the Savior Jesus was justified, that is they were declared forgiven of all the sins for which they could not receive forgiveness from the Law of Moses. In closing Paul cautioned the men and women present to be careful that they did not fail to heed the gospel message he had just proclaimed to them, lest the judgment of God that was spoken by the prophets should come down upon them.

Those closing words of Paul's sermon closed the synagogue service.

Luke reports, "Now when Paul and Barnabas were going out, *the people* kept inviting them to speak to them about these things on the next Sabbath." Paul's sermon had aroused among those in the synagogue a high degree of excitement and stirred up an intense desire to hear more – understandably so. What news he brought! What a message he delivered! The Messiah promised in the Holy Scriptures had come! He was a Savior! And what a Savior! Put to death but raised back to life! He lives and many can testify to that! In him there is forgiveness of sins! In him God forgives what the law cannot forgive! What amazing grace!

Stirred up with the good news of Jesus the Savior burning within their hearts, as Paul and Barnabas were slowly making their way out of the synagogue those who had heard Paul's sermon wanted to hear more about Jesus the Savior. And as they were exiting the synagogue, they kept inviting Paul and Barnabas to come back on the next Sabbath to tell them more. Luke informs us in Acts 13:43,

> And after the synagogue *service* had broken up, many of the Jews and of the God-fearing proselytes followed Paul and Barnabas, who, speaking with them, kept appealing to them to continue in the grace of God.

Many, but not all as shall be seen, of the Jews together with the God-fearing Greeks were so excited by the gospel message they had heard that they followed Paul and Barnabas to where they were staying. Their excitement over the gospel of Jesus indicated that they had believed the message Paul had delivered to them. Because they had become believers in the Savior Jesus, while they were walking Paul and Barnabas kept urging them to continue in the grace of God in Jesus for their forgiveness and eternal life. Having been brought to faith, they needed to continue in that faith for their salvation.

Now Paul experienced such a favorable reception even though he was sick and in spite of his somewhat repulsive appearance. His offensive appearance would have been a cause for the Galatians to turn away from him in disgust and to despise his gospel message that he preached. But because of the gospel they had heard, Paul's repulsive appearance did not drive them away. Rather they received him as an angel of God, and as if he were Christ Jesus himself![145] Such was the power of the gospel of God's grace in Christ Jesus to a people hungry for the good news of God's full and free forgiveness because of Jesus' reconciling sacrifice on the cross for the sins of all people everywhere, even there in Galatia!

People who are excited over something really good that has happened to them or who have heard something that is new and special love to talk about it and tell others. That appears to have been true of those Jews and God-fearing Greeks who were so favorably aroused by Paul's sermon. During the week following that sermon they must have been talking to many of the residents of Pisidian Antioch. The God-fearing Greeks no doubt would have been talking especially to their Greek friends and neighbors, telling them abut Paul and Barnabas, the traveling rabbis who had come to their city, and about the content of Paul's sermon. What would have particularly interested the other Greeks in the city was the fact that the good news of the Savior Jesus could apply to them also without their first having to become Jewish converts who had to accept circumcision and abide by all the laws of the Jews. The news spread like a wild fire. And since Pisidian Antioch was small in size, it would not have been difficult for the news to get around to nearly everyone in the city. It is obvious that that is what must have happened, for Luke reports, "Now when the Sabbath came, nearly all the city had gathered to hear the word of the Lord." (Acts 13:44)

Some of the Jews in the synagogue on the preceding Sabbath had not been so favorably impressed by Paul's sermon. Based on what Luke wrote in Acts 13:45 below one may safely speculate that they were probably the rulers and the rabbis of the synagogue. Luke does not say that they raised any objections during the following week. It can be assumed that they kept their thoughts pretty much to themselves. But their attitude changed dramatically on the next Sabbath day when they saw that nearly the entire population of the city turned out to hear the word of the Lord that Paul and Barnabas would speak. Seeing all those people coming to their synagogue and the size of the crowds trying to squeeze into it triggered the jealousy of those unbelieving Jews.

It is not likely that all those Greek Gentiles of Pisidian Antioch were able to get into the synagogue. There were likely to have been large numbers of them standing outside in front of it. Luke does not supply us with the details of when the Jewish rulers and rabbis began attacking what Paul and Barnabas were saying – before the service, during the service or outside after it – nor where they started arguing with Paul and Barnabas – inside the synagogue or outside of it because there was not room enough in the synagogue to hold everyone.

Whatever the exact scene may have been, the Jewish rulers and rabbis became extremely jealous of the success of the gospel that Paul and Barnabas were preaching. Being filled with jealousy, we can sense that those Jewish leaders were thoroughly aggravated that the Greeks of the city did not turn out in such large numbers to hear them speak about the Law of Moses on the Sabbath days as they were turning out to listen to Paul and Barnabas proclaim the gospel of Jesus Christ that day. Luke tells us, "When the Jews saw the crowds, they became filled with jealousy and began to speak against the things being spoken by Paul, blaspheming." (Acts 13:45) Those Jewish leaders began speaking out against the gospel of Jesus and in the process were condemning the grace of God that held out the forgiveness of sins to all who came to believe it, Greek Gentiles as well as Jews. In attacking the gospel those Jewish rulers and rabbis were not only rejecting the salvation that God was offering through the Savior Jesus, they were also slandering it and the person of Jesus who had established it with his substitutionary death on the cross to pay for all sins.

In response Paul and Barnabas spoke fearlessly, unafraid of any Jewish reprisals. They said, 'It was necessary the word of God be spoken to you first" (Acts 13:46a). It had been necessary to speak the word of God about his grace and gift of eternal life to the Jews first. They were God's chosen people to whom he had proclaimed his Word and had promised his saving grace in the person of the Messiah. And God had made the Jewish nation for the purpose of being a kingdom of priests.[146] They were to be the mediators between God and mankind to witness God's saving grace that he would accomplish through the Messiah to come. So it was necessary that the Jews be the first to hear the good news about the Savior Jesus Christ whom God had sent and did accomplish that great salvation – both for the Jews and the Gentiles as well.

But by rejecting the gospel of Jesus Christ that Paul and Barnabas were proclaiming, those Jewish leaders were rejecting the gospel's promise for themselves and declaring themselves unworthy of the eternal life that God gave through faith in that gospel. Luke reports in Acts 13:46b that Paul and Barnabas told the Jewish leaders, "Since then you reject it (the word of God) and do not consider yourselves worthy of eternal life, behold, we turn to the Gentiles!"

The Gentiles were eager to hear the gospel of the Savior Jesus. All the Jewish leaders had to do was to look around at the crowds of Greek Gentiles filling the synagogue and standing all around it to see the Gentiles' eagerness to hear the good news about Jesus the Savior. With the statement of what Paul and Barnabas would do Luke indicated what Paul would do in the future whenever Jews hardened their hearts and rejected the gospel of Jesus – he would turn to the Gentiles. As stated in Chapter 8, that appears to have been what Paul had started doing already during his ministry in Tarsus and the region of Syria and Cilicia, But here in Pisidian Antioch was the first time Luke actually reported that Paul did so.

Luke tells us in Acts 13:47 that as justification for their turning to the Gentiles Paul and Barnabas quoted Isaiah 49:6:

For so the Lord has commanded us, "I HAVE MADE YOU TO BE A LIGHT FOR THE GENTILES IN ORDER THAT YOU BRING SALVATION AS FAR AS THE END OF THE EARTH."[147]

Their choosing the words of Isaiah 49:6 fit the occasion of the Jewish leaders' rejecting the gospel and of Paul and Barnabas' therefore turning to the Gentiles. That verse of Isaiah revealed the words that God the Father had spoken in eternity to God the Son, the preincarnate Messiah and Great Servant of God, who was to come into the world. In the context of the opening verses of Isaiah 49 the Messiah spoke of his ministry among the Jews in Palestine as though he had already carried out that ministry, which would not happen for almost another 750 years. He said that he had labored among the Jews for no purpose and had spent himself for nothing. It was all in vain.[148] But God the Father told him it was too small of a thing for him to bring back those of Israel. God the Father said he would also make him a light for the Gentiles to bring salvation to the ends of the dearth. The Messiah and Savior Jesus came, taught the Jews in Palestine, fulfilled his redeeming mission, ascended into heaven, and then began through his apostles to be a light for the Gentiles to bring salvation to the ends of the earth. Being in Jesus Christ's service as his heralds, Paul and Barnabas applied the words of Isaiah 49:6 to themselves and their ministry and said as a result of the Jewish leaders' rejecting the gospel, they were turning to the Gentiles.

Luke then informs us,

48 "And when the Gentiles heard *this*, they began to rejoice and to glorify the word of the Lord, and as many as had been appointed to eternal life believed.

49 And the word of the Lord was being spread through the whole region." (Acts 13:48, 49)

Upon hearing Paul and Barnabas' declaration, the Gentiles began to rejoice. There may have even been shouts of joy ringing around the synagogue. For it was made clear to the Gentiles that God's grace and gift of salvation was theirs through faith alone in Jesus. They did not need to first become Jews through the rite of proselyte conversion that accepted circumcision and obedience to all the laws of the Jews.

Luke also reports that as many as had been appointed to eternal life believed. That was true for the Jews who had begun to believe in Jesus as well as for the large numbers of Greek Gentiles who had begun to believe in him. God had appointed them to have eternal life through faith in Jesus Christ back in eternity before the creation of the world when he elected all whom he would bring to faith during their lifetimes through the gospel of Jesus Christ by the working of the Holy Spirit. Years after this day in Pisidian Antioch Paul himself would write about this election to faith for eternal life, first in his Second Letter to the Thessalonians and then again in his Letter to the Ephesians. He would write:

> ... God chose you from the beginning for salvation by the sanctifying work of the Holy Spirit and faith in the truth. (2 Thessalonians 2:13)

> Blessed be the God and Father of our Lord Jesus Christ, who has blessed us with every spiritual blessing in the heavenly realms, since he chose us in him before the foundation of the world, that we would be holy and blameless before him. (Ephesians 1:3, 4)

Now many have followed their human reasoning to conclude that since God chose some like these Jewish and Greek Christian believers in Pisidian Antioch to be brought to faith in Jesus for eternal life, therefore God must have chosen all the rest in the world who do not come to faith in Jesus to be eternally condemned. Logically their human reasoning makes sense; their human conclusion, however, contradicts the clear, inspired Word of God, which says in the following verses:

> Say to them, "As I live," declares the Lord God, "I take no pleasure in the death of the wicked, but rather that the wicked turn from his way

and live. Turn! Turn from your evil ways! For why will you die, O house of Israel?" (Ezekiel 33:11)

This (praying for all people) is good and pleasing in the sight of God our Savior, who wants all people to be saved and to come to a correct knowledge of the truth. (1 Timothy 2:3, 4)

No one by their own thinking of choosing will come to believe in Jesus Christ for their eternal salvation. It is only by God's grace that anyone is saved through faith in Jesus, as Paul stated in Ephesians 2:8. So, it is to God's credit that any are saved. On the other hand, it is the fault of those who do not believe that they perish, for they resisted the Holy Spirit and denied their Lord Jesus who bought them and brought swift destruction upon themselves.[149] These two biblical teachings cannot be reconciled by human logic. The attempt to logically reconcile these two teachings will either end up in the heresy of synergism, that it is to a person's credit that he believed and was saved, or in the heresy that it is God's fault that he chose the person to be condemned. These two biblical teachings must be left side by side without trying to tie them logically together.

Now after Paul and Barnabas told the Jews that they were turning to the Gentiles, Luke tells us that the word of the Lord was being spread through the whole region. The Greek word for "region" means basically "country", and "land". It is best understood here as the area surrounding the city of Pisidian Antioch. Luke does not tell us by what means the gospel of Jesus was being spread, but very likely it was being spread by word of mouth. And since it was the Greek Gentiles who had turned out in such large numbers to listen to the message of Paul and Barnabas, it was probably the Greek Gentiles spreading the good news to their friends and relatives living in the city or on farms scattered around the countryside.

For how long the gospel message of Paul and Barnabas continued to spread out into the surrounding countryside is unknown. It is likely to have continued for a little while at least. During that time, since Paul and Barnabas told the Jewish synagogue rulers and rabbis that they were going to turn to the Gentiles, Paul and Barnabas would have taken the Jewish and Greek believers in Jesus to a different location for their worship services and instructional classes. In this manner a new Christian church was formed and established.

While this favorable time for Paul and Barnabas' ministry and the nurturing of the church continued, the jealousy and resentment of the unbelieving Jews of the synagogue continued to simmer and heat up. Among the synagogue members who did not believe the gospel Paul and Barnabas had preached were the socially prominent, wealthy,[150] God-fearing Greek women who were already mentioned. To those women the synagogue rulers and rabbis began pouring out their blasphemous arguments against Paul and Barnabas and the gospel of Jesus Christ. Once the minds of those women had been poisoned and stirred up, they talked and complained to their influential, wealthy husbands, who in turn had connections to the ranking men of Pisidian Antioch, the city magistrates. And since the Jews were an important part of the social and political makeup of the city, the Jewish leaders would have been complaining to those magistrates also. Being a Roman colony the magistrates probably consisted of a small group of Roman aristocrats that made a ruling oligarchy.[151] The Jewish leaders then kept stirring up the pot of discontent and slander among the prominent women and the magistrates until it boiled over. Luke says, "But the Jews incited the God-fearing, prominent women and ranking men of the city and stirred up a persecution against Paul and Barnabas, and threw them out of their district." (Acts 13:50) Using their authority, the magistrates expelled Paul and Barnabas from their area.

It is possible that that persecution of Paul and Barnabas may have included beating them with a rod. It is known from Paul's Second Letter to the Corinthians that he was beaten with rods on three occasions.[152] He was beaten once in Philippi, which was a Roman colony.[153] Being a colony, Philippi had a lictor, whose duties included apprehending criminals and administering punishment. Pisidian Antioch was also a Roman colony and a military center. It is possible that also there Paul, as well as Barnabas, was beaten with a rod by the city's lictor. That would account for the second of the three beatings.

Lystra was also a colony that persecuted Paul and Barnabas. Perhaps such a beating was administered to them there as well before stoning Paul. If so, that would make the third beating with a rod that Paul suffered and endured.

Paul and Barnabas then left. And when they left the area, Luke informs us in Acts 13:51, 52:

> 51 Then they shook off the dust of their feet against them, and went to Iconium.
>
> 52 And the disciples continued to be filled with joy and the Holy Spirit

Paul and Barnabas' gesture of shaking the dust off of their feet followed Jesus' directive to do so as a testimony against those who rejected them and the Word of God they preached and by doing so brought the judgment of God down upon themselves.[154] But when they left Pisidian Antioch Paul and Barnabas could look back upon their mission work in the city and see that it had been successful. A newly formed Christian congregation now existed there – the first Gentile church to be founded in the province of Galatia and separated from the Jewish synagogue. Precious souls had been reached and saved. That success was not their doing but the result of the Holy Spirit's working faith through the gospel of Jesus in the hearts of many who heard it. And when they left Pisidian Antioch, the Holy Spirit was continuing to fill the new Christian converts with the joy of their eternal life and salvation. As for the rejection of the gospel by many of the Jews in Pisidian Antioch and the persecution that they instigated against Paul and Barnabas, that was just another hostile reaction to the gospel that Paul would encounter from synagogue to synagogue in one city after another wherever he went. That was just one of the things that Jesus said Paul would suffer for his name.[155]

Iconium

After Paul and Barnabas shook off the dust of their feet, they started following the second part of the Via Sebaste road. They then walked east-southeast. They were unlikely to have known the exact distance to Iconium when they started out, but following the Roman road the distance would have been about seventy-five miles.[156] Iconium was the easternmost city of Phrygia,[157] which is called Konya today.[158] Walking at a rate of about 20 miles a day, it would have taken nearly 4 days to walk to Iconium. As they had done on their trek from Perga to Pisidian Antioch, they would have had to camp each night under the stars and eat the provisions they had managed to bring with them. As they walked along the Via Sebaste road, they would have gradually been descending from the 3,600-foot elevation at Pisidian Antioch to an elevation of 3,170 feet at Iconium.

Along the way if they came to a vantage point where they could look down towards Iconium, they might have been able to see that the city lay on the western edge of the vast, fertile Lycaonian plain that stretched 3 miles or more beyond the city. According to the early 1st century geographer Strabo the northern and eastern parts of the Lycaonian plain were barren. Ramsay explained the reason for that was a lack of water. By way of contrast the western and southern parts of the great Lycaonian plain that made up the Iconium plain were well watered.[159] Strabo stated regarding that part of the great Lycaonian plain that Iconium was well settled at a prosperous location that was good grazing country.[160] A mountain stream flowed into the city that made the land around it a great garden that was green with trees and was rich in produce. The water from the stream had no outlet, so it dissipated into the fertile soil as far east as the eye could see.[161] What is more, the Tcharshamba River at times brought down large amounts of water from the Isaurian mountains that inundated the land. Adding to the abundant supply of water was the large Lake Trogitis. Its water level varied considerably and sometimes rose high enough that water ran through the Tcharshamba Su[162] and flooded a large part of the plain, which was ordinarily cultivated with crops.[163]

When Paul and Barnabas drew near to Iconium, they would have been able to look back to the west towards Pisidian Antioch from which they had come and see the Taurus mountain peaks rising up more than 5,000 feet.[164] They would also have been able to see off in the distance mountains to the north and to the south. Being knowledgeable of other cities with their rugged terrains and natural fortifications, Paul and Barnabas might have noted that the city of Iconium on the western edge of the great Lycaonian plain was indefensible. It was better suited for peace than for war, and for commerce, agriculture, and the wealth that went with such enterprises.[165] Among its valuable exports were silver and copper from the mines in the mountains to its north,[166] and from its well-watered Iconium plain came apricots, grapes for the making of wine, cotton, flax, and grain.[167]

Like the other cities that Paul had visited, Iconium had a long and interesting history. Its name "Iconium" was derived from the Greek term "eikon" which meant an "image, figure, likeness".[168] [169] There were two legends for the origin of Iconium from which the city derived its name.[170] One was a Greek legend, which no doubt had its origin among the Greek immigrants who came to Iconium. The legend contended that Perseus came to Lycaonia and vanquished the opposition of the people by the power of a Gorgoneion that turned his enemies into stone. He then made the village into a city and called it Iconium after the image of the Gorgon. The other legend, probably older, appears to have been held by the native Phrygian inhabitants of Iconium. This legend was a tradition that paralleled the Noachian Flood account in Genesis 6–8. The native Phrygian Iconians prided themselves on their city having been great before the universal flood and that it was the first city to be founded after the flood. The following Phrygian legend is based on the account given in The Expositor:[171]

> King Nannakos was reigning before the great flood and lived three hundred years. He learned from an oracle that when he died, all mankind should perish. He assembled all the people at the temple and made a supplication with tears. His Phrygian subjects mourned grievously. Soon after the weeping of king Nannakos the flood occurred and all the people perished. When the earth dried up after

the flood, Jupiter told Prometheus and Athena to make images of mud. Then Jupiter caused the winds to breath into the images and made them come to life. In this way Iconium was repopulated and obtained its name of Iconium.

This Phrygian legend about the origin of Iconium is very interesting for several reasons. First, it parallels the flood account in Genesis. It has been said that the world's cultures all have their own accounts and legends of the universal flood at the time of Noah.[172] This legend of the Phrygian culture at Iconium is another. Second, archaeological excavations in 1924 around the neighboring city of Pisidian Antioch have indicated that the mounds surrounding Antioch date back to the third millennium B.C., which means there were people occupying that area only a few centuries after the Noachian flood that occurred in 2,613 B.C. Such dating of an occupation in that area harmonizes well with the Phrygian legend of nearby Iconium. Third, the ark of Noah came to rest at the end of the flood on Mount Ararat in eastern Turkey, the general region of Turkey where the Phrygian people and their legend lived.

The history of Iconium up to the time of Paul's arrival there consisted of a number of ethnic and political factors. The first Phrygian people were already present in western Anatolia by the 11th century B.C.[173] During the 8th century B.C. especially they settled everywhere in ancient Anatolia,[174] which at the time of Paul was essentially Asia Minor. They moved as far east as Iconium and infringed on that part of the Lycaonian plain.[175] This writer has not found definitive information about when Greeks migrated to Iconium. But as noted above, Greeks colonized Pamphylia and its city of Perga from the latter part of the Mycenaean Age and the Bronze Age, which was 1,600-1,100 B.C. They migrated from the Greek city of Magnesia on the western coast of Asia Minor, or what is now Turkey. It seems possible that during that same time Greeks also migrated to Iconium.

Iconium was a city of Galatia as is commonly stated. Ramsay stated that it continued to be a city of Galatia until the Roman reorganization in the 3rd century A.D.[176] The history of what nations ruled over Iconium is similar to that of neighboring Pisidian Antioch. After the death of Alexander the Great Iconium was ruled by the Seleucid dynasty. Then it was governed by the kingdom of Pergamon, and after that it came under the rule of Galatians until Mithridates VI took control of it. Pompey then liberated Iconium from Mithridates in 64 B.C. and Rome controlled it. In 39 B.C. Mark Antony, who was ruling the eastern part of Rome's empire, gave control of Iconium to Polemon of Cilicia, who was also known as Polemon II, king of Pontus. Because Polemon was incapable of ruling over it with the rest of his large dominion, three years later Antony entrusted the rule of Iconium to Amyntas king of the Celtic Galatians; he then ruled over it until he was killed in 25 B.C. at which time Iconium was again taken over by the Romans and Emperor Augustus.[177]

At one time Iconium was the chief city of a tetrachy, which consisted of 14 cities.[178] It was perhaps to that time that Ramsay referred when he said that Iconium had been a commanding center of a very wide area through the Lycaonian plain to the north and east and south to the border of Lystra[179] and had a population that was spread over 200 square miles.[180] During the reign of Emperor Claudius that began in A.D. 41 the city was granted the privilege of using his name as a prefix and the city then became known as Claudiconium.[181] Claudiconium was likely to have been the name in use when Paul came to the city in late A.D. 46 to early 47. In the latter part of Hadrian's reign, perhaps about A.D. 135, he made Iconium a colony.[182]

One would think that with such a rich ancient history archaeologists would have been busy excavating the site of Iconium to uncover its historical treasures. But that has not been the case as at other cities to which Paul traveled. This writer has found little on archaeological diggings at Iconium. But he thinks that he has learned from Conybeare and Howson what is a probable reason for that. In their book The Life And Epistles of St. Paul, the first edition of which was 1852, they reported that Iconium was destroyed repeatedly. When the Turks conquered the area and took control of Iconium, they destroyed the

Greek and Roman city and then used the city's ancient remains as building materials to construct their defensive walls that were about two miles in circumference.[183] Furthermore, this writer has learned that the tell – the mound of what was ancient Iconium, has been made into a park for a mosque at that location. As a result of these facts, this writer cannot describe what the ancient city of Iconium might have been like at the time Paul visited it with Barnabas.

After having walked and camped out under the stars for 4 days, when Paul and Barnabas arrived at the city of Iconium, they would have needed to replenish their food supplies. It is quite likely, therefore, that they went to the marketplace. In the process of shopping for the food items they needed they also would have been able to mingle with the residents of the city to get to know them, the city, and where they could find lodging.

Very quickly they would have learned the people of Iconium spoke two languages primarily – Phrygian, the language of the native inhabitants, and Greek, the language of the Greek immigrants and of commerce throughout the Mediterranean world. But they would also have heard a spattering of Latin coming from the Romans in the crowds. Since Paul and Barnabas would have known only a little of the Phrygian language that they might have picked up in Pisidian Antioch, they would have conversed with the merchants in Greek while shopping for their food supplies. From the merchants, as well as the residents who were probably standing around, they might have been able to ask where they could find a place to stay. It is also probable that if they did not see a Jewish synagogue located near the marketplace or on a busy street corner they had passed, they would have inquired whether there was a synagogue in the city and where it was located. During their shopping expedition they would have learned that the population of Iconium was made up of Phrygians, Greeks, Romans, and Jews. The Jews would have been moved there when Antiochus the Great around 200 B.C had Jewish families brought into the region of Phrygia.[184]

Another point of information that the two missionaries would have wanted to know was what was the predominant religion of the

Gentile population in Iconium. Ramsay said that it was apparent from ancient inscriptions that had been found that the religion of the Iconian people was a worship of the Phrygian Mother-Goddess Cybele, who was worshipped from Iconium and northwards for about thirty miles as the Zizimmene Mother. The name Zizimmene was derived from her supposed residence at the Zizima up in the mountains north of Iconium. It was believed that she revealed her presence by the underground wealth that she taught men how to recover. That wealth was in the copper and silver mines beside the village there. The mines had been worked from ancient times and were still productive at the beginning of the A.D. 1900s. The migrant Greeks then Hellenized the worship of the Phrygian Mother-Goddess into a worship of Athena. This religion was still being practiced in a Christianized form at the start of the 1900s.[185]

Luke had a good reason for describing Paul's ministry with Barnabas in Pisidian Antioch. It enabled Luke to describe for the first time how Paul conducted his ministry among the Jews and the Gentiles on his missionary journeys. Luke's description of Paul's ministry and sermon in Pisidian Antioch presented examples of how Paul went about preaching the gospel from synagogue to synagogue in city after city among the Jews first and then the Gentiles as well as what successes and kinds of opposition Paul experienced in place after place. Since Luke had reported those details of Paul's ministry in Pisidian Antioch, he felt no need to repeat them in connection with Paul's missionary work in Iconium, Lystra, and Derbe. Luke's description of Paul's missionary work in those last three cities was short and became so very brief that his report on Paul's work in Derbe consisted of no more than a few words in the two verses of Acts 14:20 & 21.

Beginning with Paul and Barnabas' work in Iconium Luke began painting in short, broad strokes a picture of what Paul's ministry was like during the remainder of his first missionary journey. It appears that Luke had a double purpose in writing his accounts of Paul's work in Iconium, Lystra, and Derbe. First, Luke was continuing to depict how the gospel was being spread by Jesus' bondservant and apostle

Paul. Second, Luke was depicting what Paul's missionary work was like for Paul personally as he experienced successes by God's grace overshadowed by severe trials and persecutions. Through his brief narrative strokes of what Paul personally experienced and suffered Luke was leading up to a climatic summary that Paul himself expressed in but one short sentence: "Through much tribulation we must enter into the kingdom of God" (Acts 14:22). Paul's sentence summed up to a great extent what his first missionary journey was like – much tribulation, an experience that appears to have also been Paul's earlier experience during his eight years at Tarsus and in the regions of Syria and Cilicia. Luke then described how Paul drew upon those personal experiences to prepare and to encourage the new Jewish and Gentile converts of the churches he had founded for their respective lives that they would have to face as believers in Jesus in a world full of people who reject the gospel and turn against those who believe it.

Luke reports Paul and Barnabas' ministrations in Iconium in just five and a half verses. But that short report has been the subject of much discussion and debate since the 5th to 6th centuries A.D. In a Greek manuscript dated at that time a copyist added a number of details to Luke's account in an attempt to smooth over what he thought was an inconsistency between verses 2 and 3 of Acts 14:1-5, which verses will be quoted during the following discussion. To the copyist it seemed illogical that because of opposition from the Jews Paul and Barnabas would therefore continue working in Iconium, which is what he understood those verses to mean. The effort to remedy the apparent inconsistency of Luke's text has continued to more modern times. Two scholars have suggested that the apparent inconsistency should be resolved by moving verse 3 to between verses 1 and 2. There is no real inconsistency in Luke's text, however. The verses stand correctly as they are without need of added details or shifting the position of verse 3. The supposed but non-existent problem is easily removed when one understands that Luke painted his account of Paul and Barnabas' work in Iconium in broad brush strokes. Verses 1 and 2 are simply an overview of that work and verses 3 through 6a then provide Luke's few pertinent details that surrounded that work.

In Acts 14:1 Luke reports, "Now it happened in Iconium *that* they entered the synagogue of the Jews together and spoke in this manner." This verse 1 is a brief summary statement of Paul and Barnabas' ministerial activity. On the Sabbath day Paul and Barnabas entered the synagogue together and spoke. In this manner they proceeded with their work of preaching the gospel of Jesus Christ from Sabbath day to Sabbath day. They apparently did this for a month or longer. Together they preached the gospel of Jesus the Savior as Paul had done in the synagogue of Pisidian Antioch.

In the last half of verse 1 Luke then reports that they did so, ". . . with the result that a great multitude of not only Jews but also Greeks began to believe." From Sabbath to Sabbath as the two of them together preached the good news about Jesus Christ more and more of the Jewish members of the synagogue believed Jesus was their Lord and Savior. During that same time God-fearing Greeks who were attending the synagogue services also believed. It seems apparent that those Greeks who believed must have then been sharing the good news about Jesus with their Greek friends and neighbors, so that more and more of the Greek population started coming and were believing the gospel that Paul and Barnabas were preaching. In this way a great multitude, which could also be translated as a large crowd, of Jews and Greeks believed. How many Jews and Greeks believed is impossible to say, perhaps hundreds. This large number believed, not because of anything that Paul and Barnabas did, but because of the divine power of the gospel message itself and the Holy Spirit who worked through it to bring those Jews and Greeks to faith in Jesus.

Now the following Verse 2 of Acts 14 is another summary statement. While the preaching of the gospel mentioned in Verse 1 together with its success was going on, opposition to the gospel was also arising and going on. Luke reports, "But the Jews who refused to believe stirred up and embittered the minds of the Gentiles against the brothers." No doubt stirring up an embittered, evil mind set against the brothers also took some time. It did not happen immediately and in just one week.

It should be noted that in the original Greek text the clause "the Jews who refused to believe" is literally "the Jews who were disobedient." Through the gospel God tells sinners to believe in Jesus Christ, as God did through Paul and Silas when they told the jailer in Philippi, "Believe in the Lord Jesus, and you will be saved" (Acts 16:31). That divine command to believe in Jesus is called a gospel imperative, or invitation. With that command God invites sinners to believe in Jesus for the forgiveness of t their sins and salvation from the eternal punishment they deserve for those sins. But when sinners refuse to believe in Jesus, they are rejecting God's invitation and disobeying his command to believe. They are being disobedient. Accordingly the Greek text of Acts 14:2 calls the refusal to believe disobedience. The reader may see further examples of where the New Testament calls unbelief disobedience in Acts 19:9, Romans 15:31, Hebrews 3:18, 1 Peter 2:8, 3:1 & 20, and 4:17. In these verses The Vivid English Translation Of The New Testament translates disobedience as a refusal to believe or unbelief. In John 6:29 Jesus said that believing in him was the work of God. Believing in Jesus is the greatest work of God, for it keeps the First Commandment, "You shall have no other gods besides me." Conversely, refusing to believe in Jesus is an act of disobeying that First Commandment.

In summarizing Paul and Barnabas' missionary work in Iconium and the opposition it aroused, Luke was careful to differentiate for us the various groups of people who were involved –the Jews who believed the gospel and the Jews who refused to believe the gospel; the Greeks, meaning first of all the Greeks who feared God and worshipped with the Jews on the Sabbaths, and then secondly the many Greeks who must have been the friends and neighbors of the Greeks who feared God and also came to the synagogue to hear the gospel. Then Luke tells us about the "brothers", meaning those Jews and Greeks who came to believe the gospel of Jesus Christ and became Christian brothers of Paul and Barnabas. And finally Luke mentions for us the Gentiles, who were the non-Jewish residents of

Iconium, the Greeks and the native Phrygians and the Romans of the city who were not believers in Jesus.

Understanding who the various groups of people were, we can now understand who did what to whom. The unbelieving Jews of the synagogue embittered the minds of the unbelieving Greeks, native Phrygians, and Romans in Iconium against the "brothers", the Christian Jews and Greeks. This makes it clear that the unbelieving Jews had not yet stirred up a persecution against Paul and Barnabas themselves, but only against the Jewish and Greek Christian converts. What also becomes clear is that because of the unbelieving Jews, the unbelieving Greek, Phrygian, and Roman citizens of Iconium were having their minds poisoned and turned against their fellow Jewish and Greek citizens who did believe in Jesus. The malicious antagonism of the unbelieving Jews had the effect of stirring up a religious persecution of the Christians in their city. What furthermore becomes obvious is that when the unbelieving Jews started their malicious campaign against the Christian converts in Iconium, Paul and Barnabas could no longer meet with those Christians in the synagogue. They had to find some other place where they could meet for worship, prayer, and instructional classes. In that way Paul and Barnabas founded a church made up of Jewish and Greek converts apart from the synagogue, as they had also done in Pisidian Antioch.

In spite of the unbelieving Jews arousing a persecution against the Christian converts, God had been blessing the missionary work of Paul and Barnabas to the extent that a great multitude of Jews and Greeks had been brought to faith. Having summarized this for us, Luke says in Acts 14:3, "Therefore they spent a long time speaking boldly for the Lord, who was testifying to the word of his grace by granting miraculous signs and wonders be performed by their hands." Because the Lord Jesus was blessing their missionary work with a multitude of Jewish and Greek converts, Paul and Barnabas stayed in Iconium a long time preaching his gospel. Just how long they stayed we do not know. But an estimate of a year or longer would not be beyond reason.

Throughout that entire time Paul and Barnabas spoke boldly for the Lord. They held nothing back because they were afraid for their own safety or that people who heard the truth of what God said might not like it, reject it, and turn away. They proclaimed the truth and the full counsel of God the way it was – the law that showed the people their sins and the gospel that showed them the grace of God in Christ Jesus. Unlike them, in this modern day and age there are those who shirk from preaching the true, strong doctrines of God. They are so concerned about a numerical church growth that they lack a concern for a spiritual church growth and tell the people the popular things that their itching ears want to hear. They do not tell the people the scriptural truths the people need to hear to lead them to repentance, faith, salvation, and spiritual sanctification. Such preachers need to humble themselves under God to do his will of speaking the truth and letting the results up to God, but they seem to have forgotten or had never learned that their job was to preach the truth, let the chips fall where they may, and let God take care of the results.

Paul and Barnabas spoke so boldly for the Lord because their faith rested solidly on Jesus and his promises, such as Jesus made to his disciples in Matthew 10:26-32:

> 26 Do not be afraid of them; for nothing is covered that will not be revealed, or secret that will not be made known.
>
> 27 What I say to you in the darkness, speak in the light; and what you hear *whispered* into your ear, proclaim aloud upon the rooftops.
>
> 28 And stop being afraid of those who kill the body, but who are unable to kill the soul; but rather always be afraid of him who is able to destroy both body and soul in hell!
>
> 29 Are not two sparrows sold for a cent? And not one of them will fall to the ground without *the will and consent of* your Father.
>
> 30 But even the hairs of your head are all numbered.
>
> 31 So stop being afraid! You are worth more than many sparrows!
>
> 32 Therefore everyone who will confess me before men, indeed I will confess him before my Father who is in heaven.

During the long time that Paul and Barnabas labored in Iconium the Lord Jesus himself was aiding their efforts. He was enabling them to perform miraculous signs and wonders. Through those miracles he was revealing that he was not a dead man who had been crucified but the living Lord and Savior who had been resurrected from the dead and who was enabling Paul and Barnabas to perform those miraculous signs and wonders in his name. What is more, through those miracles the Lord Jesus was substantiating that the gospel of his grace that Paul and Barnabas were preaching was his message to the Iconian people and that Paul and Barnabas were truly his messengers.

Luke was not the only New Testament writer to state that the Lord aided the missionary efforts of his messengers in the preceding manner. The gospel writer Mark wrote, "Then those disciples went out and preached everywhere, while the Lord was working with *them* and confirming the word by means of the accompanying miraculous signs" (Mark 16:20). And the writer to the Hebrews wrote, "This salvation, which at first was spoken by the Lord, was confirmed to us by those who heard, while God was bearing witness together with *them* both by miraculous sings and wonders and various kinds of powerful deeds and distributions of the Holy Spirit according to his will" (Hebrews 2:3 & 4).

Over the period of time that Paul and Barnabas were preaching the gospel while the unbelieving Jews were embittering the Gentiles of Iconium, the population of the city was becoming more and more polarized. Luke tells us in Acts 14:4, "The people of the city were divided; there were those on the one hand with the Jews, but there were those on the other hand with the apostles." The Jews' instigation of malice toward the Christians had succeeded to the extent there was an open division in the city. In the one camp were the unbelieving Jews and Gentiles; in the other were the Christian Jews and Greeks who were following and supporting Paul and Barnabas.

Luke labels Barnabas an apostle as well as Paul. Luke was not incorrect in calling Barnabas an apostle. As this writer explained in Chapter 7 in connection with Paul's first visit to Jerusalem after his conversion when he saw Peter and James, the Greek word for "apostle" had a broad and a narrow meaning. In its broadest sense "apostle" meant a delegate and a messenger, who had been commissioned and sent out as such. In its narrowest sense "apostle" meant one of the Twelve whom Jesus called and Paul whom Jesus called later.

As the unbelieving Jews stirred up more and more antagonism against the Christian Jews and Greeks, Paul and Barnabas increasingly became a focus of attention, for they were the ones preaching the gospel that was converting the great multitude of Jewish and Greek citizens of Iconium. The focus on Paul and Barnabas finally came to an ugly, malicious head. Luke tells us in Acts 14:5-7,

> 5 Now when a hostile movement of both the Gentiles and the Jews with their rulers arose to mistreat and to stone them *to death*,
>
> 6 *and* when they became aware *of it*, they fled down to the cities of Lystra and Derbe of Lycaonia and the surrounding region,
>
> 7 and there they continued preaching the gospel.

The unbelieving Gentiles and Jews incited a hostile movement against Paul and Barnabas. The participants included the unbelieving Gentiles and Jews together with their rulers, meaning the rulers of the synagogue and the ringleaders of the Gentile mob. The Greek term for "hostile movement" is "orme", which means a violent impulse and an assault. A mob was formed, and an assault got under way to mistreat Paul and Barnabas and then stone them to death. The Greek word for "mistreat" is hubrizo. It means to act and to treat shamefully. Jesus used this term when he revealed in Luke 18:32 that he would be handed over to the Romans who would then mock him, treat him shamefully, and spit on him. We know from the gospels that that shameful mistreatment consisted of his being beaten and scourged. Paul also used the Greek term to describe how Silas and he were shamefully mistreated in Philippi, at which time they were seized, dragged before the authorities and the crowd and publicly beaten with rods before being thrown into prison.[186] Understanding how this Greek term was used in those instances, it is clear that the unbelieving Gentiles and Jews of Iconium were intending to make a shameful, brutally debasing public spectacle of

Paul and Barnabas that would end with the mob stoning them to death.

In some way or another Paul and Barnabas heard this assault had gotten under way. The mob was frantically searching for them to seize them. They likely learned about it from a Jewish or Greek Christian who had become aware of the mob and its intentions. When Paul and Barnabas learned of it, they fled from Iconium to Lystra and then to Derbe. Such a mob was without reason and beyond listening. It was intent only upon a bloody, deadly course of action. Trying to speak to it would have been foolhardy. The smart thing for them to do was to move on. They were not cowards for doing so. They simply did what Jesus had told his disciples to do when they were persecuted: "Whenever they persecute you in this city, start to flee to the next." (Matthew 10:23) They were far from being cowards; they were persecuted missionaries being compelled to move on from one successful mission endeavor to the next. Since the unbelieving populace of Iconium did not want their preaching any more, they could better continue their preaching in Lystra and Derbe.

Lystra

The location of the remains of the city of Lystra was first guessed by Col. Leake in 1820.[187] In 1884-1885 Prof. Sterrett of Cornell University positively identified the site of ancient Lystra[188] when he found a pedestal epigraph, which also proved that Lystra was a Roman colony. On that large inscribed pedestal the colony of Lystra honored its colonial founder Emperor Augustus.[189] Lystra was located on the plain of Lycaonia in the center of what had been Anatolia and at Paul's time was in western Asia Minor. To the best of this writer's knowledge, as of the time of this writing an excavation of the site has never been undertaken. Plans for excavating the site were announced in 2005 by the staff of the University of Selcuk of Konya (near the site of Iconium), Turkey.[190] The site of Lystra is about 450 yards from the present Turkish village of Hatunsaray. Its mound measures about 675 yards by 600 yards with a height just under 100 feet.[191] There are very few remains of ancient Lystra that are visible above ground. Ancient Lystra "was off the main road, being situated in a secluded, charming spot among hills, and was therefore well fitted as a place of refuge,..."[192] It was reported that archaeological finds have been discovered in the area that date from prehistoric times to the Middle Ages.[193] Lystra had been in the kingdom of Galatia. When its last king, Amyntas, was killed, Lystra was taken over by Emperor Augustus, who made Lystra a Roman colony in 25 B.C.[194] Augustus made Lystra a colony to serve as a military garrison to dominate the rebellious Isaurian tribes that threatened the region. Lystra was the easternmost Roman fortified city that Augustus constructed to pacify Pisidia and Issauria.[195] Another possible reason for Augustus' making Lystra an armed garrison might have been to safeguard the precious water supply that the area provided for the fertile Iconian plain.[196] In a neighboring village of Lystra two brothers who were architects mentioned their native place of residence in an inscription that reveals those ancient people had a civic pride that touched all classes of citizens.[197] Paul himself exhibited such a pride in his home city of Tarsus.[198]

Fleeing for their lives from the unbelieving Jews and Gentiles of Iconium, Paul and Barnabas walked 18 miles to Lystra,[199] where they must have thought they would have some relative safety. They would have been able to walk that distance in one day. During their walk they would have left the easternmost region of Phrygia and entered the western region of Lycaonia. Lystra, like Derbe, was located in the western part of Lycaonia that was controlled by the Romans.

When they came to Lystra, they would have seen a temple of the pagan god Zeus standing outside of the city gates. Since Luke does not mention a synagogue or the presence of Jews in Lystra, it appears that very few Jews resided there and that the vast majority of the population of Lystra consisted of pagan Gentiles. There is a possibility that Timothy with his Jewish mother and grandmother were in the crowds that listened to Paul preach the gospel of Jesus. This is a possibility because when Paul returned to Lystra on his second missionary journey in A.D. 50 Timothy was already a believer in Jesus Christ who was well spoken of by the Christian brothers in Lystra and Iconium.[200]

The native inhabitants spoke their native Lycaonian language. Ramsay did not think that they spoke Greek, but since Paul did not speak the Lycaonian language and could only address them in Greek or Latin, which would have been spoken by the Romans in the colonial city, it seems most likely that Paul would have preached to the Lystrian people in Greek, for Greek was the universal language of the Mediterranean world at that time.

Now Luke informs us in Acts 14:8-10,

> 8 In Lystra a man was sitting, who had no strength in his feet, *having been* crippled from his mother's womb, who never walked.
>
> 9 This man[201] listened to Paul while he was speaking. When Paul fixed his eyes on him and saw that he had faith for being healed,
>
> 10 he said in a loud voice, "Stand up straight on your feet!" And he leaped up and began walking around.

Luke does not tell us how long Paul and Barnabas were in Lystra before this miraculous healing occurred. It is not likely that it happened as soon as they set foot in the city. They were more likely to have been in the city for a little while getting to know the city and its citizens. At some time after being in the city they began witnessing the gospel of Jesus to the residents. Since it appears that there was no synagogue in the city, they most likely began speaking publicly in the marketplace or by the city gate where the crowds tended to gather.

On one of those days there was a man sitting in the public place where Paul began addressing the crowd. Luke does not tell us that the man was a beggar, so perhaps he was not. On the other hand, since he was sitting in that public place where people gathered, which was the typical practice of beggars who were trying to eek-out an existence for themselves, it is quite possible that he was begging for alms and that Luke in his brief narrative style did not mention the fact.

What was of the greatest importance to Luke was the man's physical condition. Luke provides us with several important details about that. In presenting those details the medical acumen of Luke as a physician comes out. First, Luke notes that the man had a serious disability in his feet, namely that they were incapable of enabling him to stand upright. Second, the man's disability was due to a congenital problem; he had been born with the disability. Third, as a result of his disability the man had never walked. The man's physical disability, then, was a hopeless, life-long handicap that was beyond human help. Being a smaller sized city, the people of Lystra surely would have known this man and the details about his life and disability.

The man sat there listening attentively to Paul speaking. It may have been while Paul was perhaps teaching the crowd about the divine power of Jesus and how Jesus had performed so many kinds of miracles that the man began believing that Jesus surely had the power to cure his disability as well. Then apparently at the end of his address Paul fixed his eyes on him. A divine gift of the Holy Spirit enabled Paul to see that the man had been brought to faith by the gospel message and also believed that Jesus could heal his disabled feet too. Seeing that the man had such faith in Jesus, not a faith that would enable the man to be healed but a faith that simply trusted in Jesus and that Jesus could heal him if he wished to do so, Paul said in a loud voice, "Stand up straight on your feet!" And the man did! The power of the resurrected, living Lord Jesus reached out through the words of Paul and miraculously healed the man's disabled feet! How powerful and wonderful was the working of the Lord's miraculous healing! The man needed no rehabilitation to strengthen his weak feet or to teach him how to walk. No indeed! The man immediately by the miraculous power of Jesus was able to leap up and start walking around. As Jesus did in the ministries of his apostles, he enabled Paul to perform this miracle to substantiate that Paul was a spokesman for God and that he spoke the message God had for the people.[202]

We then learn from Luke:

> 11 And when the crowds saw what Paul had done, they lifted up their voice in the Lycaonian language, saying, "The gods, who have become like men, have come down to us!

> 12 And they began calling Barnabas, Zeus, and Paul, Hermes, since he himself was the chief speaker. (Acts 14"11, 12)

The crowds of Lycaonian people who had gathered to hear Paul became astounded when they saw what Paul had done. They had never seen such power! They had never seen such a miracle! They knew that could not have been the doing of a mere man. They knew that miracle had to have been the working of a god. They were pagan people. Throughout their lives they had been taught to believe in the mythological gods of the Greek pantheon. Upon seeing Paul's miracle the crowds in their excitement reverted to their native Lycaonian language, which Paul and Barnabas could not understand. So they did not know that the people were calling them the Greek gods Zeus and Hermes, whom the Lycaonians thought had become like men and had come down to them from Mount Olympus. In Greek mythology Zeus, whom the Romans called Jupiter, was the ruler of the gods. Hermes, whom the Romans called Mercury, was his son. Hermes was believed to be the messenger of the gods.[203] The Lycaonians supposed that Barnabas was Zeus, perhaps because of his better appearance and stature. They supposed Paul was Hermes because Paul had been the one doing the speaking. This association of these two mythological gods Zeus and Hermes was a common faith of the people in the area of Lystra. This is a known fact from a couple of archaeological finds in the area of Lystra. Ramsay discovered an inscription in 1909 in ruins near the city of Lystra. The inscription had been made by ancient native Lycaonians. The inscription recorded the dedication of a statue to Zeus and to Hermes. In reporting this find of Ramsay's Camden M. Cobern stated in his classic work, <u>The New Archaeological Discoveries</u>, "This (inscription) shows that these two gods were classed together in the local cult, and again illustrates the accurate local knowledge of St. Luke."[204] F.F. Bruce also mentioned the joint worship of Zeus and Hermes near Lystra as the result of an inscription and an altar that had been discovered.[205]

Now we hear next: "And when the priest of Zeus, whose temple was just outside of the city,[206] brought bulls and wreaths to the gates, he together with the crowds wanted to sacrifice *them*." (Acts 14:13). Lystra, like most cities at that time, was surrounded by defensive walls. Just outside the city gates stood a temple of Zeus. It has been thought the existence of that temple indicated that Zeus was the protector of the city. When he priest of Zeus heard the news that the gods Zeus and Hermes had come down from Olympus as men, he, most likely in the persons of his servants, had bulls decorated with garlands of flowers brought to offer as sacrifices to Paul and Barnabas.

These sacrificial proceedings in their honor took Paul and Barnabas by complete surprise. It is not clear where they were at the time, but this writer tends to think they were still teaching in the public marketplace or near the city gates. Just how they came to understand whom the people thought they were and what the people were about to do Luke does not clarify for us either. But somehow, they heard something that told them the crowd together with the Priest of Zeus was about to sacrifice the bulls to them. As soon as they heard that, they became utterly appalled. Luke informs us, "And when the apostles Barnabas and Paul heard this, they tore their robes and rushed out into the crowd, shouting, ..." (Acts 14:14) Since Barnabas was supposedly Zeus who was mentioned first in verse 12, he is named before Paul in this verse as well. Appalled and grieved over the sacrilegious, blasphemous festivities underway in their honor, they tore the neck of their robes with a quick, downward ripping yank to express how they felt. Most likely they tore the undershirt worn closest to their body, for their outer robes were a heavy material that could not be easily torn.

The Lycaonians' readiness to offer sacrifices to Paul and Barnabas confronted the two missionaries with the hard, inescapable truth about the human nature of all heathen people. Like all heathens the Lycaonians had been given a natural knowledge of God through the created universe in which they lived. They had nature to reveal to them that there is a God who is almighty, eternal, wise, and kind. And their own consciences taught them that that God was a fair and just judge who would hold them accountable for their thoughts, words, and actions. Having this natural knowledge, however, did not lead them to worship and serve the One true God of heaven and earth. Instead they turned to the worship of idols, as Psalm 96:5 says the heathen peoples do: "For all the gods of the peoples are idols, but the Lord made the heavens." In the case of the Lycaonians their spiritual ignorance even caused them to think that Paul and Barnabas, mere men, were gods. Similarly, the Romans in their spiritual ignorance confessed their emperor to be a god. This gross idolatry in which the heathen stumble about blindly shows the shortcoming of the natural knowledge of God – it does not tell people who the true God is nor what he has done in Jesus Christ to save them. For that knowledge they need to hear the Word of God, which he revealed in his Holy Scriptures.

It was for that purpose of proclaiming the truth about God to the spiritually ignorant Lycaonians that Paul and Barnabas rushed out into the crowd, shouting,

> 15 "Men, why are you doing these things? We ourselves are also men who suffer the same misfortunes[207] as you, preaching the gospel to you to turn completely away from these worthless *idols* to the living God who made the heaven and the earth and the sea and everything in them;
>
> 16 "who during the generations gone by permitted all the nations to go their own ways;
>
> 17 "and yet he did not leave himself without witness by doing good, by giving you rain from heaven and fruitful seasons, satisfying your hearts with food and gladness." (Acts 14:15-17)

Paul and Barnabas began shouting as loudly as they could to attract the crowd's attention to stop their sacrificial intentions. They tried to arrest the people's intentions by prompting them to think about what they were doing and why. There was no reason for their sacrificial festivities. Paul and Barnabas assured them that they were not gods but mere human beings. Like the Lycaonians, they suffered the same misfortunes of hardships, illness, and death. They had the same needs for food, water, and clothing. They were no different or any better than the Lycaonians. They were merely men who were proclaiming the good news about the Lord and Savior Jesus Christ, so the Lycaonian people would turn away from their worthless idols that were only imaginary gods and turn to the One, true God who really lived and existed. He was the God who had displayed such great patience with the past generations who had gone their own idolatrous ways. He did not destroy them in his anger as they deserved for doing so, and as he will do to all idolaters on the day of judgment; rather, he kept testifying to his existence by doing good. He showed his kindness by giving them rain from heaven and fruitful seasons of abundant crops, which they had been seeing year after year in the fertile Iconium plains nearby. In that way he had been satisfying their hearts with food and gladness. In addressing the crowd as Paul did in these verses, he "as a wise and careful missionary, appealed to the knowledge of natural religion, in order to build upon the beauty of revealed religion."[208]

Having directed the crowds to the One, True God, Luke tells us, "And by saying these things, they hardly restrained the crowds from making a sacrifice to them." (Acts 14:18) The Lycaonian people were so steeped in their mythological gods and so deep in their spiritual ignorance that they did not want to listen to Paul's admonition.

Now Paul and Barnabas were able to remain in Lystra for some period of time afterwards, for Luke's passing mention of "disciples" in verse 20 makes it clear that they were there long enough to preach the gospel and teach the new converts to found a church in Lystra. They were able to continue their preaching and teaching, however, only for a time. Luke informs us in Acts 14:19, "And Jews came along from Antioch and Iconium." The news that Paul and Barnabas were preaching the gospel in Lystra traveled back along the Via Sebaste highway first to Iconium and then to Pisidian Antioch. Still filled with the hatred that had motivated the unbelieving Jews to drive Paul and Barnabas out of their cities, the Jews of Pisidian Antioch traveled the seventy-five miles to Iconium, where they joined forces with the Jews of Iconium. Together they traveled the eighteen miles to Lystra. The hatred of men knows no limits, not even in long distances. Once in Lystra they began stirring up the crowds of unconverted pagan Lystrians who previously had wanted to honor Paul and Barnabas with their sacrifices. We learn from Luke, "And when they had won over the crowds and had stoned Paul, they were dragging him outside the city, believing he was dead." (Acts 14:19) The Jews from Pisidian Antioch and Iconium succeeded in stirring up the crowds of Lystrian pagans into a frenzied mob that angrily stoned Paul inside the city itself, then dragged him out of their city and dropped his lifeless looking body on the ground. Believing he was dead, they left his corpse for the vultures to dispose of.

But Paul was not dead. He must have been a bloody, bruised wreck of a man, but by the gracious providence of God he was not dead, for the Lord had mercy on Paul and preserved his life for the work he still wanted his bondservant to do. Luke tells us, "After the disciples encircled him, he got up and went into the city. And the next day he went out with Barnabas to Derbe." (Acts 14:20) The disciples were the Lycaonian converts who had been won over by the gospel and made up the new congregation Paul and Barnabas had founded. After the Jewish led mob had left Paul for dead outside the city, those disciples were able to come out to where Paul was lying on the ground and circled around him. They, too, were likely to have thought Paul was dead and had gone out to bury him in the graveyard. They must have been extremely surprised and amazed when Paul's lifeless looking body began to move and to gradually sit up. He then stood up and walked on his own power into the city. After resting for the night, he left with Barnabas to begin walking to Derbe, a distance of about eighty-one miles.[209] It would have taken them four days to walk that distance, and again Paul would have had to sleep out at night under the stars regardless of the weather. Here again Paul showed his strength and stamina and resiliency with which God blessed him. A lesser, weaker man, as some have asserted Paul had been, would never have been able to walk that distance and camp out in the elements for four days after having been stoned nearly to death. And he did so with only one night's rest before making the walk to Derbe in order to resume his work as a bondservant of his Master Jesus Christ.

Derbe

Derbe was an important frontier city in the southeast of the Roman province of Galatia and in the region of Lycaonia. Because of its importance Emperor Claudius changed Derbe's constitution and honored the city by allowing his name to be prefixed to Derbe's name. It then became known as Claudio-Derbe. Claudius probably did this in the earlier part of his reign, which began in A.D.41. It is possible that when Paul worked in Derbe with Barnabas about the latter part of A.D. 48 the city was then called Claudio-Derbe.[210] [211]

Camden M. Cobern reported that the location of the ancient city of Derbe had been fixed by Prof. Sterrett of Cornell University in 1885 where there was an artificial mound just north of the Taurus mountains on the edge of the Lycaonian plain. Cobern noted, however, that the identification of that site at the time was not absolutely conclusive.[212] In more recent times F. F. Bruce reported that M. H. Brillance in 1956 identified the site about one third of a mile north-northeast of Karaman but afterwards Brillance argued that the site was two and a half miles south-southeast from the first site he had pinpointed.[213] Other than Lystra and Colosse Derbe was the only New Testament site still unexcavated in Turkey. Then in 2013 it was reported that near Karaman actual excavations of ancient Derbe had begun and that they had begun to uncover some remains of the city. Two inscriptions have been found that mention Derbe by name and verify the site is the ancient city of Derbe. In that report of 2013 it was stated that the excavations had uncovered a stone quarry, graves, ancient walls, and a church-like structure.[214] Besides those findings a very important find has been a Roman milestone that was found in the graveyard of Kavak, which establishes the line of the Roman road from Laranda and Derbe to Lystra. A second inscribed milestone was found on the same road a mile away upon a bridge of the Tchashamba

Su.²¹⁵ The site of Derbe is a distinctive mound set out in the middle of the plain.²¹⁶

After Paul and Barnabas had arrived in Derbe, it is obvious that they remained there for some period of time, for Luke tells us in Acts 14:21 that they "preached the gospel to that city and made many disciples." Luke makes no mention of the presence of a Jewish synagogue. For that reason it would appear there were no Jews to speak of residing in Derbe and that the city, like Lystra, was a pagan city composed entirely of Gentiles. Nor does Luke mention that there was a persecution instigated against Paul and Barnabas. Therefore, we may assume that their work in Derbe moved ahead peacefully without incident, which must surely have been a relief after what they suffered in Pisidian Antioch, Iconium, and Lystra. And what was an added blessing was the Holy Spirit's working mightily through their preaching of the gospel of Jesus Christ to bring many of the pagan residents of Derbe to faith. In this way the Word of God was taken to Derbe, more souls were saved for eternal life, and a Gentile church was founded.

The Conclusion Of Paul's First Missionary Journey-The Return To Antioch, Syria

Luke informs us in Acts 14:21 & 22:

> 21 And after they had preached the gospel to that city and had made many disciples, they returned to Lystra and Iconium and Antioch,
>
> 22 strengthening the souls of the disciples, encouraging them to persevere in the faith and saying, "Through many tribulations we must enter into the kingdom of God."

In the above verses Luke gives us a brief overview of the first part of Paul and Barnabas' return trip to Antioch in Syria that would conclude Paul's first missionary journey. To begin their trip they returned first to Lystra, Iconium, and Antioch. In choosing this route

Paul revealed his commitment as a bondservant of the Lord Jesus to carrying out his work carefully and fully without regard for himself, his own comfort, or his own safety. He was in Derbe in the region of Lycaonia that was on the border of Cilicia. He could have gone south to Laranda on the Via Sebaste, then turned south on an existing road that would have taken him to the main east/west road that ran along the shores of the Mediterranean, and then walked east to his home city of Tarsus for a little rest before pushing ahead on that road to Seleucia the port city of Antioch in Syria. Had he chosen to walk that route, the total distance would have been about 261 miles. Instead, he retraced his steps from Derbe to Lystra, Iconium, and to Pisidian Antioch – a distance of 174 miles.[217] But then he had to walk about an additional 160 miles south back through the Taurus Mountains to return to Perga and then on to Attaleia where he could board a ship to sail to Seleucia the seaport of Antioch – a total walking distance of about 324 miles plus about a two-day sea voyage. We see, then, that he took the longer and harder way back to Antioch, Syria, instead of the shorter and easier way through Tarsus.

What is more, by taking that longer and harder way he was putting himself into more danger. He had already been persecuted and driven out of Pisidian Antioch, Iconium, and Lystra and even stoned and left for dead. As full of hate for Paul as the Jews and Gentiles of those cities were, if they saw him alive and in their city again, they would have wanted to kill him. In spite of that potential danger Paul returned to each of those cities.

Paul demonstrated that he surely was not a coward lacking courage. What would have given him such courage was his Lord and Savior Jesus Christ who always fulfilled his promise to Paul to be with him and to watch over him. Jesus had already delivered him from the persecutions in Pisidian Antioch and Iconium and Lystra and preserved his life from death by stoning. Having Jesus' presence and promises to protect him bolstered Paul's faith and gave him the courage to go on whatever the adversity or danger that lay before him. In light of how Paul's life and ministry proceeded and ended, it is very apparent that Paul had the faith to accept whatever happened to him as his Lord Jesus' good and gracious will for him, and that even if the danger before him were to result in his death, that was merely the doorway his Lord Jesus had chosen for him to walk through into the eternal glory that awaited him. Such a faith must have upheld Paul to his very end and being beheaded as a martyr. Paul's explicit trust in the Lord Jesus is an example for us all to maintain in and through whatever adversities and dangers Jesus may have in store for us during our lifetimes.

Aside from the faith of Paul that was just described, why would Paul knowingly take the longer, harder route to return to Lystra, Iconium, and Pisidian Antioch that put him in such danger? Luke answers this question for us – to strengthen the souls of the newly converted Christians in the churches of each of those cities and to encourage them. Those Christian men and women – so new and young in the faith – were all too aware of the persecution that had erupted in their respective city against Paul and Barnabas and the gospel of Jesus Christ. And what is more, they were still living among those hateful Jews and Gentiles. No doubt they had become the targets of the hot hatred that simmered in the hearts of the unbelieving Jewish and Gentile citizens all around them every time they stepped into the marketplace or ventured out onto the street. Having to bear such a burden each and every day was a temptation for them to forsake their newfound faith to return to their former Judaism or paganism. Understanding the strain and the pressure that those Christians were under was the reason Paul did not take the shorter, easier route but took the longer, harder, more dangerous route. For their sakes he went back through Lystra, Iconium, and Pisidian Antioch. He had to encourage those Christians to hang on and to persevere in their newfound faith.

The preceding discussion of Paul's reasons for revisiting the three congregations is justified in light of his same loving concern that he later expressed for the newly converted Christians in Thessalonica who were being severely persecuted by the Jews. Paul himself wrote in 1 Thessalonians 3:1-5:

1 For this reason (because the Thessalonian Christians were the glory and the joy of Paul and his fellow workers) when we could stand it no longer, we considered it good to remain behind in Athens alone,

2 and we sent Timothy, our brother and God's fellow worker in the gospel of Christ to strengthen and to encourage you concerning your faith

3 so that no one is troubled by these tribulations. For you yourselves know that we are destined for this.

4 For indeed when we were with you, we told you beforehand that we are destined to being oppressed, just as it has also happened as you know.

5 For this reason when even I could no longer stand it, I sent *another messenger* that I might come to know about your faith, lest in some way the tempter tempted you and our labor turned out to be for nothing.

Being so concerned about the Christian converts having to bear daily the persecution of their fellow citizens, the central theme of Paul's encouragement to strengthen those Christians in Lystra, Iconium, and Pisidian Antioch consisted of this message: "Through many tribulations we must enter into the kingdom of God." As mentioned previously, Luke had a dual purpose for writing his accounts of Paul's work in Iconium, Lystra, and Derbe – to depict how the gospel was being spread by Paul and what Paul's missionary work was like for Paul personally as he experienced missionary successes overshadowed by severe persecutions. This dual depiction of Luke's leads to his climatic summary of Paul's first missionary journey as Paul expressed it himself. Among his joyful successes there were many tribulations. About 18 years into the future and about 9 months before his martyrdom Paul recalled for Timothy in 2 Timothy 3:10 & 11 what he had experienced on his first missionary journey. He wrote:

10 Now as for you, you have followed faithfully my teaching, way of life, purpose, faith, patience, love, perseverance,

> 11 persecutions, sufferings, such as happened to me in Antioch, Iconium, and in Lystra, such persecutions as I endured. And yet the Lord delivered me out of *them* all!

To strengthen and encourage the recent converts to Christianity, Paul drew upon his own personal experiences to prepare and to encourage them for the tribulations they must also go through during their own respective journeys to the glorious kingdom of heaven that awaited them. Yes, they too were experiencing the hatred and the maltreatment of those who rejected the gospel and turned on those who believed it. As Paul wrote to the Thessalonians, Christians are destined to be persecuted and oppressed by the unbelieving and ungodly world in which they lived. Like Paul, then, they needed to be ready for such maltreatment and to accept it as part of their Christian lives. Likewise the Christians of all ages – whether missionaries or pastors or teachers or laymen and laywomen – all need to be ready and to accept by faith the hard truth that they too must enter the kingdom of God through many tribulations of persecutions and personal adversities. Many knowledgeable and mature Christians in the past have summed that up in this manner: "First the cross, then the crown!"

Now we learn from Luke in Acts 14:23,

> Then after electing by a show of hands elders for them in every church, and when they had prayed with fasting, they entrusted them to the Lord in whom they had believed.

With this one verse Luke tells us for the first time how in the apostolic church the congregations were organized and their respective public ministry was established. What was done was an example for the New Testament Church of all ages, but it was not a divine law of how and what must be done. It needs to be pointed out, however, that Paul and Barnabas employed no hierarchical authority in these congregations to establish their office of the public ministry for them by appointing elders, whom we today would call pastors, to serve their respective congregation. Paul and Barnabas merely guided the congregations in how their respective public ministry could be established for the continual teaching of God's Word in their midst.

Paul and Barnabas instructed the three churches to elect elders/pastors by a show of hands. In Acts 14:23 Luke used the Greek word cheirrotoneo, which properly means to vote by stretching out the hand and to elect.[218] Paul also used that Greek term in 2 Corinthians 8:19 for the churches electing, or choosing, an unnamed fellow Christian brother to assist with the collection of the Gentile churches.

Paul and Barnabas followed the procedure the apostles implemented for the election of the seven deacons in the church of Jerusalem, which Luke reported in Acts 6:1-7. It is apparent that Paul and Barnabas had the Christian laymen nominate men of their congregation whom they considered to be the most qualified to serve as the pastor of their congregation. When the slate of the qualified candidates had been assembled, Paul and Barnabas had the laymen elect by a show of hands which man they wanted to serve in the public ministry of the congregation. After each congregation had elected its pastor, we can assume that Paul and Barnabas also followed the example set by the apostles in the church of Jerusalem in installing the seven deacons and did what the church of Syrian Antioch did when they themselves were commissioned. Paul and Barnabas had the congregation conduct an ordination service that consisted of prayer and the rite of the laying on of hands that installed the respective men into the pastoral office of their congregation.

About fourteen years into the future in A.D. 63 Paul would write down in 1 Timothy 3:1-7 and Titus 1:5-9 what qualifications a man must have to serve as a pastor. One of the qualifications was that the man must be able to teach the Word of God and the gospel of Jesus Christ for the instruction of others, especially for those in his spiritual care. Surely Paul would have advocated in the churches of Lystra, Iconium, and Pisidian Antioch that they, too, elect men who had the biblical and spiritual knowledge to be able to teach others. In those newly founded churches there was only one way that there could have been men qualified to teach the members of the congregation. Paul, together with Barnabas, would have had to teach those men to the point that they had learned the essential, fundamental doctrines of the whole counsel of God. Paul and Barnabas would have had to do that teaching during the time they were working in those three cities. They must have kept very busy in an intensive training schedule to complete the minimum training necessary for men among the converts to be capable of teaching the other members in the church. How much time was needed for such intensive training probably varied from one congregation to another, and there is no certain way of knowing now what was the minimum amount of time they expended to accomplish that training. It is clear that Paul and his coworkers with him on his missionary journeys did indeed conduct an extensive course of training from what Paul wrote to the Thessalonians. Among the many things Paul taught the congregations was the fact that they would be persecuted. Paul wrote in 1 Thessalonians 3:4, "For indeed **when we were with you, we told you** beforehand that we are destined to being oppressed, . . ." The depth of Paul's teaching even included teaching the Christian converts about the coming of the Great Antichrist, as he did in 2 Thessalonians 2:1-12, and wrote in verse 5, "Do you not remember that **while I was still with you, I used to tell you these things?**"

Having taught the members of the congregations, having trained men for service as pastors in the public ministry of their churches, having had the men of the congregation elect a pastor and ordain him to serve their congregation, Paul and Barnabas' work for the present was brought to an end. In each of the three congregations they prayed with fasting, entrusted them into the care of their Lord in whom they had come to believe, and then they left to return to the church in Antioch of Syria.

Luke tells us in Acts 14:24-26:

> 24 And when they had passed through Pisidian, they came into Pamphylia,

> 25 and after they spoke the word in Perga, they went down to Attaleia.
>
> 26 And from there they sailed away to Antioch, from where they had been commended to the grace of God into the work that they had just completed.

From these verses we learn another reason Paul had for choosing the longer, harder route back to Antioch in Syria. He had to return to Perga for a period of time to preach the gospel there. When Barnabas and he had come from Cyprus to Perga before walking up to the cities in Galatia, they had just passed through Perga. They did not stay long enough to preach the gospel there. But there were precious souls in Perga too, who needed to hear the gospel of Jesus that they might believe and be saved. So, they remained in Perga just long enough to share the gospel with the residents there and then walked down to Attaleia to board a ship that carried them back to Seleucia, the port city of Syrian Antioch. For how long they remained in Perga and what success they had in preaching the gospel there Luke does not tell us.

Luke informs us in Acts 14:27 & 28:

> 27 Then when they arrived and gathered together the church, they began reporting all the things that God had done with them and that he opened the door of faith to the Gentiles.
>
> 28 Then they continued to spend a long time[219] with the disciples.

Paul and Barnabas had left Antioch in A.D. 46 and did not return until A.D. 49. It had been about three years since the congregation of Antioch had commended them to the grace of God and sent them on their way. Upon their return the church would have been most excited to see them again and to be able to renew their friendships with the two missionaries. Undoubtedly it was a joyous and warm homecoming celebration. The entire congregation would have been all ears to hear the stories Paul and Barnabas could tell them. But when Paul and Barnabas gathered with the congregation to report all that had happened during the three years that they were gone, they did not speak about what they had done and accomplished. No, they reported what God had done with them and through them and how he had blessed their missionary journey by opening the door of faith to the Gentiles, like the Roman Proconsul Sergius Paulus who had been steeped in magic but believed the gospel, like the crippled man in Lystra who believed and whose feet the Lord then gave Paul the miraculous power to heal, and like the Greeks and Gentiles of the cities who turned out in great numbers to hear the gospel of Jesus, many of whom believed and then began suffering the persecution of their neighbors and fellow citizens who rejected the gospel. And Paul and Barnabas would surely have reported the persecutions they suffered in Pisidian Antioch, Iconium, and Lystra, but how the Lord had delivered them from them all. Yes, to God be the glory, great things he had done! And there were more troubles to come for God to deliver his gospel and church from, as we shall see in the next chapter on the First Ecumenical Council of the apostles and elders in Jerusalem.

---

1. Acts 13:2
2. French, David H.; Roman Roads & Milestones Of Asia Minor Vol.4; p. 41; http://biaa.ac.uk/ckeditor/filemanager/userfiles/electronic_publications/Vol.%204%20The%20Roads-Fasc.%204.1.pdf
3. French, David H.; Pre-And Early Roman Roads Of Asia Minor; 10/1/2016; p. 182 http://www.dlir.org/archive/archive/files/arkeoloji_dergisi_v-5_p179-187_6bb72bd981.pdf
4. French, David H.; Roman Roads & Milestones Of Asia Minor Vol.3; p. 45; http://biaa.ac.uk/ckeditor/filemanager/userfiles/rrmam%20vol.%203%20milestones.pdf
5. Anatolianroads.org; The Anatolian Roads Project; https://anatolianroads.org/via-sebaste
6. French, David H.; Roman Roads & Milestones Of Asia Minor Vol.4; maps on p. 16 & 17; http://biaa.ac.uk/ckeditor/filemanager/userfiles/electronic_publications/Vol.%204%20The%20Roads-Fasc.%204.1.pdf
7. Strabo; The Geography Of Strabo; Book XII, Chapter 7, paragraph 3 on the webpage; published in Vol. V of the Loeb Classical Library edition, 1928; http://penelope.uchicago.edu/Thayer/E/Roman/Texts/Strabo/12G*.html
8. Davis, John D.; A Dictionary of the Bible; Baker Book House; Grand Rapids, Michigan; Seventeenth Printing, June 1969; p. 567
9. Conybeare, W. J. & Howson, J. S.; The Life And Epistles of St. Paul; Wm. B. Eerdmans Publishing Company; Grand Rapids, Michigan; Reprinted March 1974; p. 127

10. Davis, John D.; A Dictionary of the Bible; Baker Book House; Grand Rapids, Michigan; Seventeenth Printing, June 1969; p. 567
11. Conybeare, W. J. & Howson, J. S.; The Life And Epistles of St. Paul; Wm. B. Eerdmans Publishing Company; Grand Rapids, Michigan; Reprinted March 1974; p. 127
12. Wikipedia; Pamphylia; https://en.wikipedia.org/wiki/Pamphylia
13. Bruce, F. F.; The Acts Of The Apostles; William B. Eerdmans Publishing Company; Grand Rapids, Michigan; Third Revised And Enlarged Edition; 1990; p. 300
14. Anatalya Central; Perge – Ancient City; http://antalyacentral.com/historical-sites/Perge-ancient-city
15. Wikiwand; Perga; https://www.wikiwand.com/en/Perga
16. Turkish Archaeological News; Perge; https://turkisharchaeonews.net/site/perge
17. Wikiwand; Perga; https://www.wikiwand.com/en/Perga
18. Bruce, F. F.; The Acts Of The Apostles; William B. Eerdmans Publishing Company; Grand Rapids, Michigan; Third Revised And Enlarged Edition; 1990; p. 300
19. Wikipedia; Mycenaean Greece; https://en.wikipedia.org/wiki/Mycenaean_Greece
20. Ibid.
21. Wikipedia; Pamphylia; https://en.wikipedia.org/wiki/Pamphylia
22. Strabo; The Geography Of Strabo; Book XII, Chapter 7, paragraph 3 on the webpage; published in Vol. V of the Loeb Classical Library edition, 1928; http://penelope.uchicago.edu/Thayer/E/Roman/Texts/Strabo/12G*.html
23. Anatalya Central; Perge – Ancient City; http://antalyacentral.com/historical-sites/Perge-ancient-city
24. Wikipedia; Pamphylia; https://en.wikipedia.org/wiki/Pamphylia
25. Strabo; The Geography Of Strabo; Book XII, Chapter 7, paragraph 3 on the webpage; published in Vol. V of the Loeb Classical Library edition, 1928; http://penelope.uchicago.edu/Thayer/E/Roman/Texts/Strabo/12G*.html
26. Archaeology News Network: An Ancient Olive Oil Production Center In Pamphylia; https://archaeologynewsnetwork.blogspot.com/2013/08/an-ancient-olive-oil-production-centre.html#jPcm4qtaljvaUoU0.97
27. Bruce, F. F.; The Acts Of The Apostles; William B. Eerdmans Publishing Company; Grand Rapids, Michigan; Third Revised And Enlarged Edition; 1990; p. 300
28. Wikipedia; Perga; https://en.wikipedia.org/wiki/Perga
29. Bible Hub; Perga; https://biblehub.com/topical/p/perga.htm
30. Bruce, F. F.; The Acts Of The Apostles; William B. Eerdmans Publishing Company; Grand Rapids, Michigan; Third Revised And Enlarged Edition; 1990; p. 300
31. Encyclopedia Britannica; Perga; https://www.britannica.com/place/Perga
32. Wikiwand; Perga; https://www.wikiwand.com/en/Perga
33. Turkish Archaeological News; Perge; https://turkisharchaeonews.net/site/perge
34. Bruce, F. F.; The Acts Of The Apostles; William B. Eerdmans Publishing Company; Grand Rapids, Michigan; Third Revised And Enlarged Edition; 1990; p. 300
35. Turkish Archaeological News; Perge; https://turkisharchaeonews.net/site/perge
36. Bruce, F. F.; The Acts Of The Apostles; William B. Eerdmans Publishing Company; Grand Rapids, Michigan; Third Revised And Enlarged Edition; 1990; p. 300
37. Wikipedia; Perga; https://en.wikipedia.org/wiki/Perga
38. Bruce, F. F.; The Acts Of The Apostles; William B. Eerdmans Publishing Company; Grand Rapids, Michigan; Third Revised And Enlarged Edition; 1990; p. 3000

39. John's Notes; Part 3 – Antalya, Perga, Aspendos, Pisidian Antioch; http://johnsnotes.com/archives/2009TurkeyTrip-3-Transfer.htm
40. Antalya Central; Perge – Ancient City; http://antalyacentral.com/historical-sites/Perge-ancient-city
41. Bible Hub; Perga; https://biblehub.com/topical/p/perga.htm
42. Turkish Archaeological News; Perge; https://turkisharchaeonews.net/site/perge
43. Realm of History ;A Bevy Of Greek Mythology – Depicting Mosaics Uncovered At The Ancient City Of Perge, Turkey; https://realmofhistory.com/2017/07/25/greek-mythology-mosaic-perga/
44. Wikiwand; Perga; https://www.wikiwand.com/en/Perga
45. Turkish Archaeological News; Perge; https://turkisharchaeonews.net/site/perge
46. Wikiwand; Perga; https://www.wikiwand.com/en/Perga
47. Davis, John D.; A Dictionary of the Bible; Baker Book House; Grand Rapids, Michigan; Seventeenth Printing, June 1969; p. 594
48. Turkish Archaeological News; Perge; https://turkisharchaeonews.net/site/perge
49. Antalya Central; Perge – Ancient City; http://antalyacentral.com/historical-sites/Perge-ancient-city
50. Antalya Central; Perge – Ancient City; http://antalyacentral.com/historical-sites/Perge-ancient-city
51. Ibid.
52. Turkish Archaeological News; Perge; https://turkisharchaeonews.net/site/perge
53. Bruce, F. F.; The Acts Of The Apostles; William B. Eerdmans Publishing Company; Grand Rapids, Michigan; Third Revised And Enlarged Edition; 1990; p. 300
54. Wikiwand; Perga; https://www.wikiwand.com/en/Perga
55. Turkish Archaeological News; Perge; https://turkisharchaeonews.net/site/perge
56. Antalya Central; Perge – Ancient City; http://antalyacentral.com/historical-sites/Perge-ancient-city
57. Wikiwand; Perga; https://www.wikiwand.com/en/Perga
58. Turkish Archaeological News; Perge; https://turkisharchaeonews.net/site/perge
59. Conybeare, W. J. & Howson, J. S.; The Life And Epistles of St. Paul; Wm. B. Eerdmans Publishing Company; Grand Rapids, Michigan; Reprinted March 1974; p. 129
60. 2 Corinthians 11:26
61. This distance is based on measuring along the Via Sebaste as drawn on French's map of the Itinerarium Burligalense (West); French, David H.; Roman Roads & Milestones Of Asia Minor Vol.4; http://biaa.ac.uk/ckeditor/filemanager/userfiles/electronic_publications/Vol.%204%20The%20Roads-Fasc.%204.1.pdf
62. Wight, Fred H.; Manners and Customs of Bible Lands; Moody Press; Chicago, Illinois; p. 271
63. Ref. Matthew 9:17, Mark 2:22, Luke 6:37; the Greek term was "askos"; Thayer, Joseph Henry; Greek-English Lexicon of the New Testament; Zondervan Publishing House; Grand Rapids, Michigan; p. 81
64. Wight, Fred H.; Manners and Customs of Bible Lands; Moody Press; Chicago, Illinois; p. 94, 75
65. Exodus 22:26
66. Bruce, F. F.; The Acts Of The Apostles; William B. Eerdmans Publishing Company; Grand Rapids, Michigan; Third Revised And Enlarged Edition; 1990; p. 300

67. Ramsay, W. M.; St. Paul The Traveler And Roman Citizen; Baker Book House; Grand Rapids, Michigan; p. 93
68. FamTour; Via Sebaste Ancient Roman Road Day Hike; http://www.famtouralanya.com/portfolio/via-sebaste-ancient-roman-road-day-hike
69. Ramsay, W. M.; St. Paul The Traveler And Roman Citizen; Baker Book House; Grand Rapids, Michigan; p. 93-97
70. Galatians 4:13, 14
71. An ancient Greek broad-brimmed hat was called a Petasos, which dated as far back as the 5th century B.C. It was worn particularly by farmers and travelers. Wikipedia: Petasos; https://en.wikipedia.org/wiki/Petasos
72. French, David H.; Pre-And Early Roman Roads Of Asia Minor; http://www.dlir.org/archive/archive/files/arkeoloji_dergisi_v-5_p179-187_6bb72bd981.pdf
73. French, David H.; Pre-And Early Roman Roads Of Asia Minor; 10/1/2016, p. 183 http://www.dlir.org/archive/archive/files/arkeoloji_dergisi_v-5_p179-187_6bb72bd981.pdf
74. Wikipedia; Roman Roads; https://en.wikipedia.org/wiki/Roman_roads#Construction_and_engineering
75. David H. French in his paper Pre- And Early Roman Roads of Asia Minor noted earthen roads, quarried roads called roadways, and paved roads called highways; http://www.dlir.org/archive/archive/files/arkeoloji_dergisi_v-5_p179-187_6bb72bd981.pdf
76. French, David H.; Pre-And Early Roman Roads Of Asia Minor; 10/1/2016; p. 181 http://www.dlir.org/archive/archive/files/arkeoloji_dergisi_v-5_p179-187_6bb72bd981.pdf
77. French, David H.; Pre-And Early Roman Roads Of Asia Minor; 10/1/2016; p. 182 http://www.dlir.org/archive/archive/files/arkeoloji_dergisi_v-5_p179-187_6bb72bd981.pdf
78. Bruce, F. F.; New Testament History; Doubleday; New York, London, Toronto, Sydney, Auckland; 1969; p. 273
79. Strabo; The Geography Of Strabo; Book IV, Chapter 1, paragraph 13 on the webpage; published in Vol. II of the Loeb Classical Library edition, 1923; http://penelope.uchicago.edu/Thayer/E/Roman/Texts/Strabo/4A*.html
80. Bruce, F. F.; New Testament History; Doubleday; New York, London, Toronto, Sydney, Auckland; 1969; p. 273
81. Strabo; The Geography Of Strabo; Book XII, Chapter 5, paragraph 4 on the webpage; published in Vol. V of the Loeb Classical Library edition, 1928; http://penelope.uchicago.edu/Thayer/E/Roman/Texts/Strabo/12E*.html
82. Bruce, F. F.; New Testament History; Doubleday; New York, London, Toronto, Sydney, Auckland; 1969; p. 273
83. Strabo; The Geography Of Strabo; Book XII, Chapter 7, paragraph 1 on the webpage; published in Vol. V of the Loeb Classical Library edition, 1928; http://penelope.uchicago.edu/Thayer/E/Roman/Texts/Strabo/12G*.html
84. Ibid.; paragraph 2
85. Ibid.; paragraph 3
86. Ibid.; paragraph 3
87. Cobern, Camden M.; The New Archaeological Discoveries; Funk & Wagnalls Company; New York & London; 1917; p. 521; Google the following: "PDF Cobern,

Camden M.; The New Archaeological Discoveries; Funk & Wagnalls Company; New York & London; 1917"
88. Schneidervin, John C.; Christian Inconnect; An Overview Of The Book Of Genesis; http://www.christianinconnect.com/overview-of-the-book-of-genesis.html
89. Wikipedia; Antioch of Pisidia; https://en.wikipedia.org/wiki/Antioch_of_Pisidia
90. Turkish Archaeological News; Article: Antioch of Pisidia; https://turkisharchaeonews.net/site/antioch-pisidia
91. Wikipedia; Antioch of Pisidia; https://en.wikipedia.org/wiki/Antioch_of_Pisidia
92. Davis, John D.; A Dictionary of the Bible; Baker Book House; Grand Rapids, Michigan; Seventeenth Printing, June 1969; p. 40
93. Bruce, F. F.; New Testament History; Doubleday; New York, London, Toronto, Sydney, Auckland; 1969; p. 273
94. Turkish Archaeological News; Article: Antioch of Pisidia; https://turkisharchaeonews.net/site/antioch-pisidia
95. Wikipedia; Antioch of Pisidia; https://en.wikipedia.org/wiki/Antioch_of_Pisidia
96. Bruce, F. F.; The Acts Of The Apostles; William B. Eerdmans Publishing Company; Grand Rapids, Michigan; Third Revised And Enlarged Edition; 1990; p. 300
97. Wikipedia; Antioch of Pisidia; https://en.wikipedia.org/wiki/Antioch_of_Pisidia
98. Turkish Archaeological News; Article: Antioch of Pisidia; https://turkisharchaeonews.net/site/antioch-pisidia
99. Turkish Archaeological News; Article: Antioch of Pisidia; https://turkisharchaeonews.net/site/antioch-pisidia
100. Wikipedia; Men (deity) https://en.wikipedia.org/wiki/Men_(deity)
101. Cobern, Camden M.; The New Archaeological Discoveries; Funk & Wagnalls Company; New York & London; 1917; p. 534; Google the following: "PDF Cobern, Camden M.; The New Archaeological Discoveries; Funk & Wagnalls Company; New York & London; 1917"
102. Conybeare, W. J. & Howson, J. S.; The Life And Epistles of St. Paul; Wm. B. Eerdmans Publishing Company; Grand Rapids, Michigan; Reprinted March 1974; p. 136
103. Josephus, Flavius; Antiquities of the Jews 12.3.1 Josephus – Complete Works; Kregel Publications; Grand Rapids, Michigan; Twelfth Printing, 1974; p. 251
104. Josephus, Flavius; Antiquities of the Jews 12.3.3 Josephus – Complete Works; Kregel Publications; Grand Rapids, Michigan; Twelfth Printing, 1974; p. 251
105. Josephus, Flavius; Antiquities of the Jews 12.3.4 Josephus – Complete Works; Kregel Publications; Grand Rapids, Michigan; Twelfth Printing, 1974; p. 252
106. Cobern, Camden M.; The New Archaeological Discoveries; Funk & Wagnalls Company; New York & London; 1917; p. 532;Google the following: "PDF Cobern, Camden M.; The New Archaeological Discoveries; Funk & Wagnalls Company; New York & London; 1917"
107. Wikipedia; Antioch of Pisidia; https://en.wikipedia.org/wiki/Antioch_of_Pisidia
108. Ibid.
109. Turkish Archaeological News; Article: Antioch of Pisidia; https://turkisharchaeonews.net/site/antioch-pisidia
110. Edersheim, Alfred; Sketches of Jewish Social Life – In The Days Of Christ; Wm. B. Eerdmans Publishing Company; Grand Rapids, Michigan; reprinted 1974; p. 254
111. Nehemiah 8:1-8
112. Edersheim, Alfred; Sketches of Jewish Social Life – In The Days Of Christ; Wm. B.

Eerdmans Publishing Company; Grand Rapids, Michigan; reprinted 1974; p. 251, 252
113. Ibid.; p. 267
114. Gingrich, F. Wilbur; Shorter Lexicon of the Greek New Testament; The University of Chicago Press; Chicago and London; Fourth Impression 1973; p.207
115. Edersheim, Alfred; Sketches of Jewish Social Life – In The Days Of Christ; Wm. B. Eerdmans Publishing Company; Grand Rapids, Michigan; reprinted 1974; p. 250
116. Ibid.; p. 253
117. Ibid.; p. 259
118. In this manner Paul described unbelieving pagans; see Ephesians 2:12
119. Edersheim, Alfred; Sketches of Jewish Social Life – In The Days Of Christ; Wm. B. Eerdmans Publishing Company; Grand Rapids, Michigan; reprinted 1974; p. 260
120. Ibid.; p. 261
121. Ibid.
122. Ibid.
123. Ibid.
124. Ibid.; p. 262
125. Ibid.; p. 260
126. Ibid.; p. 268
127. Ibid.; p.272
128. Ibid.; p. 277
129. Lenski, R. C. H.; *The Interpretation of* The Book of Acts; Lutheran Book Concern, 1934; Assigned to The Wartburg Press, 1944; Assigned to Augsburg Publishing House, 1961; p. 514
130. Edersheim, Alfred; Sketches of Jewish Social Life – In The Days Of Christ; Wm. B. Eerdmans Publishing Company; Grand Rapids, Michigan; reprinted 1974; p. 277
131. Luke 4:17
132. Numbers 6:24-26
133. Edersheim, Alfred; Sketches of Jewish Social Life – In The Days Of Christ; Wm. B. Eerdmans Publishing Company; Grand Rapids, Michigan; reprinted 1974; p. 275
134. Ibid.; p. 268
135. Ibid.; p.267
136. Ibid.; p. 250
137. Coming to a correct understanding of what "those who fear God" and "proselyte" meant in the Book of Acts and at the time of Paul's ministry in Asia Minor and Greece is complicated by several factors. Some commentators have equated the two and said those who feared God were proselytes and converts to Judaism. But in actuality a distinction was made between the two. Furthermore, the definition of a proselyte varied from time to time and from place to place. The Aramaic Jews in Palestine where the influence of the Pharisees was so dominant were more conservative and strict than the Hellenistic Jews in Asia Minor and Greece who were more liberal. In Palestine a proselyte was a Gentile living in Palestine who had turned from paganism to Judaism and who had accepted circumcision and being bound by the laws of Moses as the requirement for his becoming a convert who was then recognized as a full fledged Jew and not a Gentile. Among the more liberal Hellenistic Jews in Asia Minor and Greece a proselyte was a Greek who had forsaken the pagan polytheism to embrace the reverence and worship of the One God of Judaism but who had not accepted circumcision and obedience to all the

laws of Moses. He remained a Greek who was recognized by the Jews as one who feared God. On top of these variations came the Rabbinic designations of the "proselyte of righteousness" which fit the Palestinian Aramaic definition, and the "proselyte of the gate" which fit the Hellenistic definition but carried the added stipulation that the proselyte was residing in Palestine, which did not fit the Hellenistic definition of what was a proselyte. What is more, the Jewish Encyclopedia includes the designations of "half-converts" and "semi-converts".

For detailed discussions on these distinctions of proselytes, the Greek term for proselyte "proselutos", the Greek terms "phoboumenoi" and "sebomenoi" which are used in the phrases "those who fear God" and "God-fearing", the following can be consulted: Thayer, Joseph Henry; Greek-English Lexicon of the New Testament; Zondervan Publishing House; Grand Rapids, Michigan; Arndt, William F. and Gingrich, F. Wilbur; Greek-English Lexicon of the New Testament and Other Early Christian Literature; The University Of Chicago Press; limited edition licensed to Zondervan Publishing House; 1957; Freidrich, Gerhard, editor; Theological Dictionary of the New Testament, Vol. VI; Wm. B. Eerdmans Publishing Company; Grand Rapids, Michigan; Jewish Encyclopedia, The Unedited Full Text Of 1906; Proselyte; Lives Transforming; First century Judaism; https://www.livestransforming.com/first-century-judaism/ Ps.89:20

138. Ps.89:20
139. 1 Sam.13:14
140. Ps.2:7
141. Isa.55:3
142. Ps.16:10
143. Hab.1:5
144. ref. Genesis 46:27
145. Galatians 4:14
146. Exodus 19:6
147. Isaiah 49:6
148. So it actually happened in history. Jesus' three-year ministry among the Jews appeared to be a failure. They rejected the Word of God that he spoke and crucified him. The words of the apostle John in John 1:11 echo what Isaiah reported that the Messiah had lamented in eternity – his labor had been in vain. John wrote: "He came to his own land of Israel, and his own people did not receive him *favorably*."
149. Acts 751; 2 Peter 2:1
150. This is the meaning of the Greek word euschemon that is translated "prominent" in Acts 13:50; see Gingrich, F. Wilbur; Shorter Lexicon of the Greek New Testament; The University of Chicago Press; Chicago and London; Fourth Impression 1973; p. 87; and Thayer, Joseph Henry; Greek-English Lexicon of the New Testament; Zondervan Publishing House; Grand Rapids, Michigan; p. 263
151. Ramsay, W. M.; The Cities Of St. Paul, Their Influence On His Life And Thought – The Cities Of Eastern Asia Minor; The Dale Memorial Lectures, In Mansfield College, Oxford;1907; A. C. Armstrong And Son, New York; Hodder And Stoughton, London, 1908; https://archive.org/details/citiesofstpaul00ramsuoft
152. 2 Corinthians 11:25
153. Acts 16:19-24
154. Matthew 10:14; Mark 6:11; Luke 9:5 and 10:10 & 11
155. Acts 9:16

156. This distance is based on measuring along the Via Sebaste as drawn on French's map of the Itinerarium Burligalense (West); French, David H.; Roman Roads & Milestones Of Asia Minor Vol.4; http://biaa.ac.uk/ckeditor/filemanager/userfiles/electronic_publications/Vol.%204%20The%20Roads-Fasc.%204.1.pdf
157. In support of Iconium being in Phrygia, not Lycaonia, the following statement was made as the sixth of the top ten archaeological finds: "6. Phrygian Altar Inscriptions – discovered in 1910 by William Mitchell Ramsay and displayed in the Istanbul Archaeology Museum – In Acts 14, Luke writes that Paul and Barnabas left Iconium and entered the region of Lycaonia. A century before Luke, Cicero had written that Iconium was in the region of Lycaonia. This made many scholars think Luke made a mistake – like saying someone left London and entered England. The discovery of these inscriptions show the people of Iconium did not speak the Lycaonian language but the Phrygian and Greek languages. This discovery confirms the accuracy of Acts 14 and is one reason William Mitchell Ramsay wrote that Luke 'is a historian of the first rank' and 'should be placed along with the very greatest of historians.' " From: Fact Bridge; Top-NT-Archaeological-Finds; Find #6; http://factbridge.org/sites/default/files/inline-files/Top-NT-Archaeological-Finds.pdf
158. Bruce, F. F.; The Acts Of The Apostles; William B. Eerdmans Publishing Company; Grand Rapids, Michigan; Third Revised And Enlarged Edition; 1990; p. 316
159. Ramsay, W. M.; The Cities Of St. Paul, Their Influence On His Life And Thought – The Cities Of Eastern Asia Minor; p. 324; The Dale Memorial Lectures, In Mansfield College, Oxford;1907; A. C. Armstrong And Son, New York; Hodder And Stoughton, London, 1908; https://archive.org/details/citiesofstpaul00ramsuoft
160. Strabo; The Geography Of Strabo; Book XII, Chapter 6.1; published in Vol. V of the Loeb Classical Library edition, 1928; http://penelope.uchicago.edu/Thayer/e/roman/texts/strabo/home.html
161. Ramsay, W. M.; The Cities Of St. Paul, Their Influence On His Life And Thought – The Cities Of Eastern Asia Minor; p. 317; The Dale Memorial Lectures, In Mansfield College, Oxford;1907; A. C. Armstrong And Son, New York; Hodder And Stoughton, London, 1908; https://archive.org/details/citiesofstpaul00ramsuoft
162. The Royal Geographical Society; Geographical Journal; London, England; 1903; p. 367, footnote of the journal; the Tcharshamba Su, or Charshamba Su, was 20 miles south of Iconium and was the largest channel but did not usually carry much water ; This info is on P.401 of the PDF copy; https://ia800302.us.archive.org/29/items/geographicaljou40britgoog/geographicaljou40britgoog.pdf
163. Ramsay, W. M.; The Cities Of St. Paul, Their Influence On His Life And Thought – The Cities Of Eastern Asia Minor; The Dale Memorial Lectures, In Mansfield College, Oxford;1907; A. C. Armstrong And Son, New York; Hodder And Stoughton, London, 1908; https://archive.org/details/citiesofstpaul00ramsuoft
164. Ramsay, W. M.; The Cities Of St. Paul, Their Influence On His Life And Thought – The Cities Of Eastern Asia Minor; p. 317; The Dale Memorial Lectures, In Mansfield College, Oxford;1907; A. C. Armstrong And Son, New York; Hodder And Stoughton, London, 1908; https://archive.org/details/citiesofstpaul00ramsuoft
165. Ibid.; p. 318
166. Ibid.; p. 337
167. Aiton, John, D.D.; St. Paul And His Localities In Their Past And Present Condi-

tion; Arthur Hall, Virtue & Vo.; London, England; 1856;[p. 155 https://books. google.com/books?id=eDQBAAAAQAAJ&pg=PA356&lpg=PA356&dq=St5.+Paul+ And+His+Localities&source=bl&ots=ESK6IKdJYV&sig= pkp8HcoDjCT9kvhB3z6VjHtK0qY&hl=en&sa=X&ved=0ahUKEwjD-tnn2qjZAhUY0mMKHcYbA0UQ6AEINjAB#v=onepage&q=St5.%20Paul%20And%20His%20Localities&f=false
168. Ramsay, W. M.; The Cities Of St. Paul, Their Influence On His Life And Thought – The Cities Of Eastern Asia Minor; p. 320; The Dale Memorial Lectures, In Mansfield College, Oxford;1907; A. C. Armstrong And Son, New York; Hodder And Stoughton, London, 1908; https://archive.org/details/citiesofstpaul00ramsuoft
169. Thayer, Joseph Henry; Greek-English Lexicon of the New Testament; Zondervan Publishing House; Grand Rapids, Michigan; p. 175
170. Ibid.; 326
171. Nicoll, W. Robertson, M.A. LL.D, editor; The Expositor; Sixth Series; Hodder And Stoughton; London; 1905; p. 198, 199
    https://books.google.com/books?id=TDU2AAAAMAAJ&pg=PA199&dq= Nannakos&hl=en&sa=X&ved= 0ahUKEwjr8ZG7qavZAhUL9mMKHbmnDMIQ6AEIKzAA#v=onepage&q= Nannakos&f=false
172. John Warwick Montgomery wrote: "The destruction of well nigh the whole human race, in an early age of the world's history, by a great deluge, appears to have so impressed the minds of the few survivors, and seems to have been handed down to their children, in consequence, with such terror-struck impressions, that their remote descendants of the present day have not even yet forgotten it. It appears in almost every mythology, and lives in the most distant countries, and among the most barbarous tribes." Montgomery, John Warwick; The Quest For Noah's Ark; Bethany Fellowship, Inc. Minneapolis, Minnesota; p.23
173. Wikipedia; Phrygians: https://en.wikipedia.org/wiki/Phrygians
174. Ancient History Encyclopedia; Phrygia; https://www.ancient.eu/phrygia/
175. Ramsay, W. M.; The Cities Of St. Paul, Their Influence On His Life And Thought – The Cities Of Eastern Asia Minor; p. 351; The Dale Memorial Lectures, In Mansfield College, Oxford;1907; A. C. Armstrong And Son, New York; Hodder And Stoughton, London, 1908; https://archive.org/details/citiesofstpaul00ramsuoft
176. Ibid.; p. 343
177. Bruce, F. F.; The Acts Of The Apostles; William B. Eerdmans Publishing Company; Grand Rapids, Michigan; Third Revised And Enlarged Edition; 1990; p, 316
178. Aiton, John, D.D.; St. Paul And His Localities In Their Past And Present Condition; Arthur Hall, Virtue & Vo.; London, England; 1856; p. 155; https://books. google.com/books?id=eDQBAAAAQAAJ&pg=PA356&lpg=PA356&dq=St5.+Paul+ And+His+Localities&source=bl&ots=ESK6IKdJYV&sig= pkp8HcoDjCT9kvhB3z6VjHtK0qY&hl=en&sa=X&ved=0ahUKEwjD-tnn2qjZAhUY0mMKHcYbA0UQ6AEINjAB#v=onepage&q=St5.%20Paul%20And%20His%20Localities&f=false
179. Ramsay, W. M.; The Cities Of St. Paul, Their Influence On His Life And Thought – The Cities Of Eastern Asia Minor; p. 335; The Dale Memorial Lectures, In Mansfield College, Oxford;1907; A. C. Armstrong And Son, New York; Hodder And Stoughton, London, 1908; https://archive.org/details/citiesofstpaul00ramsuoft

180. Ibid.; p. 340
181. Bruce, F. F.; The Acts Of The Apostles; William B. Eerdmans Publishing Company; Grand Rapids, Michigan; Third Revised And Enlarged Edition; 1990; p. 316
182. Ramsay, W. M.; The Cities Of St. Paul, Their Influence On His Life And Thought – The Cities Of Eastern Asia Minor; p. 352 & 362; The Dale Memorial Lectures, In Mansfield College, Oxford;1907; A. C. Armstrong And Son, New York; Hodder And Stoughton, London, 1908; https://archive.org/details/citiesofstpaul00ramsuoft
183. Conybeare, W. J. & Howson, J. S.; The Life And Epistles of St. Paul; Wm. B. Eerdmans Publishing Company; Grand Rapids, Michigan; Reprinted March 1974; p. 146, the second paragraph and footnote #2
184. Ibid.; p. 147
185. Ramsay, W. M.; The Cities Of St. Paul, Their Influence On His Life And Thought – The Cities Of Eastern Asia Minor; p. 330-333; The Dale Memorial Lectures, In Mansfield College, Oxford;1907; A. C. Armstrong And Son, New York; Hodder And Stoughton, London, 1908; https://archive.org/details/citiesofstpaul00ramsuoft
186. Acts 16:19-24
187. Nicoll, W. Robertson, M.A. LL.D, editor; The Expositor, Volume VI, Fourth Series; Wm. M. Ramsay; St, Paul's First Journey In Asia Minor; Hodder & Stoughton; London; 1892; Nicoll, W. Robertson, M.A. LL.D, editor; The Expositor; Sixth Series; Hodder And Stoughton; London; 1905; p. 198, 199; https://books.google.com/books?id=TDU2AAAAMAAJ
188. Cobern, Camden M.; The New Archaeological Discoveries; Funk & Wagnalls Company; New York & London; 1917; p. 525; Google the following: "PDF Cobern, Camden M.; The New Archaeological Discoveries; Funk & Wagnalls Company; New York & London; 1917"
189. Nicoll, W. Robertson; editor; The Expositor, Volume VI, Fourth Series; Wm. M. Ramsay; St, Paul's First Journey In Asia Minor; Hodder & Stoughton; London; 1892; p. 292 https://books.google.com/books?id=h6YQAAAAYAAJ&pg=PA161&lpg=PA161&dq=The+Expositor,+1892,+St,
190. The University of Selcuk of Konya, Turkey; Paper: A Plan For Archaeological Excavation of Lystra (Zoldura Hoyuk); presented between September 26 to October 1, 2005, in Torino, Italy; https://slidex.tips/download/a-plan-for-archaeological-excavation-of-lystra-zoldura-hyk
191. Ibid.
192. Cobern, Camden M.; The New Archaeological Discoveries; Funk & Wagnalls Company; New York & London; 1917; p. 525; Google the following: "PDF Cobern, Camden M.; The New Archaeological Discoveries; Funk & Wagnalls Company; New York & London; 1917"
193. The University of Selcuk of Konya, Turkey; Paper: A Plan For Archaeological Excavation of Lystra (Zoldura Hoyuk); presented between September 26 to October 1, 2005, in Torino, Italy; https://slidex.tips/download/a-plan-for-archaeological-excavation-of-lystra-zoldura-hyk
194. Bruce, F. F.; The Acts Of The Apostles; William B. Eerdmans Publishing Company; Grand Rapids, Michigan; Third Revised And Enlarged Edition; 1990; p. 319, 320

195. Nicoll, W. Robertson; editor; The Expositor, Volume VI, Fourth Series; Wm. M. Ramsay; St, Paul's First Journey In Asia Minor; Hodder & Stoughton; London; 1892; p. 292 https://books.google.com/books?id=h6YQAAAAYAAJ&pg=PA161&lpg=PA161&dq=The+Expositor,+1892,+St,
196. The University of Selcuk of Konya, Turkey; Paper: A Plan For Archaeological Excavation of Lystra (Zoldura Hoyuk); presented between September 26 to October 1, 2005, in Torino, Italy; https://slidex.tips/download/a-plan-for-archaeological-excavation-of-lystra-zoldura-hyk
197. Cobern, Camden M.; The New Archaeological Discoveries; Funk & Wagnalls Company; New York & London; 1917; p. 525 oogle the following: "PDF Cobern, Camden M.; The New Archaeological Discoveries; Funk & Wagnalls Company; New York & London; 1917"
198. Acts 21:39
199. This distance is based on measuring along the Via Sebaste as drawn on French's map of the Itinerarium Burligalense (West); French, David H.; Roman Roads & Milestones Of Asia Minor Vol.4; http://biaa.ac.uk/ckeditor/filemanager/userfiles/electronic_publications/Vol.%204%20The%20Roads-Fasc.%204.1.pdf
200. Acts 16:1 & 2
201. Lit. one
202. Ref. Mark 16:20, Hebrews 2:4
203. Ancient History Encyclopedia; Hernes; https://www.ancient.eu/Hermes/
204. Cobern, Camden M.; The New Archaeological Discoveries; Funk & Wagnalls Company; New York & London; 1917; p. 526; Google the following: "PDF Cobern, Camden M.; The New Archaeological Discoveries; Funk & Wagnalls Company; New York & London; 1917"
205. Bruce, F. F.; The Acts Of The Apostles; William B. Eerdmans Publishing Company; Grand Rapids, Michigan; Third Revised And Enlarged Edition; 1990; p. 322
206. Lit. the priest of Zeus, the one that was before the city
207. The Greek compound word is made up of the words "to suffer" and "like, same things"; it has been explained as meaning to be subject to the same incidents and exposed to the same frailties and evils, as well as to suffer like feelings with another person
208. Kretzmann, Paul E.; Popular Commentary of the Bible, New Testament, Volume I; Concordia Publishing House; St. Louis, Missouri
209. This distance is based on measuring along the Via Sebaste as drawn on French's map of the Itinerarium Burligalense (West); French, David H.; Roman Roads & Milestones Of Asia Minor Vol.4; http://biaa.ac.uk/ckeditor/filemanager/userfiles/electronic_publications/Vol.%204%20The%20Roads-Fasc.%204.1.pdf
210. Nicoll, W. Robertson; editor; The Expositor, Volume VI, Fourth Series; Wm. M. Ramsay; St, Paul's First Journey In Asia Minor; Hodder & Stoughton; London; 1892; p.295
211. Ramsay, W. M.; The Cities Of St. Paul, Their Influence On His Life And Thought – The Cities Of Eastern Asia Minor; The Dale Memorial Lectures, In Mansfield College, Oxford;1907; A. C. Armstrong And Son, New York; Hodder And Stoughton, London, 1908; p. 360 https://archive.org/details/citiesofstpaul00ramsuoft
212. Cobern, Camden M.; The New Archaeological Discoveries; Funk & Wagnalls

Company; New York & London; 1917; p. 526; Google the following: "PDF Cobern, Camden M.; The New Archaeological Discoveries; Funk & Wagnalls Company; New York & London; 1917"
213. Bruce, F. F.; The Acts Of The Apostles; William B. Eerdmans Publishing Company; Grand Rapids, Michigan; Third Revised And Enlarged Edition; 1990; p. 320
214. Biblical Archaeology ; Bible History Daily; Article: Derbe Excavations Explore Pauline Site; https://www.biblicalarchaeology.org/daily/biblical-topics/new-testament/derbe-excavations-explore-pauline-site/
215. American Journal of Archaeology; The American Journal of Archaeology and the History Of The Fine Arts, Volune VI; "Archaeological News – Lystra & Derve"; Ginn & Company; Boston; 1890; p. 343;
   https://books.google.com/books?id=b6MrAQAAIAAJ&pg=PA343&lpg=PA343&dq=archaeological+finds+at+ancient+Lystra&source=bl&ots=e_4AydbP85&sig=oTjKe_grIu14NhFdsqPm8HEhlg0&hl=en&sa=X&ved=0ahUKEwiIpNfsjMbZAhUD34MKHSx1A9I4ChDoAQhSMAk#v=onepage&q=archaeological%20finds%20at%20ancient%20Lystra&f=false
216. Holy Land Photos Blog; Excavations At Derbe Have Begun https://holylandphotos.wordpress.com/2013/09/05/excavations-at-derbe-have-begun/
217. This mileage of 174 miles is very comparable to the mileages given by Dr. Mark Wilson, director of the Asia Minor Research Center in Antalya, Turkey. He calculated the mileages using the Barrington Atlas of the Greek and Roman World. Biblical Archaeology ; Bible History Daily; Article: Derbe Excavations Explore Pauline Site; https://www.biblicalarchaeology.org/daily/biblical-topics/new-testament/derbe-excavations-explore-pauline-site/
218. Thayer, Joseph Henry; Greek-English Lexicon of the New Testament; Zondervan Publishing House; Grand Rapids, Michigan; p. 668
219. Lit. not a little time

V
THE APOSTOLIC COUNCIL

Paul's Age: 50
Date: A.D. 50

12

PAUL'S PARTICIPATION IN THE APOSTOLIC COUNCIL MEETING; PAUL'S REBUKE OF PETER IN ANTIOCH, SYRIA

P*aul's Participation In The Apostolic Council Meeting*

After Paul and Barnabas returned to Antioch, they resumed the preaching and teaching that they had been doing before being sent on Paul's first missionary journey. They were able to do that in peace throughout the balance of A.D. 49. They no doubt accepted that peaceful time as a blessing of God after the troubles and persecution they had experienced in Galatia. That continued into the early part of A.D. 50.

But that was just a peaceful interlude. A new and serious problem arose. Luke informs us in Acts 15:1,

> And when some came down from Judea, they began teaching the brothers, "Unless you become circumcised according to the custom of Moses, you cannot be saved."

The men came to the church in Antioch from Judea. Acts 15: 24 clarifies that they had gone out from the church in Jerusalem, but they did so without having been sent by its leaders. They were Jewish men who have commonly been called Judaizers. They often came from the Jewish sect of the Pharisees as Acts 15:5 shows. They accepted Jesus

Christ as the long-awaited Messiah (Christ). However, for salvation they insisted the laws of Moses must be obeyed, especially the rite of circumcision.

As we look back now at the controversy that those Judaizers incited we can see how much was at stake. First of all, the gospel of Jesus Christ itself was at stake. The insistence that the Gentile men must be circumcised to be saved emptied the all-sufficiency of Jesus' sacrificial death for sins that gained eternal salvation for all mankind, Gentiles as well as Jews. If the Judaizers' teaching would have been adopted at the Apostolic Council, the gospel of salvation by God's grace alone through faith alone in Jesus Christ would have been forever overturned, making Christianity no different from all the other religions in the world, namely another religion of works that each person must perform for himself. Secondly, the teaching of the Judaizers that the Gentiles must accept circumcision and the laws of Moses put a stumbling block in front of the Gentiles. It required them to first become full-fledged Jewish converts before they could become Christians and gain salvation. The majority of the Gentiles would not have accepted that. The Judaizers' teaching, then, if it would have been adopted and implemented, would have forever dimmed the attraction of Christ's gospel and impeded the growth of Christ's Church. If that teaching had been adopted, the Christian Church would have never become a universal faith attractive to the Gentiles in the world. Most likely the Church would have become and remained no more than another small sect of Judaism.

Now the question of whether Gentiles had to be circumcised in order to be saved and received into the Church had been debated and settled seven years earlier in A.D. 43 in connection with Peter's ministering to the Roman centurion Cornelius and his Gentile household.[1] The church of Jerusalem had pronounced then that the Gentiles need not be circumcised to be saved and to be a part of God's Church. But it is apparent those Judaizers who came to Antioch were disgruntled over Gentiles being accepted into the Church. Their dissatisfaction might have begun with that pronouncement and grew more intense as time went on. The day came that acting on their own they went to the church of Antioch, which was the main center of Gentile Christianity, and began teaching its male Gentile members that unless they were circumcised according to the custom of Moses they could not be saved. They made circumcision a requirement for salvation.

Acting on their own as they were, those Judaizers were meddlers meddling in the church of Antioch and its ministry. Since they insisted upon the Jewish custom of circumcision according to the laws of Moses, they most likely also adhered to the Jewish avoidance of Gentiles. They were, then, creating a double problem for the church in Antioch: their teaching was overturning the gospel of salvation by faith alone and their aloofness from Gentiles was making a brotherly church fellowship an impossibility.

How upsetting the Judaizers' teaching and aloofness must have been to the Gentiles in the church of Antioch! Suddenly those Gentiles were hearing that their faith in Jesus was not sufficient for salvation. They lacked the Jewish rite of circumcision according to the laws of Moses. They were, then, no better than second-class guests in the church. No doubt those Gentiles became thoroughly confused as well, because they had never heard Paul or Barnabas tell them that they must be circumcised to be saved and to be Christian members of Jesus' Church.

And how upset Paul and Barnabas must have become upon hearing what those Judaizers were teaching! For the Judaizers' teaching was in effect attacking the ministry that Paul and Barnabas had been conducting in Antioch, Cyprus, and Galatia, as well as contradicting their doctrine that a Christian was free from having to keep the laws of Moses.

Luke tells us in Acts 15:2 how Paul and Barnabas reacted to the message of the Judaizers: "Then a great deal[2] of strife and debate were raised by Paul and Barnabas against them." Paul and Barnabas did not stand for the Judaizers' teaching. They rose up against it. A great deal of strife and challenging then erupted.

Now this was Paul's first confrontation with Judaizers. He would have many more such confrontations during the course of his apostolic ministry, especially in the churches of Galatia, Corinth, Philippi,

Colosse, and Crete. In opposition to the Judaizers' teaching he and Barnabas upheld the freedom that Christians had in Christ from the Old Testament laws of Moses. The ceremonial laws like circumcision and the eating of only "clean" foods and the observance of Old Testament festivals were not obligatory for believers in Jesus. The Christians could observe those rites and festivals and restrictions if they desired to do so, but they had the Christian liberty not to observe them if they chose not to do so. Those things were adiaphora, meaning matters neither forbidden nor commanded by God for Christian believers in Jesus. However, when the Judaizers made the observance of those ceremonial laws necessary for salvation, then Paul and Barnabas stood on the liberty Christ had given to his Church from those laws and opposed the Judaizers. The truth of the gospel was at stake, not only for the Christians in Antioch but in the whole Christian Church for all ages to come. The gospel of salvation by God's grace alone and by the Christian's faith alone was being threatened and in danger of being overthrown. Only one year into the future Paul would write to the Galatian churches when they were also being upset and troubled by Judaizers: "It was for freedom that Christ set us free. Always stand firm, then, and stop being entangled again in a yoke of slavery!" (Galatians 5:1) And twelve years into the future when the Colossians were being upset by false teachers requiring abstinence from certain kinds of food and drink and were requiring the observance of Jewish festivals and Sabbaths, Paul wrote to the Colossians,

> Do not let anyone judge you in regard to eating and drinking or in the matter of a *religious* festival or a new moon festival or a Sabbath day, which are a foreshadowing of things to come, but the reality is in Christ. (Colossians 2:16, 17)

Fighting for the truth of the gospel and for the Christians' freedom from the laws of Moses, Paul and Barnabas taught and debated. But the Judaizers refused to listen and stood upon their false teaching. Luke informs us that then the church in Antioch, ". . . appointed Paul and Barnabas and some others of them to go up to the apostles and elders in Jerusalem about this controversial issue." (Acts 15:2) The church in Antioch assembled a delegation that consisted of Paul and Barnabas and some other men who no doubt were also respected leaders in the congregation. According to Galatians 2:3 Titus accompanied Paul to the Apostolic Council Meeting. Neither Luke nor Paul say Titus was an appointee to the delegation. In the coming years Titus would become a trusted coworker of Paul's in the ministry at Corinth and on the island of Crete.

In sending this delegation the church of Antioch took the right step toward insuring that the unity of the Church of Christ was preserved and that no division would splinter it. The church of Antioch was not appealing to the church of Jerusalem as a higher authority for a ruling decision by which it would then abide. It was simply sending its delegation to discuss the controversial issue, so the two churches could insure their doctrinal positions were in agreement with one another and that they stood united as one Church of the Lord Jesus Christ. Together they would then continue to walk as one. Paul would call upon the splintered congregation of Corinth to do the same thing in A.D. 56, six years into the future. Paul would write to those church leaders and members,

> Now I urge you, brothers, by reminding you of the name of our Lord Jesus Christ, that you all speak the same thing, and that there may be no divisions among you, but that you may go on being made complete in the same mind and in the same judgment. (1 Corinthians 1:10)

Paul supplies us in Galatians 2:1 & 2a with some additional details of how it came about that he went to the Apostolic Council Meeting in Jerusalem. In defense of his apostolic standing in the Church Paul referred to that Council Meeting and wrote, "Then after fourteen years I again went up to Jerusalem with Barnabas, taking Titus along also. Moreover, I went up as a result of a revelation; . . ." Paul went to the Council Meeting, not only because the church in Antioch commissioned him to go with the others, but because the Lord himself had told him in a revelation that he was supposed to attend it. We have no record of what the Lord told Paul in that revelation, but it seems apparent that the Lord considered the controversy so important to the future of his Church that he wanted Paul to go to that Council Meeting to uphold and to defend the true gospel that he had had Paul preaching and teaching already for years. Apparently, the Lord knew that the best way to nip that false teaching of the Judaizers in the bud was to have the apostles and the elders of the mother church in Jerusalem stand up together with Paul and the delegation from Antioch to condemn the Judaizers' teaching as a heresy to be rejected, not only in Antioch, but in the whole Christian Church. We are not told how Paul's receiving that revelation tied in with the church of Antioch's appointing him to go to the Apostolic Council. Perhaps Paul's revelation was a ratification that holding the Meeting was the right thing to do, or, perhaps Paul's appointment to go to the Meeting occurred in connection with Paul's disclosure of the revelation. We just do not know the order of how these things occurred.

We learn from Luke in Acts 15:3,

> "Consequently those who were sent on their way by the church were traveling through both Phoenicia and Samaria telling in detail the conversion of the Gentiles, and they continued to cause great joy among all the brothers."

Either the delegation from Antioch could not sail to Caesarea because the shipping season was still closed in what might have been January or February of A.D. 50, or the shipping season had opened in the month of March but the delegation chose to walk the overland route rather than take the sea route. Whatever the delegation's reason for walking the overland route, the men followed the main road south from Antioch down along the Mediterranean seacoast through Phoenicia and then into Samaria. As a result of Jewish Christians having fled about 18 years earlier to Phoenicia and Samaria to escape the persecution that had erupted in Jerusalem when Stephen was stoned, congregations had been formed in Phoenicia and Samaria.

The delegation from Antioch stopped along the way to tell those different Jewish Christian congregations the good news about the conversion of the Gentiles. Paul and Barnabas would have been able to relate many details about the Gentiles in Syria and Cilicia and in Galatia who had been turning from their paganism to believe in the Lord and Savior Jesus Christ. Their reports about the conversion of the Gentiles time and again were causing the Christians in Phoenicia and Samaria to rejoice and be glad.

As Paul related the good news about the conversion of the Gentiles, he surely understood that the Lord was fulfilling the promise he had made to Abraham about 2,100 years earlier. At that time the Lord had told Abraham, "In your Seed all the nations of the earth will be blessed." That Seed of Abraham Paul clarified in Galatians 3:16 was Christ Jesus, the Messiah and Savior of all people. In Abraham's Seed, Christ Jesus, the Lord said all the nations would be blessed, meaning the Gentiles in the world who would hear and accept the gospel in faith. [3] With that promise the Lord made known his gospel of salvation in Christ Jesus was intended for the Gentiles as well as for the Jews. But, as Paul himself stated in various letters of his, over the ages since the time of Abraham the gospel of Christ the Savior was a mystery that remained hidden.[4] Throughout those ages of passing generations God allowed the Gentiles to go their own ways[5] But God overlooked those ages of ignorance and gave orders for people to repent.[6] So in the fullness of time when Jesus Christ the Savior had come, Paul was given the blessing of proclaiming to the Gentiles that hidden mystery of the gospel of Jesus Christ to lead them to faith.[7] Paul was making known to them the mystery of the gospel[8] that they were fellow heirs with the Jews and fellow members and fellow sharers in the gospel promises.[9] Now with the large numbers of Gentiles in the cities of Syria, Cilicia, and Galatia turning from their paganism to believe in Jesus Christ the Savior, Paul was seeing that promise to Abraham being fulfilled. As Paul reported to the church in Antioch upon his return from his first missionary journey, the door of faith had been opened to the Gentiles.[10] Starting to see the fulfillment of that promise to Abraham and the Gentiles in large numbers being converted was indeed a cause for rejoicing then as it still is for us today who are Gentiles, for the Lord by his grace in Jesus Christ has also opened the door of faith to us and made us fellow heirs and sharers in the promise of eternal life and salvation. But at the time when Paul was walking with the delegation from Antioch to the Apostolic Council Meeting in Jerusalem and the Jewish Christians in Phoenicia and Samaria were rejoicing over the conversion of the Gentiles, the Judaizers were attempting to slam that door of faith shut in the faces of the Gentiles.

Now in Galatians 2:1 Paul sets the time of the Apostolic Council as "after fourteen years." That would be fourteen years after his brief fifteen day visit to Jerusalem that he mentioned a few verses earlier in Galatians 1:18. The three years that Paul mentioned in Galatians 1:18 would have been three years after his conversion. Those three years plus the following fourteen years tells us that the Apostolic Council met seventeen years after Paul's conversion in A.D. 33. The Council met, then, in A.D. 50.

Luke then informs us,

> Now when they arrived in Jerusalem, they were welcomed by the church and the apostles and the elders. And they reported all the things God had done with them. (Acts 15:4)

The members of the church in Jerusalem together with the apostles who were present and the elders of the church gave the delegation from Antioch a warm welcome. In this way the unity and the fellowship of the two churches were heartily expressed. It set a good example of the kind of brotherly love to be cherished and nourished among congregations and church bodies truly united in the same faith and doctrine. After the initial welcome and the Apostolic Council got under way, Paul and Barnabas made a report to the church of Jerusalem. They reported not what they had done in Antioch, Cyprus, and Asia Minor, but what God had done in those places by bringing large numbers of pagan Greeks to faith in Jesus Christ.

But, upon hearing this wonderful news, Luke informs us in Acts 15:5,

> Then some of those from the religious sect of the Pharisees who had believed stood up, saying, "They must be circumcised and commanded to keep the law of Moses."

Paul found himself and his teaching of the gospel being opposed by his former fraternal brothers – the Pharisees, among whom he had once been a rising star. These men who opposed him were like the Judaizers who had stirred up the strife and controversy in Antioch. In Galatians 2:4 Paul said they were "false brothers who were brought in secretly, such ones as slipped in to spy out our freedom that we have in Christ Jesus in order to enslave us." They had accepted Jesus as the Messiah, but they had brought with them their belief that the laws of Moses must be obeyed for eternal salvation, which included the circumcision of the men. Having this belief, they were insisting that the Gentiles who were being received into the Church must also obey the laws of Moses and be circumcised. In effect they were demanding that the Gentiles had to become Jews before they could become Christians in the Church. As previously explained, this false teaching put the true gospel of Jesus Christ and the future of the Christian Church in jeopardy. For an in-depth discussion of the Pharisees, their beliefs, and their practices, see Chapter 4.

The Pharisaic Judaizers raised this controversial issue, for it was the purpose for this Apostolic Council Meeting. It being the main order of business, Luke informs us, "And the apostles and elders gathered together to look into this question." (Acts 15:6) A private meeting was then held to discuss the issue. In attendance were the apostles and the elders. Paul in his account of this Apostolic Council Meeting mentions in Galatians 2:9 only the apostles Peter and John as being present. Whether other apostles were also in attendance we do not know. They may have been away from Jerusalem preaching and doing mission work elsewhere. Paul also mentions James was present.

James, who was an elder and the head of the church in Jerusalem, is the only elder whose name we know.

In Galatians 2:2 Paul provides us with more details of this meeting, which included himself and surely Barnabas as well. Paul tells us, "... and I laid the gospel that I preach among the Gentiles before them, and I did so privately to those having a reputation, lest in some way I am running or had run in vain." In that private meeting Paul laid out the gospel of Jesus Christ as he taught it. He surely emphasized most pointedly that he taught that observing the laws of Moses and the rite of circumcision were not necessary for salvation, because salvation was through faith alone in Jesus Christ. Therefore the Gentiles need not be circumcised or abide by the laws of Moses.

After that private meeting, the apostles and elders rejoined the main body. Luke informs us that much debate then ensued on the floor of the meeting. The Pharisaic Judaizers were standing firm on their position, arguing for its adoption by the whole assembly. At this point in the Council's meeting the future of the gospel of salvation by God's grace through faith alone and the future of the Christian Church itself were hanging in the balance. Which way would the Council go? What would tip the scale?

Luke tells us that then Peter stood up and addressed the Council's assembly and said:

> 7 Men, brothers, you yourselves understand that some time ago[11] God made a choice for himself among you, that the Gentiles hear by my mouth the word of the gospel and believe.
>
> 8 And God, the knower of hearts, bore witness by giving the Holy Spirit to them just as he also gave him to us.
>
> 9 And he did not differentiate between us and them, having cleansed their hearts by faith.
>
> 10 So why are you putting God on trial now, to place a yoke upon the neck of the disciples, which neither our fathers nor we ourselves were strong enough to bear.
>
> 11 On the contrary, we believe that we are saved through the grace

of the Lord Jesus according to which manner they are also. (Acts 15:7-11)

Peter reminded the assembly that seven years earlier in A.D. 43 God had him speak the gospel to the Roman centurion Cornelius and his Gentile household in Caesarea of Samaria. Upon hearing the gospel those Gentile people believed the gospel of Jesus, which God bore witness to by pouring out the Holy Spirit upon them as he had poured out the Holy Spirit upon the Jewish believers on Pentecost. God himself made no distinction between those Gentile believers and the Jewish believers. So why were the Judaizers making a distinction at that time and putting God on trial who had already accepted the Gentiles without their first having become Jewish converts? The Jewish believers like Peter believed they were saved by the grace of the Lord Jesus Christ alone, and so it was for the Gentile believers also.

After Peter spoke to the assembly Luke informs us in Acts 15:12,

> Then the whole assembly became quiet, and they began listening to Barnabas and Paul describing all the miraculous signs and wonders God had done among the Gentiles through them.

The whole assembly became quiet. None of the Judaizers could argue the truth of what God had done with Cornelius and his Gentile household through Peter. Peter's testimony took the wind out of the Judaizers' sails and calmed their arguments.

Then everyone in the assembly turned their attention to Paul and Barnabas once again. Earlier they had reported the successes of what God had accomplished among the Gentiles through their missionary efforts and journeys. At this time Paul and Barnabas began relating the miraculous signs and wonders God had done through their hands among the Gentiles – the blinding of Elymas the Jewish magician that influenced the proconsul Sergius Paulus, and how in Iconium the Lord had been "testifying to the word of his grace by granting miraculous signs and wonders performed by their hands." (Acts 14:3) [12] Paul and Barnabas had a good reason for recounting those miracles to the assembly. Through those miracles God himself had been bearing witness to the facts that the gospel they had been preaching was his message to the Gentiles and that Paul and Barnabas were his messengers. And in that way God also testified he was receiving the Gentiles into his Church by faith alone in Jesus Christ without circumcision and obedience to the laws of Moses.

Then Luke tells us in Acts 15:13-21:

13 And after they became silent, James began to speak, saying, "Men, brothers, listen to me! Simon[13] has just described how God was first concerned about taking from the Gentiles a people for his name.

15 "And the words of the prophets agree with this, just as it is written,

16 'AFTER THESE THINGS I WILL RETURN

AND I WILL REBUILD THE TABERNACLE OF DAVID THAT HAS FALLEN,

AND ITS PARTS THAT HAVE BEEN RAZED TO THE GROUND I WILL REBUILD AND I WILL RESTORE IT,

17 " 'IN ORDER THAT THE REST OF MANKIND MAY SEEK OUT THE LORD,

AND ALL THE GENTILES WHO HAVE BEEN CALLED BY MY NAME,[14]

18 SAYS THE LORD, WHO MAKES THESE THINGS[15] known from ages long past.'

19 "Therefore, as for me, I judge that we do not make it difficult for those from among the Gentiles who are turning to God,

20 "but that we write to them to abstain from food[16] polluted by idols and from fornication and from the meat of strangled animals and from blood.

21 "For Moses from ancient times has those who preach him in every city, and he is read in the synagogues every Sabbath."

After Paul and Barnabas finished speaking, James began to speak to the assembly as the leading elder and head of the church in

Jerusalem who was presiding over the Apostolic Council. The assembly had just heard from Peter that God years earlier had received the Gentiles of Cornelius' household on the basis of their faith alone in Jesus without circumcision and the observance of the Mosaic Law. In support of that testimony of Peter the assembly had then heard from Paul and Barnabas the miracles God had done in support of their gospel ministry to the Gentiles. In substantiation of the Lord's receiving the Gentiles as a people for himself, James then quoted Amos 9:11-12 in which the Lord had foretold centuries earlier that the Gentiles would seek him out and be called by his name. No further testimony or proof was necessary. God himself had already sealed the matter. The issue was settled.

That being the case, James then offered his recommendation on for the Council to consider. He recommended that the church would not make it difficult for the Gentiles who were turning to God through faith in Jesus Christ. Requiring them to accept circumcision and obedience to the laws of Moses would make becoming Christians difficult for them. Furthermore, James recommended that the Council write a letter to the Gentiles advising them of the Council's decision and that the Gentiles need only to abstain from food sacrificed to idols, and from consuming the meat of strangled animals and their blood, which Jewish Christians would find offensive, especially when they ate with the Gentiles in fellowship gatherings. The Gentiles were also urged to abstain from fornication in which the pagans so freely indulged, both in their daily lives and in their worship of idols, to which the Gentiles as former pagans themselves had also been accustomed to doing.

Luke tells us in Acts 15:22-29 that after James addressed the assembly:

> 22 At that time it seemed good to the apostles and the elders, together with the whole church, to select men from among them and send them to Antioch with Paul and Barnabas – Judas who is called Barsabbas and Silas, men who were leaders among the brothers.
> 23 And they sent the following letter by their hand:[17]

The apostles and the elders, your brothers;

To the brothers who are from the Gentiles throughout Antioch and Syria and Cilicia:

Greetings.

24 Because we have heard that some have gone out from us, to whom we had not given any orders, and they troubled you with words, upsetting your souls,

25 it seemed good to us, having become of one mind, to select men and send them to you with our beloved Barnabas and Paul

26 -- men who have risked their lives in behalf of the name of our Lord Jesus Christ.

27 Therefore we have sent Judas and Silas, and they can report the same things by word of mouth.

28 For it seemed good to the Holy Spirit and to us to lay no greater burden upon you except these necessary prohibitions,[18]

29 to abstain from meat offered to idols and from blood and from the meat of strangled animals and from fornication. If you keep yourselves from these things, you will do well. Farewell.

The Council adopted James' recommendation. To hand carry the Council's letter to the church in Antioch the Council selected Judas, whose surname was Barsabbas, and Silas. They would accompany Paul and Barnabas to Antioch. We will hear more about Silas in Chapter 1 of Volume II in connection with Paul's second missionary journey. The Council's letter addressed the Gentiles as "brothers", a term that at once declared a fellowship between the Jewish Christians and the Gentile Christians in Christ's Church and expressed the unity that existed between them. Together they were one Church united in the same faith, doctrine, and practice. The Council addressed its letter to the Gentiles who were not only in Antioch but were also throughout Syria and Cilicia. The Council's letter was intended to be a circular letter that was read first in the church of Antioch, which was the main center of Gentile Christianity in the regions of Syria and Cilicia. Afterwards the Council's letter was to be circulated among the congregations that Paul had established in Syria and

Cilicia during the eight years of his work in those places. The Council's addressing its letter to those Gentiles in Syria and Cilicia attests to the fact that Paul did indeed do missionary work in those areas and established Gentile congregations in those places during that time which is shrouded in silence for the most part.

The Council began its letter by acknowledging the trouble those Gentiles were put through and recognizing the spiritual upheaval that they suffered because of it. But the Council stated the church in Jerusalem was not responsible for the trouble and spiritual agony that the Judaizing troublemakers had put them through. Those men came from Judea and the church in Jerusalem, but the Jerusalem church did not send them nor sanction their false teaching. Those Judaizers had acted on their own without the consent of the church of Jerusalem.

In its letter the Council then explained what were the results of its meeting. The assembly of men had become of one mind on the issue of whether Gentile believers in Jesus had to be circumcised and obey the laws of Moses to become members of the Christian Church. As one united body the assembly had voted a resounding "No!" and preserved the unity of the Church. The Church would not be divided into a Jewish church that confessed Jesus was the Christ but demanded the observance of circumcision and the Mosaic Law to be saved and into a Gentile church that confessed Jesus was the Christ and that faith alone in Jesus Christ saved. There would be one, true Christian Church that confessed faith in Jesus Christ alone without obedience to the Mosaic Law. God's Church was one united whole in faith, doctrine, and practice. What a travesty that the Church of today is so divided! The devil has been all too successful in sewing his diabolical seeds of false doctrine and dissension and division throughout the centuries since the days of Paul and the Apostolic Council in Jerusalem.

In its letter the Council also wrote that it was sending its own delegation to Antioch with Paul and Barnabas, namely Judas and Silas. These two delegates would deliver an oral report that confirmed in greater detail the decision of the Council as stated in the letter.

What is more, the Council acknowledged what dedicated and

courageous missionaries from the church in Antioch Paul and Barnabas were. They had risked their lives to spread the gospel of Jesus Christ. In including this commendation of Paul and Barnabas the Council indicated that it was well aware of the life-threatening persecutions Paul and Barnabas had endured and suffered during their missionary work in Galatia.

The Council's letter then closed by noting what things the Gentile Christians needed to avoid and refrain from to preserve brotherly love and harmony in the Church that consisted of both former Jews and former pagans. The Council noted the Gentiles would do well if they kept themselves from those necessary prohibitions.

Paul also provides us in Galatians 2:3-10 with some additional details of how matters proceeded at the Council's meeting:

3 But not even Titus who was with me, even though he was a Greek, was compelled to be circumcised

4 because of the false brothers who were brought in secretly, such ones as slipped in to spy out our freedom that we have in Christ Jesus in order to enslave us,

5 and to whom we did not yield in submission for an hour, in order that the truth of the gospel might remain permanently with you.

6 Moreover, from those recognized to be something – whatever kind they were makes no difference to me; God does not show partiality[19] – for those having a reputation contributed nothing to me,

7 but on the other hand when they saw that I had been entrusted with the gospel for the uncircumcised[20] just as Peter *had been* for the circumcised,[21]

8 for he who was at work for Peter in *his* apostleship for the circumcised was also at work for me *in my apostleship* to the Gentiles,

9 and when they understood the grace that had been given to me, James and Cephas and John, those recognized to be pillars, gave the right hand of fellowship to me and Barnabas, that we *would go* to the Gentiles and they to the circumcised.

10 *They asked* only that we keep remembering the poor, the very thing I was also eager to do.

In addition to the decisions of the Council that were noted above, another very important decision the Council made was not to compel Paul's Christian companion Titus, who was a Greek, to be circumcised. It was likely that Paul brought Titus along with him to make an example of him both at the Apostolic Council Meeting and then in the church of Antioch when they returned there. While the debate with the false brothers, the Judaizers, was going on at the Council Meeting, there in the flesh of Titus was living proof of what God had been doing among the Gentiles. Just as God had brought Titus, a Greek by birth, to faith and accepted him without any obligation to be circumcised and follow the laws of Moses, so God had been doing with all the other Greek converts from paganism in Antioch as well as the pagans of Greek, Phrygian, Lycaonian, and Roman ancestry in the cities of Galatia. Was the Council to overturn what God had already been doing in record numbers among those pagan Gentiles? As Paul would often write later when protesting something so plainly wrong and outlandish, "God forbid!" that the Council should do such a thing. And after the Council adjourned its meeting, Titus would then be able to return to Antioch as an uncircumcised Gentile who was not required to submit to being circumcised or obeying the laws of Moses. As he, a Greek, was not compelled to be circumcised to be a member in God's Church, so all the Greeks and Gentiles wherever they might live could be assured they would not be compelled to be circumcised and observe the laws of Moses either. The matter of accepting circumcision and obedience to the laws of Moses had been settled -- they were not necessary. The Gentiles were free from those requirements. And Titus was living proof of that!

During the course of the Apostolic Council's meeting Paul did not yield for even an hour to the Judaizers. Paul as well as Barnabas stood staunchly on the truth of the gospel that salvation was by faith alone in Jesus Christ without the requirements of circumcision and obedience to the Mosaic Law. Paul had stood so firmly against the Judaizers throughout the Council's meeting to preserve the gospel for the Gentiles and for all Christians for all time. And before the Council adjourned its meeting, he was given the right hand of fellowship by the leaders of the church in Jerusalem – James and the apostles Peter and John. What was more, they divided the work of the Church with Paul, entrusting to him the mission work to the Gentiles while they continued with the mission work to the Jews. No stipulations were placed on Paul; he was asked only to remember the poor, which he already had every intention of doing.

After the Apostolic Council adjourned, Luke informs us that Paul, Barnabas, the others in the delegation from the church of Antioch, plus the Council's appointees Judas and Silas, traveled to Antioch to report the results of the Apostolic Council meeting. In Acts 15:30-35 Luke reports:

> 30 So when they were sent away, they came down to Antioch, and when they had gathered the church together, they delivered the letter.
>
> 31 And after they read it, they began to rejoice because of its encouragement.
>
> 32 Both Judas and Silas, who also were prophets themselves, encouraged and strengthened the brothers by means of a lengthy message.
>
> 33 Then after they had spent time there, they were dismissed with peace from the brothers to those who had sent them.[22]
>
> 35 But Paul and Barnabas continued to stay in Antioch teaching and preaching the word of the Lord with many others also.

When the two delegations arrived in Antioch, the whole church was gathered together. At that time Judas and Silas delivered the Council's letter to the church of Antioch. The letter was then read. It was most likely read aloud by one of the leaders of the church of Antioch for all to hear. After hearing the letter's contents, the Gentile members of the congregation began to rejoice, as did the Gentiles of Pisidian Antioch when they heard that the Lord's salvation was for them.[23] We can properly imagine that the joyous celebration of the Gentiles continued for at least a few minutes before the vocal expressions of excitement and joy died down to a dignified silence. Such a joyous outburst is understandable, for indeed a heavy burden had just been lifted from those Greek Gentiles, a burden that Peter had said the Jews themselves had been unable to bear.[24] The Gentiles learned that no greater burden would be laid on them except the few necessary prohibitions that were mentioned in the letter, which were really no burden at all. With the lifting of the burden of circumcision and obedience to the laws of Moses, the spiritual agony to which the Gentiles had been subjected was removed from them as well. In its place there arose a spontaneous emotional relief. The joy of having their eternal salvation and life in heavenly glory through faith alone in Jesus made certain rushed over them like the fast-flowing torrent of an unstoppable flash flood. It was a joy such as new converts experience when the truth of the gospel of full and free forgiveness and life everlasting begins to swell in their soul and engulf their mind and open their mouths in thankful praise.

After the reading of the letter and the initial outpouring of the Gentiles' joy, Judas and Silas addressed the church. They were prophets. The context makes clear that on this occasion they were prophets, not in the sense of proclaiming a revelation from God about some matter or future event, but in the sense of preachers proclaiming the revealed Word of God with its comforting promises that abound in Jesus Christ. They then delivered a lengthy message of encouragement for the spiritual strengthening of the congregation. The church today would benefit greatly if all preachers delivered such a message from God's Word itself that held out spiritual encouragement for the building up and strengthening of God's people rather than filling the ears of the listeners with other social concerns and political ambitions.

Luke tells us in verse 33 above that Judas and Silas then spent time with the brothers in the church of Antioch. They were then dismissed with peace from the brothers in Antioch to return to those in Jerusalem who had sent them. But it appears that Silas chose to remain in Antioch rather than return with Judas to Jerusalem, for Silas was there in Antioch when Paul chose him to replace Barnabas. And Acts 15:34, which is omitted in many early Greek manuscripts, states, "But it seemed good to Silas to remain there." Although it has been thought that a copyist later inserted this verse, it does deserve some serious consideration as being an authentic reading that lays the background for Acts 15:40 when Paul selected Silas as his fellow worker.

Paul's Rebuke Of Peter In Antioch, Syria

Sometime after Paul returned to Antioch and remained there teaching and preaching, Peter came to Antioch for a visit. Upon his arrival, Peter, a Jewish Christian, freely associated with the Gentile Christians in the church of Antioch and ate with them. He ate with them even though the meats they ate were not "clean" meats according to the laws of Leviticus 11. Peter's associating and eating with the Gentile Christians was in keeping with the decision of the Apostolic Council and in accordance with what Peter himself had done years earlier by a revelation of the Lord in the case of the Roman centurion Cornelius and his Gentile household.[25]

But then some Jewish Christians from Jerusalem arrived, who were closely associated with James, the head of the church in Jerusalem. These men belonged to a group of Jewish Christians who in Christian liberty continued to observe the ceremonial laws of their former Jewish religion, including the rite of circumcision and the eating of only clean meats. After these men arrived Peter began to exhibit a behavior that was contrary to the decision that the Apostolic Council had made not long before. Peter began to separate himself from the Greek Gentiles of the church and abstaining from their "unclean" meats. He began doing so in order to give the impression that he was upholding the Levitical law of Moses and avoiding becoming defiled by associating with the Gentile Christians and eating their unclean meats. Peter was putting on an act and being hypocritical. The other Jewish Christians of the church of Antioch, including even Barnabas himself, joined in Peter's hypocrisy of avoiding the Gentile Christians and refusing to eat with them.

Peter's separating himself from them became offensive to the

Greek Christians. Paul then felt compelled to take issue with Peter's conduct as a matter of principle for the good of the Church, because the gospel of Christ and the liberty it gave to Christians from the ceremonial laws of Moses were at stake. If Paul had not censured Peter's actions, the end result for the Christian Church would have been disastrous – the decision of the Apostolic Council would have been overturned in practice. Pressure would have again been put on the Gentile Christians to be circumcised and to observe the ceremonial laws of Moses. The true gospel of justification by faith alone without works of obedience to the law would have been jeopardized.

Paul tells us in Galatians 2:11-21 about this incident and what he was compelled to do:

11 Now when Cephas came to Antioch, I opposed him to his[26] face, because he stood condemned.

12 For before some men came from James, he used to eat with the Gentiles, but when they came, he began to draw back and separate himself, because he was afraid of those favoring circumcision.[27]

13 And the rest of the Jews joined him in his hypocrisy,[28] so that even Barnabas was carried away by their hypocrisy.

14 But when I saw that they were not acting uprightly in accordance with the truth of the gospel, I said to Cephas in the presence of *them* all,

"If you, being a Jew, are living like a Gentile and not like a Jew, how is it that you are trying to compel the Gentiles to follow Jewish customs?

¶ 15 "We, Jews by nature and not sinners from among the Gentiles,

16 knowing that a man is not declared righteous[29] as a result of works of law but by means of faith in Jesus Christ, even we have put our trust in Christ Jesus, in order that we might be declared righteous as a result of faith in Christ and not as a result of works of law, for as a result of works of law no person[30] will be declared righteous.

17 But if, while seeking to be declared righteous in Christ, we ourselves came to be found sinners *also*, is Christ a servant of sin? God forbid!

18 For if these things that I destroyed I again rebuild, I show that I myself am a lawbreaker.

19 For through law I died to law, in order that I might live for God.

20 I have been crucified with Christ; and I no longer live but Christ lives in me; and the life that[31] I now live in the flesh, I live by faith in the Son of God who loved me and gave himself for me.

21 I am not setting aside the grace of God; for if righteousness *comes* by means of law, then Christ died for no reason."

Paul's rebuke of Peter put an end to the matter of Peter's error. Though it was not Paul's intention, his rebuking Peter as he did also established clearly that he was an apostle of the Lord of equal rank with Peter. What is more, Paul's handling of the matter also showed what an insightful and knowledgeable theologian God had raised Paul up to be.

Paul did much here in rebuking Peter and at the Apostolic Council to preserve the gospel and the Church of his Master, the Lord Jesus Christ. The truth of the gospel had been defended and upheld. The future of the Church had been kept on its right course. The Gentiles did not have to follow the Jewish customs and observances of the Mosaic Law. The gospel of Jesus Christ freed them, and all people of all ages as well, from the laws of Moses.

Here in Antioch and at the Apostolic Council in Jerusalem Paul had stood up to the false teaching of the Judaizers. But the Judaizers' movement did not end here. It had only begun. The Judaizers stubbornly persisted in trying to spread their heresy. They doggedly followed after Paul westward from where they had begun in Judea and Jerusalem to nearly every city where Paul went – to Antioch in Syria, to the cities in Galatia of Asia Minor, to the city of Corinth in Greece. Time and again in place after place Paul had to stand up to the Judaizers and combat their heresy to preserve the gospel of Jesus Christ and his Church. The reader will observe this as he continues reading in the next volume, Volume II, about Paul's second and third missionary journeys that carried the gospel for the first time into Europe. And during those missionary journeys he, as an apostle and bondservant of his Lord Jesus Christ, had to be a defender of the Christian faith as well as a missionary to the Gentiles.

---

1. Acts 10:1-11:18
2. Lit. no little
3. Pelikan, Jarislav, editor; Luther's Works, Volume 4, Lectures On Genesis, Chapters 21-25; Concordia Publishing House; St. Louis, Missouri; 1964; p. 152
4. Ephesians 3:3-10; Romans 16:25, 26; Colossians 1:26, 27
5. Acts 14:16
6. Acts 17:30
7. Ephesians 3:8-10; Romans 16:25, 26; 1 Corinthians 2:1
8. Colossians 1:26, 27; Ephesians 3:3-6
9. Ephesians 3:3-6
10. Acts 14:27
11. Lit. from former days; perhaps 10 or more years earlier Peter preached to Cornelius' household
12. See also Mark 16:20 and Hebrews 2:2:4
13. Simon is Peter's Greek name; James used his Hebrew name "Simeon"
14. Lit. all the Gentiles upon whom my name has been invoked
15. Am.9:11-12
16. Lit. things
17. Lit. wrote by their hand
18. Lit. things
19. Lit. accept a face of a man
20. Meaning the Gentiles
21. Meaning the Jews; likewise v.8 & 9
22. Many early manuscripts omit v.34:"But it seemed good to Silas to remain there."
23. Acts 13:48
24. Acts 15:10
25. Acts 10 & 11
26. Lit. the
27. Lit. those from circumcision
28. Lit. joined him in being a hypocrite
29. Or, justified; likewise in the following verses
30. Lit. flesh
31. Lit. that which, or what

CPSIA information can be obtained
at www.ICGtesting.com
Printed in the USA
LVHW042349141019
634128LV00007B/2235/P